SOCIAL CHANGE AND CONSERVATION

Environmental Politics and Impacts of National Parks and Protected Areas

Edited by

Krishna B. Ghimire and Michel P. Pimbert

BJH 5051 - 9/2

First published in the UK in 1997 by
Earthscan Publications Limited

Copyright © UNRISD, 1997

A catalogue record for this book is available from the British Library

ISBN: 1 85383 415 7 (hardback),   1 85383 410 6 (paperback)

Typesetting and page design by PCS Mapping & DTP, Newcastle upon Tyne

Cover design by Gary Inwood

For a full list of publications please contact:
Earthscan Publications Limited
120 Pentonville Road
London N1 9JN
Tel. (0171) 278 0433
Fax: (0171) 278 1142
Email: earthinfo@earthscan.co.uk
http://www.earthscan.co.uk

Earthscan is an editorially independent subsidiary of Kogan Page Limited and
publishes in association with WWF-UK and the International Institute for
Environment and Development.

CONTENTS

The United Nations Research Institute for Social Development (UNRISD)

The United Nations Research Institute for Social Development (UNRISD) is an autonomous agency engaging in multi-disciplinary research on the social dimensions of contemporary development problems. Its work is guided by the conviction that, for effective development policies to be formulated, an understanding of the social and political context is crucial. The Institute attempts to provide governments, development agencies, grassroots organizations and scholars with a better understanding of how development policies and processes of economic, social and environmental change affect different social groups. Working through an extensive network of national research centres, UNRISD aims to promote original research and strengthen research capacity in developing countries.

Current research themes include: The Challenge of Rebuilding War-Torn Societies; Integrating Gender into Development Policy; Environment, Sustainable Development and Social Change; Crisis, Adjustment and Social Change; and Volunteer Action and Local Democracy: A Partnership for a Better Urban Future. New research is beginning on: Follow-Up to the Social Summit; Business Responsibility for Sustainable Development; New Information and Communications Technologies; Culture and Development; Gender, Poverty and Well-Being; and Public Sector Reform and Crisis-Ridden States. Recent research programmes have included: Ethnic Conflict and Development; Socio-Economic and Political Consequences of the International Trade in Illicit Drugs; Political Violence and Social Movements; and Participation and Changes in Property Relations in Communist and Post-Communist Societies. UNRISD research projects focused on the 1995 World Summit for Social Development included Rethinking Social Development in the 1990s; Economic Restructuring and Social Policy; Ethnic Diversity and Public Policies; and Social Integration at the Grassroots: The Urban Dimension. A list of the Institute's free and priced publications can be obtained by writing to: UNRISD, Reference Centre, Palais des Nations, CH-1211, Geneva 10, Switzerland. Fax: (41 22) 740 0791; e-mail: info@unrisd.org; World Wide Web Site: http://www.unicc.org/unrisd/

CONTRIBUTORS

Piers Blaikie	Professor, School of Development Studies, University of East Anglia, Norwich NR4 7TJ, England.
Jens Brüggemann	Project Co-ordinator, Federation of Nature and National Parks of Europe, 94475 Grafenau, Germany.
Marcus Colchester	Director, Forest Peoples Programme, World Rainforest Movement, 8 Chapel Row, Chadlington, Oxfordshire OX7 3NA, England.
Chandana Dey	Freelance researcher, 'Mitali', Santiniketan–731225, West Bengal, India.
Andréa Finger-Stich	Environmental consultant, 'Les Eaux-Vives', Vovray, 74160 Archamps, France.
Krishna B. Ghimire	Project Leader, United Nations Research Institute for Social Development, Palais des Nations, 1211 Geneva 10, Switzerland.
Sally Jeanrenaud	Doctoral scholar, School of Development Studies, University of East Anglia, Norwich NR4 7TJ, England.
Eddie Koch	Journalist, Daily Mail & The Guardian, P.O. Box 32362, Braamfontein, Johannesburg 2001, South Africa.
Chris McIvor	Programme Director Caribbean, Save the Children, 1 National Heroes Circle, Kingston, Jamaica.
James Morrison	Ethnohistorian consultant, Legal and Historical Research, 666 Brewster Street, P.O. Box 1053, Haileybury, Ontario POJ 1KO, Canada.
Michel P. Pimbert	Director, World Wide Fund For Nature — Switzerland, chemin de Poussy 14, 1214 Vernier, Geneva, Switzerland.
Jules N. Pretty	Director, Sustainable Agricultural Programme, International Institute for Environment and Development, 3 Endsleigh Street, London WC1H 0DD, England.

ACKNOWLEDGEMENTS AND A CAVEAT TO THE READER

The contributions to this volume are part of a wider international research endeavour on social change, the environment and sustainable development in general, and the associated impacts of national parks and protected areas in particular. Several participating and non-participating organizations have played an important role in the making of this book.

We are particularly indebted to Solon Barraclough, Andréa Finger-Stich, Jenifer Freedman and Sari Nissi at UNRISD, Geneva, for their advice and critical comments on the theoretical and empirical material included in the book. We would also like to acknowledge the help of Anita Tombez for her excellent typing and preparation of the manuscript.

We are grateful to WWF-International, Gland, for providing both financial and intellectual inputs at all stages leading to the production of the book. We are especially obliged to Biksham Gujja and Gonzalo Oviedo for their critical feedback on sections of the book or earlier related papers. We would also like to thank Sandra Charity from WWF-Brazil for her useful comments on parts of the book.

We have also found reviews of the book by Robert Chambers from IDS, Brighton, Vithal Rajan of Deccan Development Society, Hyderabad, and Grazia Borrini-Feyerabend from IUCN, Gland, extremely beneficial.

During the preparation of this book, we have had an opportunity to interact with a wide range of individuals, including staff from mainstream conservation organizations. While many generally thought the study to be 'timely', a few clearly rejected the implications of its findings. We wish to thank these observers whose reactions have helped us deepen our analysis and clarify the main message of the book.

With the publication of this book, our intention is not to disparage the many remarkable efforts of conservationists to save important landscapes, species and environmental processes. Our purpose is to encourage debate and imaginative thinking to ensure that conservation is also socially sustainable. For a conservation programme to be successful, a delicate balance of social and environmental exigencies is truly essential. There is simply no healthy environment without healthy livelihoods. Failure to respect social justice, as is argued in the book, not only provokes economic misery and conflict, but also makes it difficult to mobilize local participation for conservation. Environmental projects, such as those involving protected areas, should reduce local poverty and curb environmental degradation, not the contrary. Human dignity and cultural diversity should be protected as much as the environment.

Krishna B. Ghimire and Michel P. Pimbert
Geneva
January 1997

FIGURES

TABLES

I

SOCIAL CHANGE AND CONSERVATION: AN OVERVIEW OF ISSUES AND CONCEPTS

Krishna B. Ghimire and Michel P. Pimbert

Conservation in the Context of Rural Development

Environmental conservation has been a persistent theme in discourses on rural and agricultural development. The past four decades have seen the emergence of major environmental organizations such as The World Conservation Union (IUCN), the World Wide Fund For Nature (WWF) and the United Nations Environment Programme (UNEP), as well as a number of powerful environmental campaigning organizations such as Greenpeace and Friends of the Earth. Bilateral agencies, the World Bank, the United Nations Development Programme (UNDP), the Food and Agriculture Organization of the United Nations (FAO) and other United Nations organizations, Consultative Group on International Agricultural Research (CGIAR) institutions and non-governmental organizations (NGOs) from developed countries have also invested substantial sums in environmental programmes and projects in developing countries. The 1992 United Nations Conference on Environment and Development (UNCED) in Rio and the establishment of the Global Environmental Facility (GEF) and several environmentally oriented commissions and the ratification of a number of environmental conventions are evidence of the attention being given to conservation. It is commonly believed that environmental degradation and rural poverty exist in the same locality, and that environmental rehabilitation is important for poverty reduction in addition to the provision of improved production technologies and services. But the relationships between poverty and environmental health are highly complex. The social structures and processes producing poverty and environmental decay interact at all levels, from individual households in particular areas to transnational organizations, policies, institutions and markets (Barraclough, Ghimire and Meliczek, 1997). In many cases, the processes and structures that render local livelihoods vulnerable are responsible for environmental decline as well.

Many types of conservation measures have been witnessed. They can be grouped into two broad categories. First, there are those which aim at rehabilitating or improving the environmental resources in or adjacent to settlement areas to ameliorate living conditions of such social groups as farmers, pastoralists, the landless and women. Soil conservation, water retention, afforestation, agro-forestry and regeneration of forests and grasslands are some of the initiatives commonly undertaken. Second, there are programmes that seek to preserve important tracts of forest and water bodies for biodiversity protection or scientific research, sometimes combined with recreation and tourism development. Project documents and specialists in favour of this latter type of conservation measure claim that there can be numerous benefits for resident and surrounding populations (Dixon and Shermann, 1990; McNeely and Miller, 1984). The present work asserts that programmes' effectiveness can be gauged on the basis of their real capacity to reduce poverty and promote long-term environmental rehabilitation of the area.

We are concerned here primarily with this second category of conservation measures, which includes national parks, game reserves, biosphere reserves, wildlife sanctuaries, etc. In conservation discourse, these are referred to as 'protected areas' and are considered to be essential for the conservation of biological diversity (WRI, IUCN, UNEP, 1992:117). Substantial stretches of national territories are included in this protective regime and, as we shall see below, the total area is increasing.

The prominence of the protected area system in the context of rural or agricultural development is problematic because of its specific method of restricting resource use for local populations. It has customarily led to extensive resource alienation and economic hardships for many rural social groups. Some of these groups have also experienced cultural and social marginalization. It is specifically worth noting that this process is occurring at a time when numerous painful rural transformations and social conflicts are unfolding, such as growing marketization of rural economies, unemployment, widening differentiation and reduced solidarity. Undoubtedly, many of these consequences are in great part a direct result of the dominant patterns of 'development' that have focused primarily on rising income per capita, productivities and technological modernization. The core issues of rural social security and sustainable livelihoods have received secondary attention.

About this Volume

This work is an attempt to analyse the current processes of the establishment of an increasing number of protected areas with a strong preservationist orientation in the context of ongoing rural social change. While the literature on protected areas has been growing, the majority of the publications are concerned essentially with the question of how to preserve nature, wildlife in particular. With the exception of a few studies which deal with livelihood issues, aspects of human welfare are generally considered only when the primary purpose of nature preservation is threatened. The central message of this book is that local social development is also crucial in its own right. Rural people deserve to have access to the resources required to meet their basic needs, economic safety and, where possible, upward social mobility. In other words, conservation programmes are only valid and sustainable when they have the dual objective of protecting and improving local livelihoods and ecological conditions. The volume not only critically examines the content and practice of protected area management in different contexts; it also scrutinizes the origins of the concept of conservation, and its ability to fulfil social as well as environmental goals. It seeks to demonstrate that protected area management systems are not apolitical as implied by most conservationists, nor are the resultant costs and benefits equally shared among different social groups. In particular, it records and analyses how the establishment of protected areas has affected the customary rights, livelihoods, well-being, natural resources management practices and social cohesion of local people living in and around the protected areas. Policy measures to accommodate local communities' concerns, in large part due to growing social conflicts and grassroots mobilization through such initiatives as CAMPFIRE in Zimbabwe, ecotourism, extractivism and so forth have largely been ineffective because of the non-respect of local rights over natural resources, excessive reliance on market forces, institutional problems and a lack of popular participation. The book is careful to avoid simplistic recommendations. Instead, it argues for a total overhaul in the current course of conservation thinking and practice.

This introductory chapter summarizes the main issues and concepts related to the social dimensions of protected areas. It also aims to highlight how these issues and concepts are dealt with in the different chapters, as well as the central arguments that run through the book. In the second chapter, Blaikie and Jeanrenaud look at the complex relationships between human welfare and biodiversity, especially how these issues are perceived differently by a wide range of actors. Brüggemann, in the third chapter, compares the experiences of protected area management in Costa Rica and Germany. He suggests that richer countries such as Germany have not always combined social and environmental exigencies in a sound manner, but their greater financial ability and willingness to accept less rigid, 'compromise' oriented protected regimes have nonetheless helped

3

to generate less conflict among resource users than in developing countries such as Costa Rica. In Chapter IV, Colchester examines the impact of protected areas on indigenous peoples, concluding that conservationists have put the preservation of nature above the interests of indigenous peoples. Another social group negatively affected by protected areas, women, is considered in Chapter V by Dey. The emerging role of protected areas in creating employment and income, strengthening culture and protecting vital ecosystems in rural areas in France is examined by Finger-Stich and Ghimire in Chapter VI. Chapter VII by Ghimire explores the potential of protected area systems for social development based on an investigation of panda reserves in China, indicating that conservation can make a significant contribution but only when social development objectives receive as much priority as the preservation of wildlife. Koch and McIvor focus in the following two chapters on the impacts of 'green' tourism on local communities in South Africa and Zimbabwe, respectively; both conclude that surrounding communities are not only commonly excluded from park benefits but are negatively affected by their existence. Morrison, in Chapter X, deals with the situation of indigenous peoples in Canada, and suggests that their aspirations are far from met, with continuing conflicts over land and divergent interests with conservationists. In the final chapter, Pimbert and Pretty discuss the problematic nature of people's participation in protected area management and argue for fundamental changes in the present conservation paradigm.

Protected Areas as a Social Space

A vast 'undisturbed' area, with unique wildlife species and spectacular sceneries, is the typical popular image associated with protected areas. The same area may be regarded by conservationists as an ideal habitat for rare species of wildlife. For biologists and botanists, a protected area represents exceptional riches for research and scientific writing. Foresters might identify it in terms of the valuable tree species that could yield high dividends if harvested. In short, parks and other protected areas are for plants and animals.

It should be noted that ecosystems and biodiversity are continually changing. The natural phenomena and wildlife that are included within the boundaries of parks and reserves are no exception; they too are far from 'static'. One does not need to be a natural scientist to observe certain changes. The spread of disease, food scarcity, acute weather changes, multiplication in number of particular species, etc. can lead to important modifications in habitat structure and wildlife evolution. Similarly, wetlands can be transformed in a matter of a few decades through replenishing, rapid evaporation or ecological succession. Entire new islands may emerge though soil deposit or existing ones may disappear when water levels rise, leading to changes in the natural landscape and assemblages of plant and animal species.

More importantly, within the notion of 'pristine' nature that parks and reserves attempt to maintain, it is difficult to integrate the interaction of human beings with nature. It is clear that any modification in ecosystems has to take into account the specific role played by human beings — which is, after all, one of the species inhabiting ecosystems. Human beings have obviously been part and parcel of recent evolutionary processes. In fact, as we shall discuss below, most existing landmarks, including many of those considered to be 'pristine' by conservationists, have been strongly influenced by human existence and activities in one period of history or another.

Protected areas are a social space. They are socially conceived and preserved. The vocabulary involved lends support to this contention: the word 'park', for example, comes from the medieval Latin *parricus*, which means 'enclosure'. 'Reserve' also originates from the Latin *reservare*, meaning 'save'. Indeed, 'preservation', 'protection', and 'conservation' essentially imply that certain areas or natural aspects are kept away from the present demand. Similarly, 'establishment' denotes a legal event of bringing into existence and 'management' implies certain techniques of supervising the area, frequently involving a whole range of new institutions, professionals and methods. Which social forces are behind these measures? How are choices for use and protection made and related social costs reduced? It is clear that the areas included in parks and reserves retain such resources as forests, water, fertile land, minerals and wildlife. They may also represent many cultural, aesthetic and spiritual values locally. Important decisions with respect to the use and protection of certain natural resources have been made throughout human history, at times provoking long-lasting conflicts. What is probably new is the way the arguments are advanced by their proponents. A common reasoning has been that parks and reserves are for the 'common good', established and managed through 'impartial' state institutions. Commercial actors are also encouraged to participate in order to make the management of parks and reserves financially self-reliant. Numerous moral justifications — such as the equal respect of human beings for other species and protection of the natural patrimony for future generations — are presented so that conservation becomes a 'non-negotiable' issue. What is non-negotiable for one social group may, however, be altogether negotiable for others. This perception also changes over time.

Wild or Human-Managed Ecosystems?

Most parts of the world have been modified, managed and, in some instances, improved by people for centuries. The biodiversity which conservationists seek to protect may be of anthropogenic origin, since there is often a close link between moderate intensities of human intervention and biodiversity. The term 'wild' is, in fact, misleading because it implies the absence of human influence and management. The concept of wilderness as an 'untouched or untamed land is mostly an urban perception, the view of people who are far removed from the natural environment they depend upon' (Gómez-Pompa and Kaus, 1992:273).

Much of what has been considered as 'natural' in the Amazon is, in fact, modified by Amerindian populations (Posey, 1993). Indigenous use and management of tropical forests is best viewed as a continuum between plants that are domesticated and those that are semi-domesticated, manipulated or 'wild', with no clear-cut demarcation between natural and managed forest. Many plant species and populations that have long been considered to be 'wild' are actually carefully nurtured by people, albeit less intensively than those cultivated in their fields (Gómez-Pompa and Kaus, 1992; Wood, 1995). Certain large animal species would not occur in forest unmodified by humans, and important game species such as deer, tapir, monkey, collared peccary and jaguar reach much higher densities in modified areas. Home gardens planted by indigenous forest peoples and peasant communities are particularly attractive to wildlife and the populations of several species may have actually increased as a result of the crops and fruit trees planted. Species richness and the abundance of wildlife in the Sonoran desert in the United States is greater in areas cultivated by indigenous populations than in adjacent or analogous habitats that are not cultivated (Reichardt et al., 1994). Many indigenous groups have evolved ways of harvesting resources without depleting them. Biodiversity-rich areas — denser forests, relatively undisturbed grasslands, reefs and waterways — are generally found associated with territories claimed or used by indigenous peoples (Alcorn, 1994). In agricultural landscapes it is mainly local people who create and manage biological diversity (Haverkort and Millar, 1994; Salick and Merrick, 1990).

What many conservationists still refer to as 'pristine' landscapes, 'mature' tropical forest or 'untouched wilderness' are, in fact, mostly human cultural artefacts. Although this conception is slowly gaining some currency in Western societies (see, for example, EEC, 1992), conservation in developing countries is still informed by the 'wilderness myth'. Protected area management plans rarely begin with the notion that biodiversity-rich areas are social spaces, where culture and nature are renewed with, by and for local people.

Establishment, Management and Use is Informed by a Specific Ideology

The first protected areas were established during the last century. In the industrializing countries, governments began to set aside areas of particular scenic beauty or uniqueness exclusively for conservation. However, the creation of most of these protected areas involved the exclusion of local people. In the United States, for example, Yellowstone National Park was established in 1872 around a tract of hot springs and geysers in north-western Wyoming. The inhabitants of Yellowstone, mainly Crow and Shoshone native Americans, either left for reservations after intense persuasion or were driven out by the army, which then managed the park until 1916 (Utley, 1973). In Eastern and Southern Africa, conservationists usually worked in isolation from the surrounding societies and dissociated themselves from local livelihood needs. The leading conservationists were foresters from the Imperial Institute of Forestry at Oxford as well as many mammalogists, zoologists, biologists and animal traders from the United Kingdom. Their management philosophy emphasized that 'the public good was best served through the protection of forests and water resources, even if this meant the displacement of local communities' (McCracken, 1987). In Western and Central Africa, the French colonial administrators and naturalists followed a very similar policy (see Chapter VI).

This neglect of resident people in protected areas persists today. Until quite recently, few plans for protected area management made any explicit recognition of the survival need of the people living inside forests, coastal strips, wetlands and other biodiversity-rich areas earmarked for conservation. But many of these areas are heavily populated. In South America, for example, 86 per cent of national parks have people living in them and using the natural resources of the parks to some extent (Amend and Amend, 1995). In India, a study of 171 national parks and sanctuaries conducted in the mid–1980s found that there were 1.6 million people living in the 118 parks that were inhabited (Kothari et al., 1989). By 1993, some 600,000 tribal peoples were already displaced, some 20 per cent of the country's tribal population. Some suggest that as many people may be removed again if the Ministry of Environment and Forests proceeds with its plans to establish a further 150 national parks and 650 wildlife sanctuaries in the next few years (PRIA, 1993).

Land alienation for protected areas is increasing under the programmes of the Global Environmental Facility (GEF) and international conservation NGOs which promote large Yellowstone-like national parks and wilderness areas. Some remarkable exceptions apart, the basic underlying attitude is isolationist, in which both design and management seek to protect the park or reserve from surrounding society. Decisions on which land or water areas of a country should be incorporated in national parks are made by the state environmental agencies or/and expatriate conservation professionals, who also independently design and execute park management plans. Conservation in other types of protected areas (e.g. multiple-use zones) has also tended to be carried out through enforcement. Major international conservation agencies, together with groups of national elites, have often put their combined efforts behind preservationist, 'people out' approaches. Armed police forces or the army are frequently mobilized. Heavy penalties have been imposed on those who break conservation laws and regulations.

By and large, the present conservation paradigm is 'an attempt to transplant national parks, a rich country institution, to an alien setting' (Southgate and Clarke, 1993). The hasty imposition of conservation ideologies and techniques based on Western models creates artificial, idealized landscapes in which local people have no place. Indeed, an important function of the 'wilderness' offered by protected areas is to provide a temporary antidote to modern civilization. For many of the better off urbanites who increasingly sense their alienation from nature, protected areas are special institutions where rest, contemplation and the sensual experience of unspoiled wilderness are still possible. The growing interest in the world's conservation areas by relatively affluent members of developed countries is 'not a throwback to the primitive, but an integral part of the modern standard of living as people sought to add new "amenity" and "aesthetic" goals and desires to their earlier preoccupation with necessities and conveniences' (Hays, 1982:21). This statement increasingly applies to the urban elites of developing countries for whom the enjoyment of nature has also become an integral part of the consumer society.

Various Social Groups and their Differing Interests

Numerous social groups interact with protected areas. On the one hand, there are those social groups which favour the establishment of parks and reserves using the present management styles. These may include government officials, politicians, aid workers, environmentalists, commercial and tourist interests, rich merchants, large landowners, the urban population groups, etc. Different groups evoke different logics or combinations of them to justify setting up protected areas. For example, environmentalists may stress the need to protect biodiversity. Government officials may maintain that these areas are for the common public interest and for future generations. The market potential of genetic resources and of tourism development would be highlighted by international and national commercial and tourist interests. The possibility of generating foreign exchange earnings would be asserted by these groups, as well as government officials and environmentalists. The latter two groups may also emphasize the usefulness of state intervention and professionalism, if protection of the environment is to be successful. Naturally, not all groups have the same power base; nevertheless they are all likely to derive certain gains through the establishment of parks and other protected areas. Thus these groups may make compromises despite differing interests occasionally.

On the other hand, there are the local communities who suffer most of the hardships resulting from the establishment of protected areas. But local communities too are far from homogeneous. Elites are present in all societies. Sometimes they provide much-needed leadership, but frequently they exploit common folk in order to fulfil personal interests. Community members and groups are stratified by age, gender, religion, wealth, economic activities, social status, power and so forth. There are those who reside within protected areas and those who live outside them. They may be indigenous peoples, or migrants to the area. Some communities or their members may depend upon hunting and forest gathering for their livelihoods, while others may specialize in fishing. Certain communities make a living through pastoral activities and others through crop production. Similarly, sections of the local population may become more engaged in the collection of forest products and petty trading. In reality, most rural communities combine many of these activities. The distance factor is also important, as people living in areas adjacent to a park may be heavily dependent on the use of park resources. Poorer households, the landless and women from settlements quite far from the park might also be relying on the park's resources for their livelihoods. These weaker social groups are adversely affected when restrictions are imposed on resource use within protected areas (see Chapters II, IV and XI).

The main difference between local communities and some of the dominant groups mentioned above is that local communities, albeit numerically important, retain a weak power base and subsequently have little say in decision-making concerning resource use options and protected area management. Likewise, community groups, unlike the dominant actors, often lack environmentally benign justifications for many of their livelihood activities, such as slash-and-burn cultivation, farming of marginal areas, overgrazing, hunting, etc. It is true that, with the establishment of a park in a given area, some richer households within the community might also find their land appropriated and existing economic activities being disturbed, but they are likely to receive lofty compensations or will have other economic possibilities. For poorer households, however, such an occurrence may mean the loss of their entire livelihood and culture. These and other pertinent socio-environmental consequences of protected areas are more closely examined in the following section.

Major Socio-Environmental Processes and Outcomes

There are several types of protected areas, and the purpose of their establishment is very broad (see Box 1.1). There are now close to 8500 units throughout the world, widely distributed across continents. Worldwide, the growth in national parks and protected areas has been relatively rapid over the last two decades. Protected areas now exist in 169 countries, covering approximately 7,734,900 square kilometres or some 5.2 per cent of the Earth's land area (an area roughly equivalent to the size of the United States (excluding Alaska) or twice the size of India). In 115 countries, 1328 sites covering some 3,061,300 square kilometres have marine or coastal elements within them (WCMC, 1992). Strictly protected areas (national parks, strict nature reserves, natural monuments) cover 3 per cent of the Earth's surface. Of these areas, 1508 are national parks of the Yellowstone model. At least another 40,000 protected areas of various sorts have been established that do not meet the criteria of the World Congress on National Parks and Protected Areas (CNPPA), but which contribute to

Box 1.1 *The definition, categories and main functions of protected areas established by IUCN and CNPPA*

A protected area is an area of land and/or sea especially dedicated to the protection of biological diversity, and of natural and associated cultural resources, and managed through legal or other effective means (McNeely, 1993; IUCN, 1994a).

IUCN recognizes six management categories:

Category I   Strict Nature Reserve/Wilderness Area. Protected area managed mainly for science or wilderness protection.

Category II   National Park. Protected area managed mainly for ecosystem protection and recreation.

Category III   Natural Monument/Natural Landmark. Protected area managed mainly for conservation of a specific natural feature.

Category IV   Habitat and Species Management Area. Protected area mainly for conservation through management intervention.

Category V   Protected Landscape/Seascape. Protected area managed mainly for Landscape/Seascape protection and recreation.

Category VI   Managed Resource Protected Area. Protected area managed mainly for the sustainable use of natural resources.

The CNPPA has defined seven purposes for protected areas (McNeely, 1993). These are to:
1   Safeguard the world's outstanding areas of living richness, natural beauty and cultural significance as a source of inspiration and an irreplaceable asset;
2   Maintain the life-supporting diversity of ecosystems, species, genetic varieties, and ecological processes;
3   Protect genetic variation and species which are needed to meet human needs, e.g. in food and medicine;
4   Provide homes to human communities with traditional cultures and knowledge of nature;
5   Protect landscapes reflecting a history of human interaction with the environment;
6   Provide for scientific, educational, recreational and spiritual needs of societies;
7   Provide benefits to local and national economies and as models for sustainable development to be applied elsewhere.

biodiversity conservation. This brings the total land area protected up to almost 10 per cent (McNeely, 1994).

National parks and other protected areas are seen as important instruments for the conservation of biological diversity. According to the IVth World Congress on National Parks and Protected Areas (CNPPA) held in Caracas in 1992, each country should now designate a minimum of 10 per cent of each biome under its jurisdiction (e.g., oceans, forests, tundra, wetlands, grasslands) as a protected area (McNeely, 1993). Many countries have already included more than 10 per cent of their territories in protected areas, and some countries — such as Costa Rica, Honduras, Bhutan, Botswana and Tanzania — have already brought nearly 25 per cent of their national territories under protected areas, and many more are approaching this level (MacKinnon et al., 1986; McNeely, 1993; Utting, 1993; Ghimire, 1994).

The IUCN encourages its member countries to include the full range of protected area categories in their national programmes (IUCN, 1994a). For each of the six proposed categories, the IUCN recommends that the area should be managed primarily for conservation purposes and that any human use in the protected area should not conflict with that primary purpose. In this context, it is particularly noteworthy that the newly introduced category VI allows for the sustainable use of natural ecosystems but, in practice, at least two-thirds of the area must remain in its 'natural state' for inclusion in this internationally accepted category. Although this latest IUCN category was apparently designed to integrate social development concerns in protected area management, human settlements and resource use by local people are only tolerated as exceptions.

Moreover, the different protected area categories which do allow for some human use are very unevenly represented in the developed and developing countries. Category V, Protected Landscapes/Seascapes, is especially relevant here. By definition a Protected Landscape/Seascape is:

> *an area of land, with coast and sea as appropriate, where the inter-action of people and nature over time has produced an area of distinct character with significant aesthetic, ecological and/or cultural value, and often with high biological diversity. Safeguarding the integrity of this traditional interaction is vital to the protection, maintenance and evolution of such an area (IUCN, 1994a).*

Out of a world total of 2273 Protected Landscapes/Seascapes recognized by IUCN (IUCN, 1994b), over half the Category V sites are located in Europe, with 1307 sites covering 6.6 per cent of the continent's surface. This reflects the view that conservation — in Europe at least — depends on the inclusion of people, and therefore places where people co-exist with nature are worthy of special attention. In sharp contrast, however, Category V sites are under-represented in the protected area networks of the developing world: four sites for the whole of Central America (0.01 per cent of the land area), 56 in South Asia (0.09 per cent), 20 in sub-Saharan Africa (0.1 per cent), seven in the Pacific (0.03 per cent) and 175 in South America (1.1 per cent) (WCMC, 1994).

Two related conventions signed in the 1970s for protected sites are the World Heritage Convention for areas of outstanding universal value and the Ramsar Convention for wetlands. Although not an international convention, the UNESCO 'Man and the Biosphere' (MAB) programme designates biosphere reserves in which the human component is generally thought to be vital for the long-term integrity of the reserves. Similarly, the concept of 'cultural landscapes' under the World Heritage Convention explicitly recognizes the role of human agents in the continuing, organic evolution of whole landscapes (Phillips, 1995). In practice, however, the recognition of cultural landscapes and the creation of the legal basis for their management have been an exclusively Euro-centric phenomenon. This partly reflects the greater attention which has been given to the evolution of rural landscapes in Europe in particular; these have been subject to detailed scrutiny by cultural historians, geographers and human ecologists. Similar well-researched and documented analysis of national landscape types and their evolution has all too often been lacking in the developing world.

Following the 1992 Earth Summit in Rio and the ratification of the Conventions on Biodiversity, Climate Change and Desertification, many more developing countries are coming under pressure to increase areas under protected regimes. Besides the forest and wetland areas, village commons, woodlots and watershed areas are increasingly included in parks and reserves. The creation of corridors to link different protected areas by incorporating marginal lands, riverside areas and, at times, settlements is being commonly emphasized in national conservation plans (see Chapter VII). Wetland and coastal areas are also increasingly transformed into protected areas. Recently, it has become fashionable to establish cross-border parks (Koch, 1995). These measures are likely to lead to a significant increase in the national territories under protected areas, with usually severe impacts on local livelihoods and culture.

Costs to Livelihoods and Culture

The management of protected areas in developing countries all too often entails huge social and ecological costs. These are rarely perceived as likely to be significant during the process of designation but may ultimately threaten the long-term viability of protected areas themselves. The devastating consequences of resettlement schemes for indigenous peoples and peasant communities removed from areas earmarked for conservation are particularly noteworthy in this context (see Chapter IV). So are the enduring negative impacts of coercive conservation programmes implemented by the former apartheid governments of Rhodesia (Zimbabwe) and South Africa (see Chapters IX and VIII).

12

A growing body of empirical evidence now indicates that the transfer of 'Western' conservation approaches to the developing countries has had adverse effects on the food security and livelihoods of people living in and around protected areas (Ghimire, 1994; Kothari et al., 1989; West and Brechin, 1991). On several occasions, local communities have been expelled from their settlements without adequate provision for alternative means of work and income. In other cases, local people have faced restrictions in their use of common property resources for food gathering, harvest of medicinal plants, grazing, fishing, hunting and collection of wood and other wild products from forests, wetlands and pastoral lands. National parks established on indigenous lands have denied local rights to resources, turning local people practically overnight from hunters and cultivators to 'poachers' and 'squatters' (Colchester, 1994).

More insidiously, the exclusion of resident people from protected areas aggravates the loss of valuable traditional knowledge of plant, animal and microbial species used for food, medicinal and other purposes. Rural processing technologies and innovations which evolved over many generations also disappear together with the capacity for indigenous experimentation that historically produced a myriad of sophisticated agricultural and ecological management systems (Wood, 1995; Altieri, 1987).

Rebuilding the relationship between local people, and authorities and conservation organizations after a history of policing and exclusion is difficult. The use of coercive methods that are assumed to be valid for all people, all times and all places is counter-productive. These measures most often disempower local communities and directly or indirectly impose more restrictions, from total exclusion to the selective denial of access to certain resources. Denying use of resources to local people severely reduces their incentive to conserve these resources. Moreover, the current style of protected area management usually results in high management costs for governments in the South, with the majority of benefits accruing to national and international external interests.

Erosion in Traditional Resource Use and Protection

Paradoxically, the exclusion of indigenous peoples and peasants, the neglect of their knowledge and resource management institutions can, at times, lead to a gradual impoverishment of biological diversity. For example, the conservation value of national parks in East Africa has been recently questioned:

> *The implicit assumption in creating a park is that protection will maintain and most likely enhance biological diversity. In reality, the opposite may be the case. Part of the reason stems from the large role human ecology has played in shaping and maintaining the East African savannas....The biological inadequacy of protected*

areas has only become apparent in recent years (Western and Giochoi, 1993:270).

By excluding local people from protected areas, present mainstream conservation strategies for forests, wetlands, pastoral lands, semi-arid environments, and hilly and mountain areas remove the anthropogenic disturbance of ecosystems which may be essential for the generation and conservation of biological diversity. The integrity of biodiversity-rich areas can also be impaired when the historical process that has been responsible for their present character is stopped by restricting or prohibiting local use of land and other natural resources inside protected areas (see Pimbert and Pretty, 1995; Pimbert and Toledo, 1994; Wood, 1995).

As mentioned earlier, protected area management has often been based on a far too static view of ecosystem dynamics. It needs to become cognizant with, and build on, the mutually reinforcing links between local livelihood activities and the enhancement of genetic, species and ecosystem diversity (see Chapter XI). There is, of course, an upper limit to the positive effects of disturbance on diversity. The diversity of biological communities is bounded by the richness of the source pool for recolonization and, at some point, the disturbance regime becomes so severe that it makes the environment uninhabitable except for the hardiest colonizing species. However, from a conservation perspective, indigenous or local management can provide the controlled disturbance needed for the maintenance of ecosystem diversity and maximum species diversity. Strict preservation could ultimately destroy biodiversity as well as the indigenous knowledge needed for sustainable ecosystem management.

This is not to suggest that all local communities and indigenous peoples everywhere conserve biological diversity. While many indigenous peoples see clearly that their long-term survival depends on them caring for their land for the benefit of future generations, their societies are undergoing rapid change. The loss of their ancestral territories to outsiders, pressures on local communities and environments to produce a marketable surplus and the use of new technologies, like chainsaws and agricultural chemicals, have upset traditional patterns of land ownership, management and use. More generally, when referring to human impacts on biodiversity-rich areas it is important to distinguish the ecological consequences of subsistence or low external input activities geared to satisfying local needs and markets from those impacts inflicted by industrial activities fuelled by the global market and extremely powerful commercial interests (e.g., timber, mining, tourism and fishing industries, and bioprospecting agents).

Growing Social Conflict

Parks and reserves have become a major source of rural tension in most developing countries. This is due in part to the near-secretive way in

14

which decisions to establish parks and reserves are made in the capital cities by national authorities, usually with financial and technical assistance from foreign aid and conservation agencies. The following example from Nepal illustrates how opaque such park projects can sometimes be:

> *The sorry saga of Khaptad National Park unfolded slowly. It began some ten years back when a few villagers encountered some people from outside the area. In reply to the traditional, friendly inquisition by the villagers, the outsiders replied 'don't worry'. These people had actually been demarcating the boundary of the park (Rana, 1992).*

The cases in which local populations are fully involved in project design from the beginning are rare. Moreover, as human settlements in and around a park or reserve are considered a nuisance to wildlife, people are usually removed. Where this is not politically feasible, smaller, selected groups of populations, such as the indigenous, long-settled or households inhabiting the periphery, are allowed to stay. The so-called migrants, new settlers or those living in core areas are required to vacate the area. In certain states of Brazil, for example, the government has decided to allow only the 'traditional' populations to remain inside the park, provoking much internal dissension among the local population (Castell and Vereecken, 1995). This has, at the same time, made it easier for the government to intervene. The habitually negative official attitude towards the local populations means that even when some compensation is provided — such as payment for land acquisition or provision of income generating activities — a deep local suspicion prevails.

Reliance on rigid laws and coercion, at times reaching 'militaristic proportions' (Peluso, 1992a:3), often leads local populations into direct conflict with parks authorities. It is therefore not surprising that in many localities park guards and wardens are among the most detested government officials. Although sporadic in nature, organized protests and rallies, attacks on park guards, poisoning of animals and deliberate burning of forests are becoming common events in many developing countries. Strong contentions surrounding land claims have surfaced at the national level in many countries. In India, resentment by local people to protected area legislation and enforcement agencies has led to acts of sabotage and civil disobedience, setting fire to large areas or parks, alliance with insurgent movements to drive out parks guards, as well as killing wildlife to provide funds in support of these movements (Gadgil and Guha, 1992; Roy and Jackson, 1993; Kumar, 1993; Fürer-Haimendorf, 1986). This conflict in and around protected areas has often tended to take attention away from the more deep-rooted problem of overexploitation of resources by dominant urban-industrial interests. India has recently experienced a number of denotifications or boundary alterations of sanctuaries and national parks to accommodate commercial pressures (Sarkar et al., 1995).

In Thailand, the expulsion of large numbers of settlers as well as growing restrictions on resource use by local populations on the one hand, and rapid 'privatization' of park areas by tourism development involving growth in hotels, bungalows, golf courses and resorts on the other have provoked many sustained protests by local populations. Some observers describe this situation as a 'parks war' (see Handley, 1994:36). In Africa, hostile actions against parks have been recorded in South Africa, Namibia, Zimbabwe, Uganda, Kenya, as well as in many West and Central African countries (see Chapter VIII). In Latin America too, open protests have commonly occurred, namely in the southern and eastern states of Brazil, and in Ecuador, Costa Rica, Nicaragua, Guatemala and Mexico (Barraclough and Ghimire, 1995; Utting, 1993).

Given that more areas are being brought under the network of protected areas than the existing management capacity can cope with, and that the present models do not offer viable alternatives to affected populations, a large number of parks and reserves have been failures, as much on environmental as social grounds. Growing social conflict surrounding the use of natural resources has meant that parks and reserves are unable to fulfil even their narrow conservation mandate. If the degradation of natural resources outside the park or reserve and the erosion in traditional resource use and protection practices brought about in large part by the establishment of the protected area are considered, most parks and reserves would clearly have a negative environmental balance sheet. On the other hand, even for those which, at the present time, seem to be relatively successful in protecting biodiversity, the future remains far from certain because of their neglect of local and regional social exigencies. How long can a park or reserve exist when it is surrounded by discontent and sometimes hungry populations? Clearly, the prevailing conceptions and practices assure neither sustainable environmental conservation nor social gains to local populations.

What has Gone Wrong?

Differing National and International Interests and Priorities

Protected areas usually reflect the priorities of regional, national and international interests over local subsistence needs. The demarcation, management and infrastructure of protected areas all too often reinforce the interests of global conservation and those of the international leisure industry and other commercial groups. Local people often express their sense of deep frustration with these externally imposed priorities by saying that 'people should be considered before animals' (Hackel, 1993), and they often view 'wildlife conservation as alien, hypocritical, and as favouring foreigners' (Munthali, 1993).

Declaring biodiversity-rich areas as 'internationally important' conservation sites is meaningless for local resource users as long as the issues that emerge out of such declarations have not been discussed and resolved to the satisfaction of local communities. Farmers and forest dwellers who have lost land and/or traditional rights over resources cannot appreciate the value of vague 'long-term' conservation benefits for society or humanity. In their view, conservation benefits should be quantifiable — if possible immediate — with local people getting a fair share of the benefits accruing from the protected area.

In the vast majority of cases the gains of the preservationist mode of intervention have tended to be one-sided, going mainly to external groups interested in conservation and not to local people. However, it is the local communities who bear most of the hardship, through lost access to resources, damage to crops and through the physical danger presented by many wild animals. Koch and McIvor provide vivid examples of how the benefits of biodiversity conservation through tourism in South Africa and Zimbabwe are lowest or negative at the local level and highest for powerful commercial groups acting at a national or global level (Chapters VIII and IX, respectively). Ghimire's account of the scientific and international conservation interests associated with panda reserves in China also highlights the mismatch between local priorities and so called 'global conservation imperatives' (Chapter VII). The many social actors affected by conservation often have different interests, values and agendas. Blaikie and Jeanrenaud indicate how an appreciation of such differences in perspective can help to understand, and deal with, the contested meanings and priorities different actors project onto nature (Chapter II).

The priorities and diverse realities of rural people have also been largely misperceived by outside professionals who pretend to combine conservation with the satisfaction of human needs in park buffer zones and other so-called integrated conservation and development projects (ICDPs). Most of them have tended to project their own categories and priorities onto local people. In particular, their views of the realities of the poor and powerless, and what should be done, have generally been constructed from a distance and mainly for professional convenience (Chambers, 1992).

Livelihood systems are diverse in rural areas, where inhabitants commonly rely on a mix of wild foods, agricultural produce, remittances, trading and wage labour. Household decision-making continually adjusts to the changing nature of the environment and local economies. Household livelihood strategies often involve different members in diverse activities and sources of support at different times of the year. Many of these, like collecting wild foods and medicine, home gardening, common property resources, share-rearing livestock and stinting, are largely unseen by outside professionals, including those involved in planning and evaluating ICDPs.

Measures to combat poverty and hardship induced by a protected area scheme in a developing country usually emphasize the creation of full- or part-time jobs in, for example, the tourism and crafts sector. Employment and wages thus become standard forms of compensation for lost livelihoods — the many activities which make up a living. The problem is that for most rural people, and particularly for the weak and vulnerable, employment is only one component of livelihood. Informed by reductionist employment thinking, well-meaning job creation strategies substitute for other, more imaginative, approaches which might seek to sustain local livelihoods by building on a multiplicity of activities and resources. Culturally specific ways of relating to the world and organizing economic life are thus displaced in favour of the more uniform industrial-urban development model of the North (see Chapters VI and XI).

A final example of the misfit between local realities and externally defined priorities stems from the way biological diversity and wild resources used by local communities are valued in economic terms. The few economic analyses of biological diversity conducted so far have essentially focused on global values and foreign exchange elements and very little on the household use values of, for example, 'wild' foods and medicines (Scoones et al., 1992; Gujit et al., 1995). Simple economic valuations based on direct use values (for consumption or sale) (see Pearce et al., 1989) have often been misleading and too reductionist to provide a sound decision-making basis for policy makers and land-use planners. Moreover, until recently, few comprehensive local level studies were available even to begin to understand the range of ways biodiversity matters to local people, or how values fluctuate according to season or to the many viewpoints of highly differentiated local communities. The economic and social values of much of the biodiversity that nurtures people in and around protected areas have been ignored or underestimated by outside professionals. This has biased conventional resource planning in ICDPs in favour of species of commercial importance, or commodity food crops.

The priorities and needs of rural people in developing countries simply cannot be understood and met through concepts and categories derived from the urban industrial experience of the developed countries. While the above examples of professional biases are also rampant in the wider community of development planners, economists and agricultural scientists (Chambers, 1993), the problem is compounded in public and private conservation organizations because they have few, if any, sociologists or anthropologists working in the field or at headquarters. Moreover, many specialists originating from these latter groups become quickly co-opted within the dominant thinking of conservation.

Rights, Security and Territory

In many European countries, including Germany and France, the long-established order of land tenure and rights of access to resources has generally been respected in recent decades (see Chapters III and VI). British conservationists accepted the vision of nature as part of a process of 'continuity and gradual change, with man at the centre and integral to the rural landscape' (Blacksell, cited in Harmon, 1991:34). National parks in Britain thus recognized existing rights and sought to maintain the established pattern of farming and land use by rural communities.

Colonial powers carried with them to the tropics little of this respect for traditional rights and uses. International conservation organizations and national governments also have a long history of denying the rights of indigenous peoples and rural communities over their ancestral lands and the resources contained therein. For example, most of the very large area earmarked for conservation in Costa Rica is under a strictly protected regime that excludes local communities, unlike in Germany where protected area regimes represent more of a 'social compromise' (see Chapter III). This negation of the prior rights of indigenous and other local communities has been one of the most enduring sources of conflicts and violence, both in the developing world and in advanced industrialized nations such as Canada where aboriginal peoples seek greater self-determination by regaining control over territories now enclosed in the country's protected area network (see Chapter X).

As scientific documentation and understanding improve, 'wild' resources and areas are increasingly seen as the result of co-evolutionary relationships between humans and nature. Recognition of anthropogenic landscapes and 'wild' species moulded by human activity has important implications for ownership and, consequently, for rights over access to and use of biological resources found in protected areas. However, in the rush to 'exploit' the biological wealth of protected areas in the developing countries, little or no attention is given to the intellectual property rights of local communities who have shaped the 'wild' and enhanced biological diversity.

Indeed, recent advances in biotechnologies and genetic engineering have increased the commercial value of the genes and biochemical substances found in the diverse flora and fauna conserved in protected areas. Bioprospecting expeditions by Northern based institutions often use the knowledge of local peoples to identify promising drugs, biopesticides and other new 'natural' products. A very small fraction of the benefits derived from the commercialization of biological resources is retained in the country, let alone the community, where the collections take place (UNDP, 1994). Moreover, commercial companies protect their new found 'discoveries' and products with the help of patents and other intellectual property rights. These Western concepts of private property do not recognize the intellectual contributions and informal innovations of indigenous and rural peoples who have modified, conserved and managed so-called 'wild' plant and animal species (Crucible Group, 1994). Such extractivism and unfair enrichment is also implicitly encouraged by mainstream conservation interventions based on top-down

19

planning and operational procedures in which outside professionals largely neglect local knowledge, skills and rights (see Chapters II and XI).

Lack of Code of Conduct

Powerful conservation agencies and individuals, with their close contacts with national elites, have tended to design protected area management systems in a uniform manner in most developing countries. Scientific and technical expertise is provided, while pressurizing the politicians and high-level officials to make environmental protection legally binding. Many of the politicians and officials may have direct or indirect financial or other gains (e.g., strengthening of patronage relationships) to make as well, since environmental initiatives usually imply creating new projects and programmes and business opportunities. A few of them might be genuinely concerned about the deteriorating environmental health and associated long-term negative impacts on living conditions of certain population groups.

The environmental agencies and specialists might somehow be answerable to their supporters and contributors in their home constituencies, although many are not, but they are accountable for their action neither to the government nor to people in developing countries. They prescribe various environmental protection models and laws, but these are to be followed mainly by the national authorities and their people. Occasionally, politicians become unpopular by proposing strict protection measures, and may experience unfavourable electoral consequences. However, conservation organizations and influential natural scientists are not required to interact directly with the local population that is being affected, nor do they face negative electoral consequences. For instance, there exists no legal or political framework that would permit local populations to seek justice for social conflicts and misery caused by any international or national conservation organizations and environmentalists. This has in many ways allowed conservation organizations and professionals to put exclusive emphasis on narrowly defined environmental protection and neglect social needs.

Lack of Concern for Local People's Well-being

Improvement of the livelihood conditions of local people has seldom been a goal when protected areas are established. The present management systems are concerned essentially with the pure protection of flora and fauna and seek to separate local communities from their customary interactions with the local ecology. The concept of strictly protected areas is too narrow to permit integrated resource management.

A more positive attitude in establishing and managing protected areas would open doors for many socially desirable opportunities and actions. For example, preoccupation would change from 'how can people be removed from the parks and reserves in order to end encroachment and poaching?' to 'how can people achieve improved levels of living so that their reliance on the park resources is reduced and they have a real interest in protecting them?' The questions to be addressed would be: what are the resources that might be used by local communities for their subsistence and for generating income without seriously degrading the local ecosystem? How can the park administration together with other state institutions mobilize local and external resources and services in support of local efforts to increase food production and income generation? (see Chapter VI).

Any improvement in crop production, livestock raising and the local agro-ecology depends upon the park authority's full acceptance of people's customary access to land, as well as its involvement in intensifying production activities. Marginal areas or the land adjacent to the park boundary could be used for agro-forestry systems designed to increase local food availability and wood products, as well as to improve watershed conditions. Indigenous peoples, poor farmers, fisherfolk, pastoralists and women could collect numerous items without degrading the park, for example, forest foods, fibres, medicinal plants, construction materials, fuel and other useful biomass, depending upon resource availability and the existing cultural and livelihood practices (Chapters V, VII and XI; see also Cunningham, 1993a). Many of these items represent important sources of income when sold, but this is only possible when authorities allow people to enter the park and harvest resources. Park administration and protection activities may represent some employment possibilities for local populations, but only when they are given priority in recruitment. They could be assisted in running shops, itinerant businesses and producing or selling of handicraft goods. But the absence of any obligation to promote the livelihood interests of local communities within protected area management systems simply means that, even when the potential for local social development is stated in the project documents, this is not fulfilled. It often serves to attract foreign funding — which can eventually be used for non-social items (e.g., flora-fauna surveys, patrolling, official buildings and vehicles) or creating ad hoc development projects.

Bureaucracies and Local Institutions

Government, para-government and private sector organizations, together with their donors, have tended to prefer large conservation projects to less visible, small projects. The reasons are analogous to those which plague rural development projects. As Chambers states:

> *big is beautiful because big is bankable; pressures to spend aid funds are best overcome through large projects......They are usually highly visible and photogenic....They may provide opportunities*

21

for corruption at the higher levels of government. They provide contacts for local professionals and civil servants which may make it easier for them to join the brain drain to the richer world. Consultants....find large projects a source of profitable employment. Implementation can be assured where necessary through the use of foreign skills. (Chambers, 1993)

International conservation organizations acting as technical advisors or implementors of national protected area strategies spend a large proportion of their funds on expatriate salaries, planes and helicopters for survey work, international travel and meetings. A very small part of the funds managed by these institutions is invested locally in capacity building and actual field-based conservation. Meanwhile, many government departments and field stations entrusted with day-to-day protected area management are clearly underfunded and suffer from a lack of co-ordination, or rivalry, with other departments (see Chapters III and VIII). Low government staff salaries act as disincentives and all too often encourage rent-seeking behaviour, as Dey points out in her study on protected area management in West Bengal, India (Chapter V). The emphasis on state and professional control, often encouraged by suspicion and distrust of local people, means that a substantial proportion of protected area budgets must be spent on policing activities. When funding is withdrawn, protection and park management activities are jeopardized. Institutional interventions are rarely designed in such a way that at the end of the project cycle there are local institutions and skills in place to ensure the continuation of protected area management, without further need for external inputs.

The undermining of local institutions and systems of resource management is no doubt the most debilitating and enduring impact of national and international bureaucracies. They have tended to substitute for local action, thus stifling any existing initiatives and institutions. Through their radical monopoly control over management priorities and implementation, many conservation institutions and their donors have seriously impaired local and national capacities for sustainable natural resources management.

Several chapters in this book highlight the importance of local institutions for the management of wildlife and protected areas and for coping with changing economic conditions. For as long as people have engaged in livelihoods pursuits, they have worked together on resource management, labour sharing, marketing and many other activities that would be too costly, or impossible, if done alone. Local groups and indigenous institutions have always been important in facilitating collective action and co-ordinated natural resource management.

Indigenous peoples' resource management institutions probably offer the most striking evidence of active conservation. These institutions include rules about use of biological resources and acceptable distribution of benefits, definitions of rights and responsibilities, means by which tenure is determined, conflict resolution mechanisms and methods of enforcing rules, cultural sanctions and beliefs (Alcorn, 1994). Similarly, the literature on common property resources highlights the importance and resilience of local management systems for natural resources and sustainable livelihoods (Arnold and Stewart, 1991; BOSTID, 1986; Bromley and Cernea, 1989; Ostrom, 1990; Jodha, 1990; Niamir, 1990).

Limited Popular Participation

There are few examples of conservation initiatives based on indigenous knowledge and rule-making institutions. Pimbert and Pretty argue that the way conservation bureaucracies and external institutions are organized and the way they work currently inhibit this devolution of power in protected area management (Chapter XI). Moreover, despite repeated calls for peoples' participation in conservation over the last twenty years (e.g., Forster, 1973; McNeely and Miller, 1984; McNeely, 1993), the term 'participation' is generally interpreted in ways which cede no control to local people. It is rare for conservation professionals to relinquish control over key decisions on protected area design, management and evaluation. Participation is still largely seen as a means to achieve externally desirable conservation goals. This means that, while recognizing the need for peoples' participation, many conservation professionals place clear limits on the form and degree of participation that they tolerate in protected area management.

Existing conservation institutions and professionals need to shift from being project implementors to new roles which facilitate local people's analysis and planning. The whole process should lead to building or strengthening local institutions, so enhancing the capacity of people to take action on their own. This implies a new professionalism in conservation with new concepts, values, participatory methodologies and behaviour (see Chapter XI).

Review of Major Initiatives

There are now many examples of projects seeking to use local economic incentives for the conservation and sustainable use of biological diversity in and around protected areas (Kiss, 1990; McNeely, 1988; Sayer, 1991; Stone, 1991; Wells et al., 1992). Some of these initiatives are 'official accommodation responses' to the growing opposition to parks and local resource alienation. Nonetheless, a few of them are somewhat challenging the dominant conservation approaches. The main initiatives which claim to be based on more equitable power- and benefit-sharing arrangements are critically outlined below, and further analysed in later chapters.

CAMPFIRE and Related Institutions for Wildlife Management

CAMPFIRE (Communal Area Management Programme for Indigenous Resources) is often presented as the best example of community based resource management and development in Africa. This experiment for wildlife utilization in Zimbabwe has pointed to the potentials for the devolution of control over natural resource management to local communities. The idea is that the CAMPFIRE scheme should allow for the co-management of wildlife by the government, district councils and local communities, as well as return to local councils of some of the revenues earned through safari hunting and tourism. The money is then reinvested in community development projects, to compensate for the wildlife damage incurred and increase the economic incentive for local management of wildlife (see Chapter IX and Peterson, 1994). The CAMPFIRE programme does not attempt to enforce its existence in situations where local communities and government agencies are aware that it is a suboptimal use of land. In other words, the programme is driven by a desire to make wildlife a competitive form of land use.

Realizing some of the problems in the ways wildlife and other resources had been managed, the government of Zimbabwe passed an amendment to the Parks and Wildlife Act in 1982 to enable districts and local communities to gain some benefits from wildlife resources, marking the beginning of what would become known as CAMPFIRE. By 1990, CAMPFIRE was working in 12 districts, and by September 1994 in 22 districts. Operating under a concept of adaptive management, CAMPFIRE has evolved a set of principles based on experience, rather than a centrally designed programme. Conservation and government officials claim that the CAMPFIRE programme has eliminated or drastically reduced poaching, re-awakened local peoples' appreciation of the value of wildlife, increased household revenues and encouraged the use of wildlife revenues for food security in times of drought.

However, the CAMPFIRE programme has also faced many constraints. The administrative structure of local government is an outside imposition, with elected representatives, and traditional village leaders who may or may not sit on the councils. As a result, the delineation of village and ward boundaries does not necessarily correspond with the traditionally evolved communities, or with discrete ecological zones. Councils often preside over wards of high human density and low wildlife populations along with wards of low population density and substantially larger wildlife populations. In the first group, wards have high development demands and low wildlife revenues but pay few of the costs associated with wildlife. In the second group, the opposite is the case.

The main obstacles to the progress of the CAMPFIRE programme have been the councils' 'bureaucratic impulse to retain authority, the necessity for councils to raise revenues and the fact that councils do not trust local communities to make the right decisions' (Murphree, 1993). The councils have been unwilling to devolve real responsibility and power to local communities to manage their own wildlife resources. Above all, councils have not passed on to local communities the full amounts of revenue generated from wildlife management. Indeed, councils have appropriated most of the revenues generated by their communities, made promises of revenue distributions which they have not kept, ignored local needs for training and marginalized any genuine participation in wildlife planning and management by local people. The outcome has been hostility or cold indifference to the CAMPFIRE programme, mistrust of councils, increasing intolerance and resentment vis-à-vis wildlife and a continued lack of communal environmental controls.

The fundamental issue facing CAMPFIRE is whether government institutions are based on decisions made by the people or for the people (Peterson, 1994). The essential institutional profile for successful local management must bring together ownership, management, cost and benefit of wildlife in one unit. The proper administrative units for CAMPFIRE implementation are ultimately ward and village development committees. According to Murphree, effective incentives for local level sustainable management of wildlife and other common property resources must include institutional reforms that vest control and planning with local user groups, legislation that recognizes and guarantees rights for local people over the use and benefits of wild resources, and economic incentives and effective mechanisms for controlling access and the sharing of benefits locally (Murphree, 1994). McIvor argues that wider structural changes such as land distribution are especially important (see Chapter IX).

There is, however, no 'blueprint' for an ideal communal management regime over wildlife and other natural resources. The variables are so diverse and context-specific that similar initiatives elsewhere must be based on experiential learning and locally negotiated action, not on simplistic carbon copies of the CAMPFIRE programme (see Chapter VIII).

Joint Forest Management (JFM)

Joint management schemes for forest use have had some notable success in India. The chapter by Dey in this volume critically looks at what happens in practice, in particular with respect to women. Enlightened officials in several states began to realize in the late 1970s and 1980s that they could not realistically hope to protect forests without the help and involvement of local communities. About 95 per cent of India's forest lands are owned by state governments and forest protection and exclusion through policing had not proved sustainable. Considerable local resistance had created a major crisis in Indian forestry (Guha, 1989). A number of initiatives in West Bengal, Gujarat, Haryana and the Himalayan region began to evolve joint management schemes between the state and local communities. The idea was to give local people a stake

25

in the protection of the forests through the sharing of benefits, responsibilities and power.

Beginning in 1972, villagers in West Bengal formed Forest Protection Committees (FPCs) in co-operation with the Forest Department to regenerate sal (*Shorea robusta*) forests in degraded areas (Malhotra et al., 1991). The villagers protect the forest, while the Forest Department provides forestry and cash inputs. After a 10–15-year rotation, the villagers receive 25 per cent of the profits from the harvesting of sal timber. However, while the forest is regenerating, local people are free to collect a whole range of non-timber forest products used for food, fodder, fuel, fibre, household items and medicines. By 1990, 1611 FPCs had been established and were managing over 191,000 hectares of degraded sal forests. The significant increase in human population which took place at the same time and in the same districts where forest regeneration occurred is particularly noteworthy in this context.

Success in the form of biological regeneration and increased income was considered so remarkable in West Bengal and other parts of India, that the national government issued an order on 1 June 1990 requesting all states to undertake joint forestry management (Dhar et al., 1991; Campbell, 1992). More recently, the potential of extending JFM principles to protected area management were highlighted by key social actors from government departments and conservation organizations, and by social activists, in India (Sarkar et al., 1995). Major problems will need to be overcome to ensure the success of decisions to scale up and spread JFM across the land, and adapt its principles to protected area management (see Chapters V and XI). There are important discrepancies between what actually happens on the ground and how JFM is portrayed by outside professionals and institutions.

Official views of JFM are all too often based on self-deception and misleading feedback from the field. In many cases the Forest Department staff are not genuinely interested in people's participation, but merely want the co-operation of local communities to secure forest regeneration. There are examples of Forest Department pressure on the selection of village Forest Protection Committee members, though the latter is not supposed to be an extension of the Forest Department (Sarkar et al., 1995). Moreover, the Forest Department's and state-wide rigid regulations (e.g., on the choice of tree species, silvicultural practices and timber harvest time) are at odds with what is required for local-level adaptive planning. In this context, the mismatch between local and external visions of how the forest should be managed and what it should look like can be quite remarkable. Rather than encouraging forest management based on the uniform adoption of a 10–20-year timber harvest cycle, many tribal groups in West Bengal would call for further ecological succession, selective timber harvesting and species diversification within regenerating forest stands under JFM agreements. But on the whole, the attitudes and behaviour of forest officers remain paternalistic and profoundly disempowering. For example, informal comments by foresters working at different levels in the Forest Department hierarchy of the state of West Bengal often describe tribal people and their FPCs as 'ignorant', 'primitive', 'underdeveloped in all respects' and 'economically irrational' (Pimbert, 1994). The future of forests and local people depends on a radical shift from the current form of Joint Forest Protection to a more emancipatory form of Participatory Forest Management that devolves real power over key silvicultural and benefit-sharing decisions to local institutions. In that more enabling context, the granting of secure long-term tenure and rights of usufruct over trees and their products will be an essential ingredient of success. Today, many local communities dependent on the forests for their livelihoods have insecure rights and are aware that the Forest Department may take back the forests once they are regenerated and productive again.

Ecotourism

The recent conservation literature shows much enthusiasm about the prospects of 'ecotourism'. The concept itself is scarcely new, since it is basically another term for 'game' or 'nature' tourism. What is true, however, is that the significance of 'green' tourism has increased, as more areas are brought under protected area systems. The documents produced on the topic by important conservation and development agencies tend to present rather a promising picture of ecotourism. It is also considered a key source of foreign exchange earnings for the government and for the protected area, and a vital source of economic incentives for people living in or around the conservation area (Wells et al., 1992). Furthermore, ecotourism initiatives are considered to increase the environmental and cultural sensitivity of incoming tourists (Dixon and Sherman, 1990; Boo, 1990; Lindberg, 1991).

However, those studying ecotourism with a critical eye point out manifold shortcomings. As is often the case for classical tourism, ecotourism schemes tend not to be integrated with other sectors of the national or regional economy; and only a fraction of earnings generated actually reach or remain in the rural areas (Healy, 1992; Speelman, 1991; see Chapters VIII and IX). More importantly, the majority of the rural population is frequently bypassed economically even where some earnings remain in the tourist location, as they are used up by the related administration or appropriated by local elites and business people. At the same time, traditional livelihood sources and cultures are negatively affected in nearly all cases.

Koch, assessing the potential of ecotourism in the reconstruction of rural South Africa, argues that generating economic benefits and empowering rural people is only feasible when many wide-ranging reforms — such as restoration of land rights to local communities, support for new forms of land tenure, strengthening of community institutions, investment in technical and managerial skills and mandatory impact assessments of all ecotourism schemes — are carried out (see Chapter VIII). The necessary structural political and economic changes along these lines are difficult — in South Africa as in many other countries.

Extractive Reserves

The practice of 'extracting' forest resources is ancient, but a legal recognition of the populations involved as well as of the areas concerned is relatively recent. The new experience comes mainly from the Brazilian Amazon involving the use of forest extraction methods by rubber tappers, riverine dwellers, Indians and other forest-dependent people. By 1991, some 2.2 million hectares of Amazonian forest areas, inhabited by 6200 families, had been declared extractive reserves (Millikan, 1991; Hecht and Cockburn, 1990).

The extractive reserves have emerged as an attractive proposition within conservation circles because of the possibility of conserving tropical forests together with providing incomes to local populations (Reid et al., 1988; Schwartzman, 1989; Pearce, 1990). In practice, however, the overall ability of extractive reserves to protect both forests and the livelihoods of indigenous and other rural people has been limited. A major problem has been the lack of respect of the legal status of extractive reserves by powerful groups such as land speculators, cattle ranchers, loggers, mining groups and so forth. Another problem is the low and uncertain price of most extracted forest products, coupled with exploitative intermediaries (Barraclough and Ghimire, 1995).

It is estimated that, in the Amazonian region, some 300 to 500 hectares of forest areas would be needed for an average family to maintain its subsistence with present markets and technologies (ibid.). The requirement of relatively large forest areas is an inherent limitation of extractive reserves. They also need to be sparsely populated. Moreover, the country's other population groups may have conflicting aspirations and claims on the forest areas to be included in extractive reserves. For example, the entire indigenous and extractivist Amazonian Brazilian population makes about one tenth of 1 per cent of that country's population (ibid.).

The approach of extractive reserves places utmost faith on market mechanisms. The prospect of collecting forest products for sale and income is seen as an exemplary incentive to garner indigenous peoples' support for conservation. This market-driven orientation does not seek to strengthen traditional production, reciprocal and self-reliance systems which may be well adapted to local conditions. How would or should people survive if and when the extractable items became diminished, or the income generated from them did not correspond to prices for purchased necessities? Besides, an exclusive reliance on market mechanisms for the successful management of extractive reserves implies that any 'market failure' may mean the failure of the reserves as well.

A few studies looking at the prospects of forest extraction outside the Brazilian Amazon confirm many of these pitfalls. A study of resin tappers in Honduras reveals that due to insecure tenure, fluctuating prices and the breakdown of communal leadership and organization, neither the protection of forests nor the livelihood of resin tappers is ensured (Stanley, 1991). Another study in East Kalimantan, Indonesia, suggests similar tenural and community empowerment problems of rattan extractivists, given the current trend of opening the interior of Kalimantan to plantation projects, timber harvest and agricultural expansion. It has been suggested that the establishment of village reserves to allow local communities to have total control of their rattan production, rather than the establishment of large extractive reserves, might be a solution (Peluso, 1992b). Whether these village reserves would represent sufficient, sustainable livelihood sources for local communities is, however, another question. In many ways, the Joint Forest Management experiment in India is based on the notion of sustainable extraction and forest management. Yet, as discussed above, land rights are firmly vested on the Forest Department which does not wish to see community control over resources. Moreover, the prices of forest products are not guaranteed. Under these circumstances, local communities can scarcely expect fully secured livelihoods. In short, although the extractive reserves may present some prospects of sustainable resource use and forest protection in a limited number of cases, by no means do they offer a permanent solution to the widespread socio-economic marginalization and major processes of environmental degradation in rural areas.

Biodiversity Prospecting and Commercial Leases

Biodiversity prospecting (or bioprospecting) is the exploration, extraction and screening of biological diversity and indigenous knowledge for commercially valuable genetic and biochemical resources. It has become an integral part of the research and development (R&D) of large industrial corporations which market new natural products such as oils, drugs, perfumes, waxes, dyes and biopesticides (cf. Reid et al., 1993; UNDP, 1994; Baumann et al., 1996). The financial stakes are very high for the growing number of pharmaceutical corporations, biotechnology companies and their intermediaries which comb the forests, fields and waters of the developing world in search of biological wealth. For example, it is estimated that medicinal plants and micro-organisms from the biodiversity-rich developing countries contribute at least US$30 billion per year to the developed world's pharmaceutical industry (UNDP, 1994).

The first major bilateral contract for bioprospecting involved the US-based pharmaceutical giant Merck & Co. and the Instituto Nacional de Biodiversidad (INBio) of Costa Rica, a private non-governmental research institute. According to the two-year contract signed in 1991, INBio agreed to provide Merck's drug-screening programmes with

29

chemical extracts from wild plants, insects and micro-organisms mainly collected within Costa Rica's extensive protected area network, which holds a significant proportion of the region's remaining biological diversity. In return, Merck agreed to give INBio a two-year research budget of US$1.135 million, an undisclosed share of royalties on any resulting commercial products, and assistance to establish in-country capacity for drug research. Part of this money should be reinvested in conservation activities since the National Parks Agency of Costa Rica will receive 50 per cent of any royalties INBio may eventually receive and 10 per cent of its up-front payment from Merck.

The Merck-INBio agreement has been hailed as a 'model' agreement for bioprospecting and has attracted considerable attention from developing country governments, which perceive the potential to generate tangible economic benefits from biodiversity conservation. Collaborative efforts between the private and public sector have also been established. For example, three United States government agencies set up a programme in 1992 to fund 'International cooperative biodiversity groups' (ICBGs) designed to 'promote conservation of biological diversity through the discovery of bioactive agents from natural products, and to ensure that equitable economic benefits from these discoveries accrue to the country of origin' (Reid, 1994:252). The ICBGs claim to facilitate this process by linking developing country organizations and indigenous peoples with academic and industry partners in the United States such as Bristol-Myers Sqibb, Monsanto (Searle) and American Cyanamid (RAFI, 1994). It is argued that bilateral bioprospecting agreements offer positive local incentives for conservation and sustainable commercial opportunities. It is too early to assess fully the social and ecological impacts of bioprospecting. However, it is unlikely that, as currently practised in and around protected areas, bioprospecting will provide indigenous and local communities with important 'economic incentives for conservation' — as often claimed by mainstream conservation organizations and governments.

The Convention on Biological Diversity (CBD), which entered into force in December 1993, recognizes that states have sovereign rights over their biological resources, and that the terms and conditions for access to these materials are within the realm of national legislation (UNEP-CBD, 1994). Commercial contracts and other bilateral agreements for access to biodiversity are based on 'mutually agreed terms' (Article 15.4) between the national government and the bioprospecting firm. While Article 8(j) of the Convention also recognizes 'the knowledge, innovations and practices of indigenous and local communities' and specifically 'encourage[s] the equitable sharing of benefits arising from the utilization of such knowledge, innovations and practices', national legislations do not require that bioprospecting agreements be subject to the prior informed consent of local people. Negotiations at the international level are, after all, carried out by national elites on behalf of their people and bilateral agreements signed by the 'contracting parties' make little or no reference to local actors involved in biodiversity management. National sovereignty necessarily takes precedence over local control in the absence of state recognition of indigenous peoples' property rights, including the ability to control access to genetic resources within their living environments and control over production and marketing (GRAIN, 1995; Posey, 1995).

The CBD's language on intellectual property rights (IPRs) is subject to varying interpretations but does not compromise patent and intellectual property right systems based on Western concepts of property. A view from the pharmaceutical and agrochemical industry argues that the Convention may even go further than the General Agreement on Tariffs and Trade (GATT) in legitimizing industrial property regimes (Duesing, 1992). Furthermore, while the GATT-TRIPs agreement (on trade-related aspects of intellectual property rights) (Article 27.3) calls for the development of sui generis legislation for IPRs, there is considerable pressure to extend Northern-style IPRs to as many countries as possible through international negotiations in the World Trade Organization (WTO). Institutions and private corporations based in developed countries seek access to tropical biodiversity to develop, first and foremost, patented and profitable products. Patents and other IPRs are key elements in global industrial strategies for monopoly control over biological materials, knowledge and markets.

Although benefit-sharing agreements are frequently mentioned in commercial contracts between bioprospecting agents and sovereign states, the specific terms of benefit sharing are strictly confidential. Available evidence indicates that benefits shared with countries in which collections took place represent a small fraction of the annual R&D budget of the corporations involved (UNDP, 1994; RAFI, 1994). Moreover, indigenous and local people receive only a minuscule proportion of the profits generated from sales of products that embody their knowledge and resources. For example, Posey (1990) estimates that less than 0.001 per cent of the market value of plant-based medicines has been returned to indigenous peoples from whom much of the original knowledge came. And while various codes of conduct and guidelines have been developed to ensure greater equity, compensation and fair sharing of benefits between bioprospecting companies and local communities (e.g., FAO, 1993; WWF, UNESCO and Kew Gardens in Cunningham, 1993b; ASOMPS, 1992; Shelton, 1995), none are internationally legally binding. Nor are they applied in an exemplary manner in the field programmes of influential international conservation organizations involved in protected area management in developing countries.

The appropriation of local peoples' knowledge, innovations and biological resources for the purpose of commercial extraction and control may reach new heights with the leasing of protected areas. China, with its new policy emphasis on 'businesslike management' of protected areas, is seeking to lease out parks and reserves on a long-term basis to individuals and companies associated with large commercial interests, e.g.

31

tourist agencies, pharmaceutical companies, nature foundations, etc. (Chi and Liang, 1993:10–13). Similarly, 'Prime Sites for Lease in Zambian National Parks' was the title of an advertisement which appeared in the *Financial Times* of 9 August 1995. The Zambia Privatisation Agency (ZPA), an autonomous body of the Zambian government, offers competitive tender leases to foreign investors for 25 biodiversity-rich sites (5 to 105 hectares) in several Zambian national parks. The land within national parks remains the property of the government and the 10–25-year leases are available for US$100,000–300,000. In this advertisement the focus is on attracting investors for the tourism industry. However, these initiatives set convenient precedents for governments and corporations involved in bioprospecting and new natural product development. Will 'Parks for Life' (i.e., the IUCN motto for the World Congress on National Parks and Protected Areas held in Venezuela, 1992) become major instruments for the commodification of life and cultures in the brave new world of biotechnology and genetic engineering?

Changing the Current Course

Park project reports and protected area management plans usually include a long list of recommendations or action plans to be considered if the present course of activities were to be effective. The most obvious suggestions are the creation of effective legal instruments, availability of increased financial and technical assistance, establishment of new institutions and better co-ordination between those which already exist, improvement in infrastructure, undertaking of scientific research, monitoring, etc. Considerable emphasis is increasingly placed on the potential of market mechanisms to make the maintenance of parks and reserves financially self-reliant and contribute to local and regional economic development (e.g., through tourism). The importance of people's participation in protected area management is one aspect that is also now mentioned frequently. Most of these propositions are quite valid, but a major problem is that they have tended to be loaded with dominant conceptions and excessively generalized, often not suited to diverse local contexts. Inclusion of certain themes such as partnership with local people and integration of conservation activities with local and regional development has also been standardized; again problems lay in their true practice. What is especially worth mentioning is that most protected area management plans and evaluation reports avoid even referring to structural issues such as land reform, income distribution, decentralization of power, social mobilization, as well as local rights and sovereignty over resources, without which sustainable management and more socially oriented use of natural resources in rural areas is mere illusion.

A number of points are crucial here. First, the need to establish parks and reserves itself should be critically examined. The existing models and practices are concerned basically with how to increase the total surface under the national protected area network and ensure effective preservation. But how many parks and reserves should a country actually have? What proportion of the national territory should they represent, and why? In which ecological and socio-political zones should they be established? What proportion of the protected areas should be kept under a 'strictly' protected regime removed from local use, and why? These questions should be raised and addressed within the specific, unique context of each country. Unfortunately, this is rarely the case.

Logically, any environmental conservation initiative must lead to an improvement in the local ecology. Yet, as discussed above, the park's approach to conservation has frequently resulted in the degradation of a much larger surface than the area actually protected and has made local communities less responsible in their usually sustainable practice of natural resources management. It is clear that if the main intention of conservation initiatives is to improve local ecosystems, other models such as forest farming, watershed programmes, agro-forestry or even sustainable agricultural practices may be more adapted to diverse local circumstances. Parks and reserves may also fulfil this function in a limited manner if they are transformed into small ecological units such as 'village parks'.

At times, social and environmental exigencies might be at loggerheads. For example, if a forest area represents good land for crop production and animal husbandry — especially when food and income are most sought after — the locally desirable land use would certainly not be the establishment of a park or reserve where such activities would be severely controlled, if not altogether prohibited. Understandably, priorities of peasant, pastoral or fishing communities would be different from those of urban or foreign-based environmentalists. When should environmental priorities be superior to social ones? And, when should national and international needs take precedence and be imposed on local ones? Whose knowledge and whose reality should be taken into account?

Second, even when the establishment of strictly protected areas such as parks and reserves is seen as necessary, more flexible categories should be utilized. Biodiversity protection and livelihood activities do not come in to direct conflict everywhere. In mountain areas, wildlife habitat zones and settlement areas may exist at different elevations used for mutually exclusive purposes, as in the case of panda reserves in China (see Chapter VII). In semi-arid regions, cattle and many species of wildlife might intermingle and graze together. In tropical landscapes, it is sometimes difficult to determine where the settlements end and where the forests begin. In such cases, the validity of a conservation approach that seeks to separate people from the surrounding ecosystems can easily be questioned. More importantly, as pointed out above, numerous locally useful items can be extracted from forests and other protected areas without seriously degrading them. The existing protected area categories are too restrictive to allow sustainable resource use and management combining realistic

33

policies and institutions which harmonize the protection of unique species and ecosystems with the improvement of local livelihood systems.

In this respect, the present 'zoning' of parks and reserves also needs to be reviewed. The 'core' protective zones of parks and reserves have tended to be unrealistically large in relation to the 'buffer' zones where limited resource extraction is permitted. Indeed, the creation of 'buffer' zones, supposedly to allow customary resource-use activities, has usually implied further official encroachment into local woodlots and other common property resources such as marginal grazing lands, as it is the park and government officials who decide how these areas should be modified and used. If protected area management is to be made more consistent with human needs, the buffer zones must represent economically viable zones. In addition to this, local extraction of natural resources that are renewable and can be exploited without damaging the ecosystem should be considered in all zones. It is evident that this would call for institutional and policy changes. However, not to favour resource extraction because such arrangements need imaginative thinking and willingness on the part of the concerned officials is socially unjustifiable.

It is not enough to attempt to protect the landscape as such. Attention must be given instead to the ways of life of those who are the architects of the landscape, and upon whom the survival of biodiversity depends. In this connection, the concept of 'cultural landscapes' may be a more appropriate protected area category for the vast majority of socio-ecological contexts which inform, and renew, nature's diversity. The notion of 'cultural landscapes' challenges conservation NGOs and government agencies to be more holistic in their approach. After all, the management of an organically evolving cultural landscape calls for the presence of vital and sound local livelihood systems based on the use of landscape resources, although often the existing literature on 'cultural landscapes' does not recognize sufficiently many internal and external socio-economic changes that affect the concerned communities (cf. Birks et al., 1988; von Droste et al., 1995).

Third, although the design of rural development programmes to provide new sources of income and employment to the affected populations is not new in conservation planning, their actual outcomes remain extremely paltry. In part, this is due to a lack of proper orientation and reflection. Most conservation-associated rural development projects are scant, sectoral and short-term. Even where some benefits are to occur, it is the richer and more powerful individuals and social groups that benefit. They are top-down and charitable in nature, with little participation of local communities. Most of them have been initiated with the simple intention of reducing organized opposition to the establishment and expansion of protected areas (Ghimire, 1994). The lack of sensitivity to social development and human rights issues is being slowly recognized within mainstream conservation circles (Wells et al., 1992; see also Thin, 1995), but effective policy reforms and attitudinal changes are inhibited by the insidious legacy of preservationist ideologies, the professional resistance of old-school conservationists oriented towards habitat protection, and a centralized management out of touch with fast-changing rural realities (Chapters II, VII and XI). In some cases too, the wish to maintain a good 'corporate image' for fund raising purposes has encouraged an organizational culture unable to openly acknowledge and learn from past mistakes, and reorient conservation programmes accordingly (Chapter II).

Indeed, there has rarely been genuine concern for offering sustainable livelihood alternatives on the part of most conservation planners and administrators. Their firm priority has been to accomplish the objective of habitat or species protection. Most available project resources have been allocated for this purpose. Even when certain financial provisions have been made for the rural development component, much of the budget may be used for salaries, construction of office buildings, vehicle purchases, etc. (Ghimire, 1994). Moreover, no appropriate expertise has been made available in most cases. Even with the best intentions, how can an average biologist, botanist or ecologist comprehend complex local cultural norms, gender issues, social differentiation processes and so forth, which very often determine who will make gains and who will lose?

Whether the argument is that poverty is responsible for the existing pressure on the environment, or that rural people living adjacent to protected areas merit the same level of living as their urban counterparts, the related social issues should logically receive prominence in environmental and rural development planning. They should also receive attention because without sufficient care to local socio-economic improvement, the cause and action of nature conservation would, without any doubt, be ultimately frustrated. In short, the integrated conservation-development concept must approach the issue from the complex socio-cultural, economic and political angle rather than consider it as a mere means to vindicate narrow species-protection intents. More financial resources, matched with suitable expertise, must be made available to any concerted rural development initiative. Organizational cultures must nurture long-term visions and compassion for people, especially the weak and vulnerable.

Finally, a radical shift is required from imposed conservation which aims to retain external control of the management and end-uses of protected area resources, to an approach which devolves more responsibility and decision-making power to local communities. Protected areas are likely to be sustainable ecologically, economically and socially only if the overall management scheme can be made sufficiently attractive to local people for them to adopt it as a long-term livelihood strategy. As shown by a few recent experiences in participatory conservation (e.g., Pimbert et al., 1996; Wild and Mutebi, forthcoming; WWF and BSCRM, 1995; WWF and the Government of India, 1996), there is a need to combine the general validity of the ecological principles on which management plans rest with the site-specific knowledge, priorities and innovations of local communities. In that context, dialogue, negotiation, bargaining and conflict resolution are all integral parts of a long-term participatory process which continues well after the initial appraisal and planning phases.

From the outset, the definition of what constitutes a protected area, how it should be managed, and for whom, needs to be based on interactive dialogue to understand both how local livelihoods are constructed and people's own definitions of well-being. Participatory protected area management must start not with analysis by powerful and dominant outsiders, but with enabling local people, especially the poor, to conduct their own. This implies the use of participatory methodologies by staff of conservation NGOs and government agencies as well as a shift from top-down teaching to learning which is shared, lateral and based on experience.

However, the adoption of a participatory culture and changes in professional attitudes and behaviour are unlikely to follow automatically when new methods are adopted. Training of agency personnel in participatory principles, concepts and methods must be viewed as part of a larger process of reorienting institutional policies, procedures, financial management practices, reporting systems, supervisory methods, reward systems and in-house norms (cf. Thompson, 1995; Absalom et al, 1995). Institutionalizing and operationalizing participatory approaches in conservation bureaucracies will be an arduous task in which trial and error, self-critical reflection, experimentation and innovation will be critical ingredients of success. Much might be learnt from the few examples of institutional transformation in large-scale programmes dealing with rural development, agricultural research and extension, soil and water management and education (see Bawden, 1994; Hinchcliffe et al, 1995; Thompson, 1995; Scoones and Thompson, 1994; Uphoff, 1992).

Genuine popular participation should mean that the powerless develop, create and systematize their own knowledge and begin to define their own vernacular forms of conservation and management schemes. For example, indigenous peoples such as the Ye'kuana in Venezuela have developed community procedures to demarcate their territories. By delimiting sacred sites or areas of cultural and historical significance, local communities can consciously plan what is to be protected in the landscape. A complex mosaic and integrated mix of different habitats, corresponding to different community needs, priorities and abilities, may prove to be the best mechanism to conserve biological diversity in areas where local livelihoods are directly dependent on continued access to natural resources. Landscape ecologists increasingly view this patchy structure of the landscape as important for the maintenance of fundamental ecological processes and biological diversity (Baker, 1992). Disturbance resulting in patchy vegetation in various stages of recovery encourages new colonizations and enhances both habitat and species diversity (Reice, 1994).

Some indigenous and local communities have outlined more clearly how outside organizations and professionals interested in the biodiversity on their lands should behave, and what their rights and obligations are towards local people. For example, the Kuna of Panama and the Inuit Tapirisat of Canada have established guidelines to ensure that research carried out on their territories is controlled by the local communities. Such community controlled research (CCR) may allow indigenous peoples to better manage access and use of, for example, ethno-botanical knowledge which is increasingly targeted by bioprospectors working for pharmaceutical companies (Posey and Dutfield, 1996). The Kuna produced an information manual which includes guidelines for scientific researchers as well as a presentation of Kuna objectives with respect to forest management, conservation of biological and cultural wealth, scientific collaboration and research priorities. However, their territories have also been continuously invaded by loggers, ranchers and squatters, and internal solidarity is receding in the face of market and other external pressures (Barraclough and Ghimire, 1995). These are issues commonly confronted by most indigenous groups and forest-dependent communities.

The combination of participatory rural appraisal and local-level ecological and economic valuation methods in conservation and land-use planning can provide a better understanding of local realities and aspirations (Gujit et al., 1995). This adaptive planning approach can strengthen local peoples' initiatives to sustain their livelihoods and the environments on which they depend. For example, the results of local economic valuations of biological diversity can be of direct use to indigenous and local communities in defence of their knowledge, rights of access and use of 'wild' resources. They can be the starting point of negotiations with powerful outside institutions to enhance local natural resource management structures. Local peoples' involvement in the social production of conservation (i.e., its knowledge base, funding priorities, management plans and end uses) through democratic fora is essential for resolving conflicts and reconciling conservation with local livelihoods (see Chapter VIII).

Such models demand the new forms of accountability which are increasingly being called for by organized groups within civil society. For example, the International Alliance of the Indigenous Tribal Peoples of the Tropical Forests has recently engaged in a dialogue with major conservation organizations, including IUCN and WWF-International, to establish joint principles guiding conservation in indigenous territories. These popular initiatives can be interpreted as calls for political action and organization against Western conservation ideology and centrally based dominance. They pose new challenges for conservation organizations and governments.

In short, any new concept and practice related to environmental protection has to be relevant to the day-to-day life of the common people in the area. For this, it must, at the least, guarantee livelihood security, including rights to local resources. Local rights of access and usufruct over genetic and biological resources, territorial control and security are all essential to empower indigenous and rural people to resist the drives of commercial organizations to appropriate resources and the biodiversity on which local livelihoods depend. The conservation of biological diversity partly hinges on effecting policy changes that strengthen local livelihoods by guaranteeing and enforcing these rights. Technical and financial assistance for activities such as ecotourism, extractivism, etc. could be a useful restitutive measure, but these schemes can by no means represent full alternatives. They could be 'additional' to the existing livelihood activities based on farming and other existing primary-resource-harvesting activities. People should not feel that government is 'taking an arm while giving a finger in return'. The social purpose of the establishment of protected areas should be that the above order is reversed. They should truly seek to empower local communities, strengthen local institutions and assist them to acquire necessary financial and technical means. The government officials, environmental organizations and conservationists should be directly accountable to local populations. The idea should be that nature protection initiatives such as parks and reserves should be managed by the local people themselves. In any event, if the ultimate goal of an environmental programme is to achieve better local living conditions and ecology, local communities should be in a better position to assess what is good for them than American biologists, British conservationists, German and Scandinavian foresters, or members of European aristocracies and preservationist organizations. The principal challenge is how local resources, skills and efforts could be mobilized and strengthened. The role of the state, rural development NGOs, conservation organizations and environmentalists should be collaborative and facilitating, not domineering as is currently the case.

To sum up, it can be said that the 'success' of parks and other types of strictly protected areas is measured basically in environmental terms, if not on the narrow basis of species protection. What is the social purpose of establishing a park or reserve? Major political issues of how many of the natural resources should be protected and used, and for what specific purposes, are usually reduced to simplistic technical and financial matters, or to problems of encroachment and poaching by local people. The present models are simply not designed to combine amelioration of local ecology and livelihoods; and they ignore their own social sustainability. There is therefore much need for debate and for imaginative people-centred initiatives. These are, however, unlikely to come from mainstream conservation bureaucracies; nor are they likely to happen without strong social pressure and mobilization at the grass roots.

References

Absalom, E, R Chambers, S Francis, B Gueye, I Guijt, S Joseph, D Johnson, C Kabutha, M Rahman Khan, R Leurs, J Mascarenhas, P Norrish, M P Pimbert, J N Pretty, M Samaranayake, I Scoones, M Kaul Shah, P Shah, D Tamang, J Thompson, G Tym and A Welbourn (1995), 'Sharing our concerns — Looking into the future', *PLA Notes*, No 22, London, pp 5–10.

Alcorn, J B (1994), 'Noble savage or noble state? Northern myths and southern realities in biodiversity conservation', *Ethnoecologica*, Vol 2, No 3, pp 7–19.

Altieri, M A (1987), *Agroecology: the Scientific Basis of Alternative Agriculture*, Westview, Boulder.

Amend, S and T Amend (1995), *National Parks without People? The South American Experience*, IUCN, Gland.

Arnold, J E M and W C Stewart (1991), *Common Property Resource Management in India*, Tropical Forest Paper No. 24, Oxford Forestry Institute, Oxford.

ASOMPS (Asian Symposium for Medicinal Plants, Spices and other Natural Products) (1992), *The Manila Declaration*, developed at the Seventh Asian Symposium for Medicinal Plants, Spices and other Natural Products, Manila.

Baker, W L (1992), 'The landscape ecology of large disturbances in the design and management of nature reserves', *Landscape Ecology*, No 7, pp 181–194.

Barraclough, S and K Ghimire, (1995), *Forests and Livelihoods: the Social Dynamics of Deforestation in Developing Countries*, Macmillan, London.

Barraclough, S, K Ghimire and H Meliczek (1997), *Rural Development and the Environment: Towards Ecologically and Socially Sustainable Development in Rural Areas*, UNRISD/UNEP, Geneva.

Baumann, M, J Bell, F Koechlin and M P Pimbert (1996), *The Life Industry: Biodiversity, People and Profits*, Intermediate Technology Publications, London.

Bawden, R J (1994), 'Creating learning systems: a metaphor for institutional reform for development', in I Scoones and J Thompson (eds), *Beyond Farmer First: Rural People's Knowledge*, Intermediate Technology Publications, Agricultural Research and Extension Practice, London, pp 258–263.

Birks, H H, H J B Birks, P E Kaland and D Moe (eds) (1988), *The Cultural Landscape — Past, Present and Future*, Cambridge University Press, Cambridge.

Boo, E (1990), *Eco-Tourism: The Potentials and Pitfalls*, WWF-US, Washington, D C.

BOSTID (Board on Science and Technology for International Development) (1986), Proceedings of the Conference on Common Property Resource Management (Annapolis, Maryland, 21–26 April 1985), National Academy Press, Washington, DC.

Bromley, D W and M M Cernea (1989), *The Management of Common Property Natural Resources*, Discussion Paper No 57, The World Bank, Washington, D C.

Campbell, J (1992), *Joint Forest Management*, The Ford Foundation, New Delhi.

Castell, F and M Vereecken (1995), *Influence de la Création de la Station Ecologique Jréia-Itatins sur la Dynamique Agraire de la Communauté de Despraiado (Sao-Paulo – Brazil)*, unpublished thesis, Centre National d'Etudes Agronomiques en Régions Chaudes (CNEARC), Montpellier.

Chambers, R (1992), *Rural Appraisal: Rapid, Relaxed and Participatory*, Discussion Paper No 311, Institute of Development Studies, Brighton.

— (1993), *Challenging the Professions: Frontiers for Rural Development*, Intermediate Technology Publications, London.

Chi, W and C Liang (1993), *Impact of National Parks and Natural Protected Areas on Chinese Society and Environment*, mimeo, Rural Development Institute and Forestry Institute, Beijing.

Colchester, M (1994), *Salvaging Nature: Indigenous Peoples, Protected Areas and Biodiversity Conservation*, UNRISD/WRM/WWF, Discussion Paper No 55, UNRISD, Geneva, September.

Crucible Group (1994), *People, Plants and Patents: The Impact of Intellectual Property Rights on Trade, Plant Biodiversity and Rural Society*, International Development Research Centre (IDRC), Ottawa.

Cunningham, A B (1993a), 'Development of a conservation policy on commercially exploited medicinal plants: a case study from Southern Africa', in O Akerele, V Heywood and H Synge, *Conservation of Medicinal Plants*, Cambridge University Press, Cambridge, pp 337–358.

— (1993b), *Ethics, Ethnobiological Research and Biodiversity: Guidelines for Equitable Partnerships in New Natural Products Development*, WWF-International, Gland.

Dhar, S K, J R Gupta and M Sarin (1991), *Participatory Forest Management in the Shivalik Hills: Experience of the Haryana Forest Department*, Sustainable Forest Management Working Paper No 5, Ford Foundation, New Delhi.

Dixon, J and P Sherman (1990), *Economics of Protected Areas: a New Look at the Costs and Benefits*, Earthscan, London.

von Droste, B, H Plachter and M Rossler (eds) (1995), *Cultural Landscapes of Universal Value — Components of Global Strategy*, Gustav Fisher Verlag, Jena.

Duesing, J (1992), 'The Convention on Biological Diversity — its impact on biotechnology research', *Agro-Food Industry Hi-Tech*, No 3, pp 19–23.

EEC (European Economic Community) (1992), 'Council directive', 92/43/EEC, *Official Journal of the European Communities*, No L 206/7, Brussels, 22 July.

FAO (Food and Agriculture Organization of the United Nations) (1993), *International Code of Conduct for Plant Germplasm Collecting and Transfer*, Rome.

Forster, R R (1973), *Planning for Man and Nature in National Parks*, IUCN Publications, New Series No 26, Morges.

Fürer-Haimendorf, C (1986), Statement to the Fourth International Conference on Hunting and Gathering Societies (London, 8–13 September).

Gadgil, M and R Guha (1992), *This Fissured Land: an Ecological History of India*, Oxford University Press, Delhi.

Ghimire, K (1994), 'Parks and people: livelihood issues in national parks management in Thailand and Madagascar', *Development and Change*, Vol 25, January, pp 195–229.

Gómez-Pompa, A and A Kaus (1992), 'Taming the wilderness myth', *Bioscience*, Vol 42, No 4, pp 271–279.

GRAIN (Genetic Resources Action International) (1995), 'Towards a biodiversity community rights regime', *Seedling*, Vol 12, No 3, pp 2–14.

Guha, R (1989), *The Unquiet Woods: Ecological Change and Peasant Resistance in the Himalayas*, Oxford University Press, Oxford and New Delhi.

Gujit, I, F Hinchcliffe, M Melnyk, J Bishop, D Eaton, M P Pimbert, J N Pretty and I Scoones (1995), *The Hidden Harvest: The Value of Wild Resources in Agricultural Systems*, IIED, London.

Hackel, J D (1993), 'Rural change and nature conservation in Africa: a case study from Swaziland', *Human Ecology*, No 21, pp 295–312.

Handley, P (1994), 'Parks under siege', *Far Eastern Economic Review*, 20 January.

Harmon, D (1991), 'National park residency in developed countries: The example of Great Britain', in P C West and S R Brechin (eds), *Resident Peoples and National Parks: Social Dilemmas and Strategies in International Conservation*, University of Arizona Press, Tucson, pp 33–39.

Haverkort, B and D Millar (1994), 'Constructing diversity: the active role of rural people in maintaining and enhancing biodiversity', *Ethnoecologica*, Vol 2, No 3, pp 51–64.

Hays, S (1982), 'From conservation to environment: environmental politics in the United States since World War Two', *Environmental Review*, No 6, pp 19–29.

Healy, R G (1992), *The Role of Tourism in Sustainable Development*, mimeo (circulated at Bellagio Conference on Ecotourism, 8–12 February 1993).

Hecht, S and A Cockburn (1990), *The Fate of the Forest*, Penguin, London.

Hinchcliffe, F, I Gujit, J N Pretty and P Shah (1995), *New Horizons: the Economic, Social and Environmental Impacts of Participatory Watershed Development*, Gatekeepers Series No 50, Sustainable Agriculture Programme, IIED, London.

IUCN (World Conservation Union) (1994a), *Guidelines for Protected Area Management Categories*, IUCN, Gland.

— (1994b), *1993 United Nations List of National Parks and Protected Areas*, IUCN, Gland.

Jodha, N S (1990), *Rural Common Property Resources: Contributions and Crisis*, ICIMOD, Kathmandu.

Kiss, A (ed) (1990), *Living with Wildlife: Wildlife Resource Management with Local Participation in Africa*, Technical Paper No 130, The World Bank, Washington, D C.

Koch, E (1995), *Dead Cows, a Long Bicycle Ride, the Fence of Fire and a Man on the Run: Linking Human Livelihoods, Transfrontier Conservation and the Protection of Biological Diversity in Southern Africa*, mimeo, UNRISD/GEM, Geneva.

Kothari, R, P Pande, S Singh and R Dilnavaz (1989), *Management of National Parks and Sanctuaries in India*, status report, Indian Institute of Public Administration, New Delhi.

Kumar, S (1993), 'Taiwan accuses princess of smuggling rhino horn', *New Scientist*, 16 October, p 11.

Lindberg, K (1991), *Policies for Maximizing Nature Tourism's Ecological and Economic Benefits*, WRI, Washington.

MacKinnon, J, K MacKinnon, G Child and J Thorsell (eds) (1986), *Managing Protected Areas in the Tropics*, IUCN, Gland.

Malhotra, K C, D Deb, M Dutta, T S Vasulu, G Yadava and M Adhikari (1991), *Role of Non Timber Forest Produce in Village Economy: A Household Survey in Jamboni Range, Midnapore District, West Bengal*, sponsored by the Ford Foundation in collaboration with the Government of West Bengal, Indian Institute of Biosocial Research and Development, New Delhi.

McCracken, J (1987), 'Conservation priorities and local communities', in D Anderson and R Grove (eds), *Conservation in Africa — People, Policies and Practice*, Cambridge University Press, Cambridge.

McNeely, J A (1988), *Economics and Biological Diversity: Developing and Using Economic Incentives to Conserve Biological Resources*, IUCN, Gland.

— (ed) (1993), *Parks for Life: Report of the IVth World Congress on National Parks and Protected Areas*, IUCN, Gland.

— (1994), 'Lessons from the past: forests and biodiversity', *Biodiversity and*

Conservation, Vol 3, No 4, pp 3–20.

McNeely, J and K Miller (1984), *National Parks, Conservation and Development: the Role of Protected Areas in Sustaining Society*, Smithsonian Institution Press, Washington, D C.

Millikan, B (1991), *The Social Dynamics of Deforestation and the Challenge of Sustainable Development in Rondônia, Brazil*, mimeo, UNRISD, Geneva, June.

Munthali, S M (1993), 'Traditional and modern wildlife conservation in Malawi — The need for an integrated approach', *Oryx*, No 27, pp 185–187.

Murphree, M W (1993), *Communities as Resource Management Institutions*, Gatekeeper Series No 36, IIED, London.

— (1994), *The Evolution of Zimbabwe's Community-Based Wildlife Use and Management Programme*, mimeo, Tanzanian Community Conservation Workshop, Dar-es-Salaam, 8–11 February.

Niamir, M (1990), 'Community forestry: Herders' decision making in natural resource management in arid and semi-arid Africa', *Community Forestry Note* 4, FAO, Rome, p 25.

Ostrom, E (1990), *Governing the Commons: The Evolution of Institutions for Collective Action*, Cambridge University Press, New York.

Pearce, D, A Markandya and E Barbier (1989), *Blueprint for a Green Economy*, Earthscan, London.

Pearce, F (1990), 'The rainforests — finding solutions that everyone can work and live with', *Development Forum*, Vol XVIII, No 5, September–October, pp 12–13.

Peluso, N L (1992a), *Coercing Conservation: The Politics of State Resource Control*, mimeo, Berkeley.

— (1992b), 'The political ecology of extraction and extractive reserves in East Kalimantan, Indonesia', *Development and Change*, Vol 23, No 4, pp 49–74.

Peterson, J H (1994), 'Sustainable wildlife use for community development in Zimbabwe', in M M R Freeman and U P Kreuter (eds), *Elephants and Whales: Resources for Whom?*, Gordon and Breach, Reading.

Phillips, A (1995), 'Cultural landscapes: An IUCN perspective', in B Von Droste, H Plachter and M Rossler with A Semple (eds), *Cultural Landscapes of Universal Value: Components of a Global Strategy*, Fisher-Verlag, Berlin.

Pimbert, M P (1994), *Field Observations on Joint Forest Management in West Bengal and Report on an International Workshop on JFM Co-organised by the Ford Foundation, the WWF–UNESCO–Kew Gardens People and Plants Initiative, the Government of West Bengal, the Indian Institute of Biosocial Research and Development and the Society for the Promotion of Wastelands Development* (7–18 November 1994), mimeo, WWF-International, Gland.

Pimbert, M P and J N Pretty (1995), *Parks, People and Professionals Putting 'Participation' into Protected Area Management*, UNRISD Discussion Paper No 57, UNRISD-IIED-WWF, Geneva.

Pimbert, M P and V Toledo (1994), 'Indigenous people and biodiversity conservation: myth or reality?', *Ethnoecologica*, special issue, Vol 2, No 3, Mexico, p 96.

Pimbert, M P, I Ahmad, A Ahmad, R Ahmad, Z Ali, A Aleem Chaudhry, B Gujja, S A Hasnain, K Haye, A Hussain, U Khalid, S N Khurshid, D Malik, M Merchant, Z Parveen, A Munaf Quaim Khani, J Shah, S Tariq, A Tahir Virk, A Zaidi and S Uz Zaman (1996), *Community Based Planning for Wetland Conservation: Lessons from the Ucchali Complex in Pakistan*, WWF-Pakistan, The Punjab Wildlife Department of the Government of Pakistan and WWF-

International, Lahore, Pakistan.

Posey, D A (1990), 'Intellectual property rights and just compensation for indigenous knowledge', *Anthropology Today*, Vol 6, No 4, pp 13–16.

— (1993), 'The importance of semi-domesticated species in post contact Amazonia: effects of Kayapo Indians on the dispersal of flora and fauna', in C M Hladik, A Hladik, O F Linares, H Pagezey, A Semple and M Hadley (eds), *Tropical Forests, People and Food: Biocultural Interactions and Applications to Development*, Man and Biosphere Series, Vol 13, UNESCO, Paris, pp 63–71.

— (1995), *Indigenous Peoples and Traditional Resource Rights: a Basis for Equitable Relationships?*, proceedings of a workshop held at the Green College Centre for Environmental Policy and Understanding (Oxford, 28 June 1995), Oxford University, Oxford.

Posey, D A and G Dutfield (1996), *Beyond Intellectual Property Rights: Towards Traditional Resource Rights for Indigenous and Local Communities*, IDRC and WWF-International, Ottawa and Gland.

PRIA (Society for Participatory Research in Asia) (1993), *Doon Declaration on People and Parks: Resolution of the National Workshop on Declining Access to and Control over Natural Resources in National Parks and Sanctuaries* (Dehradun, 28–30 October 1993), Forest Research Institute, Delhi.

RAFI (Rural Advancement Foundation International) (1994), *Bioprospecting/Biopiracy and Indigenous Peoples*, RAFI Communique, Ottawa, November.

Rana, D S (1992), 'The case of Khaptad: park or people?', *The Rising Nepal*, 10 January.

Reice, S R (1994), 'Non-equilibrium determinants of biological community structure', *American Scientist*, Vol 82, No 5, pp 424–435.

Reichardt, K L, E Mellink, G P Nabhan and A Rea (1994), 'Habitat heterogeneity and biodiversity associated with indigenous agriculture in the Sonoran desert', *Ethnoecologica*, Vol 2, No 3, pp 21–34.

Reid, W V (1994), 'Biodiversity prospecting: strategies for sharing benefits', in V Sanchez and C Juma (eds), *Biodiplomacy: Genetic Resources and International Relations*, ACTS Press, Nairobi.

Reid, W V, J N Barnes and B Blackwelder (1988), *Bankrolling Successes: A Portfolio of Sustainable Development Projects*, Environmental Policy Institute and National Wildlife Federation, Washington, D C.

Reid, W V, S A Laird, C A Meyer, R Gamez, A Sittenfeld, D H Janzen, M A Gollin and C Juma (1993), *Biodiversity Prospecting: Using Genetic Resources for Sustainable Development*, WRI, Washington, D C.

Roy, S D and P Jackson (1993), 'Mayhem in Manas: the threats to India's wildlife reserves' in E Kemf (ed), *Indigenous Peoples and Protected Areas — The Law of Mother Earth*, Earthscan, London.

Salick, J and L C Merrick (1990), 'Use and maintenance of genetic resources: crops and their wild relatives', in R C Carroll, J H Vandermeer and P M Rosset (eds), *Agroecology*, McGraw-Hill, New York, pp 517–548.

Sarkar, S, N Singh, S Suri and A Kothari (1995), *Joint Management of Protected Areas in India*, Indian Institute of Public Administration, New Delhi.

Sayer, J (1991), *Rain Forest Buffer Zones: Guidelines for Protected Area Managers*, IUCN, Gland.

Schwartzman, S (1989), 'Extractive reserves in the Amazon', in J O Browder (ed), *Fragile Lands of Latin America: Strategies for Economic Development*, Westview Press, Boulder.

Scoones, I, M Melnyck and J N Pretty (1992), *The Hidden Harvest: Wild Foods and Agricultural Systems: A Literature Review and Annotated Bibliography*, IIED and WWF-International, London and Gland.

Scoones, I and J Thompson (eds) (1994), Beyo*nd Farmer First: Rural People's Knowledge*, Agricultural Research and Extension Practice, Intermediate Technology Publications, London.

Shelton, D (1995), *Fair Play, Fair Pay: Laws to Preserve Traditional Knowledge and Biological Resources*, WWF-International, Gland.

Southgate, D and H L Clarke (1993), 'Can conservation projects save biodiversity in South America?', *Ambio*, No 22, pp 163–166.

Speelman, N (1991), 'Regional marketing as a means to balanced development of the tourist industry in marginal areas', *World Leisure and Recreation*.

Stanley, D (1991), 'Communal forest management: the Honduran resin tappers', *Development and Change*, Vol 22, No 4, October, pp 757–779.

Stone, R D (1991), *Wildlands and Human Needs: Reports from the Field*, World Wildlife Fund, Washington, D C.

Thin, Neil (1995), *Recurrent Comments by Social Development Advisers on WWF JFS Proposals and Meetings*, mimeo, Edinburgh University, 17 January.

Thompson, J (1995), 'Participatory approaches in government bureaucracies: facilitating the process of institutional change', *World Development*, Vol 23, No 9, September, pp 1521–1554.

UNDP (United Nations Development Programme) (1994), *Conserving Indigenous Knowledge: Integrating Two Systems of Innovation*, UNDP, New York.

UNEP-CBD (1994), *Convention on Biological Diversity*, text and annexes, UNEP Interim Secretariat for the Convention on Biological Diversity, Geneva.

Uphoff, N (1992), *Learning from Gal Oya: Possibilities for Participatory Development and Post-Newtonian Science*, Cornell University Press, Ithaca.

Utley, R M (1973), *Frontiers Regulars: the United States Army and the Indian, 1866–1891*, Macmillan, New York.

Utting, P (1993), *Trees, People and Power: Social Dimensions of Deforestation and Forest Protection in Central America*, Earthscan, London.

WCMC (World Conservation Monitoring Centre) (1992), *Global Biodiversity: Status of the Earth's Living Resources*, Chapman and Hall, London.

— (1994), *Data Sheet Compiled by the World Conservation Monitoring Centre*, Cambridge.

Wells, M, K Brandon and L Hannah (1992), *People and Parks: Linking Protected Area Management with Local Communities*, World Bank, WWF-US and US Agency for International Development, Washington, D C.

West, P C and S R Brechin (eds) (1991), *Resident Peoples and National Parks: Social Dilemmas and Strategies in International Conservation*, University of Arizona Press, Tucson.

Western, D and H Giochoi (1993), 'Segregation effects and impoverishment of savanna parks: The case for ecosystem viability analysis', *African Journal of Ecology*, No 31, pp 269–281.

Wild, R and J Mutebi (forthcoming), *Conservation through Community Use: Establishing Resource Use and Joint Management at Bwindi Impenetrable National Park, Uganda*, People and Plants Discussion Paper, UNESCO, Paris.

Wood, D (1995), 'Conserved to death. Are tropical forests being over-protected from people?', *Land Use Policy*, Vol 12, No 2, pp 115–135.

WRI, IUCN, UNEP (1992), *Global Biodiversity Strategy*, WRI, IUCN and UNEP, place of publication unknown.

WWF and BSCRM (1995), *Planning for Conservation: Participatory Rural Appraisal for Community Based Initiatives*, report on the Participatory Rural Appraisal (PRA) Training Workshop (Ostritza, Bulgaria, 14–22 June 1993), Bulgarian Society for the Conservation of the Rhodopi Mountains (BSCRM) and WWF-International (WWF), Gland.

WWF and the Government of India (1996), *Participatory Management Planning for Keoladeo National Park, Bharatpur, India*, WWF-India, New Delhi.

II

BIODIVERSITY AND HUMAN WELFARE

Piers Blaikie and Sally Jeanrenaud

Introduction

'Biodiversity'[1] is perceived and valued differently by a wide range of actors. These contested meanings and competing interests have profound implications for protected area management.

While policy makers and writers at the international level perceive a synergy between biodiversity conservation and human welfare as an unproblematic 'vision' of conservation, from the level of practice their supposed relationship more often appears as mere rhetoric. There have been formidable political problems in the way of negotiating biodiversity conservation at the international level. There has also been serious questioning of the capability and will of many states to formulate and implement conservation policies on the ground. At the local level, conservation efforts have led to the definition and management of biodiversity

1 As used in the Convention, the term has the following definition (IUCN, 1994): '"Biological diversity" means the variability among living organisms from all sources including, *inter alia*, terrestrial, marine and other aquatic ecosystems and the ecological complexes of which they are part; this includes diversity within species, between species and of ecosystems'. Thus biodiversity is the variability of life in all forms, levels, and combinations. It is not the sum of all ecosystems, species and genetic material, but rather represents the variability within and among them. Biologists usually consider it from three different perspectives:

- genetic diversity: the frequency and diversity of different genes and/or genomes; this includes variation both within a population and between populations;
- species diversity: the frequency and diversity of different species;
- ecosystem diversity: the variety and frequency of different ecosystems.

resources, usually in the name of the state, and this in turn has precipitated struggles over those resources. Finally, there are crucial ambiguities, inconsistencies and contradictions in the formulation and practice of biodiversity conservation, particularly in the role of science and 'facts' in the biodiversity discourse (Mann, 1991). Thus, while the contemporary debate about biodiversity appears to represent elements of a new moral dimension about 'human–nature' relationships, it is also a testimony to familiar political–economic divisions. These involve divisions between international, national and local interests; between North and South; between science and politics. They involve power relations at the local level deriving from differences of class, ethnicity and gender.

Bearing these issues in mind, it is easy to see that the analysis of the relationship between biodiversity and human welfare cannot only be a matter of scientific research. While scientific methods may be powerful ways to identify and present the problems of biodiversity erosion, they are not the only ones. The issue of biodiversity involves resources, which are the focus of commercial exploitation and livelihoods on the part of different actors. The debate is thus highly politicized. Furthermore, within the academic and international policy-making environment, it is important to be critically aware of the social forces that withdraw and confer credibility to various scientific ideas. Scientific 'facts' about biodiversity are used to support various intellectual projects, upon which reputation, promotion and consultancy fees depend (see the section on Actors in Biodiversity Conservation, below). Therefore biodiversity discourses are engaged in at many different levels and by a wide cast of protagonists. Different people have specific interests in very particular natural resources or species for certain purposes. 'Nature' is not only perceived and valued from various cultural and ideological perspectives; powerful economic incentives are also involved in shaping and conserving special aspects or constituents of nature. By no means all of these different interests and normative notions about biodiversity concern human welfare, although they may be invoked in its name.

However, an analysis of biodiversity and human welfare must not confine itself to the economic concerns of the actors involved. It must also involve a critical review of the ideas and ideologies of biodiversity. In other words, it is naive to expect that one can 'read off' notions about biodiversity from the structural position which actors hold, or that they will create and use ideas that somehow are explicable in terms of their being instrumental to their economic interests. Rather, different actors create their own ideas about biodiversity, appropriate and adapt others, and experience and use them in different ways in different arenas. It is thus necessary to focus on the ideas themselves as well. A section on different paradigms for biodiversity conservation is devoted to this task, bearing in mind that actors will use parts of these paradigms, sometimes in an eclectic and contradictory manner, in pursuit of their own 'projects'.

The main objective of this chapter is to contribute to a more consistent and effective strategy for the conservation of biodiversity, and to identify clearly who conservation will and should benefit, and how. For a more effective policy to emerge, the vision must be deconstructed into its (often contradictory) parts, and deepened to accommodate social dynamics. This requires changes both within and outside the conservation movement. The conservation movement itself must take up the challenge to recognize and work with the political economy of biodiversity erosion and conservation. This change mainly implies the development of effective policies at the international, state and local levels, but at the same time understanding the political and institutional obstacles which stand in its way. These obstacles must not be characterized simply as 'lack of political will', corruption or administrative inefficiency and thus considered to be external to the policy-making process. They must be worked with and tackled in other arenas from that of biodiversity conservation alone — for example in trade and tariff agreements, the structure and volume of international aid to developing countries and human rights for indigenous peoples — in short, a number of enduring political issues revolving around human welfare, but which may be only indirectly related to biodiversity conservation itself.

Biodiversity and Human Welfare

The notion of 'welfare' is subject to multiple interpretations, and may be identified here as ways in which different values of biodiversity are appropriated by different actors. There is a growing recognition of the need to accommodate qualitative and indigenous concepts of the values of biodiversity with a particular emphasis on the ways in which these appropriated values are distributed. In addition, the range of measures of welfare has been steadily extended, as illustrated by the increasing sophistication of the Human Development Index (HDI), published annually by the UNDP.

Most of the methodological and scientific references which mention the connections between biodiversity and human welfare have done so in very general terms. The discourse usually focuses on the benefits of biodiversity to 'mankind' over long time periods and on a global scale. It is useful, however, to identify the different values of biodiversity in principle, and then to go on to identify who appropriates each of these values. Brown and Moran (1993) identify these as:

- direct and instrumental/use values;
- indirect instrumental/use values;
- non-instrumental intrinsic value.

Direct and Instrumental/Use Values

These are concerned with the enjoyment and satisfaction derived from the use of biological resources. Because they involve the consumption of such resources, their realization is thus a major factor in the possible depletion of resources. Direct values can be decomposed into two types.

Consumptive Use Values

These refer to the values that are placed on those products that are consumed directly without passing through a market. These are clearly of greatest importance to rural populations in developing countries, where biological resources are most often collected and used (often from the 'wild', or areas not subject to the rights and obligations of private property). These products include a vast array of wild animals, insects, fish, fibres, resins, medicinal plants, fuelwood, fruits, fungi, dyes, gourds, construction materials and so on. Consumptive use values also refer to cultural, religious and recreational values involved in the consumption of the resource (for example, the importance of whale meat in Inuit cultures, or of hunting in the initiation rites of many African pastoral peoples).

The loss of this consumptive use value of biodiversity can come about for a number of different reasons. Population pressure on forest areas can convert them into privately held agricultural land, which may well result in increased aggregate food supplies, but a reduced variety of resources for subsistence. Such encroachment on forests and common property or open access resources also typically impacts on those who have least access to private property. For the poor and politically weak, the erosion of consumptive use values of biodiversity usually arises for three main reasons: first, through a redistribution of those resources towards more powerful incomers at the expense of less powerful groups; second, through a widespread conversion from consumptive to productive use values through an extension and deepening of the market for many of these resources; and third, through overuse, which tends to lead to a decline in their aggregate supply on the remaining de jure common property and de facto open access resources. All three processes commonly operate together in an agrarian political economy; the purely biological issues of diversity and supply of different resources is only part of the picture.

Productive Use Values

These are assigned to resources which are harvested and sold in the market, and thus appear in national income accounts. They are generally valued at the point of production, and involve a range of resources similar to those used for direct consumption, although they may vary depending on location. In some cases they may involve domesticated agriculture and a short list of specialized crops or products (such as a few tree species which are recognized to be commercially useful), but in other cases the same products may have both consumptive and productive values (for example, commercial and subsistence-based culling of the same wild animals).

Productive use values therefore contribute to welfare by providing monetary income to those who can appropriate this value through the effective realization of private property rights which may already exist in their favour, or through the acquisition of these rights. It is often the case that entrepreneurs may secure agreements with the state that overlay or directly overturn existing customary rights to resources, which had hitherto been enjoyed by local groups in the agrarian political economy. These groups include forest dwellers, farmers and pastoralists who had previously been able to exploit these resources locally, gaining both productive use value through their sale and consumptive use value.

Technological change continually creates opportunities to enhance productive use values. The development of genetic material for new varieties of domestic crops and medicinal research are just two examples. In such cases, the ownership of intellectual property rights over existing resources must be clarified, often leading to struggle over these resources and the value attributed to them.

Indirect Instrumental/Use Values

These refer to the functions and services of ecosystems which have value for society in general, rather than functions and services limited to the specific user(s). (They nevertheless have important social and economic implications for direct values.) Indirect instrumental use values are not consumed or traded in the marketplace; they are thus public goods. Conservation of biological resources has the following indirect values:

- providing the support system for harvested species by photosynthetic fixation of solar energy and its transfer into food chains which involve harvested species;
- ecosystem functions involving reproduction –a variety of ways are recognized in which wild biological resources may contribute to the productive use values of domesticated resources (Prescott-Allen, 1986), including: wild species forming the genetic resource for the breeding of new domesticates; wild pollinators being essential for domestic crops; and wild enemies of pests controlling attacks on domestic crops;
- maintenance of hydrological regimes, including the recharging of water tables and the buffering of extreme hydrological conditions, which might otherwise precipitate drought or flood;
- soil and water conservation by the regulation of water flows, the provision of suitable environments for the creation and maintenance of soil and its fertility through storage and cycling of essential nutrients;
- absorption, breakdown and dispersal of harmful pollutants (air and water pollutants, organic wastes);

- the provision of the aesthetically and culturally preferred environment for human habitat.

It is clear that the contributions of these indirect use values to human
welfare are substantial, even if their measurement is both practically and
methodologically very difficult. Indirect use values are diffuse and
distributed widely between populations, both at present and in the
future. The erosion of these functions may not result from the reduction
of biodiversity per se. For example, there are numerous examples of the
adverse impacts of soil erosion and declines in the productivity of rangelands, but the physical processes involved usually do not revolve around
a local or regional reduction in biodiversity.

Option Values
These refer to the future uses of both direct and indirect values. The future
is uncertain but the extinction of species is all too certain. The future paths
of socio-economic (including technical) change are also uncertain, and
the aggregate effects of unforeseen developments — such as the implications of climatic change for natural resource use, and for biodiversity in
particular — cannot be known at the present time. Although we do not
know its value, we do know that there is a positive value for maintaining
the option of genetic diversity. Society in general may thus be willing to
pay for the option of preserving a reservoir of genetic material which
may contain such valuable possibilities as teosinte (annual Central
American fodder grass, closely related to and possibly ancestral to maize).
There are also other options which society may be prepared to pay for —
such as having future access to a given species or ecosystem, even though
people cannot specify what they might be, or even contemplate ever visiting, reading about, or benefiting from them in any way.

Non-Instrumental Intrinsic Value

Many, particularly but not exclusively from 'deep ecology' movements,
would argue that all species have an intrinsic value, that biodiversity is a
moral condition, and its conservation a moral responsibility, since non-
human species have rights too. Therefore this value is non- or even
anti-anthropocentric, and has no connection with human welfare other
than (and this will be important to Gaians and others in the ecology
movement) that the act of discharging a moral responsibility might be
argued to contribute to human welfare.

Different Values of Biodiversity Accrue
to Different People

While this brief introduction points to general categories of value and to

51

their contribution to human welfare, it hides a complexity of particular and contradictory interests. For example, while 'charismatic' species such as the elephant may inspire awe and wonder among the urban middle class of the North, they may be regarded as a pest by agricultural communities in the South. While biodiversity clearly provides material benefits to commercial companies, new developments in the biotechnology industry may be at odds with the ethical or aesthetic values of other groups, and may even undermine the material subsistence of some. The point is that different actors appropriate different values from different aspects of biodiversity, and gain access to different functional benefits. Identifying different values of biodiversity, and determining to whom they might typically accrue, is a complex task because of the number of combinations of value, benefit, uses, and level of realization, and definitions of biodiversity. The different combinations can be illustrated by a case study from the Nepalese terai (drawn from both authors' professional experience there, Ghimire (1992) and Brown (1994)).

The pressures for conversion of land to agricultural use in the Nepalese terai are formidable. Population densities are still about half those on the Indian side of the border (a few kilometres away), but the Middle Hills of Nepal are experiencing extreme land pressure, and out-migration to the terai is rapidly gaining pace (Brown, 1994; Ghimire, 1992; Blaikie et al., 1980). It is mostly the very poor who encroach on the forest (the *sukhumbasi*, literally 'those with no place to go'), and they are punished by eviction, crop burning and other acts of violence. However, forest resources are being used and biodiversity reduced by other, more powerful, groups such as timber contractors and their clients in the local political hierarchy (the *pradhan panch*, or village headman, for example). Thus the issue of biodiversity is also a struggle over the meaning and classification of those resources (for example, whether the land is demarcated as official state forest or agricultural land for settlement). The text of 'biodiversity' is, at the local level, one of naked struggle over resources. The costs of conserving the forest are also borne, at least theoretically, by the Nepalese state, in terms of the opportunity costs of foregone timber and grain exports to India. But here again, the local political economy of Nepal prevents all but the smallest proportion of those revenues from reaching the national accounts and being used to further human welfare through the provision by the state of educational and health facilities in the area. Questions of who bears the real costs of conservation, and whether the offsetting of those costs by international funding would ultimately benefit the least powerful local people, have to be kept in mind. Table 2.1, adapted from Brown (1994), indicates the variety of interests in biodiversity, the different values accruing to different people and the different meanings attaching to 'biodiversity'.

This helps to unravel some of the complex issues and competing notions of the values of biodiversity.

1   There are different actors who relate in different ways to the resources in question, and they often do so in relation to specific resources in particular instances in their daily lives (for example, at the point of consumption).
2   Actors therefore may define 'biodiversity' in different ways and at different levels.
3   They bring to bear on these definitions their culture, their material circumstances and their experience of biodiversity.
4   They engage in the issue often in contradictory ways, expressed in struggles over the meaning and control of biodiversity between themselves and with outside parties. Diverse activities such as 'poaching', evictions, commercial negotiations and academic arguments at international workshops are examples of these struggles.

This illustration reveals a common pattern of the distribution of the costs of biodiversity degradation. Loss of livelihood and habitat through the depletion of the species used in local consumption and in petty commodity production are borne by the majority of rural populations, especially the poorest groups. The indirect values of biodiversity — underwriting regional ecological maintenance of natural systems — are borne by a wider spectrum of local people, although compensatory adjustments to these costs can always be made more easily by the more wealthy, who can 'buy their way out of trouble', or offset the costs of biodiversity loss by such means as purchasing fertilizers where the provision of natural fertility fails, or tubewells where water from public sources for drinking and irrigation dry up or become polluted, and so on (Seddon et al, 1979). In other words, some are able to compensate for the failure of public goods by private purchase. It is thus inadequate to impute the impact of degradation on human welfare costs only in terms of those costs — it is also necessary to consider how those costs will be met in a given, and usually unequal, political economy. The impact of biodiversity degradation upon human welfare must be set within the political economy as a whole.

Actors in Biodiversity Conservation

While some groups (for example, rural populations) enjoy direct benefits from biodiversity, biodiversity impinges on the lives of other actors in more contingent and indirect ways. In this section attention is turned to two such groups of actors involved in biodiversity issues.[2]

---

2 The authors consider a fuller range of actors in *Biodiversity and Human Welfare*, Discussion Paper No. 72, UNRISD, Geneva, February 1996.

Table 2.1 *Interest Groups and Stakeholders in Grassland Conservation in the Terai*

Group	Scale of influence	Source of power	Interests/aims	Means
Indigenous people	Local	Very limited	Livelihood maintenance; use protected areas for subsistence needs, minor trading of products; thatch, fodder, building materials, fuel, wild foods, plant medicines, hunting and fishing	Subsistence farming, minor marketing; legal and illegal extraction of resources from protected areas
Migrant farmers	Local	Limited	Livelihood maintenance; use protected areas for subsistence needs; thatch, fodder, fuel, building material	Cash farming plus subsistence; legal and illegal extraction of products from protected areas
Local entrepreneurs	Local	Many hold official positions locally	Profit; commercial gain; range of small enterprises — tourist- and non-tourist-based	Small business enterprises, buying and selling to tourists
Tourist concessions	National/some international	Lobbying or may hold official positions	Profit, commercial expansion; some of revenue may be earned overseas; control tourists staying in protected areas overnight	Tourism revenues; concessions from government
Government conservation agencies	National	Administrative and supervisory	Conserving wildlife and facilitating tourist development	Enforcing park boundaries; imposing fines

Conservation pressure groups	Local/ national some inter-national links	Lobbying, may have personal contacts, international funding	Conserving biodiversity but with considerations for local livelihoods	Lobbying, publicity
International conservation groups	International	International funding 'green conditionality'	Conserving biodiversity; limited interests in human welfare	International legislation, lobbying
Central government	National	Political and administrative growth	National development; economic growth	Legislation, bureaucracy, budget allocation

Source: Brown, 1994.

State Functionaries

State functionaries are involved in the regulation of the use of natural resources and in the formulation and implementation of policy. They do not form a homogeneous group, since they occupy different places in the administration (from First Secretary to forest rangers). They control access to biological resources through official means (for example, police, forestry officers, district-level officials, chairmen of the village council, local chambers of commerce, etc.). Their role and effectiveness in implementing biodiversity conservation will depend on the degree of technical and administrative competence of the civil service. Also, environmental protection agencies (including those in many developed countries) may not be adequately staffed, so that legal work, routine monitoring and basic administration become bogged down by delays.

For many government servants, the issue of biodiversity is probably of little direct interest, impinging on their lives only in contingent and indirect ways — through a series of regulations or bureaucratic procedures, for example. For many, the main preoccupation is to keep their jobs. For example, a local customs officer responsible for monitoring the export of live species from a developing country at a remote airport experiences the 'biodiversity issue' in a highly contingent and indirect manner. At the same time, his or her professional performance is actually quite important to biodiversity conservation. On a meagre, post-structural-adjustment government salary, customs officers are required to distinguish different species of parrot, for example, a task for which they have neither the training nor the personal commitment.

It is only through consideration of their contingent relationship with biodiversity that an understanding of their actions can be constructed. The welfare of the customs officers may be served better by extracting 'bureaucratic rent' (or bribes) and allowing through for export all manner of rare species threatened with extinction. It is very often the case that income earned at the margin by the disposal of (rather than the conservation of) rare and endangered species is more attractive to those who control these resources through the exercise of formal and informal political power.

There are opportunities for the collection of bureaucratic rent on the part of strategically placed officials in biodiversity conservation projects and programmes — for example, in the issuing of hunting licences, the inspection and monitoring of the CITES agreement, and customs inspections where live species, ivory and trophies may be exported. Moreover, the monitoring and reporting systems for many developing countries are inadequate. For example, forestry officials in Cameroon have very few vehicles to visit forest sites, and often have to hitch lifts with workers from the foreign timber companies. Many officials are in a contractually inferior position in negotiations with foreign firms which may not be too concerned about keeping to conservation guidelines. There are too many cases of large-scale illegal smuggling either connived at or run by official bodies to minimize their impact. Most instances are highly sensitive and are not officially documented (or the documentation is suppressed). But there is sufficient evidence that biodiversity conservation is seriously compromised in many countries — especially but not exclusively in the South.

For example, Ellis (1994) reports that South Africa's policy of destabilization of neighbouring countries was closely associated with the rise of South Africa as a leading intermediary in the international ivory trade. South African traders, acting in partnership with or under the protection of officers of the South African Military Directorate, imported raw ivory from Angola, Mozambique and elsewhere and exported it to markets in the Far East. This was a source of income both for the South African secret services and for the individuals associated with them. There is evidence that counter-insurgency specialists are currently using Mozambique as a base for operations inside South Africa, and that they continue to have an interest in ivory and rhino horn. Former officers of counter-insurgency units have also found employment as game wardens in national parks. Ellis shows how the South African conservation lobby has been used by some of the specialist counter-insurgency units of the South African Defence Force, and how the proposals for the large new game parks along the border between South Africa and Mozambique have important implications for politics and national security, as well as biodiversity conservation.

The implementation of CITES and the environmental clauses of the International Tropical Timber Agreement (ITTA) are markers for the future implementation of the UNCED Biodiversity Convention. Current research by the American Social Research Council (directed by Weiss and Jacobson) on the implementation and compliance with international accords shows, however, that signing agreements may be no indication of a country intending, or actually undertaking, to implement them. It is clear that biodiversity conservation may not be of much professional or personal concern to many state functionaries at all — and this applies even to personnel in wildlife protection and forestry agencies in many developing countries.

International Conservation Groups

International conservation organizations influence biodiversity conservation and management at an ideal or theoretical level through conservation policy prescriptions. They may also affect it in an applied manner, although political bargaining at the policy formulation level, and interpretation and implementation of policies on the ground, act as filters to their ideas.

Global conservation policies are largely promoted by international agencies such as IUCN, UNEP and WWF. Broad policies are set out in documents such as the *World Conservation Strategy* (IUCN, UNEP, WWF,

1980), *Caring for the Earth* (IUCN, UNEP, WWF, 1991), and other papers such as *Global Priorities for the Year 2000* (WWF, 1994). During the last decade there has been a notable shift in their policies away from the classical emphasis on nature preservation towards ideas of sustainable development, which include the more populist and neo-liberal approaches to conservation (see Approaches to Conservation, below, for further discussion).

Study of the dynamics of the policy process reveals some of the contested meanings of 'biodiversity conservation' among policy makers at the international level. A simplistic model of policy development is a function of the 'rational' policy process, by which (non-problematic) objectives are set and resources are allocated. However, we question here whether interactions about concepts, ideologies and strategies follow an orderly cycle of hypothesis, testing and adaptation in the same way as manuals outline the project cycle, for example. This image of the policy process has long been criticized as a poor model of what actually happens (Clay and Schaffer, 1984). Instead, we suggest, the development and promotion of conservation policies can become the currency of politicking, manoeuvre and professional rivalry. Two key influences shaping policy within WWF — the struggle between different approaches to conservation, and differences between the fundraisers and policy makers — illustrate this claim.

People-oriented approaches to biodiversity conservation are now more or less universally accepted as part of efforts aimed at conservation.[3] However, it appears that despite the UNCED mandate for such approaches, the institutional climate is less favourable towards neo-populist policies now than it was just a few years ago. For example, WWF International established a Biodiversity, Protected Areas and Species Conservation Programme in 1991 to help promote a community-based conservation approach. This unit was eliminated in January 1995 during a 'downscaling' exercise, despite widespread protest. To many outside groups the work of this unit represented a new and more socially oriented approach to conservation, and had led many people to believe that WWF was transforming itself.

Many critics claim that this reveals a deeper ideological struggle between the classical and populist approaches to conservation at the international level. For example, Ehringhaus (cited in Tickell, 1995) reported that WWF is divided into two contending schools of thought: the traditionalists who believe that conservation encompasses only animals, plants and protected areas; and a group that subscribes to more holistic people-oriented philosophy. The recent WWF decision is seen as a reaffirmation of the traditionalists' power. However, we suggest that there may be several other dimensions to this policy discourse.

Although many conservationists may not accept the more radical

---

3 They appear in many international policy documents such as *Caring for the Earth* (IUCN, UNEP, WWF, 1991); the *Global Biodiversity Strategy* (WRI, IUCN, UNEP, 1992); *Parks for Life* (CNPPA, 1992) and *A Guide to Agenda 21* (UNCED, 1992).

implications of the populist's model, the central management has made it absolutely clear that WWF remains firmly committed to community-based conservation. While a few traditionalists do remain, very few international conservationists would now dare voice the 'fortress mentality' of a couple of decades ago. WWF has long been a supporter of people-focused conservation, and has every intention of continuing to promote it (Martin, 1995). The official reason for the downscaling at head-quarters was decentralization, and the rationale of re-allocating resources to build up this approach in the field, rather than at the international secretariat which needed to be streamlined.

A further explanation may be the influence of the neo-liberal approach on global conservation policy at the time of the downscaling. The proponents of this approach tend to perceive the emphasis on grass-roots work as naive. There are some powerful internal and external forces pushing to bring economics closer to conservation. For example, WWF has recently made 'green accounting' a special policy issue. The growing economic emphasis resonates with the approach of the World Bank's Global Environmental Facility (GEF), which has a leading role in financing biodiversity conservation projects. According to Chatterjee and Finger (1994) there have been various confrontations between the neo-populist and neo-liberal approaches to conservation. Those who promote the latter have more political power within institutions and are either alienating or partly co-opting the former. The successful development of certain policies appears to be related to the degree of 'constituency-building' within organizations. This involves various tactics and strategies, including deliberate internal consensus-building and special modes of institutional discourse. The example above indicates a mutual constitution of ideologies, personalities and institutional practices, and their influence on policy practices.

Conservation ideologies are not the only forces shaping policy. Organizations consist of many intersecting struggles, and disjunctures of knowledge and interests between actors, which play their part in shaping strategies and agendas. Another key dynamic within WWF is the tension between its 'conservation' and its 'fundraising' cultures. Some policy staff have voiced the fear that policy is not driven by field issues, but rather by donors' concern for the 'charismatic and extinction-prone mega-vertebrates' (pandas, tigers, rhinos, whales, etc.). These have become the symbols of the international conservation movement, and many organizations find it easier to raise money through manipulating their images rather than promoting the organization's actual policy or field work (Bonner, 1994). Indeed, institutional survival may depend on these public relations exercises.

While fundraisers and public relations staff may argue that emotive appeals to save 'flagship' species or the undifferentiated rain forest enrol the public opinion of the North by providing a powerful image and entry point to more complex (and important) 'projects', their objectives and criteria of success are different from those of policy and field staff. The business side of the organization values donations; number of members; 'perceived effectiveness'; quotes in newspapers; and maintaining a high profile. A pervasive informal rule is 'don't upset the donors'. In this sense it can be argued that policy development is constrained by its 'dialogue' with the donors, and biodiversity conservation becomes, in part, a construct of the fundraisers.

Approaches to Conservation

Three distinct intellectual paradigms framing the general approach to conservation, and to biodiversity conservation specifically, can be distinguished. Each has profound and pervasive effects both on the international discourse about conservation and on the actual policies themselves in different countries. Table 2.2, adapted from Biot et al.'s (1995) review of research on land degradation and conservation, applies to biodiversity conservation as well. These paradigms also have fundamentally different approaches to human welfare, and assume different sets of relations between civil society, the market and the state.

It is apparent that international conservation policy and practice are undergoing an unusually rapid transformation. Contemporary conservation ideology, at least on paper, represents an evolution away from predominant concern for nature preservation to sustainable use of natural resources with stronger emphasis on livelihoods and, in more general terms, human welfare. Policies which once viewed people as a threat to nature now regard people as potential partners in sustainable development. Most institutions appropriate and use theories — or, more usually, parts of theories — to persuade others and enrol them in their particular 'projects'. It is not surprising therefore that policy and strategy statements are eclectic in their theoretical exposition. For example, the World Bank's *Development Report 1992*, while taking a neo-liberal economic approach to the environment and conservation, also weaves strongly neo-populist strands of thought throughout (the links between poverty and environmental degradation, for example). It is thus to be expected that, while the genealogy of conservation paradigms may be traced to a relatively pure set of mutually consistent principles, policy and strategy documents are hybrid.

Two of the three paradigms (the 'classic' and 'neo-populist') can be traced back to historical themes within early conservation. While the 'classic model' was always predominant, its history also includes popular environmental movements resistant to colonial regimes and destructive 'development', as well as conflicting views about conservation within many colonial regimes (Grove, 1987). Much of the contemporary interest in 'people-oriented' conservation has its roots in the historical struggles and strategies of local groups to protect their environments and liveli-

Table 2.2 *Three conservation paradigms*

Variable	Classic approach	Populist approach	Neo-liberal approach
Peasant behaviour	Ignorant, irrational, traditional	Virtuous, rational community-minded	Rational, egocentric
Diagnosis of environmental problem	Environmental solutions	Socio-political solutions	Economic solutions
Immediate causes of environmental problems	Mismanagement by users	Mismanagement by state, capitalists, TNCs, big business	Poor government policies and bureaucratic rules and regulations
Structural causes of degradation	Over-population, backwardness, lack of foresight, ignorance	Resource distribution, inappropriate technologies	Inappropriate property rights, institutions, prices, and rapid population growth
Institutional prescription	Top-down centralized decision-making	Bottom-up participation	'Market' policies, property rights, resource pricing, self-targeting safety nets
Academic discipline; profession	Physical sciences; bureaucrat	Sociology; activist, NGOs	Economics; development professional
Gender orientation	Gender-blind	Virtuous but victimized women	Gender myopia
Research framework	Systematic empiricism	Rapid/participant rural appraisal, community as unit of analysis	Methodological individualism
Orientation to market	Not considered	Exploitation	Pareto optimality and externalities
Models of peasant society	Conservative, paternalistic	Egalitarian	Democratic/liberal
Views of collective action	Deficient	Essential and unproblematic	Conditional rationality/ political entrepreneurs
Technology	'Fortress conservation'	Agronomic techniques of conservation	Not specified

Source: adapted from Biot et al, 1995.

hood interests, and in the more populist thinking of the nineteenth century. The reasons for the early predominance of the classic conservation paradigm and subsequent growth of the neo-populist and neo-liberal approaches are complex, but are deeply embedded within world political–economic change (especially decolonization in the South) and the social dynamics of conservation in particular countries.

The 'classic' approach focuses on environmental (rather than social) solutions to perceived environmental problems. It has been argued that this approach is embodied within the traditional (exclusionary) national parks and protected area systems. The state plays a major and leading role in defining the conservation problem, formulating policy, then implementing it. It promotes 'its own' science, appeals to a (particular) scientific interpretation of the problem, and attempts to use state power and the institution of state property to impose its policy on civil society. The issues of human welfare hardly appear on the agenda at all, and the ways in which inevitable conflicts arise with state appropriation of biological resources which it considers necessary for conservation, are resolved by coercion.

The central policy tool of this paradigm is the protected areas system, in which the conservation of entire ecosystems to prevent loss of wild species is planned. Parks and other protected areas are seen as the key instruments in conservation.

Many writers (including Nash, 1970 and Runte, 1979) have examined the inappropriate and widespread export to countries in the South of the concept of the national park as it developed in the United States — with vast areas of natural beauty set aside and preserved from human exploitation, for the enjoyment of visitors. Boundaries were drawn around special places and phenomena, setting them aside from the 'ravages' of ordinary use (Hales, 1989). However, analysis has shown that this model of a national park is a product of an affluent culture, emerging in the context of nearly boundless wealth and space, and usually in sparsely populated areas, with urban populations no longer subsisting directly from the land (Nash, 1970). This original conceptualization of the national park, now embodied within IUCN's framework, tends to exclude resident people and use of resources from parks. As a model for countries with entirely different circumstances, it is known to have caused enormous social deprivation and suffering.

A central critique of the classic approach to conservation refers to its colonial origins in developing countries. Several authors have drawn attention to the mythical dimensions of colonial conservation, suggesting that protected area policies may reveal more about western eco-cosmologies and subliminal notions about 'human–nature' relationships than 'objective' ecological science. Anderson and Grove (1987), for example, examine the wider psychological function of the African environment in the European mind. To understand how and why European ideas have shaped conservation policies in the past and present, we have to understand how nature's eternity was seen to be symbolized in Africa, and how man has sought to rediscover his lost harmony with nature. Marks (1984) has suggested that European-shaped preservationist policies hold vast acreages of land hostage to such romantic and Arcadian myths.

Contemporary ecologists and conservationists should thus be aware of the deep and reiterative relationship between science and the values of society. Conservation policies will inevitably symbolize the views and values of their authors and cultures and in this context may be analysed as social constructions. International policy needs to be open to other eco-cosmologies which may have different views about the relationships of the human and natural worlds.

In many cases the establishment of national parks has been (and continues to be) closely tied to elitist interests. For example, in the words of Colonel Mervyn Cowie, an early preservationist instrumental in the establishment of the Serengeti Park in East Africa, protected areas were designed to provide '... a cultured person's playground'. He believed that the natives had very little interest in the parks; in fact the main purpose of the parks was to 'protect nature from the natives' (Cowie cited in Gilges, 1992). Some parks also served important economic functions. For example, Mackenzie (1987) examines the essential role of wildlife (particularly ivory) and subsidies provided by the 'Hunt' in the economic survival of colonial regimes. He illustrates how the 'hunting ethos' and ideas about conservation became intimately connected to the structures of privilege and power of the new rulers of Africa.

The discourse of fortress conservation mentality also changes the way we think about people living in the vicinity of reserves. 'Hunters' become 'poachers'; 'settlers' become 'squatters' and 'land clearing for agriculture' becomes 'deforestation'. Local people are acutely aware of these changes in their perceived status. For example, according to the Bakweri people from the Etinde forest reserve in Cameroon, 'Protected area legislation turns the locals into thieves' (Jeanrenaud, 1991). The term 'buffer' zone also clearly expresses a defensive posture where 'nature' needs to be protected from people.

The 'neo-populist' approach has emerged within the last fifteen years as a response to the failures of the 'classic' approach. It is exemplified in more 'people-oriented' conservation programmes such as integrated conservation and development projects (ICDPs), joint or co-management schemes. These attempt participatory modes of project formulation and implementation. The approach has derived from a political reaction and opposition to big business, the authoritarian state, dispossession through capitalist expansion and technological change, and bureaucratic inefficiencies. In policy terms, the approach seeks to remould the interface between the majority of society (small farmers, pastoralists, petty traders, artisans etc.) and the state. This is done by acknowledging their own agendas and their own technical knowledge, adapting plans to local conditions, and facilitating conservation through dialogue, participatory action and enabling policies at international, national, and local levels. This paradigm has become the new conventional wisdom, particularly in international discourse, although there are still important lags in its succession from the state-led authoritarian 'classic' predecessor. The necessary profound reorientation of scientists and other development professionals takes time, and, in the view of some, faces formidable opposition from conservative professional interests (Chambers, 1993).

However, this paradigm too has to be explored and thought through 'on the ground'. There are emerging contradictions and problems in converting a new idea into successful conservation practice. First, it requires a high degree of skilled and committed personnel. Second, there will be competition for resources among a variety of interests, which may well be in conflict with the scientifically set agenda of biodiversity conservation. Groups of unequal power will be pursuing their own interests, and it may well be difficult for the institution charged with facilitating the conservation to preserve a level negotiating field (e.g. foreign logging companies may be able to win concessions from the state in the face of customary rights of local cultivators and forest dwellers). Third, biodiversity conservation may be against the short-term interests of much of the local population. Put simply, most people may not want conservation, because the economic costs are too high. A process of 'environmental brokerage' with effective and seemingly fair incentives and mutually agreed sanctions is clearly one way of progressing beyond these problems — but it is easier to recommend than to deliver on the ground. Finally, the neo-populist paradigm is being challenged by the resurrection of the neo-liberal approach.

The 'neo-liberal economic' approach focuses on economic benefits and costs of biodiversity erosion and management. It emphasizes the central role of the market in regulating the use of natural resources and a more limited role for the state, which should retreat from intervention to fulfilling the role of standard-setting, and 'refereeing' the proper functioning of markets. The state should remove 'perverse' incentives which encourage non-sustainable use of resources and encourage instead the internalization of environmental costs. This approach has come about in part from a deeper understanding of the limitations of real-world bureaucracies and the reduced control which the state and its functionaries have over citizens; and in part from the resurrection of a pricist counter-revolution and the dominance of economics in policy making. As McNeely says, 'current institutions, research and legislation have failed to conserve the level of biological diversity required for the welfare of society' (1988:38).

While this approach undoubtedly provides a degree of rigour, there are acknowledged problems. As with any mono-disciplinary approach, other considerations which have been analysed by political science and anthropology are not well integrated (although there are economic approaches to 'political' issues, such as the consideration of transaction costs, game theory and collective action, to name a few). There are many reasons, however, more usually captured by other social sciences than by economics, which may inhibit market-efficient behaviour. First, there may be rent seeking, regulatory capture on the part of governments, and a range of structurally conditioned agendas of consultants, international agencies and NGOs which all produce very much 'second-best' outcomes. It is a heroic assumption indeed that institutional development will necessarily evolve in a benign and environmentally friendly manner. In so many cases, market-led competition does not and cannot lead to efficient outcomes. There may also be collusion and interpenetration of state employees and policy makers with business, NGO and elite interests.

Second, in conditions of great scientific uncertainty and insufficient information about the future actions of other parties, it has proved difficult to broker the preconditions for a global market for biodiversity. It also implies the transfer of very large sums of money, and the size of the Global Environmental Facility (GEF) bears witness to national political pressures acting upon country negotiators. There are similar institutional and political difficulties in the fair regulation of markets at the state and local level.

Third, there are formidable practical and technical problems in executing the preconditions for a proper valuation of biodiversity and the capture of the market. The principal steps are, first, to estimate what the benefits of biodiversity might be — and, although a start has been made conceptually, there is a growing awareness that pricing can only capture some values for a variety of conceptual and data-related reasons (see WWF, 1993; McNeely, 1988, and Brown and Moran, 1993 for reviews). The second task is actually to capture these benefits. It is all very well for economists to calculate what the benefits should be — that is, if the markets existed and people responded to them. It is quite another for resources to be created from these hypothetical values which few can grasp and recognize, let alone pay for. Education at all levels, international pressure, pump-priming funds are some of the perennial suggestions for progress in this area. The third task is to seek institutions for the distribution of benefits. These comprise simple compensatory benefits for resettlement, alternative livelihoods, rents, and the much more important and complex issue of markets for environmental benefits for biodiversity and conservation in general. Clearly, this task is one of the most problematic. While there are neo-liberal theories concerning the conditions of appropriate institutional innovations for environmental management, there are important questions remaining about the past record for the formation of such institutions, as well as the grounds for optimism about future ones. The fourth task is to identify who the beneficiaries should be. The fifth task is to see that benefits (through whatever institutional delivery mechanism) actually accrue to the owners of biodiversity (or its components), as identified above.

Conclusion

The initial identification and definition of the biodiversity problem has come from natural scientists in the industrialized countries of the North. The problem has a complex scientific basis, and issues of definition, measurement and understanding of processes are marked by a lack of empirical data, and are subject to the individual discretion of scientists themselves. This is not specific to scientific research on biodiversity, although the degree of disagreement and 'talking past each other' is related to the complexity of the research field and the variety of under-standings of the subject. Other issues such as 'sustainability' suffer from similar problems.

> *Unfortunately, it is easier to add up ways in which the concept of biodiversity can be misused than it is to present a simple solution to the extremely complex problem of measuring and maintaining biological diversity. The public is unclear on the concept and scientists cannot give a simple answer. (Rodda, 1993)*

The privileging of certain species, ecosystems and habitats for conserva-tion over others is not, and cannot, be expected on scientific grounds alone. These judgements themselves are constructed within the scientific professions, and subject to personal discretion. Moreover, 'biodiversity' is interpreted in different ways by different actors outside these professions altogether. Many actors have a fragmentary and contingent interest in the issue of biodiversity (e.g. a specific ecosystem or a short list of species of plant or fish). Some may be involved in biodiversity through promoting symbols of conservation (e.g. single-issue campaigns in the North), while others may campaign for the preservation of their own livelihoods in the face of forest clearance, dam construction and flooding, or (ironically) the creation of a national park.

It may thus be useful for policy makers, international opinion-form-ers and decision makers to:

1 Accept that the project of biodiversity conservation is political from its very conception — even from within the natural sciences; it is an arena of competing interests and ideas;
2 Accept a plurality of definitions, but define them carefully and understand where they are coming from by attributing them to those involved;
3 Be prepared to link biodiversity with other issues, while recognizing that there are other issues involved which intersect with (some of) the aims of biodiversity, but which may not share the same final goals; human rights — particularly of indigenous people — income distribution, rights to clean water, education, shelter, etc., and human welfare are all related to biodiversity and its various values,

but these other pressing issues have agendas and goals other than those of biodiversity conservation.

The issue of biodiversity comprises a number of discourses at the global, regional, national and local levels. At each, different but intersecting definitions and meanings of biodiversity circulate, and are linked to the 'projects' of other actors. Hence, at the global level, the main policy issue from the scientific point of view is the conservation of global biodiversity and the governorship of the global commons. However, in the negotiation of international agreements, it is the persistent inequalities in wealth and the control and use of biodiversity resources between the North and South which invade the scientific agenda with political concerns. At the local level, the discourse may consist of a struggle between peasant farmers squatting illegally in the forest, forest dwellers and the state with interests in foreign exchange from timber exports — all of whom value and use differently the resources that collectively contribute to biodiversity. These discourses refer to the same physical resources, but the varied actors attach very different meanings to those resources. This has two main implications. First, since 'biodiversity' means many things to many people, it has become a bandwagon, and the rigour and precision of debates have become seriously eroded. Some policy makers may believe that they are conserving biodiversity in establishing a national park; while a warden may see theft, the displaced see dispossession. Biodiversity conservation may be all of these.

Second, although to some degree the lower levels of biodiversity conservation contribute to conservation at the higher levels in an additive manner, they involve different actors and concerns. Partly, this has to be accepted, and advocacy for conservation pursued at a variety of different levels. This disjuncture also causes serious problems in implementing conservation (conceived at the international level but implemented on the ground). Some of these problems can be eased by adopting decentralized, flexible, locally negotiated programmes. However, the call for participatory conservation has to be realistically appraised.

There are currently three main paradigms for environmental conservation — the classic/authoritarian, the neo-populist and the neo-liberal. Strategy and policy statements usually tend to use the language of more than one, although one often tends to dominate. At present, debate on conservation at the international level reflects a shift away from the classic to the neo-liberal and populist approaches. In terms of biological conservation, the two most opposed and mutually exclusionary are the classic and neo-populist. There is currently a strong call for a new professionalism and new approach to conservation which would take more account of the implications of the distribution of costs of conservation. It is increasingly recommended that local knowledge and expertise (both technical and political) be accessed and harnessed to manage natural resources through participatory programmes. While the people-oriented approach to conservation has gained credence among international policy makers and development professionals worldwide, there is a growing backlash against it as the full implications of the populist approach start to be thought through. The assumption of community and consensus in the practice of participatory conservation is far from problem-free. The plurality of understandings, and the variety of competing interests (some of them decidedly anti-conservationist) beg the question of the equal nature of the negotiations between outside agencies and local people. The former have their scientific agendas, and the latter have all sorts of contingent interests in biodiversity conservation. Frequently, there is disagreement between the two parties and also among local people themselves. How far can, or should, the outside agency push its own agenda? It is helpful for conservation agencies to consider 'advanced' participation as a best-case scenario, but also own up to their own agenda and become environmental brokers between all relevant actors.

The economic approach to environmental conservation takes a very different perspective. The conceptual problems of measuring the value of biodiversity and the political reality of appropriating it still remain formidable obstacles to the realization of efficiently functioning markets for biodiversity. While it may be possible to remove the 'perverse' incentives to degrade the environment at the national level, the operation of market signals which reflect the true value of conserving biodiversity at the local level may seem a far distant reality.

There are strong pragmatic and political grounds for paying detailed attention to the impact of biodiversity erosion and conservation upon human welfare, particularly in cases where conservation efforts may affect local people directly. The pragmatic grounds are that coerced and enforced conservation tends to fail in the long run. The political grounds are that other considerations — such as the abuse of human rights and the accentuation of inequalities — are related to environmental degradation, and so conservation efforts must be seen to address these issues too, and not to exacerbate them.

References

Anderson, D and R Grove (eds) (1987), *Conservation in Africa: People, Policies and Practice*, Cambridge University Press, Cambridge.

Biot, Y, P M Blaikie, C Jackson and R Palmer-Jones (1995), *Rethinking Research on Land Degradation in Developing Countries*, Discussion Paper No 289, The World Bank, Washington, DC.

Blaikie, Piers and Sally Jeanrenaud (1996), *Biodiversity and Human Welfare*, Discussion Paper No 72, UNRISD, Geneva, February.

Blaikie, P M, J Cameron and D Seddon (1980), *Nepal in Crisis: Growth and Stagnation at the Periphery*, Clarendon Press, Oxford.

Bonner, R (1994), 'Western conservation groups and the ivory ban wagon', in M R Freeman and U P Kreuter (eds), *Elephants and Whales: Resources for Whom?*, Gordon and Breach Science Publishers, Basle.

Brown, K and D Moran (1993), *Valuing Biodiversity: The Scope and Limitations of Economic Analysis*, CSERGE GEC Working Paper 93–09, University of East Anglia, Norwich, and University College London.

Brown, K (1994), *Conservation or Development in Nepal's Terai? Resolving Land Use Conflicts in Asia's Last Land Frontier*, CSERGE Working Paper GEC 94–23, University of East Anglia, Norwich.

Chambers, R (1993), *Challenging the Professions: Frontiers for Rural Development*, IT Publications Ltd, London.

Chatterjee, P and M Finger (1994), *The Earth Brokers*, Routledge, London.

Clay, E J and B B Schaffer (1984), *Room for Manoeuvre An Exploration of Public Policy in Agricultural and Rural Development*, Heinemann Educational Books, London.

CNPPA (Congress on National Parks and Protected Areas) (1992), *Parks for Life*, Report of the IVth World Congress on National Parks and Protected Areas, IUCN, WWF, Gland.

Ellis, S (1994), 'Of elephants and men: politics and nature conservation in South Africa', *Journal of Southern African Studies*, Vol 20, No 1, March, pp 53–69.

Ghimire, K (1992), *Forest or Farm? The Politics of Poverty and Land Hunger in Nepal*, Oxford University Press, New Delhi.

Gilges, K (1992), *Bioreserves: Land-Use Surrounding National Parks in Savanna Africa*, unpublished MSc thesis, Oxford Forestry Institute, Oxford.

Grove, R (1987), 'Early themes in African conservation: The Cape in the nineteenth century', in Anderson and Grove, op cit.

Hales, D (1989), 'Changing concepts of national parks', in D Western and M Pearl (eds), *Conservation for the Twenty-First Century*, Oxford University Press, Oxford.

IUCN (World Conservation Union) (1994), *A Guide to the Convention on Biological Diversity*, IUCN, Gland.

IUCN/UNEP/WWF (1980), *World Conservation Strategy: Living Resource Conservation for Sustainable Development*, IUCN, UNDP and WWF, Gland.

— (1991), *Caring for the Earth*, IUCN, UNEP, WWF, Gland.

Jeanrenaud, S (1991), *A Study of Forest Use, Agricultural Practices, and Perceptions of the Rainforest, Etinde Rainforest, S W Cameroon*, report submitted to the Overseas Development Administration, London.

Mackenzie, J M (1987), 'Chivalry, social Darwinism, and ritualised killing: The hunting ethos in Central Africa up to 1914', in Anderson and Grove, op cit.

Mann, C (1991), 'Extinction: Are ecologists crying wolf?', *Science*, Vol 253, 16 August, pp 736–738.

Marks, S (1984), *The Imperial Lion: Human Dimensions of Wildlife Management in Africa*, Bowker, Epping, United Kingdom.

Martin, C (1995), *Restructuring and Community Participation*, memorandum to all WWF National Organizations and Chief Executive Officers, WWF International, 2 March.

McNeely, J A (1988), *Economics and Biological Diversity: Developing and Using Incentives to Conserve Biological Resources*, IUCN, Gland.

Nash, R (1970), 'The American invention of national parks', *American Quarterly*, Vol 22, No 3.

Prescott-Allen, R (1986), *National Conservation Strategies and Biological Diversity*, report to IUCN, Gland.

Rodda, G H (1993), 'How to lie with biodiversity', *Conservation Biology*, Vol 7, No 4, pp 1959–1960.

Runte, A (1979) *National Parks: The American Experience*, University of Nebraska Press, Lincoln, Nebraska.

Seddon, D, P Blaikie and J Cameron (1979), *Peasants and Workers in Nepal*, Aris & Philip, Warminster.

Tickell, O (1995), 'Animal passions', *The Guardian*, 1 February, p 5.

UNCED (United Nations Conference on Environment and Development) (1992), *A Guide to Agenda 21*, A Global Partnership, Geneva, March.

The World Bank (1992), *World Development Report 1992: Development and the Environment*, Oxford University Press, New York.

WRI, IUCN, UNEP (1992), *Global Biodiversity Strategy Guidelines for Action to Save, Study, and Use Earth's Biotic Wealth Sustainably and Equitably*, WRI, IUCN, UNEP, Washington, DC.

WWF (1993), *Economic Analysis of Conservation Initiatives*, WWF-International, Gland.

— (1994), *WWF's Global Priorities to the Year 2000*, WWF-International, Gland.

III

NATIONAL PARKS AND PROTECTED AREA MANAGEMENT IN COSTA RICA AND GERMANY: A COMPARATIVE ANALYSIS[1]

Jens Brüggemann

Introduction

It is frequently assumed that the management and administration of protected areas tend to be more effective in rich industrialized and technologically advanced countries of the North rather than in poor developing countries. Rich countries should be more capable of providing the economic, technical and human resources necessary for effective conservation in protected areas. Through a comparison of the experience of establishing and managing national parks and other protected areas in the Central American republic of Costa Rica and the Federal Republic of Germany, this chapter suggests that the above assumption does not necessarily hold.

Significant parts of both countries' territory have been declared protected by law for nature conservation purposes. However, there are important differences between protected areas in Costa Rica and Germany — in size, conservation objectives, management/administration practices as well as social and economic impact.

In Costa Rica, national parks and biological reserves have legally been designated as strictly protected areas following closely the recommendations of the World Conservation Union (IUCN). They are administered by

---

1 The author is indebted to Krishna Ghimire, Sari Nissi and Michael Weigelt for comments on an earlier draft.

the National Parks Service with a strong emphasis on the conservation of natural processes and cover about 10 per cent of the Costa Rican land territory. In addition there are other protected areas, such as wildlife refuges or forest reserves, which serve different goals of conservation and sustainable resource use. Because a significant proportion of the population living in rural areas depends on the use of natural resources, social conflicts have frequently arisen in the course of establishing protected areas and conservation mandates have been partly compromised.

Germany's 11 national parks cover an area equal to about 2 per cent of the national territory, whereby most of the national park area belongs to the marine waddensea on the North Sea coast. Only small reserves are being strictly protected for nature conservation. The regional or Länder governments are responsible for administering protected areas within their boundaries. In addition to national parks, biosphere reserves and nature parks are also important categories for conserving large culturally shaped landscapes. They cover about one fifth of the German territory. The large protected areas are the result of a compromise between conservation goals and the interest of different resource users. Conflicts were mediated by a strong institutional structure, in part privileged by strong economic and administrative capacity, but conflicts were often resolved at the expense of nature protection.

The following sections will trace the historical processes of protected area establishment in the two countries, and will consider in particular their effectiveness on the ground vis-à-vis their expressed conservation and social objectives. Some of the concrete experiences of establishing and managing protected areas, and the contrasts between the 'modern' and more traditional or restrictive approaches to protection will then be considered in the specific cases of the Bavarian Forest National Park and South-East Rügen Biosphere Reserve in Germany, and the Central Pacific Conservation Area and Tortuguero Conservation Area in Costa Rica.

History of National Parks and Protected Areas Establishment in Costa Rica and Germany[2]

In Costa Rica, the first isolated conservation initiatives were recorded in the first half of this century. For example, in 1913 the summit of Poás Volcano was declared protected. In 1939 a law prohibited the use of resources in national forests. The term 'national park' appeared for the first time in legislation in 1945 concerning a two-kilometre-wide forest strip along the Pan-American Highway. The summits of all volcanoes

---

2 This chapter is based on interviews conducted in Costa Rica over the last four years in the course of several research projects (Brüggemann, 1991; Brüggemann and Salas Mandujano, 1992; Utting, 1993). In Germany, interviews were conducted with experts and other persons, especially during field visits to Rügen in November 1993 and to the Bavarian Forest in January/February 1994. Secondary sources provided valuable background information.

were declared national park areas in 1955 with the law that created the Costa Rican Tourism Institute (ICT) which was to administer these areas. But none of the first conservation initiatives were implemented effectively (Boza and Mendoza, 1981:24).

Historically, Costa Rica was sparsely populated and only a relatively small indigenous population inhabited the forests. At independence from Spain in 1821, there were about 65,000 inhabitants, living mainly in the Central Valley. Most of the country remained under dense forest cover. However, the expansion of coffee production during the nineteenth century in the Central Valley initiated a process of spontaneous agricultural colonization. The state supported this process with several incentives, such as the granting of land rights. Towards the end of the nineteenth century, a railway connecting the capital San José with the Atlantic harbour of Limón was constructed and forests were cleared for United Fruits banana plantations in the Atlantic zone. The development pattern of expanding subsistence and export-oriented agriculture at the expense of forests led to large-scale deforestation. From the 1950s onwards, deforestation again accelerated as a result of the promotion of cattle ranching for beef exports to North American markets.

During the 1960s, the foundations for establishing and managing national parks in Costa Rica were laid. Cabo Blanco Absolute Nature Reserve was created in 1963. The International Convention for Flora, Fauna and Natural Scenic Beauty Conservation, an initiative by the United States to create national parks and reserves, which had been signed by Latin American countries in the 1940s, was ratified in 1966 (Rodríguez, 1993:72–73). The Forestry Law of 1969 defined the criteria for different categories of protected areas. National parks and biological reserves are strictly protected areas which exclude, by definition, human settlements and resource use. In order to establish these areas according to the law, the state had to acquire the property rights, i.e., buy out land owners and evict settlers. In some protected areas, for example in wildlife refuges, resource-use regulations were issued for conservation purposes; and in others, such as forest reserves and protection zones, with the intention to sustain ecological processes and sustainable production.

After initially protecting areas of scenic, historical and cultural value for national pride and public education and recreation (volcanoes, beaches of Manuel Antonio and Cahuita), the emphasis shifted towards protecting representative examples of biological resources and ecosystems for scientific reasons. Rodríguez (1993:82) argues that the systematic establishment of national parks (Table 3.1) was a direct outcome of recommendations and exchanges of ideas from the 1972 Stockholm United Nations Conference and the 1972 World Conservation Union–National Parks Conference held in Yellowstone.

The National Parks Service (SPN) was elevated from a department within the General Directorate for Forestry (DGF) to a directorate of the Ministry of Agriculture (MAG) in 1977. The budget rose from Colones 5

Table 3.1 *National parks and biological reserves in Costa Rica (1993)*

Protected area	Year established	IUCN category	Land extension (ha)	Marine extension (ha)	Total extension (ha)
Irazú Volcano NP	1955	V	2,309		2,309
Cabo Blanco ANR	1963	I	1,172	1,790	2,962
Cahuita NP	1970	V	1,068	22,400	23,468
Santa Rosa NP	1971	II	37,117	78,000	115,117
Poás Volcano NP	1971	II	5,600		5,600
Manuel Antonio NP	1972	–	683	55,000	55,683
Guayabo NM	1973		218		218
Rincón de la Vieja NP	1973	II	14,084		14,084
Isla Guayabo/Negritos BR	1973	I	144		144
Isla Pajaros BR	1973		4		4
Barra Honda NP	1974	V	2,295		2,295
Tortuguero NP	1975	II	18,947	52,265	71,212
Chirripo NP	1975	II	50,150		50,150
Corcovado NP	1975	II	54,539	2,400	56,939
Isla del Coco NP	1978	II	2,400	97,235	99,635
Braulio Carrillo NP	1978	II	45,899		45,899
Carara BR	1978	I	4,700		4,700
Hitoy Cerere BR	1978	I	9,155		9,155
Isla del Caño BR	1978	IV	200	2,700	2,900
La Amistad NP	1982	II	193,929		193,929
Palo Verde NP	1982	II	16,804		16,804
Lomas Barbudal BR	1986	IV	2,279		2,279
Guanacaste NP	1989	II	32,512		32,512
Marino Bellena NP	1989	IV	110	5,375	5,485
Arenal NP	1991	II	2,920		2,920
Juan Castro Blanco NP	1992	II	14,258		14,258
Tapantí NP	1992	IV	6,080		6,080
TOTAL (27)			519,576	317,165	836,741

Note: ANR: Absolute Nature Reserve; BR: Biological Reserve; NM: National Monument; NP: National Park
Sources: SPN (1993:113–114); except IUCN Categories: IUCN (1994a)

million (US$ 0.6 million) in 1976 to Colones 15 million (US$ 1.75 million) in 1978. Moreover, some parks received special grants and special allotments were granted for single parks (Boza and Mendoza, 1981:25). This reflected the growing importance within the government of SPN — which had previously relied on extraordinary support: between 1970 and 1974, the then First Lady Karen Olsen de Figueres was a 'godmother' of the parks programme, securing for the SPN aid from ministries, autonomous institutions, municipalities, the Legislative Assembly and international agencies (ibid.). SPN eventually turned some of the forestry reserves and protection zones into national parks which implied that it took over the administrative authority from DGF.

The consolidation and expansion of the national parks system was mainly possible because SPN could tap international finance. Leading national conservationists founded the National Parks Foundation (FPN) in 1979 to channel essentially foreign donations for the establishment, protection and development of national parks to the proposed ends. This way donations did not have to pass through the state apparatus (Boza, 1987). The economic crisis in the 1980s put severe restrictions on the state budget, but the administration of the parks system was nevertheless able to benefit from the debt crisis at the end of the 1980s via the mechanism of 'debt for nature swaps'. International conservation organizations bought Costa Rican dollar-denominated debt titles at a huge discount on the secondary market and had the Costa Rican state convert these debt titles into local currency to be invested by local organizations — in most cases FPN — in conservation programmes. The Costa Rican government converted foreign debt into domestic debt and saved on debt service in hard currency; the conservation organizations could multiply their investments. Between 1987 and 1989, US$ 36 million in local currency was released for conservation purposes and debt titles of US$ 75 million were cancelled (Brüggemann, 1990).

Towards the end of the 1980s, DGF and SPN were moved from MAG to the newly created Ministry of Natural Resources, Energy and Mines (MIRENEM). A new concept of regional conservation units was promoted. Similar to the concept of biosphere reserves, the idea was to establish a large conservation area by linking strictly protected areas — such as national parks and biological reserves — with a buffer zone of different protected areas for sustainable resource use. It was a move towards integrating the different state authorities and national and international NGOs operating in the region, and towards decentralizing administration and management to the regional level under the overall auspices of SPN (MIRENEM, 1990).

The regional conservation units 'La Amistad' and 'Cordillera Volcánica Central' were recognized by UNESCO as biosphere reserves in 1982 and 1988. They were the first large conservation areas established in Costa Rica. La Amistad includes four national parks and one biological reserve administered by SPN, two forest reserves and two protection

Table 3.2 *National parks and biological reserves in Germany (1994)*

Protected area	Year established	IUCN-category	Land extension (ha)	Marine extension (ha)	Total extension (ha)
Bayerischer Wald NP (BSR 1981)	1970	II	13,100		13,100
Berchtesgaden NP (BSR 1990)*	1978	II	21,000		21,000
Vessertal/Thüringer Wald BSR	1979	IV,V	17,242		17,242
Mittlere Elbe BSR	1979	V	43,000		43,000
Schleswig-Holsteinisches Wattenmeer NP (BSR 1990)	1985	V			285,000
Niedersächsisches Wattenmeer NP (BSR 1992)	1986	V			240,000
Hamburgisches Wattenmeer NP (BSR 1992)	1990	V			11,700
Vorpommersche Boddenlandschaft NP	1990	V	39,700	40,800	80,500
Jasmund NP	1990	V	2,500	500	3,000
Müritz NP	1990	V	31,346		31,346
Sächsische Schweiz NP	1990	V	9,300		9,300
Hochharz NP	1990	V	5,868		5,868
Schorfheide Chorin BSR	1990	V	129,100		129,100
Spreewald BSR	1991	V	48,463		48,463
Südost Rügen BSR	1991	V	10,900	12,600	23,500
Rhön BSR	1991	V	166,674		166,674
Pfälzer Wald BSR	1992	V	179,800		179,800
Harz NP	1994	V	15,800		15,800
SUBTOTAL National Parks					716,614
SUBTOTAL Biosphere Reserves					1,204,379
TOTAL (18 different areas)					1,350,193

Note: BSR: Biosphere Reserve; NP: National Park * Extension of Berchtesgaden Biosphere Reserve 46,800 hectares.
Sources: Burger (1991); Ständige Arbeitsgruppe (1995); FNNPE (1994); IUCN (1994a)

zones administered by DGF, one wildlife refuge administered by the Wildlife Directorate (DGVS) and nine indigenous reserves[3] administered by the semi-autonomous National Commission for Indigenous Affairs (CONAI). Even though an inter-institutional management strategy was drawn up for La Amistad (MIRENEM et al., 1990), lack of co-operation set back the implementation of coherent management policies.

In recent years MIRENEM has attempted to provide for the legal basis for the 'National System of Conservation Areas' (SINAC). However, due to opposition from the agricultural sector and government institutions which stand to lose authority with the changes proposed, MIRENEM has been struggling with the formal implementation of the concept of conservation areas. The concept represents a shift from simply emphasizing strict protection without and against human interference towards integrating resident people's needs in buffer zones.

In Germany, the history of protecting landscapes dates back earlier than in Costa Rica. The Drachenfels, to the south of Bonn, was the first area to be declared protected, besides private hunting grounds, as early as 1836, and in 1921, the culturally shaped landscape Lüneburger Heide was declared the first nature park (Plachter, 1991). There are currently 86 nature parks in Germany — relatively large protected areas where resource-use practices shaped landscapes of aesthetic value and where recreation is a major management objective. It was not until 1970 that the first of 11 national parks was established. Five national parks are also listed as biosphere reserves. UNESCO has designated 12 biosphere reserves in Germany. But only a small proportion of the German territory is strictly protected for conservation. Strictly protected areas are usually very small nature reserves. Even within most of the national parks only part of the area has received a strictly protected status. This is in part an explanation why most German national parks do not meet the international criteria for the national park category (Table 3.2).

Historically, there have been many initiatives in Germany with relevance for conservation. For example, Ernst Haeckel introduced the concept of ecology in 1866. One of the first preoccupations of conservationists which translated into legislation was the protection of birds (Plachter, 1991). The concept of sustainable forestry was developed during the nineteenth century. The importance of forests in stabilizing slopes was recognized. However, German forestry has always been oriented towards sustaining timber production with little value assigned to biological diversity.

A wider concept of nature conservation was proposed by Ernst Rudorff in the 1880s. By that time, the modernization in agriculture had caused a visible change in the landscape and the effects of the industrial

---

3 Indigenous reserves were established in Costa Rica in 1978 to protect the culture, life systems and methods of resource use of the 30,000 indigenous people. However, the reserves could not prevent further marginalization of the indigenous population (see Wunderlich and Salas Mandujano, 1991).

revolution, for example contamination of air and water, began to be felt by the urban population. The growing population in the industrial centres demanded food while at the same time the rural population declined. Land use became more intensive: community agricultural lands were reparcelled, agriculture became mechanized and eventually managed with chemical inputs. However, after a discussion in the Prussian parliament in 1898, the proposal to establish national parks similar to Yellowstone was dismissed. It was believed that Germany did not have large wilderness areas (as in the United States) left. Moreover, the Parliament decided against large areas being taken out of productive use so that only relatively small areas were protected as nature monuments (see, for example, Plachter, 1991).

The desire to establish absolute nature reserves without human interference has been weak in Germany compared to approaches and concepts of 'managing' natural or culturally shaped landscapes for desired ends — a more utilitarian perspective. Especially for upper class, urban-based people, nature historically played an important role as a space for recreation and enlightenment, as a balance to the process of industrialization. The Nazi regime (1933–1945) appropriated the issue of conservation and issued the first national conservation law in 1935. As a result, some landscapes and parts thereof were protected, but the term 'national park' was not assigned to these areas — perhaps due to the ideological baggage of the concept, which had developed in the United States (Schurig, 1991:366).

The utilitarian perspective towards the protection of natural resources and the divide between 'landscape managers' and 'conservationists' continued after the Second World War when Germany was split into the socialist East and the capitalist West.

In East Germany, conservation was considered an integral part of the socialist mode of production. But this approach seemed to be innovative, it was not much different from 'landscape managing' in West Germany: the goals of conservation — the preservation of flora, fauna and ecosystems — were subordinated to economic requirements. Nevertheless, several landscapes were given legal protection. The first German biosphere reserve was established in East Germany in 1979. However, protected areas had also been used as hunting grounds by leading figures of the political elite, while ordinary 'workers' and 'peasants' would have been prosecuted for hunting in conservation areas (Schurig, 1991). The island of Vilm, a protected area since 1936 and now part of the South-East Rügen Biosphere Reserve, was reserved as a holiday resort for the political elite only.

Just before unification in 1990, a national park programme was passed in the East German parliament. On the initiative of a few conservationists who participated in the popular movement which brought down the government, five national parks were created as virtually the last act of the outgoing parliament. State ownership of land facilitated their establishment. However, the previous experience with protected areas left many East German citizens with a degree of suspicion towards these new parks.

In West Germany, the establishment of national parks was discussed by the government beginning around 1954. However, a representative of the Federal Ministry of Food, Agriculture and Forestry dismissed these ideas. Nature was seen as a human-made landscape which required management for conservation (see Bibelriether, 1992).

One result of this approach of conserving primarily the aesthetic quality of agriculturally shaped landscapes was the initiation of a programme of nature parks at the end of the 1950s, a major objective of which was the management of important cultural landscapes for recreation without interfering in agriculture and forestry. The strong peasant lobby succeeded in protecting its resource-use rights. The concept of nature parks in itself actually provided few conservation benefits, but the absence in many cases of professional administrations and the lack of financial resources put further constraints on management. Neither the federal nor state governments provided sufficient support. In many cases private conservation organizations were founded for administering nature parks.

In West Germany, the responsibility for conservation and protected areas was vested in the state governments, a practice which was extended to all of Germany after unification in 1990. The Federal Conservation Law, passed in 1976 and currently under revision, provides only general guidance. The law established several categories of protected areas, including nature reserves (strictly protected), most of them relatively small, often parts or zones of larger protected areas, and national parks (only partially strictly protected) which may contain human inhabitants (IUCN, 1992:172–173). Biosphere reserves are not yet a legal category at the federal level.

As each of the 16 Länder of the unified Germany is in charge of conservation within its territory and draws up its own conservation laws, there are no uniform regulations and practices with respect to the management and protection of protected areas. For example, the Waddensea area on the North Sea coast is protected in three national parks, with three different administrations and little communication between them. The two Bavarian national parks fall under the auspices of two different ministries.

The creation of a protected area follows a lengthy process of planning and negotiations between public authorities, institutions, interested groups and experts which usually lasts for several years. With the establishment of a protected area, conservation orders — a set of prohibitions and regulations precluding, for example, drainage, removal of landscape features or the construction of buildings — are enacted. However, the establishment of a protected area does not automatically exclude hunting (IUCN, 1992:166).

Specific Case Experiences

Some of the complex issues concerning the establishment, management and local community integration of national parks and reserves in Costa Rica and Germany can be exemplified by looking at two protected areas in each country (Figures 3.1 and 3.2). Established only recently, the Tortuguero Conservation Area in Costa Rica and the South-East Rügen Biosphere Reserve are examples of a 'modern' approach towards protected areas, as far as it has been implemented. This 'modern' conservation approach attempts to combine strict nature protection and sustainable development over a relatively large area. The other two areas, the Bavarian Forest National Park in Germany and the Carara Biological Reserve in the Central Pacific Conservation Area, could be characterized as having followed a more restrictive approach to conservation over a relatively small area.

Germany

The Bavarian Forest National Park and the South-East Rügen Biosphere Reserve are both recognized as 'Biosphere Reserves' under UNESCO's Man and Biosphere Programme. The Bavarian Forest National Park is the oldest national park in Germany, while Rügen Biosphere Reserve was established in the former East Germany just before unification in September 1990. While Rügen is still in the process of building up structures for protection, management and sustainable development, the Bavarian Forest can count on the experiences of being a national park for 25 years.

Bavarian Forest National Park
The parliament of the state of Bavaria decided in 1969 to establish the first national park in Germany — the National Park Bavarian Forest. It covers an area of 13,100 hectares of state forest in south-eastern Germany on the border with the Czech Republic. The stimulation of tourism in this economically less well-developed, marginal area had been one policy consideration. Communication, employment and education possibilities were low when the park was created. Meanwhile the situation has improved and tourism rose considerably after the establishment of the park. The park receives around 1.5 million visitors annually. In the wider region of the park tourism has contributed a greater share to regional income than has agriculture (Unger, 1993).

The forest with spruce, fir and beech trees had been relatively undisturbed on 80 per cent of the park area until the mid-nineteenth century. The forest was used economically to some extent in the past as firewood for glass manufacturing, timber production and the collection of minor forest products (cones for firewood, mushrooms, berries). In 1970, the annual logging rate was 65,000 cubic metres.

Initially the Forestry Department within the Bavarian Ministry of Agriculture and Forestry wanted to continue logging activities even after the area was declared a national park. The construction of 115 kilometres of access roads for heavy machinery was also planned. Although these plans already went against international criteria for national parks, a preparatory study was undertaken by a landscape planner in view of developing the park as a tourist attraction. The study proposed open-air enclosures in the park for animals which live or used to live in the Bavarian Forest, trails for visitors and better road connections for cars. These management objectives were typical for nature parks (Bibelriether, 1991:48–49).

Due to the initiatives of the park administrators, the lobbying of the important German non-governmental conservation organization BUND (Bund für Umwelt- und Naturschutz in Deutschland[4]) in Bavaria, as well as a few politicians, conservation objectives triumphed as the priority of the park. Against the opposition of foresters and hunters, who often were the same persons and who belonged to the politically active local elite, the construction of further access roads in the park was blocked and hunting was effectively prohibited. Logging activities were halted and gradually reduced to zero.

The principal objective of park management is non-interference in natural processes. For example, trees uprooted by storms remain on the site where they fall. No measures have been taken against the bark beetle pest since the mid–1980s except in a 500-metre-wide strip bordering a productive forest. Despite the widespread impact of acid rain, the forest has got a more diverse structure and the diversity of fauna and flora is high (Bibelriether, 1985; 1991).

The park is well equipped and well staffed. About 140 staff of the forestry department, who had worked in the forests before the establishment of the national park, were transferred to the park administration. Installations such as the information centres for visitors and school classes have received international recognition and served as a showcase for other protected areas. The Bavarian state assigned approximately US$ 4.75 million for investments in the park during the first ten years. The annual budget in the mid–1980s was approximately US$ 545,000 (ABN, 1985:100). At present, with an annual budget of approximately US$ 6 million, it has the highest park budget in Europe (IUCN, 1994b).

A second important source of financial and political support for the park was the immediate establishment of an organization of friends of the first German national park, mostly business people and other fairly wealthy or politically important people interested in nature conservation. Financial contributions to this organization are tax deductible. The NGO has supported the park administration in many aspects and contributed to financing the employment of 14 park rangers for visitor assistance.

---

4 Union for Environmental Protection and Nature Conservation in Germany.

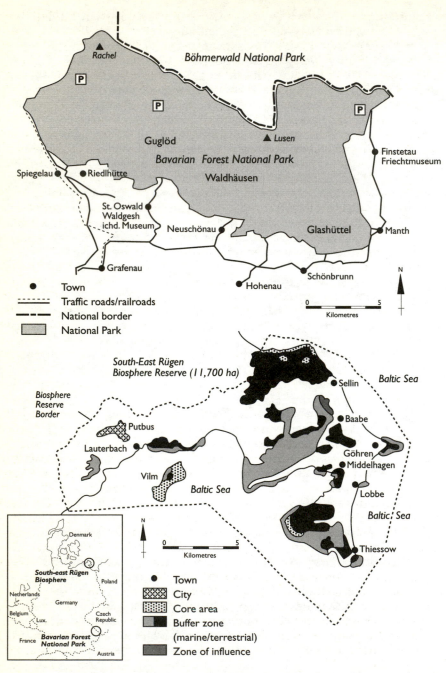

Figure 3.1 *Bavarian Forest National Park and South-East Rügen Biosphere Reserve, Germany*

The park was established practically without local participation, which was possible because of state ownership and the non-incorporation of private property in small enclaves. A few private holdings on clearings within the area were not acquired by the state. The park invested in environmental education programmes and established visitor centres in the communities bordering the park. Even though the local economies benefited from tourism development induced by the national park, restrictions on activities within the park boundaries have been met with resistance. Former foresters and hunters oppose the park because they had to give in to the authorities and stop their practices. Local residents complained because they were no longer able to collect mushrooms and pick berries in the park. While the regulations did not harm their principal livelihood sources, the national park has been criticized because it has led to restrictions on individual freedom and customary habits.

In spite of the approval of the park by outsiders and by segments of the local population, local representatives still complain that the input of communal authorities is not taken sufficiently into account in decisions concerning the park. Many oppose the proposal, currently under discussion, of enlarging the park to include state forests bordering at the west. The fear of losing authority to the park administration is one reason, the lack of interaction between the authorities of the park and the communities another. The non-existence of a buffer zone, where the authorities would support resource-use practices in accordance with conservation objectives, limits the value of the park and puts into question its designation as a UNESCO biosphere reserve, which the park was granted in 1981.

South-East Rügen Biosphere Reserve

Since its establishment in October 1990, the South-East Rügen Biosphere Reserve has been managed and developed according to the objectives of UNESCO biosphere reserves. The objective of the reserve is to protect the culturally shaped, pre-industrial landscape located in the south-east of the largest German island, Rügen, which encompasses an area of 96,200 hectares in the Baltic Sea and is connected to the mainland by a dam constructed in 1936 (see Figure 3.1). The South-East Rügen Biosphere Reserve has an overall extension of 23,500 hectares whereby more than half of the reserve covers marine areas. It is divided into three zones. The strictly protected core area is small, with an area of 360 hectares. The buffer zone encompasses 3750 hectares. Both zones are nature reserves according to the law, and the rest of the biosphere reserve, the buffer zone, is a protected landscape where the objective is to develop sustainable resource use practices for the 11,500 people living within the reserve. Besides the natural value of dynamic coast formations and natural beech woods, the south-eastern part of Rügen has had a particular historical development since the thirteenth century when monks and peasants settled there and engaged in agriculture, fishery and seafaring quite independently from the rest of the island.

The beech woods on the small island Vilm belong to the core area and as a primary forest have a high value for conservation. The island Vilm became a conservation area in 1936 and from 1959 onwards Vilm was reserved, as mentioned above, as a holiday resort for high-ranking offi- cials of the former East German regime. Since 1990 the buildings on the island serve as the base of the Federal Environment Ministry's International Conservation Academy (INA).

The National Park Office within the Ministry of Agriculture is respon- sible for administering the biosphere reserve and nine other large conservation areas in the state of Mecklenburg-Vorpommern. These ten conservation areas, including three national parks, extend to 3.4 per cent of the state's land surface of 23,800 square kilometres. Mecklenburg- Vorpommern is sparsely populated, with 1.9 million inhabitants or 82 persons per square kilometre. Because local unemployment rates in communities close to the conservation areas have been as high as 50 per cent since unification, about 3000 people migrate each month to other parts of Germany in search of employment (Jeschke, 1993:39). The National Park Office does not have sufficient resources; its budget is centrally administered and distributed among the parks and reserves. For example, there are only 76 permanent staff for all the large conserva- tion areas. Without the additional support of 'Zivis'[5] and ABM workers[6] it probably would not be possible to manage any of the parks or reserves. The South-East Rügen Biosphere Reserve has a permanent staff of six, plus four 'Zivis', four ABM workers and two additional staff.

Tourism on Rügen dates back to the turn of the last century. The south-eastern peninsula had 35,000 beds, i.e., 40 per cent of all tourist beds on the island on 5 per cent of its surface. But the great economic potential for local communities, the cultural heritage and the natural beauty, are beginning to suffocate under mass tourism. Pollution due to traffic on the small alleys of the island is one of the problems. During the high season in the summer of 1993, a peak of 15,000 cars were counted each day on the access road to the south-eastern peninsula. The large number of camping caravans is another problem; for example, the waste of chemical toilets is disposed of with virtually no control. Moreover, modern leisure activities such as mountain biking have become problem- atic; bikers have tended to go off-road and have destroyed a special lawn, one of the shrines of the area.

The economic opportunity perceived by many investors in the course of German unification has had several impacts. Construction of hotels and holiday resorts has boomed, while the inhabitants of Rügen face a severe scarcity of housing. The new buildings are not always compatible with the historical architecture of the area. Most of the reserve adminis-

---

5 'Zivis' are young men who fulfil community service as national duty instead of military service. Their subsistence costs are met by the Federal Office for Community Service.
6 ABM workers are — often highly qualified — unemployed persons. They are given short-term contracts and paid by the unemployment office.

tration's work is related to commenting on construction proposals as part of the official procedure to grant permits. However, in some cases investors have not waited for construction permits or have not adhered to conditions laid down in the construction permit.

Economic investments in former East Germany and on Rügen in particular are restricted to a large extent due to 'restitution' demands of former landowners who were expropriated by the former East German government. Unclear land rights have been a major disincentive for investments in land, but land prices have nevertheless reached high levels. The price of one square metre has ranged from 200–2000 DM in the region of the biosphere reserve. During the socialist regime, land had little monetary value.

Because of the slow pace of economic development, local community representatives and businessmen often see the biosphere reserve as a major restraint to town and country planning, agriculture and fishery. In agriculture, the administration is trying to convince peasants to extend the use of energy on their fields. For extensive grassland use without pesticides and fertilizers, peasants are granted a subsidy of 400 DM per hectare. This measure already had the effect of many wild flowers coming up again, much to the pleasure of tourists in the area.

The reserve came into existence because of the lobbying of several individuals from within the popular opposition movement at the end of the 1980s, and one of the proponents of the biosphere reserve was a priest from a village within the reserve who later became the Minister of the Environment in the state of Mecklenburg-Vorpommern. However, it is wrong to give the impression that the reserve was established as a result of public discussions and consultations. Conflicts between the reserve administration and the local people have arisen on different occasions. Nevertheless, the existence of the reserve is now accepted. There are several Rügen NGOs which are concerned by the continued unsustainable development on the island. They encompass a wide range of different interest groups, including the administrators of the biosphere reserve, to work for regional economic development while conserving the natural and cultural heritage of the island.

Costa Rica

The Tortuguero Conservation Area in the northern Atlantic zone of Costa Rica reveals the difficulties involved in moving from a restrictive approach of conservation towards 'sustainable development and conservation with a human face' in a relatively large area. A similar approach is being implemented in the Central Pacific Conservation Area with the Carara Biological Reserve. These cases exemplify the social conflicts surrounding conservation measures.

Central Pacific Conservation Area

The Central Pacific Conservation Area was formally established by Ministerial decree at the end of 1993. Situated south-west of the capital San José on the Pacific coast, the area includes four protected areas. The core of the area is Carara Biological Reserve which protects on 4700 hectares the last intact forest of a climatic transition zone between a drier region in the north (Guanacaste) and a more humid region in the south of Costa Rica. Carara still has a rich diversity of species. The whole area is the habitat of, for example, Scarlet Macaws which migrate between Carara and forest patches in the protection zone on the slopes of the Turrubares mountains to the east and the protected mangrove forests at the coast. The biological diversity of the area is threatened because the forest of Carara is like an island amidst an area of extensive agricultural practice which contributes to habitat loss: land use around the reserve is dominated by pastures for livestock (approximately 75 per cent) and basic grains production. Moreover, forest fires during the summer, poaching and pressures resulting from visitation endanger the survival of many species.

Carara Biological Reserve was created in 1978 after the state gained possession of a vast area which belonged to a large landowner who had died without heirs. The Agrarian Development Institute (IDA) established settlements for peasants in an attempt to counter the pressing problems of land shortage in the area. Of this large holding, IDA transferred 7600 hectares of natural forest and some deforested areas to the National Parks Service (SPN) which in turn established the biological reserve. In 1983, however, almost 3000 hectares of secondary forests were segregated after having been invaded by land-seeking peasants.

Although nobody lived inside the forest and the land rights seemed clear, the creation of the reserve neglected the needs of employees of the former landowner. They had traditionally planted basic grains on the marginal land in the south for their subsistence, and had used the forest to hunt and to collect minor forest products. The establishment of the reserves led to alienation of these lands. The restrictions concerning the reserve were made public, but the state authority SPN did not make any effort to incorporate the local community in the protection of the reserve, nor did they explain to them the sense of the reserve. The aggressiveness and abuse of power of some park guards with respect to hunting during the early years aggravated the frictions between communities and reserve administration. Although hunting by neighbours declined over time, the activities of professional poachers from outside the area rose. Poachers could earn around US$100 for a tropical bird on the black market while tourists paid up to US$5000 for them (*Tico Times*, 1991:7).

Even though a management plan for Carara was developed in 1983 (Cifuentes et al., 1983), the reserve remained under-staffed and under-equipped well into the 1990s. Park guards have experienced difficulties controlling the reserve to contain poaching. Moreover, during the dry season they are required to combat fires, often resulting from agricultural practices outside the reserve or deliberately ignited by poachers to distract attention from their activities.

It is true that the establishment of IDA settlements around the reserve restrained the pressure to invade the remaining forest. However, although the settlements around the reserve counted on technical and financial assistance of government institutions like IDA and MAG, and a rural development project of the European Community (EC), the results have not satisfactorily improved the living conditions of the settlers. Besides poor soils and the inadequacy of the technical package offered to settlers, little effort has been made to develop activities that took into account the location of these settlements right next to the reserve: animals coming from the reserve often destroyed agricultural production on fields close by.

Moreover, a conflict arose between the EC project, which supported a co-operative settlement, and SPN concerning the construction of a road through the northern part of the reserve to connect the production area with the coastal tarmac road. The road was eventually built after an environmental impact study had been carried out to justify the proposal. The more expensive alternative of constructing a bridge over the river was neglected. The road is not only used for marketing the products of the co-operative. It also allows tourists to visit the area: visits to the reserve rose from 5000 in 1987 to 15,000 in 1990 and about 40,000 in 1993, mostly foreign tourists, arriving on tours organized by travel agents from the Metropolitan Area of San José. Tour operators offer one-day packages to the Pacific beach with a stop-over at Carara. According to a study in 1990, the visits exceed by far the capacity of the reserve administration to manage them (Cifuentes et al., 1990).

Except for an entrance fee of US$ 2 (which was raised to US$ 15 for foreigners in September 1994), practically no economic benefit remains within the region. Due to the pressure of SPN, the Costa Rican Tourism Institute (ICT) and the private tourism sector began to support the reserve administration at the end of 1992 with financial contributions and the employment of three park guards (*Tico Times*, 4 December 1992). To take advantage of tourism, a shop could be established at the entrance of the reserve to rent out boots and to sell handicrafts and local drinks. This shop could be run by the surrounding communities, but the law of the National Parks Service simply prohibits any commercial activity within the limits of national parks or biological reserves.

Plans for the Central Pacific Conservation Area foresee the establishment of migration corridors to connect Carara Biological Reserve with the other protected areas in the mountains of Turrubares and the mangroves at the coast. One study proposed to enlarge the reserve by 2500 hectares (Lara, 1992), which would require the resettlement of peasants. Contrary to previous practice where land rights were simply reimbursed, the state institutions announced that they would attempt to find alternative land for the peasants affected. But resettlement would have a significant social impact for the local population. During preliminary studies in the course of establishing the 'Conservation Area', two researchers asked a local peasant whether he knew about the proposed resettlement scheme. The peasant nodded and asked:

'Where are you going to send us to?'
  'We don't know.'
'Will there be forest?'
  'Probably not, I believe.'
'Will there be [small, wild] animals?'
  'No.'
'And will there be rivers?'
  'No, well ... maybe.'
'If that's the case, I don't want to go there.'

(compiled after an interview with William Alpizar, 12 April 1993)

State agencies and private organizations have become more aware of social aspects of conservation, planning to work more closely with local populations and to strengthen environmental education. But so far there has been little interaction between conservation and development with the exception of a tree nursery and reforestation project (of an NGO based in San José) in the south-east of the reserve and an alternative land-use project which promotes iguana-raising instead of cattle in the communities to the north of the reserve. The project is managed by a foundation and linked to the national university's wildlife management programme. An 'Iguana Park' with enclosures, forest trails, restaurant and souvenir shop was recently created. The park provides some employment for the local communities. Moreover, peasants are offered incentives for reforestation of trees that provide habitat and nutrition for iguanas. However, the effects of the project deserve further study: while iguana-raising has proven to be very successful, peasants have complained that some released iguanas are destroying their agricultural crops.

Tortuguero Conservation Area

The conservation area comprises of the Tortuguero National Park at the Caribbean coast, the Barra del Colorado Wildlife Refuge at the border with Nicaragua and a protection zone along the coast which should function as a corridor between the other two areas, a buffer zone and several small protected areas. The Tortuguero area forms part of the bi-national conservation project 'SI-A-PAZ' (International System of Protected Areas for Peace) with Nicaragua.

The forests of the wet and humid northern Atlantic zone have been colonized mainly over the past two decades. Because the climatic conditions constrain traditional agriculture (except for the existence of banana plantations for export), pastures for cattle ranching have been established. While pastures are an economically viable land-use system, they require a relatively large land area and are considered to cause soil compaction.

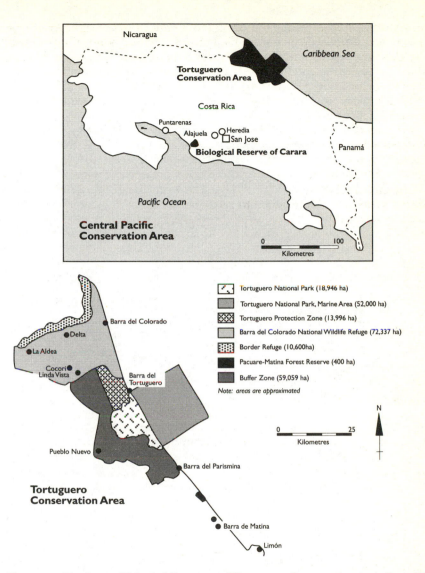

Figure 3.2 *The Carara Biological Reserve and Tortuguero Conservation Area, Costa Rica*

Logging companies have been in the area for almost 50 years, but there are still around 88,000 hectares of dense lowland rainforests with high biodiversity left, for example, inside the Tortuguero National Park (MIRENEM et al., 1991).

Tortuguero National Park was created in 1970 and currently extends on an area of almost 19,000 hectares; the area belongs almost completely to the state. Until recently, the park had a staff of fewer than 20 persons and most of their activities were related to protection within park boundaries. Equipment was insufficient and tourism infrastructure was still poorly developed by 1990 (MIRENEM, 1990). In 1992 nearly 20,000 tourists came to Tortuguero, almost all of them foreigners (SPN, 1993). Between July and October the park administration is extremely busy in controlling the beaches to protect turtles laying their eggs.

The Barra del Colorado Wildlife Refuge was created in 1985 by ministerial decree. The refuge extends over an area of 92,000 hectares. Supported by international organizations, the selection of the area was apparently made by state officials of the Forestry Directorate/Wildlife Service on the basis of old aerial photos from the 1960s which did not show the actual extent of human settlements. Barra del Colorado may be an extreme case, but in the past it was common to declare protected areas according to technical criteria without consideration of the social reality on the ground (Brüggemann, 1991). However, the declaration of the refuge did not have much impact until 1988 when the state began to inform the inhabitants about resource use restrictions in the refuge:

> The land owners can continue to work the land already cleared and apt for agriculture, but the decision of clearing more forest land or changing resource use depends on the use capacity of the soils. Squatters and customary owners can no longer obtain the legal property right, cannot modify resource use, clear forests nor can they participate in reforestation projects. (Brooijmans and van Sluys, 1990:92, own translation)

Peasants within the area of the refuge, totalling several thousand persons, organized with the support of a lawyer and formed a committee against the wildlife refuge. The organization successfully halted the enforcement of the regulations as well as attempts to evict squatters and other peasants without formal land rights. As a consequence, Barra del Colorado remained for some time merely a 'paper park'.

Land rights are traditionally linked to making use of the land by clearing the forest. Historically peasants would obtain a possession right to unused land which they would begin to cultivate. This applied to clearing virgin forest areas as well as to squatting on private holdings of large landowners if not evicted immediately (squatters' rights). After ten years of peaceful occupation, land titles (property rights) could be obtained from the National Register. However, not many peasants registered their property because it was costly, time-consuming and not really seen as necessary by peasants (Brooijmans and van Sluys, 1990; Brüggemann and Salas Mandujano, 1992).

In 1986, a new Forestry Law was passed making it necessary to obtain permits to cut trees. The requirements for the permit included a certificate of the land title, two cartographic maps, a topographic map, the approval of the municipality, a forest inventory and a note from the sawmill to receive the wood (Brooijmans and van Sluys, 1990:89). Due to the fact that most farmers lacked formal title, they were effectively excluded from cutting trees legally, both for on-farm use and for sale. Moreover, the requirements for the permits disfavour small peasants with few resources because of the costs involved. As a consequence, logging has continued mainly illegally. Logging companies bought large areas in the northern Atlantic zone and obtained titles through various means — even within the wildlife refuge. This way they could ask for permits to extract timber and they were also able to buy logs cheaply from neighbours who did not have permits. Furthermore, reforestation incentives established under the forestry law of 1986 were mainly geared to large landowners or companies and disfavoured smallholders. State moves to regulate resource use for conservation had rather the opposite effect. Timber extraction in the area accelerated in 1987–1988. This is also related to the fear of many peasants that the whole area would be declared a national park, thereby inhibiting resource use on an even wider scale (Brooijmans and van Sluys, 1990).

The state and international conservation organizations involved in activities related to the conservation of the tropical rainforest in the area shifted their attitude towards a more participatory approach. With financial support from the European Communities, MIRENEM and the regional government developed in conjunction with IUCN the 'Conservation Strategy for Sustainable Development of the Llanuras de Tortuguero' (MIRENEM et al., 1991). The studies feeding into the strategy considered biological as well as livelihood issues. The strategy was — at least partially — discussed at different levels of regional civil society including with peasants. The basic idea of the conservation strategy is to create a biosphere reserve by zoning the northern Atlantic zone. The zones consist of strictly protected core areas and buffer zones where restrictions on resource uses would operate.

The actual implementation has been rather disappointing for two reasons. First, in the course of preparing the strategy, peasants and landowners had high hopes of receiving grants and subsidies for (sustainable) development projects. Secondly, there was strong opposition from the larger producers of the Atlantic zone and their organizations (banana producers, loggers, cattle ranchers, etc.) and the agricultural union who feared restrictions on resource use or who wanted to benefit from incentives. The opposition to the conservation strategy was organized with the aims of legalizing the land tenure status for people working the land, and ensuring livelihood possibilities, as well as promoting incentives for sustainable production.

Banana companies were interested in expanding their production area towards areas within the Barra del Colorado Wildlife Refuge, offering in the early 1990s up to Colones 200,000–250,000 per hectare (about US$ 1500–1850) — a very high price for the area, perhaps ten times what conservationists could offer. However, since the imposition of quotas on banana imports by the European Community, this pressure has eased.

The European Community supported the implementation of the conservation strategy. Small community development projects were begun in six communities in conjunction with most segments of the local population. Sanitation, health and education projects received the highest priority from the inhabitants, as well as communal credit. After perceiving the benefits of the first activities, the local population asked the authorities to increase their vigilance and control of illegal fishing, for example, because the techniques employed destroyed the stock of fish they were living on (Jiménez, Project Co-Director, personal communication, 26 October 1994).

Conclusions

There are important differences with respect to historical origins and objectives of national parks and protected areas in Costa Rica and Germany. In Costa Rica, the issue of conservation was marginal in relation to preoccupations concerning development and making use of the natural resource base for much of this and the past century. The establishment of the first protected areas was to some extent related to the influence of North American scientists working in Costa Rica. The model adopted for protected areas followed closely the Yellowstone conservation concept. In Germany, conservation was discussed at the highest political level beginning at the end of the nineteenth century. But the concept adopted for protected areas was that of managing landscapes essentially for recreational purposes (nature parks). Hence, while the concept of strict nature conservation was practised in Costa Rica's national parks and biological reserves right from the outset, the establishment of the Bavarian Forest National Park meant a revolution in German conservation practice.

Up until 1994, the Bavarian Forest National Park remained the only national park in Germany which was classified as a category II protected area according to IUCN criteria (IUCN, 1994a). It is well managed compared to other German protected areas. In Costa Rica, most national parks adhere to the national park definition. Nevertheless, there are huge discrepancies in the administrative and management capacities between national parks and similar areas in Costa Rica. Compared to the rigid legislation, the implementation of management policies is weak in many areas.

Strictly protected areas have so far been used by the Costa Rican government as an instrument of preventing further environmental degradation. Assigning protected areas was considered a means of stopping forest clearance. In Germany, the establishment of national parks as an instrument to prevent industrial or intensive agricultural resource use has only recently been discussed in relation to the abandoned military training areas following the withdrawal of troops in the course of German unification (Strunz, 1991). Instead, German national parks can be labelled 'parks of compromise' because their creation is a compromise between conflicting resource-use interests.

Both approaches to protected areas, strict protection and compromise, have encountered problems. The value of conservation may be reduced in 'parks of compromise'. Depending on the degree of resource use allowed, the conservation category may just become cosmetic. The management of a German protected area is thus a tricky balance between conservation objectives and other interests. And still, even with compromises, protected areas in Germany suffer from a lack of acceptance among the local population. In Costa Rica, the establishment of many strictly protected areas has only partially translated into conservation benefits. The enforcement of the protected area status has required the input of considerable financial and human resources. Compared to the enormous amount of money spent in Costa Rica for land acquisition, relatively few resources have remained available for management purposes. In some cases logging, hunting or agriculture have continued and conflicts have arisen. The establishment of strictly protected national parks and biological reserves did not prevent further forest clearance outside these areas. Widespread land degradation outside protected areas ultimately threatens the biological diversity to be protected in national parks and biological reserves.

Conflicts in relation to the creation of protected areas have had much greater social impact than in Germany. The establishment of national parks and biological reserves has affected the livelihood security of many peasant families in Costa Rica (as shown in the case studies above). Reimbursement of lost land rights for peasants has generally been insufficient, with many of them losing their resource base without compensation. Consequences have included peasant proletarization, migration to urban centres and greater poverty (Brüggemann, 1991).

Due to a wide-ranging social security net in Germany, levels of poverty are different from those in Costa Rica and other developing countries. The state provides for the basic needs of its citizens. Moreover, Germany has developed institutional arrangements which, in principle, allow peasants, landowners, investors and other affected parties to appeal against plans and regulations. Institutional arrangements and the concept of private property enjoy legitimacy. Conflicts between conservation and private resource-use interests are mediated, at times at the expense of conservation objectives.

Even with well-developed institutions, the legal base for conservation and conservation practice varies between the single states of the Federal Republic of Germany. And even within states there is often no coherent parks policy. In Costa Rica, the legal base for protected areas management is coherent and there is only one state agency responsible for national parks and biological reserves. However, the lack of coherent government policy on conservation and environmental protection — i.e., proposing national parks in one area and allowing deforestation or polluting industries in an other — and intra- and inter-ministerial conflicts are similar in both countries.

Comparing the administration of national parks and similar areas between Costa Rica and the state of Mecklenburg-Vorpommern in Germany, it becomes obvious that they have similar 'practical' problems such as, for example, the constant shortage of funds and staff. But in both cases there are innovative approaches of generating and utilizing extraordinary support. Debt-for-nature swaps and international donations for tropical forest conservation were used in Costa Rica, NGOs are heavily involved in conservation and the National Parks Office in Mecklenburg-Vorpommern 'employed' Zivis and ABM workers paid for by other German government institutions.

A common concern in many German and Costa Rican national parks and other protected areas is tourism. In Germany some parks and reserves have developed programmes for visitor guidance, visitor information and environmental education. The Bavarian Forest National Park is a good example. The South-East Rügen Biosphere Reserve, on the other hand, which came into being only recently, is still looking for an adequate management policy. The reserve is overwhelmed by the masses of visitors. In Costa Rica, many national parks have had similar experiences in recent years, following governmental promotion of tourism increasing numbers of foreign tourists. The case of the Carara Biological Reserve is no exception (Brüggemann, 1993). Park managers in Costa Rica tend to lack experience in dealing with visitor pressure.

There are mainstream conservationists who are critical of tourism because of some negative impact on ecosystems. On the other hand, in both countries tourism is perceived as an opportunity for protected areas consolidation and regional development. Until recently, the experience in Costa Rica has shown that the park administration hardly benefited from entrance fees or taxes on tourism; regional development benefited even less. Without tourism, it would have been very difficult, if not impossible, to develop and consolidate the first German national park in the Bavarian Forest.

The role of protected areas in regional development is important. In Costa Rica, the National Parks Service has only recently begun to look beyond protection. The new approach of creating large conservation areas, similar to the biosphere reserve concept, can be considered as a positive step towards integrating conservation needs and local resource use requirements.

To sum up, it is wrong to imply that richer countries such as Germany have combined social and environmental exigencies in a perfect manner and that poorer countries like Costa Rica should copy them as models. The success of a protected area depends on its ability to adapt to local needs and to resolve conflicts. Despite a common philosophical origin and conservation intent, each park can have its specific history and character. Some of these experiences are valuable to other parks in different socio-economic and ecological contexts, but not all of them are worthy of replication.

Instead of having only experts trying to adapt the reality to conservation ideals, the exchange of practical experience between parks in different structural conditions could yield important benefits; developing and industrialized countries could learn from each other. However, richer countries would have to take the lead in making available more financial and technical resources for sustainable management of protected areas in countries of the North and the South.

References

ABN (Arbeitsgemeinschaft ehrenamtlicher und beruflicher Naturschutz e V) (ed) (1985), 'Nationalparke: Anforderungen, Aufgaben und Problemlösungen', *Jahrbuch für Naturschutz und Landschaftspflege*, No 37, Bonn.

Bibelriether, H (1985), 'Zur Vereinbarkeit von natürlicher Entwicklung und wirtschaftlicher Nutzung in Nationalparken – am Beispiel des Nationalparks Bayerischer Wald', in ABN (ed), op cit, pp 24–30.

— (1991), 'Das größte Naturwaldreservat Mitteleuropas', in *Nationalpark*, No 71, 2/91 (Sonderheft Deutsche Nationalparke), pp 48–51.

— (1992), 'Vom Naturschutzpark zum Naturpark', in *Nationalpark*, No 76, 3/92 (Sonderheft Deutsche Nationalparke).

Boza, M (1987), 'El sistema de parques nacionales en Costa Rica: un ejemplo de posibilidades para la conservación en un país en desarrollo', *Biocenosis*, Vol 3, Nos 3–4, pp 85–101.

Boza, M and R Mendoza (1981), *National Parks of Costa Rica*, INCAFO, Madrid.

Brooijmans, W J A M and F R van Sluys (1990), 'La Lucha por los Recursos Naturales', in W G Wielemaker (ed), *Colonización de las Lomas de Cocorí, Atlantic Zone Programme*, CATIE, Turrialba.

Brüggemann, J (1990), *Incentives or Restrictions for Tropical Forest Conservation?*, unpublished M Phil dissertation, Institute of Development Studies, University of Sussex, Brighton.

— (1991), *Initiativen zum Schutz des Tropenwaldes in Costa Rica: Umweltpolitik mit Sozialen Konflikten*, Final Report, Arbeits- und Studienaufenthalte in Asien, Afrika und Lateinamerika (ASA)-Programm 1990, Berlin.

— (1993), 'Auf der suche nach dem grünen paradies: tourismus und naturschutz in Costa Rica', in N Häusler et al (eds), *Unterwegs in Sachen Reisen Tourismusprojekte und Projekttourismus in Afrika, Asien und Lateinamerika*, ASA-Studien No 26, Breitenbach publishers, Saarbrücken.

Brüggemann, J and E Salas Mandujano (1992), *Population Dynamics, Environmental Changes and Development Processes in Costa Rica*, report prepared for UNCED/ UNRISD, Geneva.

Burger, H (ed) (1991), *Nationalpark*, No 71, 2/91 (Sonderheft Deutsche Nationalparke).

Cifuentes, M et al (1983), *Reserva Biológica Carara, Costa Rica*, Plan de Manejo y Desarrollo, CATIE, Turrialba.

— (1990), *Capacidad de Carga Turistica de la Reserva Biológica Carara*, CATIE, Turrialba.

FNNPE (Federation of Nature and National Parks of Europe) (1994), *Directory of National Parks in Europe*, FNNPE, Grafenau.

IUCN (World Conservation Union) (1992), *Protected Areas of the World: a Review of National Systems*, Vol 2: Palaearctic, Vol 4: Nearctic and Neotropical, IUCN, Gland and Cambridge.

— (1994a), *1993 United Nations List of National Parks and Protected Areas*, IUCN, Gland and Cambridge.

— (1994b), *Regional Reviews of Protected Areas*, IUCN, Gland and Cambridge.

Jeschke, L (1993), 'Erfahrungsbericht aus den Großschutzgebieten Mecklenburg-Vorpommerns', in Föderation der Natur- und Nationalparke Europas — Sektion Deutschland e V (FÖNAD) (ed), *Schutzgebiete in den neuen Bundesländern — Chancen für Regionalentwicklung und Naturschutz*, Tagungsbericht, Morsak Verlag, Grafenau, pp 39–42.

Lara, Oscar (1992), *Diagnostico para la Elaboración de una Estrategía para la Conservación y Desarrollo Sostenible de la Región Pacifico-Central, Costa Rica*, SPN, San José.

MIRENEM (Ministry of Natural Resources, Energy and Mines) (1990), *Estudio de Diagnostico de las Areas Protegidas en Costa Rica* (preliminary version), MIRENEM, San José.

MIRENEM, et al (1990), *Estrategia para el Desarrollo Institucional de la Reserva de la Biosfera 'La Amistad'*, MIRENEM, MIDEPLAN, CI/OAS, San José.

MIRENEM et al (1991), *Estrategía de Conservación para el Desarrollo Sostenible de Llanuras de Tortuguero, Borrador (Octubre)*, MIRENEM, IUCN and JAPDEVA (Junta de Administración Portuaria y Desarrollo de la Vertiente Atlántica), San José.

Plachter, H (1991), *Naturschutz*, Gustav Fischer Verlag, Stuttgart.

Rodríguez, S (1993), *Conservation, Contradiction and Sovereignty Erosion: the Costa Rican State and the Natural Protected Areas (1970–1992)*, PhD thesis, University of Wisconsin, Madison.

Schurig, V (1991), 'Politischer Naturschutz: Warum wurde in der DDR (1949–1989) kein Nationalpark gegründet?', in *Natur und Landschaft*, Vol 66, Nos 7/8, pp 363–371.

SPN (Servicio de Parques Nacionales) (1993), *Parques Nacionales de Costa Rica*, MIRENEM/SPN, San José.

Ständige Arbeitsgruppe der Biosphärenreservate in Deutschland (ed) (1995), *Biosphärenreservate in Deutschland: Leitlinien für Schutz, Pflege und Entwicklung*, Springer-Verlag, Berlin and Heidelberg.

Strunz, H (1991), 'Nationalpark-Inflation?', in *Nationalpark*, No 71, 2/91 (Sonderheft Deutsche Nationalparke), pp 68–72.

Tico Times (1991), '1991–1992 Guide to Costa Rica', San José.

Unger, K (1993), 'Nationalparke als strukturpolitischer Faktor - Beispiel 'Bayerischer Wald'', in FÖNAD (ed), *Schutzgebiete in den neuen Bundesländern - Chancen für Regionalentwicklung und Naturschutz*, Tagungsbericht, Morsak Verlag, Grafenau, pp 25–30.

Utting, P (1993), *Trees, People and Power: Social Dimensions of Deforestation and Forest Protection in Central America*, Earthscan, London.

Wunderlich, V and E Salas Mandujano (1991), *El Impacto de la Colonisación Agraria en los Territorios Indios en el Sur de Costa Rica*, ASA-Programm 1990, Berlin.

IV

SALVAGING NATURE: INDIGENOUS PEOPLES AND PROTECTED AREAS

Marcus Colchester

Wilderness and Preservation

And in future what a splendid contemplation... when one... imagines them as they might be seen, by some great protecting policy of government preserved in their pristine beauty and wildness, in a magnificent park, where the world could see for ages to come, the native Indian in his classic attire, galloping his wild horse, with sinewy bow, and shield and lance, amid the fleeting herds of elks and buffaloes... A nation's Park, containing man and beast, in all the wild and freshness of their nature's beauty! (Catlin, 1841, reprinted 1989:vii).

The idea that humankind, or to be more accurate mankind, is apart from nature seems to be one that is deeply rooted in Western civilization. In contrast to the 'animistic' religions of many indigenous peoples, which, to use our terms, see culture in nature and nature in culture (Hultkrantz, 1967; Lowie, 1970; Eliade, 1972; Colchester, 1981; 1982b), Judaeo-Christian traditions tell of an origin in which man was given dominion over the beasts. Indeed, even the most ancient of the world's epics, the Tale of Gilgamesh, recounts the primordial struggle between kingly civilizations and the forests, the source of all evil and brutishness (Sinclair, 1991).

In ancient Greece, untamed nature was perceived as the domain of wild, irrational, female forces that contrasted with the rational culture ordered by males. In this world view, not only was nature a dangerous threat to the city state, but the wilderness beyond was peopled by barbarians, the epitome of whom were the Amazons — long-haired, naked, female savages who represented the antithesis of Greek civilization.

These precepts endure to this day. In the Middle Ages in Europe, the image was sustained of an ordered world of culture managed by civilized men, bounded by a chaotic wilderness peopled with savages, the abode of pagan warlocks and witches who drew their power from the dangerous, evil forces of nature, the realm of Beelzebub himself (Duerr, 1985). Similar images continue to sustain the views of fundamentalist Christian missionaries who perceive the shamanism of indigenous peoples as 'devil worship', and believe that as 'Commandos for Christ' they have a God-given role to 'reach the lost until they have reached the last', in 'Satan's last stronghold' (Stoll, 1982; Colchester, 1982a:386 ff; Hvalkof and Aaby, 1981; Jank, 1977; Lewis, 1990).

Pioneering Christian fundamentalists brought these same views of nature to the New World, where they found them strongly reinforced. Beset from the first by naked, long haired 'salvages'[1] who knew nothing of Christ or modesty, their precarious frontier world depended on a taming of nature as they sought to wrest a living from a hostile wilderness. As one local poet wrote in 1662, the forests of the New World were:

> *A waste and howling wilderness,*
> *Where none inhabited*
> *But hellish fiends and brutish men*
> *That devils worshipped. (in Sinclair, 1991:50).*

The notion that their society had a 'manifest destiny' to tame the wilds became a fundamental truth and political imperative (DiSilvestro, 1993).

Dissenters from this society, alienated by its crassness and greed, sought refuge in its antithesis. For romantics such as the artist George Catlin, the noble Indians — whose guiltless lives were being undermined by disease, firewater and land-grabbing — were perceived as a part of wild nature itself — not evil, but unstained, part of an ancient world as yet untainted by the white man (Catlin, 1841). The ascetic recluse Thoreau likewise found that 'In wildness is the preservation of the world' (cited in DiSilvestro, 1993:25). These views echo an equally long counter-tradition, which sees human civilization as flawed and unfulfilling. Just as Gilgamesh, epic king of the first city of Mesopotamia, lamented 'in the city man dies with despair in his heart' (in Sinclair, 1991:6), so Thoreau was to write nearly four millennia later 'Our lives need the relief of [the wilderness] where the pine flourishes and the jay still screams ... little oases in the desert of our civilization' (cited in Ussher, no date).

---

1 The word – which is cognate with the French *sauvage* and Spanish *selvaje* – means, literally, forest-dweller. Its pejorative notion derives entirely from the prejudice against such people.

There thus emerged in late-nineteenth-century America, as a counterpoint to a view of the wilds as evil and opposed to society, a new tradition of wilderness as a refuge from the ills of civilization, as something to be preserved for the recreation of the human spirit. John Muir, one of the main forces in the national parks movement in the United States, argued vehemently and successfully that wilderness areas should be set aside for recreation to fulfil an emotional need for wild places. In the view of these conservationists, as they have come to be known, wilderness is 'primitive and natural' (DiSilvestro, 1993) a resource that is not for use but to be preserved untouched (Redford and Stearman, 1993b:428).

As well as laying the basis for the national parks programme in the United States, these views of nature powerfully shaped the global pattern of conservation. In the United States this view of conservation and nature remains as deeply embedded as ever. Wilderness is still revered by Americans as a place to rediscover the purpose of life, while for many 'wildness' *is* biodiversity (DiSilvestro, 1993:xvii). The notion that nature and human society are inherently antagonistic and incompatible rationalizes the intense sense of alienation that underlies many American versions of 'deep ecology' and motivates many members of groups such as Earth First! (Taylor, 1991). For such 'deep ecologists', 'wilderness means extensive areas of native vegetation in various successional stages, off limits to human exploitation'. They justify such exclusion on the grounds that 'most of the Earth has been colonized by humans only in the last several thousand years' (Wild Earth, 1992:4).

The Yosemite State Park and the Yellowstone National Park were the first results of this approach, and the philosophy of national parks as excluding humankind was eventually given a basis in law. As Gómez-Pompa and Kaus (1992:271) have noted, according to the 1964 US Wilderness Act, wilderness is a place 'where man himself is a visitor who does not remain'.

Since the concept of a 'national park' was born, it has spread throughout the world — and with it the basic premise that nature must be preserved free from human interference. Bernard Grzimek, whose campaigns to conserve wildlife in East Africa made the Serengeti Plains into one of the most well-known protected areas on the planet, was single-mindedly dedicated to excluding the indigenous Maasai cattle herders from their lands. 'A National Park,' he argued, 'must remain a primordial wilderness to be effective. No men, not even native ones, should live inside its borders' (cited in Adams and McShane, 1992:xvi). By the 1970s, this vision of protected area management had come to dominate the conservation movement. The World Conservation Union (IUCN), defined a national park as a large area 'not materially altered by human exploitation and occupation, where ... the highest competent authority of the country has taken steps to prevent or eliminate as soon as possible exploitation or occupation of the whole area' (cited in West, 1991:xvii).

One curious aspect of this view of nature is that even where such lands are inhabited by indigenous people, they are sometimes still considered to be wilderness. The contradiction can be sustained because of a common perception that indigenous peoples are 'of nature' — wild, natural, primitive and innocent. When Europeans contacted indigenous people in North America, the long-haired Indians fitted perfectly the European notion of wildness, as unruly, uncontrolled, feminine forces in league with the devil (Amselle, 1979). The image, though modified, was maintained in the era of 'romanticism', where indigenous peoples were considered natural and blameless 'savages', lost to civilizations in the wild woods — *sans dieu, sans loi et sans roi* (godless, lawless and kingless) (Hemming, 1978). To some extent these images are retained to this day and lie behind conservationist policies of 'enforced primitivism', whereby indigenous peoples are accommodated in protected areas so long as they conform to stereotype and do not adopt modern practices (Goodland, 1982).

In the Old World, the roots of the protected-area movement have rather different origins. Game reserves for royal hunts first appear in recorded history in Assyria in 700 BC (Dixon and Sherman, 1991:9). By 400 BC royal hunts were established in India under Ashoka (Gadgil and Guha, 1993). The Moguls reinforced this tradition in India where the idea gained a wider currency among the ruling elite. The Normans introduced the same idea to England in the eleventh century and enforced the concept of royal forests with such enthusiasm that by the reign of Henry II nearly 25 per cent of England was classified as royal hunts. Local people bitterly objected to the restrictions on their rights that these royal forests imposed (Westoby, 1987) and it is presumed by many that the myth of Robin Hood has its roots in popular resistance by Saxon yeomen to the impositions of Norman rulers.

However, while the definition of areas as royal forest served to reinforce social inequities, it did not imply the wholesale extinction of local ownership or other rights (Rackham, 1989). On the contrary, these traditional rights were too long-recognized and deeply vested for the conquerors to be able to ignore, and the royal forests were thus defined as yet another layer of special rights that did not completely extinguish the complex web of prior rights of use, access, transit and ownership.

The way national parks have been established in Britain owes much to this long tradition of overlapping rights. What has emerged is a practice of landscape conservation rather than wilderness preservation, which respects the long-established order of land tenure (Harmon, 1991). National parks in Britain thus not only fully recognized existing rights but also seek to maintain the established farming system. Moreover, they formally involve in their management local government bodies, and special mechanisms ensure that local residents have a direct influence in decision making.

Conservation notions spread overseas with the extension of the colonies, but brought with them little of this respect for traditional rights and uses. For example, the establishment of protected areas for wildlife conservation in India was founded on the forest department's experience, reinforced by the concerns of colonial sportsmen and native aristocrats, who wished to preserve game for hunting. The model for wildlife conservation that was adopted in India was based on experience in the United States, treating the local people as 'poachers' and 'encroachers' rather than as local owners with prior rights to the areas. The tribal residents of many of the areas favoured for wildlife preservation were held responsible for the decline in local fauna, particularly as some were by then involved in a lucrative trade in game birds and feathers and shifting cultivation was held in opprobrium (Tucker, 1991).

It thus transpired that despite the very different historical trajectories of the conservation movement, the needs and rights of indigenous peoples were to receive short shrift. National parks and other protected areas have imposed elite visions of land use which result in the alienation of common lands to the state. What is equally clear is that the Western conservationists' concept of wilderness is a cultural construct not necessarily shared by other peoples and civilizations which have quite different views of their relationship with what we call nature.

Indigenous peoples are thus perplexed by Western views of what conservation means (Alcorn, 1993:425). For example, Ruby Dunstan of the Nl'aka'pamux people of the Stein Valley in Alberta, Canada, who have been fighting to prevent the logging of their ancestral lands, has remarked:

> *I never thought of the Stein Valley as a wilderness. My Dad used to say 'that's our pantry'. We knew about all the plants and animals, when to pick, when to hunt. We knew because we were taught every day. But some of the white environmentalists seemed to think if something was declared a wilderness, no-one was allowed inside because it was so fragile. (Cited in Ussher, undated)*

Indigenous Peoples' Rights

There are no commonly accepted definitions of who indigenous peoples are. In its most literal sense the term 'indigenous' implies only long-term residence in a given area (Figure 4.1). Yet in international law the term has begun to be used in a more precise way to apply to culturally distinct ethnic groups, who have a different identity from the national society, draw existence from local resources and are politically non-dominant (ICIHI, 1987). In a like vein, the World Bank identifies as indigenous peoples 'social groups with a social and cultural identity distinct from the dominant society that makes them vulnerable to being disadvantaged by the development process' (World Bank, 1990). The International Labour Organization (ILO), whose Conventions treat both indigenous and tribal peoples, places more emphasis on the notion of prior residence in an area,

101

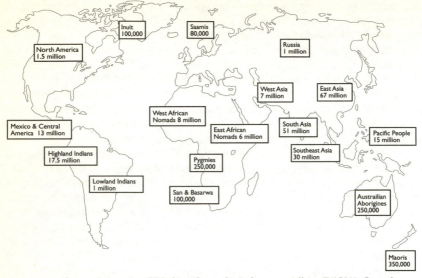

Source: International Working Group for Indigenous Affairs (IWGIA), Copenhagen

Figure 4.1 *Indigenous peoples worldwide*

before conquest, colonization or the establishment of present state boundaries. However, the ILO stresses self-identification as the fundamental
criterion for determining to whom the Conventions apply.

For their part, many ethnically distinct and marginal peoples are
increasingly adopting the term 'indigenous' to describe themselves
because of the rights that they believe are associated with such a term —
rights to their lands and territories; to maintain their cultural traditions,
religions, languages and practices; to exercise their customary law; to
govern themselves through their own institutions; to represent themselves
through their own organizations; to control their own natural resources; to
self-determination; and the recognition of their right to be different.

What most indigenous peoples themselves demand is the right to
self-determination in accordance with the International Covenants on
Civil and Political Rights and on Social, Cultural and Economic Rights.
The latest draft of the Universal Declaration on the Rights of Indigenous
Peoples, being developed by the United Nations Commission on Human
Rights, recognizes that indigenous peoples have such rights. International
law, specifically the ILO's Conventions 107 and 169, clearly accepts the
right of indigenous peoples to the use and ownership, either collective or
individual, of their traditional lands. The law establishes the principle
that 'aboriginal title' derives from immemorial possession and does not
depend on any act of the state (Bennett, 1978). The ILO Conventions also
establish firmly that indigenous peoples cannot be relocated except
according to national law for reasons of national security, economic development and their own health. According to Convention 107, if they are

102

relocated, they shall be 'provided with lands of quality equal to that of the lands previously occupied by them, suitable to provide for their present needs and future development'.

International law also goes some way towards defining how states and outside institutions should go about interactions with indigenous peoples. ILO Convention 169 notes the need to respect and safeguard indigenous peoples' customs and institutions and obliges states to consult the peoples concerned through their representative institutions. International law regarding indigenous peoples is unique in a number of respects, perhaps the most important being that it recognizes collective rights.

The examination of the relationship between conservationists and indigenous peoples, summarized below, takes these internationally agreed legal norms as its starting point. Unfortunately, conservationists have in the past had a very different starting point and, in general, still have a long way to go before a respect for these rights is incorporated into their programmes. Indigenous peoples are particularly indignant of the fact that it is precisely because the areas that they inhabit have not been degraded by their traditional resource-use practices that they are now coveted by conservationists who seek to limit their activities or expel them altogether from their customary lands. As one Karen facing eviction from the Thung Yai wildlife sanctuary in Thailand noted:

> *When we moved into these forests over two centuries ago, Bangkok was just a small village surrounded by lush vegetation. Over these many years, we Karen have protected our forest lands out of respect for our ancestors and our children. Maybe if we had cut down the forests, destroyed the land, and built a great city like Bangkok, we would not now be faced with possible eviction. (Cited in Thongmak and Hulse, 1993:167)*

The Social Impacts of Wilderness Preservation

An unhappy truth which conservationists have only recently come to admit is that the establishment of most national parks and protected areas has had negative effects on their prior inhabitants. So powerful has been the notion that conservation is about preserving wilderness that conservationists have been intensely reluctant to admit that indigenous peoples and other local residents have any rights in protected areas. The fact is, however, that like it or not, most protected areas are inhabited. Recent figures for Latin America suggest that 86 per cent of protected areas in Latin America are inhabited (Kemf, 1993; Amend and Amend, 1992). Worldwide, according to IUCN's figures for 1985, some 70 per cent of protected areas are inhabited (Dixon and Sherman, 1991).

The world's first national park at Yellowstone had originally been conceived as a preserve for both nature and Indians. But the prevailing view of Indians, at the time that the park was created in 1872, was that they were 'sneaking red devils'. The resident Shoshone of Yellowstone were thus expelled, not altogether 'willingly', and subsequent records suggest that there were violent conflicts between park authorities and the Shoshone: as many as 300 people were killed in clashes in 1877 and nine years later administration of the park was turned over to the US Army (Kemf, 1993:5–6).

As it had commenced, so it was to go on. Relocation, often forced, of indigenous peoples has been a recurring necessity in order to establish protected areas in the image chosen for them. One of the most grotesque examples of this process was documented by Colin Turnbull in his book *The Mountain People*, which described the consequences for the hunting and gathering Ik of their expulsion from their traditional hunting grounds by the establishment of the Kidepo National Park, in colonial Uganda. Obliged to adopt subsistence agriculture in the barren highlands neighbouring the park, the Ik suffered prolonged famine leading to a total collapse of society and the disappearance of all mores except naked self-interest. Traditions of food-sharing vanished as the Ik slowly died of hunger while seeking to delay the inevitable through 'poaching', begging and prostitution (Turnbull, 1972).

Forced relocation to make way for national parks has been a particularly severe problem for indigenous peoples in watershed forests — which are often afforded strong protection to conserve soils — and thus prevent the siltation of downstream engineering projects. Thus the Dumoga-Bone National Park in Sulawesi, Indonesia, while noted as a successful example of buffer zone management by IUCN (Sayer, 1991:44), in fact required the expulsion of the indigenous Mongondow people, who had been forced up the hillsides by the agricultural settlement and irrigation projects in the lowlands (*Down to Earth*, 1989).

National parks established to protect mountain gorillas in Zaire, Uganda and Rwanda have also entailed the expulsion of Batwa 'pygmies', whose extremely marginal position in the local political economies has resulted in them being apparently entirely ignored by subsequent attitudinal surveys of affected people (Hannah, 1992:34; Wells et al., 1992:76). Nevertheless, the Batwa achieved international notoriety with the feature film *Gorillas in the Mist*, in which they are explicitly blamed for the murder of the conservationist Diane Fossey, thus perpetuating the myth that conservation in Africa can only be achieved through violent confrontation with indigenous peoples (Adams and McShane, 1992).

Forced relocations are not a thing of the past. In Uganda, mass expulsions of forest-dwellers and peasant settlers have recently been carried out under a project funded jointly by the World Bank, European Community, DANIDA and NORAD to create a wildlife corridor between the Kibale Forest Reserve and the Queen Elizabeth National Park. Completely contrary to the norms on relocation under development projects of the World Bank and the Development Assistance Committee, some 30,000 indigenous people in the Kibale Forest Reserve and Game Corridor were expelled without warning, leading to serious human rights violations, mass impoverishment, burning, looting, the killing of live-stock, and deaths of indigenous peoples (Feeney, 1993). Shortly after the evictions, the chief technical adviser from the European Community reported that 'this successful operation ... has opened up the possibility of the frustrated elephant population of Kibale once more being free to migrate between the Queen Elizabeth National Park and the forest' (cited in Feeney, 1993:4).

According to the World Bank, which itself subscribes to the wildlands approach to conservation, 'resettlement is particularly important when the local people's activities are fundamentally incompatible with the preservation objectives of Wildland Management Areas' (Ledec and Goodland, 1988:97). Yet it is far from clear whether the social, political and environmental problems incurred by transplanting people out of protected areas are justified even in strictly environmental terms. Not only do they create a difficult political environment for the protected area to function within, but they also disrupt neighbouring environments into which the people have been displaced.

The study of forced resettlement has become something of a science due to its increasing frequency as an adjunct of 'development' programmes — the World Bank, for example, expects forcibly to relocate at least 3.1 million people between 1986 and 1996 (World Bank, 1993). As one Bank study has noted, forced relocation can 'be expected to cause multidimensional stress' (World Bank, 1982). These stresses include 'psychological stress' including the 'grieving-for-a-lost-home syndrome', 'anxiety for the future' and 'feelings of impotence associated with the inability to protect one's home and community from disruption'. These stresses may become so great as to cause problems under the second cate-gory of stress: 'physiological', discernible as an actual increase in health disorders. While such conditions may be reversible, the stress factors that come under the rubric of 'socio-cultural stress' may not be. The 'cessation of a range of familiar and satisfying economic, social and religious activi-ties which are tied to the oustee's old home' is related to an overall breakdown in society, particularly political structures (Scudder and Colson, 1982; Partridge et al., 1982). The leaders of the oustee communi-ties find themselves in a 'no-win situation', since they lose legitimacy if they approve the removal of their people against the will of the majority, but also if they oppose the removal, because ultimately they are proved powerless (World Bank, 1982). Societies that are removed from their lands not only lose the economic basis for their survival, but also experience 'a major reduction in their cultural inventory due to a temporary or perma-nent loss of behavioural patterns, economic practices, institutions and symbols' (Scudder and Colson, 1982:271).

Materially most oustees are substantially worse off following removal from their original areas. The fact that compensation is usually inadequate (Scudder and Colson, 1982:270) is compounded by the fact that cash compensation is often squandered improvidently by people unused to land markets. Indigenous peoples, unaccustomed to dealing with land as a saleable commodity, frequently fall easy prey to the unscrupulous. Summarizing the experience of years of work trying to mitigate the impact of forced resettlement programmes, Thayer Scudder of the University of California has noted that 'forced resettlement is about the worst thing that you can do to a person short of killing him' (cited in Claxton, 1986).

The environment, too, often suffers as a result of forced relocations. Traditional balances between humans and their environments are disrupted. People are confined to small and inappropriate land areas; traditional social institutions and patterns of land management and tenure, which used to regulate access to resources, are undermined. Short-term problem-solving behaviours replace long-term planning. The net result is environmental degradation (Colchester, 1987a).

Although resettlement has been and continues to be one of the most common means of dealing with indigenous peoples in protected areas, alternatives have long been tried. Continued residence by indigenous peoples has sometimes been tolerated, often to encourage tourism, on condition that the people maintain a 'traditional' lifestyle and do not change the way they hunt or farm. Such policies, referred to as 'enforced primitivism' by the World Bank (Goodland, 1982), which rejects them, were quite vigorously applied by the apartheid-based regimes of southern Africa. As Robert Gordon (1985) has documented, the policies were based on racist concepts which advocated that 'we must treat the Bushman as fauna and realize that he is incapable of assimilating European ideas'. Accordingly, the last group of Bushmen in South Africa were allowed to live by the Gemsbok National Park, where they were expected to survive on government handouts and by 'traditional' hunting. The experiment in preserving the Bushman 'race' was not a success, as the Bushmen not only sought to change their way of life — they wanted clothes, improved housing and hunting dogs — but also intermarried with other local Africans. After some years one of the park wardens noted with disgust 'their desirability as a tourist attraction is under serious doubt, as is the desirability of letting them stay for an indefinite period in the park. They have disqualified themselves' (cited in Gordon, 1985:32).

Conservationists now face another problem. As a result of their success in generalizing a conservation model that excludes people, national parks legislation in many countries necessarily requires the removal of residents — such laws are the norm in South America for example (Amend and Amend, 1992). As a result, conservationists may find that they are legally obliged to resettle people from national parks even though there is no evidence that their presence poses a threat to the local ecosystem or biodiversity.

A case in point is the Korup National Park in the Cameroon, a 126,000-hectare forest inhabited by about one thousand people and used by several thousand more. According to the legal decree under which the park was established, these villagers will have to be resettled (Sayer, 1991:36). But researchers developing a management and resettlement programme for the park have been sharply divided about both the necessity and advisability of the resettlement. Early surveys suggested that with the exception of one community in the very south of the proposed park, which engaged in a vigorous trade in bushmeat across the border to Nigeria, the levels of hunting, farming and gathering were probably sustainable. Subsequent, more detailed research did not disprove this, although levels of hunting were found to be higher than previously thought (Infield, 1988:45). On the other hand, these studies revealed that hunting was the single most important source of cash for the majority of villagers, representing more than half of their meagre income, yet the restrictions imposed by parks regulations meant that development of alternative means of generating a cash income would also be illegal (Infield, 1988). The World Wide Fund For Nature (WWF) thus felt obliged to argue that 'the presence of villages within the park whose inhabitants are involved in hunting, trapping and agriculture is incompatible with the operation of the park', and the organization advised a voluntary resettlement programme based on creating incentives to relocate to neighbouring forest areas with better soils, where roads, community development initiatives and improved services would be provided (Republic of Cameroon, 1989). It remains unclear whether this programme will be successful (Sayer, 1991:38), especially as the government has been unwilling to pay compensation to villagers for the abandonment of homes, crops and fruit trees.

At the same time, the imposition of restrictive legislation and the threat of relocation, which has now hung over these people's heads since 1981, has created a hostile attitude towards the park (Infield, 1988). Surveys showed that 'many, perhaps all, of the thirty villages within the Park and three kilometres from its boundary claim traditional rights to land and natural resources within the Park itself' (Devitt, 1988). One specialist looking into the managerial aspects of the park advised against resettlement, arguing that the local political disruptions would foment greater antagonism to the park and make management and policing untenable or very costly. The specialist also pointed out that the same laws that made resettlement from the park necessary would also apply in the buffer zones to which people were relocated, making their presence there equally illegal (Ruitenbeek, 1988).

The world over, conservationists are now beginning to realize that the strategy of locking up biodiversity in small parks, while ignoring wider social and political realities, has been an ineffective strategy. So long as polluting and unsustainable land-use patterns prevail outside, the future of the parks is in jeopardy (DiSilvestro, 1993). At the same time, the establishment of protected areas without taking into account the needs, aspirations and rights of local peoples may create ultimately insoluble social problems, threatening the long-term viability of the parks quite as much as the perceived threats which caused them to be established in the first place (Sayer, 1991:1).

For example, resentment among Sherpas at the imposition of the Sagarmartha National Park (Mt Everest) and the undermining of traditional commons management practices led to an acceleration of forest loss. Local elders estimated that more forest was lost in the first four years after the park's creation than in the previous two decades (Sherpa, 1993:49). In India, resentment by local people to national parks legislation and enforcement agencies has caused increasing problems. In some cases, as Gadgil and Guha (1993) note, villagers have responded by setting fire to large areas of national parks, such as the Kanha National Park of Madhya Pradesh. This kind of 'incendiarism' has occurred widely in India (Fürer-Haimendorf, 1986; Roy and Jackson, 1993).

In Africa, over a million square kilometres of land have been set aside as national parks and game reserves (Hitchcock, 1990), yet they have been remarkably unsuccessful at protecting wildlife. Commenting on the problems confronting national parks in Central Africa in his book entitled *The Imperial Lion*, Stuart Marks argues:

> *Materialistic Northerners have sought to preserve African landscapes in the only way they could, by separating them from daily human activities and setting them aside as national parks where humans enter on holiday... Wildlife protection, like other imposed policies, has always carried with it the implications of force, of quasi military operations, and of sanctions (cited in West, 1991: xviii).*

Similar conclusions have been reached by Adams and McShane about conservation programmes in Africa (1992:xv, xvii). Madhav Gadgil (1992:268) has found that the assertion of state control over natural resources in India, led to 'severe conflicts with the local populations attempting to maintain their customary rights to resources. In the process, the local traditions of resource conservation have been increasingly disrupted or have broken down altogether', a finding echoed by Roy and Jackson (1993:160). Janis Alcorn (1993:424) has drawn similar conclusions about protected-area strategies in Latin America.

Many Third World environmentalists — in countries such as Ecuador, Venezuela, Indonesia and the Philippines, for example — believe that national parks are often purposefully established as a means of denying local people's rights and reserving the areas for future exploitation. In India, conservation groups have realized that protected areas from which tribal peoples have been expelled are unusually vulnerable, deprived as they are of their first line of defence.

Conservationists have fought shy of admitting the underlying reason why the classic approach to protected-area management has failed. They have chosen instead to impose their vision, their priorities and their values of landscape, nature and society on other peoples, securing their endeavours through the power of the state and its right of eminent domain. Almost by definition, therefore, conventional protected areas have been at odds with indigenous peoples' rights to self-determination and territorial control.

The Politics of Parks

Conservationists have begun to realize that plans to protect species and habitats most often go awry if social dimensions are ignored or local communities are marginalized. Yet the very politics of conservation tends to militate against an adequate involvement of local people. Since classic conservation is so often a policy that is introduced either by outsiders to a region or foreigners to a country, it seeks legitimacy and authority by making alliances with government. For obvious reasons, since they lack local constituencies or power bases, such conservationists tend to see 'policy-makers' as their target group (Reid and Miller, 1989:vi) and hope that, by winning them over to their point of view, they can assure real changes on the ground by changing the legal status of land and obliging local players to change their activities. The result is that classic conservation approaches tend to reinforce existing divisions between local people and government, thereby increasing alienation and conflict rather than resolving them.

This is made most starkly apparent with regard to rights to land. Most national parks legislation alienates protected areas to the state, thereby annulling, limiting or restricting local rights of tenure and use. This alone makes collaboration between indigenous peoples and conservationists nigh impossible, for land rights are not just dry legal concepts: they express the deep connections between peoples and their environments, they establish the framework that regulates community use of the environment, and they are vested in local political institutions that provide the alternative to direct state management of resources. The denial of indigenous peoples' land rights is thus not just contrary to both customary and international law, it tears at the fabric of indigenous society and its relations with the environment. Yet conservationists continue to be shocked and affronted by the vehemence with which local people respond to the imposition of protected areas, and tend to assume that this hides an intention to deplete or destroy natural resources.

One example is the Loagan Bunut National Park in Sarawak, which was designed to protect Sarawak's only natural lake (Sayer, 1991:56). The lake is the customary property of the Berawan people of Long Teru, who have complex regulations governing who has rights to fish the lake and its rivers (Colchester, 1987b). Correctly noting that agricultural development, road-building and logging seriously menaced the Berawan's lands, government officials moved precipitately to define the area as a national park. The fact that their lands were increasingly under threat was not news to the Berawan — Iban and Malaysian Chinese settlers had been taking over their lands for many years and logging, too, had taken its toll, with soil pollution causing a decline in fish stocks, leaving the Berawan with a seriously reduced resource base on which to survive.

Despite being fully aware that the area was important to the Berawan for fishing, and despite proposals that it would be better to develop the area as a biosphere reserve, where the people could retain certain rights, instead of as a national park, which would extinguish them (WWF-Malaysia, 1985:23), in late 1986 the National Parks and Wildlife Office went hurriedly ahead with plans to define the area as a national park. The Berawan found themselves served with a notice that they should file claims for compensation for the extinction of their customary rights by May 1987. At the same time a proclamation was circulated, noting that erecting buildings, hunting, cutting vegetation and clearing land were all to be prohibited in the park, and punishable by a fine of M\$ 2000 (US\$ 570) and up to one year in jail. At the stroke of a government pen, they were to become poachers and squatters on their own lands. Predictably, the Berawan reacted strongly against the proposal. They asserted that they could not and would not relinquish control of their traditional territory. 'No amount of money can compensate these losses because we depend on the land and the lake for our survival' (cited in Colchester, 1989:64).

Intentionally or not, conservation efforts which ignore or deny local rights and concerns often serve to bolster state interests which have little or nothing to do with conservation. A well-documented example of this is the WWF's flagship programme in China to preserve the panda (Schaller, 1993) in which no effort was put into studying the relations of local communities — which included both Han and ethnic minorities — with their local environment, nor were these groups involved or consulted in decision-making. The main destroyer of panda habitat, logging, has largely continued unchecked; poachers have been dealt with unpredictably, negligent laissez-faire alternating with extreme severe punishment (Schaller, 1993). A number of ethnic minority communities were threatened with forced resettlement (*Survival International News*, 1986), though the ill-planned efforts came to nothing (Ghimire, 1994).

The Save the Tiger programme in India, another of WWF's highly publicized initiatives, has been just as controversial. Launched in 1973, the project has expanded to include more than 2500 square kilometres of forest. Most of the reserves have followed India's typical pattern of denying or heavily circumscribing local peoples' rights, and this by itself has led to much hardship and resentment. But protection has increased tiger numbers, causing more direct problems to the local residents. According to Gadgil and Guha (1993:234), nearly a thousand human lives have been taken by tigers in the past 20 years in the Sunderbans alone.

Resentment of the local people to the impositions of the tiger programme has increased their susceptibility to various insurgencies. In the south of Madhya Pradesh, for example, 52 villages of Maria tribals were evicted from the lands in 1984 to make way for the Kutru Tiger and Buffalo Reserve (Fürer-Haimendorf, 1986). As a consequence, the Maria are alleged to have sided with Naxalite insurgents, who have long championed tribal rights (Banerjee, 1984), having commenced as a revolutionary land reform movement among the Santal tribal people of West Bengal (Duyker, 1987).

The imposition of state controls on indigenous peoples not only leads to tensions between state agencies and local communities, but it also serves to undermine indigenous systems of resource control and management. Indeed, this may be the explicit purpose of the protected area legislation. For example, the law establishing the National Integrated Protected Area System in the Philippines, while it claims to have the 'preservation of ancestral domain and customary rights within protected areas as a management objective', aims to put protected areas under 'close management, control and study' so that 'experts' can decide the location, timing and quantity of natural resources extraction by local communities (DENR, 1992:14). The result is the erosion of local systems of decision-making and the substitution of indigenous institutions with those of what Robert Hitchcock and John Holm call the 'bureaucratic State'. In Botswana, 'it is foreign aid organizations, their academic advisers, NGO leaders and top ranking civil servants who are actually deciding the substance and rate of social change among the San'. These pressures, as much as land loss and economic problems, are undermining San culture and identity (Hitchcock and Holm, 1993:331).

Nancy Peluso (1992:47) notes that the conventional conservation approach alienates lands to the state, and the state may then go on to legitimize serious human rights abuses against those who resist state control in the name of an internationally sanctioned conservation ethic. It is alleged that since 1989, the Kenya Wildlife Service under its director Richard Leakey has declared a virtual 'war' on ivory 'poachers' and has summarily killed, without charge or trial, hundreds of indigenous peoples. Likewise, in the Central Africa Republic, French soldiers have admitted to a 'take no prisoners' policy in eliminating poaching, even killing off wounded poachers brought down by their guns. Mainstream conservationists pay little attention to these social costs and indeed help to finance some of the agencies which perpetrate such human rights abuses. At the same time, they apparently perceive the state and the armed forces as neutral mediators in conflicts over natural resources and advocate the 'systematic' involvement of national security forces in conservation programmes (Peluso, 1992:66–67).

It is very doubtful if such a hard-line approach to nature conservation achieves its objectives, in the long term. More usually, as Peluso argues, the result is to intensify social and political conflict:

> *which causes environmental degradation and ultimately fails to achieve the goals of international conservation interests. Nevertheless, the state may not 'lose'. Even if conservation goals are not achieved, the state may succeed in strengthening its capacity to govern via the use of force. (Peluso, 1992:52)*

Society and Biodiversity

If the track record of the state indicates that it cannot be relied on to defend biological diversity, the question that then occurs to conservationists is whether any other institutions, such as indigenous ones, can. Many have argued that indigenous societies do live in harmony with their natural environment and are thus its best guardians; this is an argument that many indigenous peoples themselves have used to bolster their demands for a recognition of their rights to their lands. Indeed, much of the support that indigenous peoples have been able to recruit in the industrialized North results from this belief that indigenous peoples are both closer to nature and motivated by a conservation ethic.

In general, indigenous communities have developed ways of life remarkably attuned to their local environment. Many indigenous peoples' environments are less modified and degraded than surrounding areas. Since they are often oriented primarily towards self-sufficiency, and only secondarily to the generation of surplus for trade, their traditional economies and technologies are often environmentally appropriate. Their long association with their territories has resulted in indigenous peoples' developing strong ties to their lands, expressed both in customary law and in complex religious and symbolic schemes, and extremely detailed knowledge of their resources. Such knowledge may be deeply coded within traditional lore handed down and refined from generation to generation so that the practical justification for certain customs may not be immediately apparent either to researchers or the local people themselves (Alcorn, 1989; 1994). Crucially, many indigenous peoples see clearly that their long-term survival depends on them caring for their land: for example, 'the traditional view of Borneo natives is that natural resources are held in trust for future generations' (King, 1993:167).

This combination of a long, past association with their environment and a commitment to remaining there in the future equips indigenous peoples very well for prudent management in the present. However, indigenous societies almost everywhere are undergoing rapid change and it is not clear whether the balance that these societies have, in general, maintained with their environments can endure under these changing circumstances. In the first place, many indigenous peoples have lost much of their ancestral territory to outsiders, and this had led to too many people being concentrated on too little land, upsetting traditional patterns of land ownership, management and use. Rising indigenous populations have likewise increased local pressure on the environment. Increasing demands for cash, some externally imposed and some internally generated, also place a heavier burden on local economies and environments to produce a marketable surplus. New technologies, like steel tools in place of stone ones, chainsaws, shotguns, agricultural machinery and transportation, new crops and agrochemicals, may radically change land use. At the same time traditional value systems, social organizations and decision-making processes may be transformed — and not just as a result of outside impositions. All these forces tend to upset indigenous peoples' relations with their environments and may result in over-intensive land use and environmental degradation.

Ever since ecology became a fashionable science, it has been argued not just that indigenous societies have traditionally maintained relatively stable relations with their environments — an observable reality — but that this balance is a condition that indigenous peoples consciously strive for and maintain. For example, the Colombian anthropologist Reichel-Dolmatoff (1976) interprets the Tukano Indians' concepts of vital energy and belief in the dangers attendant to the excess consumption of foods or indulgence in sex as analogous to ecologists' concepts of energetics and negative feedback. Similarly, McDonald (1977) has argued that the system of food taboos found in many Amazonian societies is a kind of 'primitive environmental protection agency' (cf. Ross, 1978). It has even become commonplace in some circles to accept that indigenous peoples are, in their own way, fully cognizant of the dangers of environmental exploitation and it has even been claimed that they have their own 'conservationist cosmovision' (Seijas and Arvelo-Jimenez, 1979).

This may overstate the case. As the Kuna Indian, Nicanor Gonsalez, points out:

> *What I have understood in talking with indigenous authorities, indigenous groups and individuals is that they are familiar with the laws of nature. They are not conservationists; rather, they know how to interrelate humans and nature... In this sense, then, I don't believe that you can say that indigenous people are conservationists, as defined by ecologists. We aren't nature lovers. At no time have indigenous groups included the concepts of conservation and ecology in their traditional vocabulary. We speak, rather, of Mother Nature. (Cited in Redford and Stearman, 1993b:427)*

Claims that indigenous peoples consciously moderate their populations and use of resources in response to environmental depletion have never been empirically demonstrated. On the contrary, detailed field research to establish the links between indigenous belief systems and actual patterns of resource use have shown how tenuous the connections really are. Reading a conservation ethic into religious symbolism or indigenous belief systems is highly subjective, and many studies show little correlation between beliefs prescribing certain practices and actual behaviour. Typically, in Amazonia, prohibitions on eating certain foods are honoured in the breach. Lacking centralized processes of decision-making, neither do these egalitarian societies succumb to the 'tyranny of custom' (Colchester, 1981; Hames, 1991). Many Amazonian Indians, it has been found, have an opportunist rather than conservationist attitude to the environment and achieve ecological balance because their traditional political systems and settlement patterns encourage mobility. Indians thus move their villages, fields and hunting expeditions to fresh areas once nearby localities are exhausted because it requires less effort than does getting diminishing returns from their present locations. Balance is thus achieved unintentionally by negative feedback rather than through a conscious concern with excessive use. Market demands and other pressures that sedentarize and enlarge these communities, thus disrupting traditional residence and settlement patterns, coupled with new technologies such as outboard engines that cut travel times and machines to process crops, may upset these negative feedback cycles and cause Indian communities to overexploit their locale (Colchester, 1981).

Similarly, Robert Harms's studies among the Nunu of Central Africa have revealed that the balance they achieve with their environment is not the result of a concern to prevent the overuse of the environment but, on the contrary, is the unintended consequence of their system of land tenure through which local villages claim exclusive rights to certain areas of forests, rivers, ponds and swamps (cited in Adams and McShane, 1992:34). As in Amazonia, it is the societies' political systems and settlement patterns that result in balance. One conclusion from a recent review of the available literature on Amazonian societies is that 'Amazonian tribal populations make no active or concerted effort to conserve fish and game resources. At the same time, it is clear in most cases there may be no need for a conservation policy, because current local subsistence demands on resources have not led to severe resource shortages.' (Hames, 1991:182)[2]

Unfortunately, there seems to be a lack of comparably detailed studies of indigenous systems of resource use in other areas. In general, it can be observed that, in contrast to the very scattered and acephalous peoples of Amazonia, more densely settled indigenous peoples have increasingly strict rules regulating access to and use of natural resources. Common

---

2 It may be objected that it is unfair and irrelevant to suggest that many indigenous systems of resource-use management are unintentionally and indirectly conservationist rather than expressly so, if their effect is to balance society with the environment. The point of labouring this distinction, between what anthropologists call manifest and latent function, is that under circumstances of rapid social and economic change people are less likely to consciously modify their practices and knowledge to improve resource management if they do not perceive the connections.

lands may be subject to clan or household ownership and access controlled by the authority of community elders, chiefs or other political authorities. In these circumstances, conscious management of resources to avoid over-exploitation may be explicit and highly effective (Shiva et al., 1991). Conservationists who worry that indigenous conservation systems will break down with the failure of belief systems (Redford and Stearman, 1993a:252) may be focusing on the wrong risk. The main threats will come from the breakdown of community political systems, systems of land tenure and rights allocations. Certainly such systems cannot be divorced from the same people's belief and value systems, but many societies — notably those in Africa — show a remarkable continuity in their political and land management systems after undergoing fundamental religious conversions.

These conclusions may likewise be relevant to progressive conservationists and community development specialists who have begun to step up their efforts to secure indigenous resource management systems in changed circumstances. These attempts have, in general, focused principally on technical innovations — agroforestry systems, non-timber forest product exploitation, etc. — or have focused on the documentation of indigenous knowledge systems. Their efforts would be better directed towards understanding the politics of community resource management.

There are those purists who will nevertheless object that any human interference in ecosystems will cause a depletion of biodiversity (Redford and Stearman, 1993a:252) and thus argue for the protection of virgin areas as wilderness. Leaving aside for the moment the ethical and cultural shortcomings of such an approach, these arguments are suspect for a number of technical reasons. In the first place, it is now increasingly realized that climax systems are not the norm — 'nature is increasingly perceived as being in a state of continuous change' (Gómez-Pompa and Kaus, 1992:272). Indeed, under certain circumstances, human interference with ecosystems may enhance biological diversity. Conservationists are beginning to realize that the Serengeti's grassland ecosystem, for example, is in part maintained by the presence of the Maasai and their cattle. With the Maasai's expulsion from their lands, the Serengeti is increasingly being taken over by scrub and woodland, meaning less grazing for antelopes (Adams and McShane, 1992; Monbiot, 1994).

It can also be argued that conservationists have been no less selective than indigenous peoples about what biodiversity to prioritize for conservation. Big mammals are prized by conservationists and indigenous peoples alike, for rather different reasons, but indigenous peoples may be more concerned to preserve crop diversity and the quality of their watershed forests.

The reality that conservationists have been reluctant to face is that the choices are not between pristine wilderness and human use but between different kinds of use and between different kinds of political control. Conservationists are increasingly realizing that the exclusion of local

115

communities from decision-making and control is against everyone's best interests. The challenge is to find new ways of involving local people in management.

Parks for People: Management Alternatives

It would be most unfair to suggest either that the conservation community has had a monolithic approach to protected-area management or that all members of that community have been insensitive to the needs and rights of indigenous peoples. As early as 1975, IUCN passed a resolution at its Twelfth General Assembly in Kinshasa, Zaire, recognizing the value and importance of 'traditional ways of life and the skills of the people which enable them to live in harmony with their environment'. The resolution recommended that governments 'maintain and encourage traditional methods of living' and 'devise means by which indigenous people may bring their lands into conservation areas without relinquishing their ownership, use or tenure rights'. The same resolution also recommended against displacement and stated 'nor should such reserves anywhere be proclaimed without adequate consultation'.

The same resolution was recalled in 1982 at the World National Parks Congress in Bali, Indonesia, which affirmed the rights of traditional societies to 'social, economic, cultural and spiritual [but, significantly, not political] self-determination' and 'to participate in decisions affecting the land and natural resources on which they depend'. While explicitly avoiding endorsing indigenous peoples' right to full self-determination or recognizing their rights to own and control their territories, the resolution advocated 'the implementation of joint management arrangements between societies which have traditionally managed resources and protected area authorities'.

At the same time, owing to the work of UNESCO's 'Man and the Biosphere' programme, the notion of biosphere reserves was developed. The basic strategy of these is one of containment through zoning, whereby a fully protected 'core zone' which excludes human occupation or use is cushioned from the outside world by a 'buffer zone' (Sayer, 1991:2).

An early example of a national parks management project which sought to assure compensatory benefits for local people in a 'buffer zone' is the Amboseli National Park in Kenya. Created on lands traditionally used by Maasai pastoralists, the park denied the local Maasai access to dry-season grazing lands and watering points, though this was essential to their cattle-based livelihood. Many conflicts resulted, and the Maasai began to show their resentment by spearing rhinos, lions and other wildlife (Talbot and Olindo, 1990:70). Under a project funded by the World Bank, the core conservation zone remained off limits to Maasai but a surrounding buffer zone was developed where watering points were

116

established outside the park. Benefits were also promised through the payment of a compensation fee for loss of access, tourism development outside the park and a share of lodge royalties to the local district council for a school and a dispensary. As Hannah (1992) notes, the project is widely cited as a successful example of 'integrated parks management', notably by the World Bank (Ledec and Goodland, 1988).

However, the project has not been without serious problems, as the World Bank has subsequently admitted (Talbot and Olindo, 1990; Wells et al., 1992:70). As Lee Hannah notes, the system began to break down in 1981 (Hannah, 1992:25). The water supply system began to deteriorate. Compensation fees went unpaid. The school was inappropriately located. Little tourism developed outside the park. Royalties accrued to central government and the local district council but failed to trickle back down to the local level (Peluso, 1992; Hannah, 1992; Talbot and Olindo, 1990). Consequently, in contrast to the relatively smoother acceptance of conservation management in the Maasai Mara Reserve further west, at Amboseli conflicts between parks management and the Maasai persist. Maasai continue to enter the park to water their cattle. The difference, according to Talbot and Olindo (1990:73), is that in the Mara, the Maasai have been more effectively involved in decision-making, which has accorded more respect to traditional authorities. In Amboseli, by contrast, the management process had 'received considerably more attention from development agencies so that a new social and political order had significantly disrupted the traditional authority system'. In Amboseli, decision-making took place at district council level and implementation by-passed the local elders.

> *Therefore, the Maasai actually living in the areas adjacent to the reserve were not really represented in negotiations and their co-operation was not secured. When it came to the distribution of benefits, the Mara region Maasai knew what they were owed and were in a position to demand it, unlike those in Amboseli. (Talbot and Olindo, 1990:74)*[3]

In a useful review of buffer zone experiences in tropical moist forests, Jeff Sayer has concluded that the results of buffer zone 'projects' have been largely disappointing (1991:4). Most have been initiated and directed by outsiders, have been of short duration, and have focused on ambitious but untried technologies to secure increased economic benefits for local people from buffer zone areas, in the hope that they would not then impinge on the core zones, which were off limits. These 'ecodevelopment projects' have 'frequently pursued objectives which were inconsistent with the aspirations of the very people they were trying to help' (Sayer,

---

3 By contrast, Hannah believes that the Amboseli project 'dealt with traditional leadership in an effective way' (1992:29).

1991:24). They have suffered from paying too little attention to social and political constraints faced by both local communities and national conservation agencies. A severe limitation on many buffer zone projects is that government conservation authorities rarely have jurisdiction over the lands outside park boundaries. Sayer (1991:4) observes that the best buffer zone projects 'have not been short-term aid projects but initiatives taken by local community groups or resource managers who have made creative attempts to solve the day-to-day problems which they faced'. One favoured approach, partly pursued in the Amboseli experiment, has been to share benefits and profits from the parks with local residents.

Creating employment in national parks as guides, trackers, porters and through other tourism services has been another means by which conservationists have sought to defuse local opposition and reconcile conflicts of interest. In the south-western corner of the Central African Republic, for example, the WWF (USA) has been seeking to establish a complex of two protected areas, the Dzangha-Sangha Dense Forest Special Reserve and the Dzangha-Ndoki National Park. The area, which contains numerous rare mammals — including elephants, primates and forest antelopes — is inhabited by both Aka 'pygmies' and various Bantu and Oubangian peoples and has been subjected to low intensity logging and serious over-hunting. According to the assessment of WWF, 'if an effective wildlife management programme is not initiated, the wildlife populations will be exterminated in the Dzangha-Sangha region within 5 years as a result of poaching' (Carroll, 1992:69).

Starting from a recognition that 'in all projects dealing with the management of natural resources, it is absolutely necessary to gain the support of the local population' (Hunsicker and Ngambesso, 1993:231), the aim of the project is to curb logging and 'poaching' and promote an alternative local economy based on ecotourism. This should generate both revenue for local community-based development groups and employment for individuals. Accordingly, the project has helped set up the *Association Communautaire de Yobe-Sangha* (ACYS), a local legally incorporated non-governmental organization run by local leaders and villagers, which receives 40 per cent of tourist takings and advises the parks' management. At the same time, in an attempt to break the Aka's dependency on low wages in the timber industry and demoralization in the sedentarized communities promoted by Catholic missionaries, the project is trying to encourage 'pygmies' to act as guards, guides and lodge staff. Aka women take tourists on collecting tours while 'pygmy' hunters use their tracking skills to help tourists spot animals (Carroll, 1992).

However, the central government continues to permit foreign companies to log in the area (Colchester, 1994a). Local political leaders and government officials maintain their illegal but highly lucrative trade in ivory, skins and bushmeat, through traditional patron–client networks. Since the protected areas threaten not just their business interests but also their political paramountcy and control of the local villagers and client 'pygmy' groups, they have worked hard to undermine the project and corrupt the parks personnel. At the same time, it is not yet clear whether the attempts of WWF to break the Aka's dependency on villagers, loggers, wildlife traders and missionaries will actually liberate them or only create an alternative dependency on expatriate conservationists (Sarno, 1993). Neither the Aka nor the ACYS have decision-making authority in the running of the reserves, though the latter does decide for itself how its revenues will be spent.

Ecotourism has now become big business and profit-sharing with local people has been a popular way by which conservationists have hoped to reconcile indigenous peoples with protected areas. However, the process has proved more difficult than might have been expected. In his study of national parks in Nepal, Michael Wells suggests that most of the profit from ecotourism in Nepali parks is enjoyed by trekking and tourism ventures based in the capital and overseas, with even the national parks agency able to recoup only a quarter of its management costs in visitors' fees. Local people certainly benefit from tourists, but much less than expected, while the social and environmental costs are far from negligible in terms of pollution and littering, overgrazing by pack animals, fuelwood depletion from heating water and cooking, and the introduction of western mores and values (Wells, 1993).

Indigenous people are far from unaware of the potential social costs of increased dependency on tourism, and all are not prepared to abandon their customary rights and ways in exchange for a temporary gain in cash income. As one Maasai told the author George Monbiot, when informed that the Director of the Kenya Wildlife Services had recommended that they keep fewer cattle and make money from tourism instead:

> *We know there is money to be made from tourism. We already have tourists staying on our lands in tented camps. And, yes, they bring us an income. We don't need the Kenya Wildlife Service to tell us that. But you can tell Dr. Leakey this. We don't want to be dependent on these tourists. We are Maasai and we want to herd cattle. If we stopped keeping cattle and depended on tourists, we would be ruined when the tourists stopped coming. (Cited in Monbiot, 1994)*

Giving people a share of the profits that can be made from conservation in exchange for extinguishing their rights and their local political autonomy, and transforming their way of life, may not seem like a very fair deal to many indigenous peoples. A number of conservationists are beginning to realize that the short-term problems of relinquishing to indigenous peoples control of decision-making in protected areas may be worth it in the long term. Lee Hannah (1992:1) notes that a strong consensus is emerging in conservation circles that African parks 'must involve local people in management decisions', although this has been hard to apply in practice. The World Bank has drawn similar conclusions (Ledec and Goodland, 1988:98).

Adopting an approach of 'conflict management', joint-management programmes seek a compromise between indigenous and conservation interests. Elizabeth Kemf (1993), who carried out a review of indigenous peoples in protected areas for WWF and IUCN, suggests that such an approach must start from an assessment of the basis for these conflicts and then establish procedures, first, for communication between local peoples and parks managers and, second, for ensuring that benefits or compensation accrue to the local people (Kemf, 1993).

In fact, 'joint management' conservation initiatives have proven very difficult as they have to bridge very wide cultural divides, as well as accommodate both the divergent priorities of the various players and the local political and economic realities. The majority of 'joint management' schemes are actually joint in name only. The lack of political power and financial resources means that local communities are more usually very junior partners in decision-making.

Conservationists aiming for local participation, like all outsiders engaged in rural development, face hard choices in defining the most culturally appropriate structures. The facile advice that conservationists should respect local systems of decision-making may obscure the fact that traditional decision-making is sometimes vested in leadership structures which marginalize women and lower castes or classes, or lower-status ethnic groups. Top-down projects which work through the local elites may sometimes be very successful in conservation terms (Ntshalintshali and McGurk, 1991) but may reinforce and even exacerbate class and gender inequities (Hannah, 1992).

A widespread problem facing conservationists and aid agencies alike is that local political elites strongly object to their client groups, with whom they have long established and profitable ties, benefiting from targeted development initiatives. Since they do not recognize the prior rights of indigenous communities to their own resources, measures adopted to compensate a loss or secure a people's livelihood may be interpreted as positive discrimination or even racism.

In 1989, Canadian conservationists and indigenous peoples allied themselves around a 'Canadian Wilderness Charter', which brought activists together to push for both native rights and protected areas. However, tensions soon emerged within the movement because of the very different perspectives of participants on what constituted wilderness and what priority should be given to native livelihoods (Morrison, 1993; Davey, 1993:204).

Recognition of Territorial Rights

One of the most loudly heralded steps towards a conservation approach that starts with a recognition of indigenous land rights was taken in

Australia in 1985, when the federal government, which also legislates for the Northern Territory, agreed to recognize Aboriginal ownership of Ayers Rock if they would immediately lease the rock back to the government as a national park. As John Cordell has noted somewhat caustically of this deal:

> *After decades of struggle, the Anangu actually held the title for about thirty-five seconds before relinquishing their ancestral rights to the state for the next ninety-nine years (1993:105).*

Uluru, as the Anangu refer to Ayers Rock, is one of four Aboriginal areas to which they have gained title in exchange for allowing them to be designated as national parks, the others being Kakadu, Gurig on the Cobourg Peninsula and Nitmiluk (Katherine Gorge). Under the agreements setting up the parks, Aborigines not only legally own the areas, but also share power on the governing boards or participate in the day-to-day management.

A number of observers have questioned the reality of the equal partnership aspired to in the setting up of these parks. Cultural and political differences have meant that the Aborigines have effectively been relegated to junior partners in management.

Detailed research carried out by Sally Weaver (1991) in the Gurig and Kakadu National Parks modifies this impression. In these cases, she found that in the first place recognition of ownership had been made conditional on the definition of the areas as national parks. Effective involvement of Aboriginal owners in management was neither achieved nor sought. Whereas Aborigines actually sought control of overall planning and policy decisions — rather than day-to-day management — they were more often cast in the role of rangers, which they resented. Aboriginal authority, she found, was continually squeezed by a tendency for government and parks agencies to extend their political–bureaucratic power base. Despite this, relations between parks field personnel and Aborigines was good owing to a genuine interest in and respect for the Aborigines among the staff. Weaver's study usefully stresses 'the inherently political nature of the relationship between parks and indigenous peoples' and she found that 'there was much less power-sharing between parks agencies and Aboriginal owners than government rhetoric and legislation suggested'(Weaver, 1991:331). Nevertheless, she noted a discernible trend of improving relations between Aborigines and parks agencies, with a gradual increase in Aboriginal control as more formal and structured interactions were instituted.

Recognition of indigenous peoples' ownership rights is hard for the old school that fears 'conceding too much control to local communities' (Sayer, 1991:10). Thus, whereas IUCN now recommends that, as far as buffer zones are concerned, 'land rights of local people should take precedence over those of distant resource users [and] laws should guarantee access to forest resources for forest people, whilst placing restrictions upon over-exploitation of these resources or clearance of the land' (Sayer,

1991:17), it remains sceptical that land rights should be recognized within protected areas themselves.

In sum it is clear that conservationists remain reluctant to relinquish or even share power over protected areas. Stung by the criticisms of their socially insensitive and politically blind approach, conservationists have been readily persuaded to admit that local people's needs should be taken into account. They have been far more reluctant to recognize indigenous assertions, backed by international law, of their rights to own and control land and exercise their authority over their own domains (West and Brechin, 1991:xvi).

However, despite these bleak prognostications, conservationists are claiming some real successes in creating conservation zones which enjoy the full support of indigenous peoples. A notable example has been developed in the unlikely context of West Papua, a Dutch colony annexed with brutal violence by Indonesia in the 1960s. In stark contrast to the inhabitants of neighbouring Papua New Guinea, land rights are not effectively recognized in West Papua (Barber and Churchill, 1987) and national parks legislation similarly denies land ownership rights to residents. Despite these formidable legal obstacles, WWF — through a ten-year long conservation programme — has been able to develop two protected areas which, with local and now national government approval, secure local peoples' rights over their resources.

The first such project established a management plan for the Hatam people, part of whose lands had been designated the Arfak Mountains Strict Nature Reserve. The plan is based on a recognition that while Indonesian law and conservation practice does not recognize the land rights of local people, such recognition is absolutely necessary for the conservation project to be successful and have local acceptance. WWF field staff thus developed a management plan which involved the local communities in demarcation of the reserve, expressly permitted traditional hunting (without modern weapons), and divided the reserve and surrounding areas into 16 'nature reserve management areas' run by village committees, which are authorized by the local government to enforce the reserve's regulations within their areas (Craven and Craven, 1990; Mandosir and Stark, 1993). In addition, the WWF team initiated a butterfly ranching scheme to provide a cash income to the villagers. The project presently relies on outside technicians to advise on the ranching practices and to label, price, package and market the butterflies, which are then exported through the parastatal company PT Inhutani II. The latter has, unfortunately, a very questionable record in dealing with indigenous peoples. Attempts to stabilize shifting cultivation have not been so successful. The WWF is certainly not complacent about the long-term viability of the scheme (Mandosir and Stark, 1993).

Legalized indigenous control of their commons will not by itself ensure either the sanctity of these areas from invasions and disruptions or that indigenous economies do not overwhelm their environmental base. Effective management requires procedures to enforce agreed regulations (Hannah, 1992:55). The challenge is to find means by which the indigenous peoples' own institutions can agree to or develop for themselves such controls (cf. Sherpa, 1993). Moreover, only in a few situations is it likely that indigenous institutions can effectively secure their areas from outside pressures, without outside assistance. This implies the necessity of defining a role for the state in securing indigenous territories as conservation areas. The point has been forcefully made by Janis Alcorn who, while arguing the case for the need to recognize indigenous lands as an effective way of preserving biodiversity, emphasises the need to take account of wider political and economic pressures as well.

Conclusions

As this review has attempted to make clear, indigenous peoples face four major problems inherent in the classic conservationist approach. In the first place, mainstream conservationists have put the preservation of nature above the interests of human beings. Secondly, their view of nature has been shaped by a cultural notion of wilderness sharply at odds with the cosmovision of most indigenous peoples. Thirdly, conservationists have sought authority for their regulation of human interactions with nature in the power of the state. And last but by no means least, conservationists' perceptions of indigenous peoples have been tinged with the same prejudices that confront indigenous peoples everywhere. The result, as we have seen, is that indigenous peoples have suffered a fourfold marginalization due to conservationist impositions.

The evidence is also clear that these impositions have violated internationally agreed norms, particularly regarding indigenous rights to land and to just compensation in the case of forced removal in the national interest. Evolving norms regarding indigenous control of land use and self-determination have also been regularly broken.

The realization by the conservation community that respect for the rights of indigenous peoples is not just a matter of pragmatism but is also a matter of principle, has been long in coming. However, it is becoming clear that, with the protected-area model of conservation anyway proving unviable, more radical approaches to nature conservation based on bottom-up processes of decision-making should be given more serious attention.

It is time that conservationists began to start their work in areas inhabited by indigenous peoples from the assumption that they are dealing with local people with legitimate rights to the ownership and control of their natural resources. The creation of protected areas may not be the most appropriate option in such circumstances, as in most cases indigenous ownership rights are denied by protected-area legislation. However, there will be cases, especially in countries which do not respect indigenous tenure or traditions, where the creation of protected areas may offer the only legally available means of securing indigenous occupancy and use rights, if not ownership.

But there is a risk that the pendulum could swing too sharply the other way, towards assumptions that once an area is under indigenous ownership and control the problem is solved and that all indigenous systems of land use are inherently sustainable. This is patently not the case. Indeed, many indigenous communities are fully aware of the fact that as pressure on their lands from outside intensifies and as their own economies and social organization change to accommodate their increasing involvement in the market economy, they need to elaborate new mechanisms to control and use their resources. Ecologists, social scientists, lawyers and development advisers may have relevant knowledge to contribute to such indigenous communities to help them achieve this transition. Their role, however, is to act as advisers to indigenous managers rather than directors of indigenous ventures (see Colchester, 1982c).

In Amazonia, for example, the practice of recruiting technical advisers to indigenous organizations has a 20-year history and has led to some notable successes in securing lands against outside intrusions. The practice has been somewhat less successful in promoting verifiably 'sustainable' systems of resource management while generating a surplus for the market.

Probably the most difficult aspect of working with indigenous peoples has been in identifying the appropriate indigenous institutions through which to mediate with outsiders. Many indigenous peoples have confronted similar problems in deciding in which institutions to vest authority for governing their own novel activities, be they oriented to conservation or to the market. Especially among relatively acephalous societies such as Amazonian Indians and 'pygmy' groups in Central Africa, the lack of central authorities creates tricky problems in the reaching of binding agreements both among themselves and with outsiders. On the other hand, the risk with more centralized and hierarchical societies is of vesting undue authority in their leadership and thus exaggerating conflicts of interest within the communities. There are no generalizations that can be made about how to solve these problems, except that the decisions should be made by the people themselves.

The trouble is that the mainstream conservation organizations are simultaneously being drawn in two conflicting directions. On the one hand, their field experience is persuading them that vesting control of land and natural resources in indigenous peoples' institutions makes conservation sense. On other hand, the current fashion of treating environmental issues as global problems is encouraging state and international interventions. As conservation becomes a global concern, substantial funds have become available for conservation organizations to implement and manage protected-area projects in Third World countries and to act as consultants for the development agencies who have assumed responsibility for managing the global environment (Abramovitz, 1991). This exaggerates the inherent top-down tendency in conservation, which results from the fact that money for conservation is in the North while most biodiversity is in the South and from the policy of 'global triage' which tends to select priority areas for conservation on the basis of technical criteria (Colchester, 1994b:11).

Conservation organizations have traditionally derived their funding from the establishment and have sought to impose their visions through the power of the state. Globalizing conservation only strengthens this tendency. Highly motivated conservationist consultants come to occupy the political space within the state that indigenous representatives have been striving to enter themselves, while at the same time, the conservation institutions, bidding for lucrative consultancies and protected area 'projects', adjust their management style to the exigencies of the international agencies that fund them rather than the indigenous communities whose territories they are seeking to conserve. While substantial conservation budgets are lavished on satellite mapping systems, helicopters, jeeps, offices and official salaries, indigenous peoples are increasingly marginalized from decision-making.

The challenge is to find a means of making conservation organizations accountable to what is for them an unfamiliar constituency — indigenous peoples — so that they are obliged to treat indigenous peoples' concerns with the seriousness they deserve. The experience in Canada, Australia and Amazonia already suggests that this will only come about through the mobilization of indigenous peoples themselves. These cases also suggest that there are grounds for guarded optimism about the outcome. Reconciling indigenous self-determination with conservation objectives is possible if conservation agencies cede power to those who are marginalized by current development and conservation models.

If there is one lesson that it seems to the author that conservationists need to learn, it is that decisions about conserving nature are by definition political — they are about the exercise of power in the making of decisions about the use of scarce natural resources with alternative ends. For whose benefit are resources to be used or conserved? Who has authority to make such decisions? Who has the power to contest them? In whom should authority over natural resources be best vested to ensure that they are prudently managed for the good of future generations?

> *I know of no safe depository of the ultimate powers of the society but the people themselves, and if we think them not enlightened enough to exercise that control with a wholesome discretion, the remedy is not to take it from them, but to inform their discretion.*

(Thomas Jefferson, 1820, cited in *The Economist*, 18 December 1993)

References

Abramovitz, Janet N (1991), *Investing in Biological Diversity: US Research and Conservation Efforts in Developing Countries*, World Resources Institute, Washington, DC.

Adams, Jonathan S and Thomas O McShane (1992), *The Myth of Wild Africa: Conservation without Illusion*, W W Norton and Co, London.

Alcorn, Janis B (1989), 'Process as resource: The traditional agricultural ideology of Bora and Huastec resource management and its implications for research', *Advances in Economic Botany*, No 7, pp 63–77.

— (1993), 'Indigenous peoples and Conservation', *Conservation Biology*, Vol 7, No 2, June, pp 424–426.

— (1994), 'Noble savage or noble state? Northern myths and southern realities in biodiversity conservation', *Etnoecológica*, Vol 2, No 3, pp 6–19.

Amend, Stephan and Thora Amend (eds) (1992), *Espacios sin Habitantes? Parques nacionales de America del Sur*, IUCN, Gland.

Amselle, Jean-Loup (ed) (1979), *Le sauvage à la mode*, Le Sycomore, Paris.

Banerjee, Sumanta (1984), *India's Simmering Revolution*, Zed Books, London.

Barber, Charles and Gregory Churchill (1987), *Land Policy in Irian Jaya: Issues and Strategies*, Report No INS/83/013, United Nations Development Programme (UNDP), New York.

Bennett, Gordon (1978), *Aboriginal Rights in International Law*, Occasional Paper No 37, Royal Anthropological Institute of Great Britain and Ireland, London.

Carroll, Richard W (1992), *The Development, Protection and Management of the Dznagha-Sangha Dense Forest Special Reserve and Dzangha-Ndoki National Park in South-Western Central African Republic*, WWF (USA), Bangui.

Catlin, George (1989), *The Manner and Customs of the North American Indians*, 1841, reprinted as Peter Matthiessen (ed), *North American Indians*, Penguin Books, Harmondsworth.

Claxton, Nicholas (1986), *The Price of Progress*, Central Television Documentary, London.

Colchester, Marcus (1981), 'Ecological modelling and indigenous systems of resource use: some examples from the Amazon of South Venezuela', *Antropologica*, No 55, pp 51–72.

— (1982a), *The Economy, Ecology and Ethnobiology of the Sanema Indians of South Venezuela*, PhD dissertation, University of Oxford.

— (1982b), 'The cosmovision of the Venezuelan Sanema', *Antropologica*, No 58, pp 97–122.

— (1982c), 'Amerindian development: The search for a viable means of surplus production in Amazonia', *Survival International Review*, Vol 7, Nos 3 and 4 (41/42), Survival International, London, Autumn/Winter.

— (1987a), *The Social Dimensions of Government-Sponsored Migration and Involuntary Resettlement: Policies and Practice*, paper prepared for the Independent Commission on International Humanitarian Issues, Geneva.

— (1987b), *Interim Report from the Upper Baram River, 4th Division, Sarawak, Malaysia: Cultural Situation of the Teru Berawan*, Survival International, mimeo.

— (1989), *Pirates, Squatters and Poachers: The Political Ecology of Dispossession of the Native Peoples of Sarawak*, Survival International and INSAN, London and Petaling Jaya.

— (1994a), *Slave and Enclave: The Political Ecology of Equatorial Africa*, World Rainforest Movement, London and Penang.

— (1994b), *Salvaging Nature: Indigenous Peoples, Protected Areas and Biodiversity Conservation*, Discussion Paper No 55, United Nations Research Institute for Social Development (UNRISD), Geneva.

Cordell, John (1993), 'Who owns the land? Indigenous involvement in Australian protected areas', in Kemf, op cit.

Craven, Ian and Mary Ann Craven (1990), *An Introduction to the Arfak Mountains Nature Reserve*, WWF (Indonesia), mimeo, Jayapura.

Davey, Sheila (1993), 'Creative communities: planning and comanaging protected areas', in Kemf, op cit.

DENR (Department of Environment and Natural Resources) (1992), *The NIPAS Law: a Primer*, Department of Environment and Natural Resources/Conservation International/Foundation for Sustainable Development Inc, Manila.

Devitt, Paul (1988), *The People of the Korup Project Area: Report on Phase 1 of the Socio-Economic Survey*, WWF (UK), mimeo, Godalming.

DiSilvestro, Roger L (1993), *Reclaiming the Last Wild Places: a New Agenda for Biodiversity*, John Wiley & Sons, New York.

Dixon, John A and Paul B Sherman (1991), *Economics of Protected Areas: a New Look at Benefits and Costs*, Earthscan Publications, Ltd, London.

Duerr, Hans Peter (1985), *Dreamtime: Concerning the Boundary between Wilderness and Civilization*, Basil Blackwell, Oxford.

Duyker, Edward (1987), *Tribal Guerrillas: the Santals of West Bengal and the Naxalite Movement*, Oxford University Press, Delhi.

Eliade, Mircea (1972), *Shamanism: Archaic Techniques of Ecstasy*, Bollingen Series LXXVI, Routledge and Kegan Paul, London.

Feeney, Tricia (1993), 'The impact of a European Community project on peasant families in Uganda', *Oxfam Briefing*, No 6, Oxfam, Oxford, July, pp 1–7.

Fürer-Haimendorf, C von (1986), *Statement*, at the Fourth International Conference on Hunting and Gathering Societies (London, 8–13 September).

Gadgil, Madhav (1992), 'Conserving biodiversity as if people matter: a case study from India', *Ambio*, Vol 21, No 3, May, pp 266–270.

Gadgil, Madhav and Ramachandra Guha (1993), *This Fissured Land: an Ecological History of India*, Oxford University Press, Delhi.

Ghimire, Krishna B (1994), *Conservation and Social Development: a Study Based on an Assessment of Wolong and other Panda Reserves in China*, Discussion Paper No 56, United Nations Research Institute for Social Development (UNRISD), Geneva, December.

Gómez-Pompa, Arturo and Andrea Kaus (1992), 'Taming the wilderness myth', *BioScience*, Vol 42, No 4, April, pp 271–279.

Goodland, Robert (1982), *Tribal Peoples and Economic Development: Human Ecological Considerations*, The World Bank, Washington, DC.

Gordon, Robert J (1985), 'Conserving Bushmen to extinction in Southern Africa', in Marcus Colchester (ed), *An End to Laughter? Tribal Peoples and Economic Development*, Survival International Review, No 44, London, pp 28–42.

Hames, Raymond (1991), 'Wildlife conservation in tribal societies', in Margery L Oldfield and Janis B Alcorn (eds), *Biodiversity Culture, Conservation, and Ecodevelopment*, Westview Press, Oxford, pp 172–199.

Hannah, Lee (1992), *African People, African Parks: an Evaluation of Development Initiatives as a Means of Improving Protected Area Conservation in Africa*,

Conservation International, Washington, DC.

Harmon, David (1991), 'National park residency in developed countries: the example of Great Britain', in West and Brechin, op cit, pp 33–39.

Hemming, John (1978), *Red Gold: The Conquest of the Brazilian Indians*, Macmillan, London.

Hitchcock, Robert K (1990), 'Wildlife conservation and development among rural populations in southern Africa', *International Third World Studies Journal and Review*, Vol 2, No 1, pp 225–232.

Hitchcock, Robert K and John D Holm (1993), 'Bureaucratic domination of hunter-gatherer societies: A study of the San in Botswana', *Development and Change*, Vol 24, No 2, pp 305–338.

Hultkrantz, Ake (1967), *The Religions of the American Indians*, University of California Press, Berkeley.

Hunsicker, Philip M and Fidele Ngambesso (1993), 'Banking on a nature reserve', in Kemf, op cit.

Hvalkof, S and P Aaby (eds) (1981), *Is God an American?*, IWGIA/Survival International Document No 43, London and Copenhagen.

ICIHI (Independent Commission on International Humanitarian Issues) (1987), *Indigenous Peoples: a Global Quest for Justice. A Report for the Independent Commission on International Humanitarian Issues*, Zed Books, London.

Infield, Mark (1988), *Hunting, Trapping and Fishing in Villages within and on the Periphery of the Korup National Park*, Korup National Park Socio-Economic Survey, Paper No 6, WWF (UK), Godalming.

Jank, M (1977), *Culture Shock*, Moody Press, Chicago.

Kemf, Elizabeth (ed) (1993), *Indigenous Peoples and Protected Areas: the Law of Mother Earth*, Earthscan Publications, Ltd, London.

King, Victor T (1993), *The Peoples of Borneo*, Blackwell, Oxford.

Ledec, George and Robert Goodland (1988), *Wildlands: their Protection and Management in Economic Development*, The World Bank, Washington, DC.

Lewis, Norman (1990), *The Missionaries*, Penguin, Harmondsworth.

Lowie, Robert H (1970), *Primitive Religion*, Liveright, New York.

Mandosir, Sius and Malcolm Stark (1993), 'Butterfly ranching', in Kemf, op cit.

Marks, Stuart A (1984), *The Imperial Lion: Human Dimensions of Wildlife Management in Central Africa*, Westview Press, Boulder, Colorado.

McDonald, D R (1977), 'Food taboos: a primitive environmental protection agency (South America)', *Anthropos*, No 72, pp 734–748.

Monbiot, George (1994), *No Man's Land: an Investigative Journey through Kenya and Tanzania*, Michael Joseph, London.

Morrison, James (1993), *Protected Areas and Aboriginal Interests in Canada*, WWF (Canada).

Ntshalintshali, Concelia and Carmelita McGurk (1991), 'Resident peoples and Swaziland's Malolotja National Park: a success story', in West and Brechin (eds), op cit.

Partridge, William L, Antoinette B Brown and Jeffrey B Nugent (1982), 'The Papaloapan Dam and Resettlement Project: human ecology and health impacts', in Art Hansen and Anthony Oliver-Smith (eds), *Involuntary Migration and Resettlement: The Problems and Responses of Dislocated People*, Westview Press, Boulder, Colorado, pp 245–263.

Peluso, Nancy Lee (1992), 'Coercing conservation: The politics of state resource control', in R D Lipschutz and K Conca (eds), *The State and Social Power in Global Environmental Politics*, Columbia University Press, New York.

Rackham, Oliver (1989), *The Last Forest: The Story of Hatfield Forest*, J M Dent & Sons Ltd, London.

Redford, Kent H and Allyn Maclean Stearman (1993a), 'Forest-dwelling native Amazonians and the conservation of biodiversity: interests in common or in collision?', *Conservation Biology*, Vol 7, No 2, pp 248–255.

— (1993b), 'On common ground? Response to Alcorn', *Conservation Biology*, Vol 7, No 2, pp 427–428.

Reichel-Dolmatoff, Gerardo (1976), 'Cosmology as ecological analysis: a view from the rain forest', *Man*, Vol 11, No 3, pp 307–318.

Reid, Walter V and Kenton R Miller (1989), *Keeping Options Alive: the Scientific Basis for Conserving Biodiversity*, World Resources Institute, New York.

Republic of Cameroon (1989), *The Korup Project: Plan for Developing the Korup National Park and its Support Zone*, Ministry of Planning and Regional Development, Cameroon.

Ross, E B (1978), 'Food taboos, diet and hunting strategy: the adaptation to animals in Amazon cultural ecology', *Current Anthropology*, Vol 19, No 1, pp 1–36.

Roy, Sanjoy Deb and Peter Jackson (1993), 'Mayhem in Manas: The threats to India's wildlife reserves', in Kemf, op cit.

Ruitenbeek, H Jack (1988), *Resettlement of Inhabitants in Korup National Park, Cameroon*, Korup Research Note No 1, author's mimeo.

Sarno, Louis (1993), *Song from the Forest: my Life among the Ba-Benjelle Pygmies*, Bantam Press, London.

Sayer, Jeffrey (1991), *Rainforest Buffer Zones: Guidelines for Protected Area Managers*, IUCN Forest Conservation Programme, Cambridge.

Schaller, George B (1993), *The Last Panda*, University of Chicago Press, Chicago.

Scudder, Thayer and Elizabeth Colson (1982), 'From welfare to development: a conceptual framework for the analysis of dislocated people', in Art Hansen and Anthony Oliver-Smith (eds), *Involuntary Migration and Resettlement: the Problems and Responses of Dislocated People*, Westview Press, Boulder, Colorado.

Seijas, H and N Arvelo-Jimenez (1979), 'Factores condicionantes de los niveles de salud en grupos indigenas venezolanos: Estudio preliminar', in E Wagner and A Zucchi (eds), Unidad y Varieded, Instituto Venzolano de Investigaciones Cientificas, Caracas, pp 253–271.

Sherpa, Mingma Norbu (1993), 'Grass roots in a Himalayan kingdom', in Kemf, op cit.

Shiva, Vandana, Patrick Anderson, Heffa Schüking, Andrew Gray, Larry Lohmann and David Cooper (1991), *Biodiversity: Social and Ecological Perspectives*, World Rainforest Movement, Penang.

Sinclair, Andrew (1991), *The Naked Savage*, Sinclair-Stevenson, London.

Stoll, David (1982), *Fishers of Men or Founders of Empire? The Wycliffe Bible Translators in Latin America*, Zed Books, London.

Talbot, L and P Olindo (1990), 'Amboseli and Maasai Mara, Kenya', in A Kiss (ed), *Living with Wildlife: Wildlife Resource Management with Local Participation in Africa*, The World Bank, Washington, DC.

Taylor, Bron (1991), 'The religion and politics of Earth First!', *The Ecologist*, Vol 21, No 6, November/December, pp 258–266.

Thongmak, Seri and David L Hulse (1993), 'The winds of change: Karen people in harmony with world heritage', in Kemf, op cit.

Tucker, Richard P (1991), 'Resident peoples and wildlife reserves in India: the prehistory of a strategy', in West and Brechin, op cit.

Turnbull, Colin (1972), *The Mountain People*, Simon and Schuster, London.

Ussher, Ann (no date), *The Invention of Wilderness*, mimeo.

Weaver, Sally M (1991), 'The role of Aboriginals in the management of Australia's Cobourg (Gurig) and Kakadu National Parks', in West and Brechin, op cit.

Wells, Michael (1993), 'Neglect of biological riches: the economics of nature tourism in Nepal', *Biodiversity and Conservation*, Vol 2, No 4.

Wells, M, K Brandon and L Hannah (1992), *People and Parks: Linking Protected Area Management with Local Communities*, The World Bank/WWF/ USAID, Washington, DC.

West, Patrick C (1991), 'Introduction', in West and Brechin, op cit.

West, Patrick C and Steven R Brechin (eds) (1991), *Resident Peoples and National Parks: Social Dilemmas and Strategies in International Conservation*, University of Arizona Press, Tucson.

Westoby, Jack (1987), *The Purpose of Forests*, Basil Blackwell, Oxford.

Wild Earth (1992), *The Wildlands Project: Plotting a North American Wilderness Recovery Strategy*, Cenozoic Society/Wild Earth, Canton, New York.

World Bank (1982), *The Relocation Component in Connection with the Sardar Sarovar (Narmada) Project*, mimeo, The World Bank, Washington, DC.

— (1990), *Indigenous Peoples in Bank-Financed Projects*, Operational Directive No 4 20, The World Bank, Washington, DC.

— (1993), *Mid-Term Progress Report of Projects Involving Resettlement*, The World Bank, Washington, DC, August.

WWF (World Wide Fund for Nature) Malaysia (1985), *Proposals for a Conservation Strategy for Sarawak*, report prepared for the government of Sarawak by the WWF (Malaysia), Kuala Lumpur.

V

WOMEN, FOREST PRODUCTS AND PROTECTED AREAS: A CASE STUDY OF JALDAPARA WILDLIFE SANCTUARY, WEST BENGAL, INDIA[1]

Chandana Dey

Introduction

In India today, resident human populations and wildlife are competing for and depending on the very same resource base. Policy makers, many of whom are also conservationists and thus interested in maintaining the natural environment, face the dilemma of providing sufficient livelihood opportunities for human populations, while allowing biodiversity to maintain itself and regenerate. This chapter examines one wildlife sanctuary in Eastern India (Figure 5.1) to see how feasible it is to reconcile wildlife conservation with the interests of the forest-dependent community that relies on the sanctuary for its livelihood. It concentrates on the

1 This is a shorter version of a more detailed report. Copies of this draft report can be obtained by writing to UNRISD, Palais des Nations, CH-1211 Geneva 10, Switzerland. I am indebted to Mr Tapobrata Bhattacharya and Ms Manjari Chaudhuri for all the hard work they put in during the fieldwork and report production. I am also grateful to Mr Heerak Nandi for the research help he offered in Calcutta. I wish to extend my thanks to the Chief Conservator of Forests, Government of West Bengal, and the Assistant Chief Conservator of Forests, whose support enabled me to undertake the research in the sanctuary areas, as well as the Forest Department officials in the Jaldapara Sanctuary who were extremely generous with their time to explain the problems of Jaldapara to us.

role played by non-timber forest products (NTFPs)[2] in the lives of women, the landless and tribals who live in nearby villages, and examines how these groups have been affected by the establishment of the sanctuary. It also explores possibilities for policy makers to involve forest-dependent people more integrally in wildlife conservation, thus improving their living conditions.

Although many people depend on forest products, the two groups hardest hit by the sealing off of forest tracts in protected areas are women and tribal communities. This is aggravated by the fact that marginal areas accessible to these groups are shrinking (Agarwal and Narain, 1990). Villagers are forced to search for fuelwood and fodder, albeit illegally. In many cases, this is combined with the collection of NTFPs, which provide a vital source of food, medicine and other useful items.

The reservation of forests has a long history. The colonial regime realized that forest wealth should be tapped, and the Forest Acts of 1878 and 1927 facilitated the acquisition of forests by the state. The 1927 Act refused to acknowledge that forest residents had any legitimate right over forest produce by virtue of their residence in the forest (Arora, 1994). This policy continued after independence with the National Forest Act (1952), which also sought to ensure a sustained wood supply for nascent industries (Desai, 1991).

As state control over forests has strengthened, community control has simultaneously weakened. Forest policies have benefited certain urban elites and further marginalized poor forest dwellers. While urban contractors have been given licenses to cut down forests, forest dwellers have been stopped when they try to collect forest products essential for their livelihood. Grazing of cattle within reserved forests and protected areas has become a punishable offence (Mistry, 1992). For most tribals, cattle represent a major source of income, and are an important measure of wealth, as they can be sold quickly for cash in times of need (*Report of the Commissioner*, 1990). Government policies to find alternatives to forest products and cattle-raising as sources of income for tribals have been only partially successful. Most tribals have thus become landless labourers with part-time employment; they still need to consume and sell forest products to be able to survive (*Report of the Commissioner*, 1990).

The relationship between forest authorities and forest-dependent communities deteriorated further, with forest authorities convinced that the rapid deforestation taking place was due mainly to poor people cutting down trees and thus the forests needed to be protected from them. Forest communities, however, felt increasingly helpless and angry. While contractors could come and fell trees legally, forest residents were

---

2 The Forest Department considers timber and polewood as the 'major' products; therefore all other forest products are known as 'minor' ones. These products are numerous, bring the government revenue and play a very major role in people's lives, especially for income and employment. The term 'minor forest products' covers a range similar to 'non-timber forest products'.

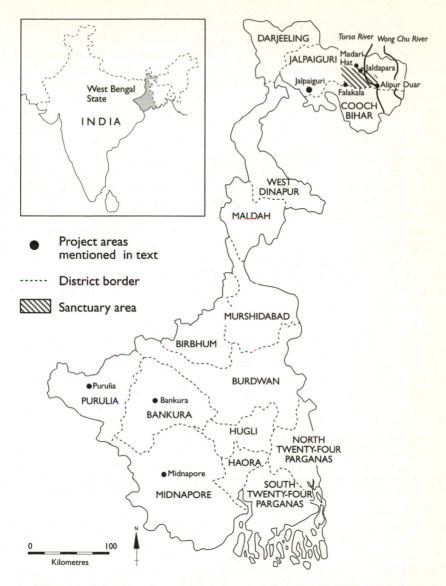

Figure 5.1 *West Bengal state and the location of Jaldapara Wildlife Sanctuary*

punished if they collected forest products, and dead twigs and leaves which did not harm forest ecology and biodiversity (Agarwal, 1988). Thus, even the relationship between the tribals and forests began to change: earlier, the forest had been a common treasure to be used carefully and protected; now that community control had declined, the forests became a 'resource' to be exploited.

133

National forest policy changed significantly in the 1970s as the government began to appreciate that there was a tremendous firewood and fodder scarcity in the rural areas. Social forestry thus became adopted as an important plank of national forest policy. However, social forestry remained a top-down policy and did not achieve many of its aims. There was virtually no participation by villagers at the local level, and almost no consultation with forest dwellers on project design and implementation, which were launched by the various state Forest Departments.

During the same period, a different type of forest regeneration programme had started, which later became known as Joint Forest Management (JFM). Interestingly, JFM began as an initiative of an individual district forest officer (DFO), which covered just 11 villages in the Arabari block in the district of Midnapore in the south-west of West Bengal. This area had been covered with luxuriant sal (*Shorea robusta*) forests until the 1930s. By the early 1970s, the forests were almost totally denuded and the villagers had begun to migrate to other areas to look for work.

Under the Arabari experiment, local people were offered the incentive of shared profits from the sale of major and minor forest produce after certain forested areas had been protected by the villagers for a period of ten years. Forest Protection Committees (FPCs) were formed to patrol the forests. During the ten-year protection period, the forests were coppiced regularly, so that the trees could grow properly; this provided fuelwood and fodder to FPCs at nominal rates (Viegas and Menon, 1991).

The forest protection programme in Arabari was adopted as a state-wide policy in the late 1980s when the JFM also spread to other states in India. In West Bengal, women members of FPCs, traditionally the chief collectors of fuelwood and fodder, were given a prominent role as they were found to be better forest guardians than men (Chatterjee, 1991). Today, almost half of all forest land and more than 70 per cent of the sal forests are covered by JFM. In 1990, a total of 191,756 hectares of forest land came under the aegis of 116 FPCs (Chatterjee, 1991).

A review of JFM initiatives carried out in 1990 found that the previously fuel-starved households were in fact provided with sufficient fuel to meet their needs. Even after a few years of forest protection, there was an enormous harvest of NTFPs. With the increased commercialization of several NTFPs, the FPCs can make enough money to guarantee a higher income to their member households. In the Arabari project, it was estimated that the commercial value of the forest, which was nil in 1972, stood at Rs 90 million in 1988.[3] As the FPCs were entitled to 25 per cent of this, the 'beneficiary share' stood at Rs 22 million and each family was likely to earn Rs 4195 annually (at the values in 1988) in perpetuity (Chambers et al., 1989).

The success of JFM illustrates that co-operation between the government and the people can work, if there is genuine consultation from the

---

3 In 1988, the exchange rate was approximately 1 US dollar = 14.5 Indian rupees, and 32 Indian rupees in 1993.

earliest stages. It also shows that communities can reap many benefits from forests, and that this can be combined with providing revenue to the government. The early positive results indicated that the people of Arabari and the other villages covered by the JFM schemes considered the forests as their own resources and took steps to protect them from further degradation. The JFM initiatives gave women members a leading role in forest protection. Another advantage of JFM was a decline in migration: families were able to stay together as incomes were rising from the sale of forest produce to meet livelihood needs.

But JFM schemes raise some controversial issues regarding the question of ownership and rights. Before forests became state property in the nineteenth century, they were communally owned and maintained. Forest dwellers enjoyed certain rights over forest products. A government-supported scheme, such as the JFM, assumes that forests and forest products belong to the state. It is the government which decides to share the profits with the village communities. Supporters of tribal rights would argue that, as forest dwellers are increasingly ejected from their homes and livelihoods, the state has some responsibilities towards them. Realistically, however, the state government of West Bengal has few avenues open, since the possibilities for land redistribution are extremely limited. That is the reason why many groups today assert that, for forest regeneration programmes to be successful, income earned from all NTFP should belong entirely to forest-dependent communities and that forest dwellers themselves should decide the form and content of protection schemes (Arora, 1994; Chambers et al., 1989; *Report of the Commissioner*, 1990).

The lesson of the Arabari experiment for policy makers is that forests cannot be protected without the active co-operation and participation of the people who depend on them (Poffenberg, 1990). The recent legislation regarding protected area management, the Forest Conservation Act (1980) and the Wildlife Protection Act (1972), specifically make afforestation in sanctuaries illegal. However, as a result of the success of JFM schemes, the Joint Protected Area Management (JPAM) initiatives are considering how to transfer JFM principles to protected areas. Legislation is not the only barrier: the present hostility between forest dwellers and sanctuary authorities makes it difficult for any joint scheme to be considered or implemented (IIPA, 1994).

The Importance of NTFP in the Village Economy

There is a growing body of evidence that NTFPs play a vital role in the lives of poor families, especially those living in forests and on the fringes of forest areas. While fuel and fodder are the main products collected by both tribal and caste households, tendu and sal leaves are also collected for sale. This income represents a substantial part of the cash earnings of the poorest households. Tendu leaves are used to wrap bundles of local cigarettes, known as *bidis*; and sal leaves are generally woven into disposable plates.

While there is not much dispute over the importance of NTFPs, the increased commercialization of these products raises many difficult questions. A study of NTFP collection in several villages in Orissa, for example, showed that the 'access to minor forest products (MFP) and the amount collected was indicative of the distribution of power in the village' (Fernandes et al., 1988). Minor forest products were found to represent between 50 and 70 per cent of total food intake of the households surveyed. It was also discovered that poor families often deprived themselves of certain food products, like mahua flowers and sal seeds, because they could sell these items and thus increase their household income. The poorest families were able to get less nutritionally valuable NTFP than the richer households.

This study also examined the performance of several government-run purchasing co-operatives, which were established with the aims of eliminating middlemen from the sale of NTFPs and buying the products directly from the collectors. These government organizations were found to have hired the erstwhile middlemen as functionaries; the prices paid to collectors for NTFPs were not the same as market prices and the government thus continued to levy a 'tax' on the NTFPs collected (Fernandes et al., 1988).

The processing of several NTFPs in small cottage industries leads to increases in the prices of some products (Poffenberg, 1990). The *lac* industry in the state of Karnataka is one example (FAO, 1991). *Lac* is an encrustation produced by a certain insect on a number of trees. It can be made into lacquer, and this is then made into items such as vases, bowls, toys, games, etc. While the collection of NTFP is arduous and time-consuming, and frequently poses dangers to the health of the collectors, such home-based industries increase workloads even further. It will be seen below that women tend disproportionately to carry out both collecting and processing tasks.

Gender and Forests

The FAO's community forestry case studies have emphasized the importance of NTFP as a source of income, employment, food, nutrition and medicinal herbs for women, the landless and tribals (FAO, 1987, 1989, 1990, 1991 and 1992).

Women forest-goers often have to decide whether it is worth their while to spend the entire day collecting and then processing NTFPs (SPWD, 1992). Women's participation in such extraction and processing activities tends to decline as they become more mechanized and as processing is organized in factory-type establishments (FAO, 1991). Even when women do work in factories, they tend to be paid less than men.

It has been argued that rural women relate to the environment in an intimate manner, often differently from men (Shiva, 1989). Several criteria can be employed to assess the closeness of the relationship between women and forests: first, the question of dependence and survival; second, the division of labour and actual forest-related jobs (who does what); third, the place that the forest plays in popular culture, and the different roles ascribed to the forest (e.g., the traditional role of hunting, or the forest divinities, and how the forest is portrayed in literature, songs, stories, etc.); finally, the amount of time that women (and men) spend in forest areas and their knowledge of tree species, plant life, forest products, etc.

Much information relating to the third and fourth points comes from the hill societies in northern India. As hill agriculture is particularly dependent on forests and commons, it is natural to find that women forest dwellers have especially close ties with the forests. This is also reflected in politically motivated initiatives, such as the Chipko movement where women took the leading role and which focused on saving trees that were being cut by contractors from outside the region (Kumar, 1993).

Some studies undertaken in preparation of social forestry programmes have found that women know of more tree species than men in the same community, and would choose different trees if they were consulted about afforestation programmes (SPWD, 1992). This particular gender divide presumes that men are more interested in the commercial possibilities from afforestation, whereas women consider issues such as nutrition, fuel requirements and income generation. Fuelwood collection and head-loading have become chief income-earning possibilities for rural women, mostly due to economic necessity (Agarwal, 1988). Many women would prefer income-generating activities other than cutting trees to collect and sell the wood. On the other hand, some studies of afforestation schemes among poor and landless farmers do show that both men and women value commercially valuable trees and look at them as investments, which can be sold for cash if and when needed (Burgess, 1992). While women may in some cases desire tree species which suit kitchen gardens and other household requirements, a family may decide to plant only saleable trees, especially if land and income are scarce.

There is also evidence of an increasing gender division concerning knowledge and expertise of the forest. As male migration increases, leaving more female-headed rural households, many rural women are forced to take over tasks which were previously shared by other (male) household members (Rodda, 1991). One of the main time-consuming and increasingly difficult tasks is to locate fuel sources. As a result of deforestation, combined with population pressures (i.e., more households requiring fuel), women in some rural areas spend the greater part of the day in search of fuelwood. One author claims that the inability of some women to provide fuel to cook meals has led to mass suicides (Agarwal, 1988). It has also been discovered that increasing fuel scarcity has led families to cook less frequently and change their dietary patterns, affecting their health status (Agarwal, 1987). Such deprivation has led many rural women to investigate other forms of nutrition which are considered 'free', and many of these foods come from the forest.

The JFM schemes which have tried to involve women in FPCs have found that women tend to guard the forests better than men, and the participation of the former is essential for project success (Chatterjee, 1991). But recent research conducted in the district of Bankura, for example, shows that although FPCs are supposed to have one male member and one female member from each household, women are excluded in practice (Sarin, 1994). In other words, forest protection has further marginalized rural women. According to this research, the male members of FPCs do not worry about where women find fuel. They are preoccupied with getting enough wood for their houses and agricultural implements, and forest protection has supplied enough wood for these requirements.

A study of the tribes in the neighbouring state of Bihar found that men and women share a variety of tasks and responsibilities (Kelkar and Dev, 1991). It is thus a fallacy that, even in indigenous societies, only men hunt and only women gather. In some Indian tribes, women participate in a traditional hunt. Moreover, men take part in the collection of forest products and share in other tasks such as the preparation of meals and child-rearing (Kelkar and Dev, 1991). While it may be true that women greatly depend on the environment, much more research is necessary to understand the relative importance of the environment for women and men in the cultures of different communities.

Tribals and Forests

In 1987, the tribal population in India consisted of about 54 million people, out of the total population of 800 million (Government of West Bengal, undated). Tribals are mainly concentrated in the hilly forested regions of the country. The definition of 'tribal' is debatable, and the degree of assimilation into mainstream caste groups has also varied (Finger-Stich, 1991).[4] Tribals traditionally formed the majority of forest communities who had little or no agricultural land but who depended on forest products for their survival. The changes in property relations in the colonial period were accompanied by other transformations, such as increased transportation and communication infrastructures, with improved access to previously isolated forest areas. These developments helped commercial interests to exploit forest resources and further undermined the position of the tribals (*Report of the Commissioner*, 1990).

---

4 The British enacted special laws for the tribal communities and a list of 'scheduled districts' was drawn up in 1833. These special provisions continued under the colonial régime, and in 1935, 'backward' tribes were included in the provincial legislatures. After independence, the constitution of India continued the dual treatment of tribal areas and tribal communities, and in 1950, the specific areas inhabited by different tribes were noted down. Therefore, concessions for members of Scheduled Tribes were granted only if they were living in areas designed for those tribes. In 1976, these restrictions were lifted, so that tribal groups could receive their due privileges wherever they resided. However, these definitional changes have meant that census data on scheduled tribes and castes have been somewhat distorted and must therefore be interpreted with care (Kulkarni, 1991).

Once forest-based communities were uprooted, they did not find it easy to adapt to the existing economic and social system. They also found that their cultural traditions were threatened (Thekaerkara, 1991). Frequently, there was also land alienation due to the influx of non-tribals onto newly cleared forest land, and tribals were forced into marginal, less fertile areas. A recent study of land alienation found that 80 per cent of tribal land had passed over to non-tribals, and that scheduled tribes were generally unaware of laws protecting them against alienation of their lands (Karuppaiyan, 1990).

Many accounts of the tribal–forest interface prior to colonial times indicate that the ecology of forest areas was able to support not just the biological diversity but also the human population. A respect for trees and wildlife is still an integral part of most tribal cultures. The imbalance between forests and people began when forests became state property. The decline in forest areas exacerbated the problem. The tribal communities still depended on the forests for their livelihoods but there were fewer forests and more demand for the same forest resources. The ecology of the area did not just support the flora and fauna but the forest dwellers also. Studies of different tribes mention that they normally consider trees as spirits and worship them, and that much of tribal culture is still woven around the forest (Das, 1991; Fernandes et al., 1988).

Such a harmonious relationship between people and the forest can only be seen in very isolated forests today. With the increase of poaching and timber felling, both threats which came from outside the region, the government decided to establish areas to protect the wildlife species from the threat of extinction. These policies, which began in the colonial period, continued after independence. Such protection in the form of national parks and sanctuaries curtailed the traditional rights of forest dwellers to collect forest products as they had in the past. No attempt was made to protect the forests with the help of the people who knew the forests best; instead the prevailing philosophy to this day contends that forests have to be protected from the people.

Women, Forests and Social Relations at the Local Level: the Case of Jaldapara Sanctuary

The General Context

West Bengal is India's fourth most populous state, with a population of 68 million in 1991. The average population density of the state is 766 persons per square kilometre but there are considerable variations between districts. Nearly 75 per cent of the total population lives in rural areas. The district of Jalpaiguri, where the sanctuary of Jaldapara is situated, is one of the four least densely populated districts of West Bengal.

According to the latest figures provided by remote sensing imagery, forests cover approximately 14 per cent of the land area of the state of West Bengal (Government of West Bengal). The per capita extent of forest area is slightly lower than the national average. There are three main forest areas in West Bengal: the deciduous forests in the south-west (where JFM is being practised), the mangrove forests in the Sunderbans delta (the delta area of the river Ganges), and the forests of the Himalayas and the foothills of this mountain range, which is known as the Dooars. The Jaldapara sanctuary is located in this last area (see Figure 5.1). In the northern forests, the most important trees are deodar, birch, firs, and oak, while sal trees predominate in the Dooars. The forests of the south-west and the Sunderbans estuarine area are under more pressure from population and livestock than are the forests in the north of Bengal, and are considerably more depleted (Bose, 1970).

In terms of population composition, the district of Jalpaiguri has the second largest percentage of scheduled castes (34 per cent) and the largest percentage of scheduled tribes (22 per cent) of the state. If taken together, the scheduled castes and the scheduled tribes account for more than 50 per cent of the population of the district. The Madari Hat Block (where Jaldapara sanctuary is located) has a total population of about 500,300, of which 100,900 people are tribals. The ethnic composition of the villagers in the sanctuary area is equally varied. There are several tribes, including the Oraon, Munda and Kheria, but these are not indigenous to the region. Some of the tribes originated in neighbouring Nepal, such as the Lepchar and the Mongar. There is still a small enclave of the Toto tribe, who retain much of their original lifestyle and have not been incorporated into the rest of the ethnically mixed villages. In the Jalpaiguri district, there are 21 forest villages[5] where the population of around 300,000 is mostly tribal. The district also has a high percentage of the cattle population compared with the rest of the state (Government of West Bengal, undated).

Since the early 1970s the state government, led by a coalition of communist parties, has attempted to improve the living conditions of the rural poor through credit arrangements, tenancy rights and land redistribution (Kohli, 1987). Village councils (*panchayats*) have also played an important role in channelling development funds to the countryside (Mallick, 1993). Political consciousness among the majority of women, the landless and tribals still remains low despite concerted attempts not only by formal political parties, but also by underground movements, NGOs, women's associations and tribal organizations.

Today, 32.48 per cent of West Bengal's forests have been declared wildlife protected areas. These fall under 16 wildlife sanctuaries, 2 tiger reserves, 1 national park and 2 intended national parks. Jaldapara is one of 20 protected areas, and among the oldest. The need to create a sanctuary to protect the grassland ecosystem and the rhinos from the threat of

---

5 The British brought in people to work as labourers in the forest. They were then settled inside the forest. People living in these villages have special rights and privileges, and are the responsibility of the Forest Department.

poaching was felt as far back as the 1920s (Das, 1966). The sanctuary was established in 1941 and ten years later came under the Cooch Behar Forest Division. At first, the sanctuary consisted of about 100 square kilometres of forest and grassland; this area was subsequently doubled as it was felt that the wildlife of Jaldapara needed a larger area in which to propagate (interview, senior official). Today, the sanctuary straddles two districts: Cooch Behar and Jalpaiguri.

Although the rhinos have made Jaldapara famous, there are many other mammals in the sanctuary. The elephants and tigers are both transient; among the permanent residents are hog deer, swamp deer, chital, wild buffalo, jungle cats and leopards. Other common animals are the Indian hare, the hispid hare and the pygmy hog.

There are two distinct ecological zones within the sanctuary, the *bhabar* lands and the swamp lands, which explains why it is home to so many different animal and bird species. The fertile *bhabar* lands contain coarse sand and pebbles washed down by the swiftly flowing Himalayan rivers. Apart from the monsoon season, the rivers run underground, with the exception of the river Torsha. These rivers then reappear on the surface where the plains begin, creating swamps.

There is a large variety of trees in the sanctuary and the undergrowth is dense. The riverain forests consist of *sisu* (*Dalbergia sisoo*), *chatim* (*Alstonia scholaris*), *khair* (*Acacia catechu*) and *simul*. There are also a variety of riverain grasses, including thatch, *hogla*, *khagra* and *purandi*. The dry mixed forests contain different trees, such as *simul*, *sinduri*, *jarul*, and grasses. Lastly, there are sal forests towards the east of the sanctuary in Baradabri and the Salkumar forest.

The field research took place in two villages. The first, Nutanpara, is one of four villages under the *panchayat* of Salkumar II. The population of the *panchayat* is around 11,000, or approximately 700 families. About 30 per cent of the village is dependent on the forests. The second site, Purba Khairbari, is a mainly tribal village which was chosen in order to investigate whether tribal women depend more on NTFP than inter-caste families. The second main difference between the two villages was the location relative to the sanctuary (Figure 5.2): Nutanpara is situated in the heart of the sanctuary, and is further from the two big market towns of the area. Purva Khairbari is located closer to the town of Madari Hat, and the sanctuary forests are less closely guarded than near Nutanpara. The population of Purva Khairbari consists of around 250 families.[6]

---

6 The research involved group interviews with nine families in Purva Khairbari and individual interviews with 18 women in Nutanpara. We needed special permission to enter the sanctuary and to visit Nutanpara. The women were both too busy and too nervous to answer our questions sufficiently. They also chose to withhold information which would harm them. We had to promise not to pass over any information to the forest authorities before they would agree to the interviews. There were two informal chats with the men of the village at the local tea shop. During one of the conversations the *panchayat pradhan* (head) was present, so we were not able to discuss the *panchayat* activities as openly as we would have liked.

The Village of Nutanpara

General Socio-Economic Conditions of Women in the Village

Interviews with 18 women revealed that half had no land or extremely marginal holdings. Some 38 per cent of the women came from share-cropper families, who cultivated very small plots. As there is little irrigation in the area, crops depend on rainfall. The chief crops are paddy, jute, wheat, tobacco and seasonal vegetables. When paddy yields were compared, most plots in Nutanpara yielded 6–7 maunds per bigha[7] according to the interviewed villagers, while in Burdwan, the most affluent district of West Bengal, paddy yields are much higher. Although most families claimed that they needed 7 bighas of land in order not to have to buy rice from the market (in years of adequate rainfall) most had far less land. The women from landless families had to buy rice daily.

The only way they could get the necessary cash was from the sale of wood, which they collected each day in the forest. The time spent inside the forest depended in large part on the proximity of their homes, with families who lived nearest the forest (some of the women surveyed lived only 500 metres away) requiring less time than the women who lived further away. The latter could spend up to six hours per day collecting wood. The twigs and branches, neatly tied together with rope, are carried on the head — a practice referred to as 'head-loading'. First, a head-protection set (made up of flattened leaves) is placed on the head, and then the bundle of wood (locally referred to as *bojha*) is hoisted onto the head. These *bojhas* weigh anywhere between 45 and 60 kilograms. Even fairly elderly women were part of the forest collection group. Three of the women interviewed in Nutanpara were members of the same family. The household head, a landless labourer, had two wives; one wife was temporarily at home looking after the baby, and the other wife went daily to collect wood from the forest. The mother had to make separate cooking arrangements while staying with the family and therefore had to collect wood for herself. Neither daughter-in-law was prepared to fetch wood for the old lady.

After collection, the wood is sorted into two piles: the better branches and logs are stacked up and once they reach a certain height (known locally as a *pili*), they are sold for cash. It normally takes a family a month to collect a *pili*, which can usually be sold for 60–100 rupees. Most families do not own vans (cycle-rickshaws) so they are unable to benefit from higher prices at Madari Hat market. The usual custom is for better-off families with access to transportation to buy wood from poorer ones.

The inferior twigs are kept for cooking. Most families used around half a *bojha* for cooking each day. The average cooking time was three to four hours for a family of four. Most people eat rice as the substantial part of their meal and combine it with some vegetables, when they can

---

7 One maund is about 36 kilograms. One bigha is the same as 0.68 of a hectare.

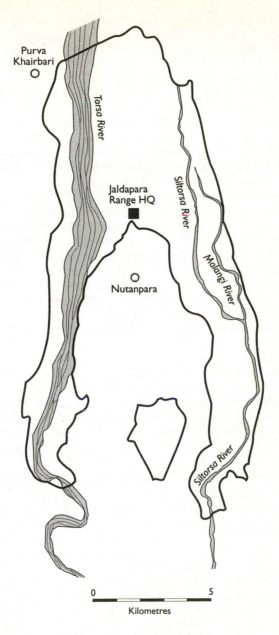

Figure 5.2 *Jaldapara Wildlife Sanctuary*

afford them. Those with land grow vegetables (tomatoes, aubergines, garlic, potatoes) for their own consumption and for sale. Those families with land normally consumed their own rice. Landless families sometimes sell their day's collection of wood by the *bojha*, to earn the income necessary to purchase rice from the market. In 1992 the price of a kilogram of rice was 6.50–8 rupees, out of their income of 10 rupees for the sale of 1 *bojha* of wood.

The families with more than 7 *bighas* of land did not generally engage in fuelwood sale. The women from these families also visited the forest less frequently, two to three times a week. However, forest-going duties are normally divided between family members: the older sons and daughters go in search of fodder for their animals, while the women leave in groups in search of firewood.

Livestock ownership partially depended on the extent of land ownership. According to the sanctuary officials, the villages around the Jaldapara sanctuary maintain about 40,000 cattle (interview). The need for fodder collection and grazing generates conflicts between livestock and wildlife. Fodder collection is prohibited by the Wildlife Act (1972), and cattle are considered one of the main threats to the sanctuary. According to the sanctuary official, the cattle bring in noxious weeds which are extremely harmful to wild animals. During fieldwork in the sanctuary, there was a much-feared anthrax epidemic which had supposedly killed one elephant.

Most families interviewed in Nutanpara know that domestic animals must be tethered and that grazing of cattle is strictly prohibited within the sanctuary. Fines are high and cattle can be seized if caught. While most families denied going to the forests to collect fodder, several young boys with baskets strapped to their backs were witnessed, carrying leaves, returning home at the same time as the women with their bundles.

Women's Dependence on Forest Products

Interviews with 18 women from different households revealed that about 22 per cent were dependent on the forest for their main source of income. The women of Nutanpara were generally reticent about giving information on what they collected from the sanctuary forests for fear of prosecution. One of the items collected is *pipli*, a fruit that is dried and can be used as a seasoning (similar to pepper). The potential income from *pipli* sale is negligible —Rs 5–6 a kilogram — when it can be sold to people from outside the village. There seem to be no possibilities for the women to market this or any other product themselves. The village of Nutanpara is cut off from the nearby towns; hiring of vans is expensive and, most importantly, people are fined if they are caught transporting forest items.

When asked about fruit availability, the women mentioned fruits like *kul*, *amloki* and *bugri*, which were consumed in the forest. The *tutu* leaf is also eaten to quench thirst. Most of the women surveyed collected mushrooms: the families who collected most were tribal, and they also engaged in occasional sales. Some of the other women said that they would not recognize the edible ones from the poisonous ones. Moreover, wild mushrooms are available only in the monsoon season. We also asked about the potatoes and other edible tubers in the forest. The women said that these were found too deep underground and that tools were required to dig them up. As taking tools into the forest was forbidden, they could not be collected. Nevertheless, a vast number of forest items are regularly collected from the forest and consumed (Table 5.1). These products are not sold, however, as the village market is small and the women are afraid to be seen transporting anything from the forest. Wood sales play a far more important income-generating role than NTFP collection, and the women were thus more busy stockpiling wood than other forest products.

While in Nutanpara, we were struck by the massive availability of bamboo, a commodity which has become scarce in other parts of the state. Bamboo house walls are a common feature of villages in north Bengal and bamboo poles are used as stilts for many two-storied houses. However, when the women were asked if they knew bamboo-weaving,

Table 5.1 *NTFP: Nutanpara village*

Month/Season	NTFP	Use	Sale /Consumption
March/spring	*Shimul* cotton (from the *shimul* flower)	To stuff pillows and mattresses	Sold (1 palla cost 100 rupees)
March	*Paskol*	Fruit	Consumed
March	*Kul*	Fruit	Consumed
March	*Amloki*	Fruit	Consumed
June/July/rainy season	Mushrooms	Vegetable	Consumed
June/July	*Titli*	Vegetable/ condiment	Consumed
June/July	*Boyera* and *haritaki*	Medicines	Sold (price not known)
September/ October	*Pipli*	Medicines/ condiment	Sold/ Consumed
December	*Chhon* grass	For house roofs	Consumed
Year-round	*Chhim* (river plant)	Vegetable (like spinach)	Consumed
Year-round	Small river crabs, snails, shrimps and frogs	Food	Consumed

most did not. Bamboo work is traditionally a low-caste occupation, and as some of the women interviewed came from the scheduled caste group called the Rajbangshis, this may have accounted for the negative response. Bamboo poles are sold and represent a substantial source of income for many families.

All the women in the survey maintained that the forest had been denser ten years back and that their forest-going time had thus been about half as long as it is at present. They also said that certain tree species like *khair* and *sisoo* were hardly seen these days; these valuable hardwoods are the main species felled for the illicit timber trade.

Most women recognized that it was the pressure of firewood collection which caused forest degradation. However, most of them also said that the illicit felling was responsible for the loss of the valuable trees, and that they were only collecting dry twigs and leaves. The forest authorities, while sympathetic to the villagers in general, claim that villagers also cut down living trees. According to the Forest Department, a common way to kill a tree is to strip the bark; the tree then dies and male villagers cut the tree and tell the women exactly where to find the wood. The women then collect the logs and claim that the tree was already dead when they found it (interview).

It was virtually impossible to determine the extent of the illicit timber trade, as this is an extremely well-hidden subject. The small town of Madari Hat has more than twenty furniture shops; the shopkeepers claim that they buy the wood from wholesale markets; the wholesalers say that they get the wood, legally, through auctions; it is extremely hard to find out how much of this trade is in fact legal.

The Forest Department is responsible for 'cutting down' operations — the cutting of some trees for sale. Ironically, the main trees which are felled are the *khair* and the *sisoo*. These large trees are cut to allow grasslands to expand, and this habitat is crucial for the survival of the rhino population of Jaldapara. The Wildlife Division cannot directly sell these trees; they are taken by the Cooch Behar Forest division and then auctioned.

The proximity of the forest to people's homes naturally affects the relationship between the villagers and the wildlife. Of the 18 women interviewed, about 28 per cent said their crops had been trampled by elephant herds and their houses destroyed. The compensation for destruction of property remains a paltry 50 rupees, even though, today, the value of certain crops runs into several hundreds of rupees. Compensation is higher only when someone is killed; however, as many of these accidents occur at night, inside the forest, people are unwilling to report them.

All of the women interviewed, especially those in Nutanpara, expressed great fear of going into the forest. They tend to go in groups, and leave forested areas well before dusk. They maintained that hardship and sheer necessity forced them to enter the sanctuary, though they were all aware of its illegality. Most of them had encountered forest guards;

146

some had been fined and all of them feared the great chance of its happening. Over the past year, the Forest Department had introduced a battalion of women forest guards — often the spouses of existing forest guards who had been given temporary contracts. One of the problems encountered in the past was that male forest guards were forbidden from striking women forest offenders.

The recently introduced Eco-Development Plan is a small step towards lessening the hostility between the forest authorities and the forest-dependent communities. The Plan had only been in effect for the past year in Jaldapara. Only very limited information on the scope of the projects was available. The village of Nutanpara had received funds for the construction of a fish-pond: some of the women interviewed had got a few days paid labour for digging this pond. The main beneficiaries were the two families whose land was used for the pond. The Forest Department was under the impression that the fish would be shared by the whole village, though the villagers were unaware of this aspect of the programme. Under the Plan, fuel-efficient stoves had been distributed to other villages in the *panchayat*, and efforts had also been made to introduce mushroom cultivation.

The chief weakness of the Plan seems to be the lack of any consultation with the people it is meant to benefit. The projects are chosen by a committee consisting of Forest Department officials and *panchayat* committee members. There are no independent village representatives on this committee. Whether a project is given to the most needy is arbitrary and really depends on the *panchayat pradhan* (head). Projects may simply be allotted to friends or to people who will vote for the *panchayat* in the next election. The budget of the Plan is also not large enough to make it into anything very significant. In 1993–1994, the Plan outlay of 1 million rupees concentrated on wells, fish-ponds and smokeless stoves. Ironically, the landless poor represent the main social group excluded from the Eco-Development Plan.

The Village of Purva Khairbari

The Evolving Relationship between Tribals and the Forest
A vast number of forest products are available within the sanctuary (Table 5.2). Most NTFPs are available and thus collected in the monsoon season by both men and women. Most NTFPs are collected for personal consumption; if items are found in bulk, they are then sold. The villagers of Purva Khairbari seemed in a better position to sell forest produce as they are in fairly close proximity to two major selling centres, the towns of Madari and Hashimara. If the villagers can get *pattas* (passes issued by the Forest Department which allow collection of certain items) it is financially worth their while to pay the bus fare to Hashimara to sell at the market there. However, *pattas* are provided only occasionally, at the discretion of the District Forest Officer.

Table 5.2 *Chief non-timber forest products in Purva Khairbari*

NTFP	Use	Season	Consumed/Sold	Market price
Shimul	Cotton wool	March	Sold	Rs 20–30 per kg
Totola	Flower for Buddhist worship		Sold	Not known
Kul, amlaki, kadam	Fruit	Spring	Consumed and sold	Rs 4–5 per kg
Dumur	Fodder, food	Spring		Not known
Jungli alu (wild potato)	Grows under roots of trees	Year-round	Consumed	Not known
Githa	A bitter-tasting tuber	Year-round	Consumed	Not known
Baby bitter gourds (*karela*)	Vegetable	Monsoon	Consumed and sold	Rs 4–5 per kg.
Mushroom (*chatu / kukri*)	Vegetable	Monsoon	Consumed and sold	Not known
Betel leaf (*paan*)	Eaten after meals as digestive	Spring	Consumed and sold	4 *paans* for 1 rupee
Taranju	Vegetable (in stews)	Spring	Consumed by humans and elephants, and sold	Handful for a rupee
River spinach	Vegetable	Year-round	Consumed and sold	1 rupee a handful
Dudhia	Vegetable like string beans	Year-round	Consumed	Rs 4–5 per kg
Cone of bamboo	Pickled	Monsoon	Consumed and sold	1 *pau* (250 grams) sells for 5 rupees
River fish, crabs, snails, etc.	Food	Year-round	Consumed and sold	

All the *adivasis* (tribals) in the survey formed a relatively homogeneous group: they are landless and depend on the sale of firewood as their primary source of income (Table 5.3). When possible, they work as agricultural labourers. Generally wage work is available only for two months in the year. These families are discouraged from moving to other areas — there is stiff competition everywhere for the existing jobs.

The tribal families in the survey seemed to be more mobile than the mixed caste families, visiting the neighbouring *hats* (markets) and even making trips to Bhutan to sell some of their goods. Most families were keen to sell forest items for cash, and were either not interested or unable to wait until price increases would bring them greater income from sales. Many interviewees also admitted that it would not be cost-effective for them to process or add value to NTFPs: for example, it takes so much time to make pillows out of *shimul* cotton that they prefer merely to collect and sell the raw material.

In Purva Khairbari, women keep the cash earnings from wood sales and buy the food for the household. However, these earnings are not substantial enough to make any savings; and they cannot refuse to hand over some of the money to the men, who normally spend it on village-brewed alcohol.

As has been mentioned, tribal men and women enjoy a different relationship with the forest from non-tribal families. This difference invariably affects their ties with the forest authorities because their very survival is at stake. The sanctuary forest around Purva Khairbari is less closely patrolled than the forests near Nutanpara.

Tribal men, especially the Oraons and Mundas, still take part in a traditional hunt during the month of March. Although the men in the survey were reluctant to admit to it, they all regularly take part. However, they claimed that they only hunt deer, rabbits and pigs; elephants and rhinos are not poached. Once an animal is caught, the meat is divided up inside the forest. The men denied ever having been caught, even though the Forest Department designates extra guards during this month. Women and children do not participate in the traditional hunt.

The families interviewed all maintained that the forest had been more dense ten years ago. Most of them had neither heard about nor benefited from the Forest Department's Eco-Development Plan. When asked about their views on forest regeneration, they seemed very enthusiastic about afforestation undertaken by the Forest Department within the sanctuary. 'If the Forest Department grew trees', they said, 'this would give us work and save the forest'. All interviewees and their families were fond of trees and had a close rapport with the forests around them.

Comparisons Between Nutanpara and Purva Khairbari

Although the samples in the two research sites were very different, it is possible to make some initial comparisons when we amalgamate the results of the surveys.

Table 5.3 *Dependence of the villagers of Purva Khairbari*
on wood sales

Number of house-holds	Landless	Chief income from forest (wood sales)	Chief income from agricultural labour	Both men and women go to forest	Only men go to forest	Only women go to forest
9	8	7	2	7	0	2

NTFP and Gender

In Nutanpara, about 90 per cent of the women regardless of social class go to the forests. None of the husbands of the women interviewed had to collect wood from the forest. In Purva Khairbari, both men and women go to the forest to collect wood and NTFP. The income from wood sales is the chief income source for most landless families. Both men and women know the forest thoroughly, though women may know more tree species than men.

NTFP Collection Versus Agricultural Labour

Families in Purva Khairbari prefer going to the forest to looking for agricultural labour (referred to locally as *hajra-mujra*) because they like being masters of their own time. *Hajra-mujra* involves the entire day of work, under the close supervision of the landlord. Moreover, the income from wood sales is more dependable and lucrative than agricultural labour. In Nutanpara, on the other hand, landless families expressed a distinct preference for agricultural labour. This may be because forest dependence is associated with the poorest segments of the village, especially the scheduled castes and the tribal families. Agricultural labour is considered an occupation with higher status. It is also interesting to note that employers in Nutanpara prefer women labourers, because they work longer and harder (group interview of men).

Value Attached to Forests

The surveys brought out distinct, attitudinal differences regarding the value attached to forests and forest items. For non-tribal families, forests are a place where people are forced to go because of the non-availability of fuel and alternative work opportunities. Frequently, in the course of interviews, the Nutanpara women said that given a chance to work elsewhere, and if they could find an alternative fuel supply, their visits to the forest would cease. The tribal families prefer to go to the forests because they know them so well. The monsoon season is the one time when most families of Nutanpara do not go to the forests because of the heavy rains. That is one of the reasons why women have to stockpile the wood during the pre-monsoon months. However, the tribals of Purva Khairbari mentioned the monsoon as being the most fertile season for NTFP collection. The largest number of products are available (see Table 5.2), for both consumption and sale. Families also collect wood regardless of the weather.

Importance of Market Ties
The families in Purva Khairbari have explored the market potential of NTFP more thoroughly than villagers in Nutanpara, because of its location closer to market centres. The profit they make is worthwhile and compensates for a day not spent in the forest. Of course, it is the provision of *pattas* that makes this possible; this opportunity does not seem available to the Nutanpara inhabitants. Although the reasons for this crucial difference were not made clear to us, one major factor may be that the Forest Department cannot afford to consistently ignore the traditional rights of tribals with regard to the forest. However, we also felt that as the tribal families of Purva Khairbari seem more enterprising than the families in Nutanpara, they have attempted to explore all avenues open to them (legal and illegal) to collect as much as possible from the sanctuary forests.

Policy Issues and Alternatives

Field research confirmed that the sanctuary forests of Jaldapara are considerably affected by constant use of villagers living nearby. The research also showed that NTFP plays a predominant role in women's lives. It accounts for the major share of family income for the poorest families, who normally do not possess any land. For these families, agricultural labour is only available for a few days in the entire year. Fuelwood is also collected by the well-off families when there is no alternative fuel supply. While most people interviewed said that illicit felling was largely to blame for forest denudation, they believed that the pressure exerted on the forests by the villagers, themselves, was also a contributory factor.

The official government policy is implemented by the wildlife division of the Forest Department through a carrot-and stick-approach. On the one hand, the Forest Department has started an eco-development component of its new management plan, to try and convince people to stay away from the forests. Various development projects are being instituted to offer forest villagers alternative non-forest-based income. On the other hand, traditional measures of forest protection have been strengthened: fines have been increased; punishment is severe; the forests are regularly patrolled and even a 'women's battalion' has been added.

The eco-development plan is the product of collaboration between the *panchayat* committees and the Forest Department. The eco-development committee forms proposals for the various villages within and bordering the Jaldapara sanctuary. These proposals are then sent to the district forest officer (DFO), who decides on how far the budget can be stretched. The main projects in 1993–1994 consisted of minor irrigation works, fish ponds, mushroom cultivation and distributing smokeless, firewood-saving stoves. As was mentioned above, few people benefited immediately from the fish pond located in the village of Nutanpara — although benefits may increase in future.

The villagers know that the forests are getting denuded but feel helpless against the odds. Some of them have no livelihood source other than the sale of firewood. They are restricted to collecting only dry twigs and leaves, because of the strict rules enforced by the sanctuary. However, they see larger-scale illicit felling taking place with no penalties imposed on the offenders. If local villagers are used for the illicit felling business, they are paid the normal agricultural wage, while the fellers gain enormous profits. It thus seems clear to most people that the Forest Department is clamping down on the easiest victims, namely the villagers, while the real offenders are not caught. This naturally creates more resentment against the forest authorities.

It is very difficult to get accurate information on the extent of timber felling within the sanctuary. However, it seems likely that there is some connivance with some forest officials, at least at the local level, in order for the illegal timber trade to go on at all. Since the sanctuary is state property, none of the villagers look on the forests as their own. To some extent, they 'use' a resource which is near at hand.

The hardship entailed in daily survival does not seem to have led to much communal unity in the villages studied. Most women pursue their lives in individual ways, apart from going into the forest in groups. Within the forest, women guard their sticks and twigs carefully. If it is necessary for them to leave their wood piles overnight in the forest, they are never sure of finding them again.

Alternatives Perceived by Women
Most of the women surveyed, particularly from Nutanpara, said that the increase in restrictions imposed by the Forest Department had led to a significant decline in their visits to the forest. Moreover, given alternative income-earning possibilities, their trips to the forest would further decrease, as they would not have to resort to wood sales to survive.

One Nutanpara resident remarked that in previous years, the forest authorities had provided paid work within the forest; now this work was no longer available. Given the availability of bamboo in the gardens surrounding most houses, the women also expressed an interest in learning handicrafts if such products could then be sold.

According to the *panchayat pradhan* of Madari Hat, the majority of tribals whom he knows are not solely concerned with the pursuit of money. They are content to live fairly simply. If their immediate needs (food, clothing, home-brewed alcohol) are met, they do not always strive to better this lifestyle. The idea of increasing income through NTFP processing is not immediately attractive as it requires a lot of extra hard work. Forest product collection is considered less arduous than closely supervised daily labour.

Forest Legislation: a Barrier to any Further Positive Change

Although there is currently a lot of thinking in official circles about the most realistic and feasible means to continue protected-area schemes, in view of increasing pressures from the human and livestock populations, the Forest Department is trapped by its own legislation. Most forest legislation is basically inimical to the interests of the forest dwellers. From the point of view of forest-dependent communities, the Wildlife Protection Act (1972) and the Forest Conservation Act (1980) represent the most controversial legislation. The latter states that 'no forest land or any portion thereof may be used for any non-forest purpose'. It specifically notes that afforestation is not permissible on forest land under strictly protected regimes.

The Forest Conservation Act has been designed to protect forests, and in practice has completely marginalized the livelihoods and the possibilities of development efforts for all forest-dependent people. In reserved forest areas, it is now illegal to build roads, hospitals and other types of infrastructure. These acts also assume that all forest produce, major and minor, belongs to the government. Although most state governments have established Forest Development Corporations (FDCs) and similar organizations to purchase NTFPs directly from the collectors and assure them a fair price, the de facto result is that the government imposes a 'royalty' on NTFP income. All these rules and regulations make it very difficult for forest-dependent people to get a fair deal, and this naturally creates a lot of conflict between the government and the people.

Finally, the Forest Conservation Act places great discretionary powers in the hands of fairly junior officers, forest guards and beat guards. Recent years in Jaldapara have seen several incidents where villagers entering the forests at night have been shot at and arrested. Local officials maintain that these 'terror tactics' are necessary to protect the forests; others feel that they can only work in the short term. While senior officers in the forest department headquarters are cogitating on the best methods to protect wildlife sanctuaries, great resentment is building up between the people and the local sanctuary authorities.

Conclusions

The Jaldapara sanctuary has had a profound impact on the lives of the people living around it. It is the only existing tract of forest land in the area, and no buffer zone exists between the sanctuary and the adjoining villages. Hence, the majority of the villagers must enter the forests daily in their search for fuel and the collection of NTFP which is the main livelihood source for the poorest families.

This survey reveals several differences in the relationship with the forest between tribal and mixed caste families. In brief, the tribal families of Purva Khairbari know the forests more intimately and collect more NTFP than the mixed caste families of Nutanpara. Their average incomes are also somewhat higher, as both men and women go to the forests and sell wood in the market. The Nutanpara families know the forests less well; here, the wood collection and sale is left to the women, while the men attempt to find work elsewhere.

As women frequent the forests more, they know more tree species than the men. Tribal women certainly feel close to trees and the forests around them; they have also shown more enthusiasm for the potential of social forestry. The gender differences, however, seem less marked than the ethnic differences when it comes to people's relationship with the forest.

The efficacy of stringent regulations on the forest-going habits of people is also a matter of controversy. Fines have increased and rules are now stricter, in an attempt to reduce the level of human interference in the sanctuary. Earlier, *pattas* used to be given for wood and NTFP collection; today, these permits are merely discretionary measures, which are informal, temporary arrangements. The very strict nature of the rules (where fines are now equal to several days' earnings) has meant that people are going to the forests less often and for shorter periods. Another effect has been that responsibility has been shifted: the wealthier families are now buying their fuelwood from the landless families; the latter are therefore significantly more likely to be caught and fined for collecting wood.

The main impact of the stringent regulations has been the increase in tension between the villagers and the Forest Department. Even though the Forest Department is attempting to carry out its Eco-Development Plan, it has not aroused much enthusiasm on the part of the recipients. Firstly, the projects have been almost 'foisted' on the people; there certainly does not seem to have been any people's participation in the design of the projects. Secondly, the villagers feel that the Forest Department is not trying its utmost to stop the illicit timber-felling trade, which (in the people's view) is the root cause for the current forest decline. Lastly, the local Forest Department officers carry out their punishments with such severity that these often exceed the bounds of legal action.

Another factor working against the promotion of NTFP as a viable income source is that forest-dependent families find NTFP processing too time-consuming to guarantee them a higher standard of living. However, if NTFP collection can be combined with afforestation schemes, there seems more likelihood of success. Furthermore, among mixed-caste families, even forest-dependency seems to be linked to status. The women of Nutanpara much preferred the expansion of other, preferably agricultural, activities to increase incomes, rather than developing forest-based activities. The forest is looked on as the last resort.

One of the major issues which emerges from this research is whether

NTFP collection can become an additional income source for poor families living in and around protected areas. Firstly, there is the question of the types and quantities of NTFPs that can be collected without damaging the biodiversity and ecological balance of the protected area. In Jaldapara, for example, villagers are allowed to collect *chhon* grass, used to thatch house roofs, for three days every winter. But the Forest Department is uncertain whether this harms the animals in the sanctuary or not. Another stumbling block for considering NTFP collection as an income source is the lack of ready markets. In other areas where potential NTFP income is enormous, the collectors are not getting a fair price and most of the profits are going to private traders or the government.

The hostility and suspicion between the villagers and the forest authorities make the running of the sanctuary highly problematic. It seems unlikely that the present level of resource use is going to decline significantly. What then are the practical solutions that can be set into motion, in order to maintain the current level of biodiversity within the sanctuary, without endangering the livelihoods of the people in the neighbouring villages?

The study suggests that a more viable alternative is the promotion of social forestry, especially designed to meet the needs of landless families in fringe areas of the sanctuary. Although some Forest Department officials claim that Jaldapara cannot be reduced in size because of the habitat requirements of the wildlife population, in actual practice, the animals avoid the fringe areas because of the high level of contact with humans. In these areas a programme like the Joint Forest Management could be attempted. However, the present Forest Conservation Act makes afforestation in sanctuary areas illegal.

The real success of the JFM lies in recognizing the vital importance for poor, landless households of ownership of trees. Recent studies show that trees represent not just a good income source but also a certain security (Chambers et al., 1989). In Nutanpara, for example, most families with even minute kitchen gardens have planted *supuri* (betel nut) trees. The latter are fast-growing trees with high commercial value. There are also other tree species which may take longer to grow but which will produce fodder, fruit, shade and other essentials for a village household.

Another reason to consider growing trees as a good investment for tribal families, is the tribals' wealth of knowledge about the forest. Any afforestation programme, properly researched and conducted, would seem to be in good hands if left with forest-dependent families such as the ones surveyed in Nutanpara and Purva Khairbari. The strength of the JFM approach is that projects are generally undertaken after a series of discussions between the Forest Department and the people. In the current scenario, dialogue is missing entirely; the people are rarely consulted, even when it comes to projects meant for them.

However, the problems between people and protected areas stem not merely from economic and environmental sources. There is also the issue of social justice. It is ironic that the forests once belonged entirely to the people and were then summarily taken away; now that some joint management partnerships are taking place, they are often considered benevolent acts on the part of the state. NTFPs, at least, should belong entirely to forest-dependent families, instead of being considered a source of revenue for the government. Local villagers cannot perpetually remain the sole scapegoats for the damage that is being done to the forests of Jaldapara.

References

Agarwal, A (1988), 'Beyond pretty trees and tigers in India', in D C Pitt (ed), *The Future of the Environment*, Routledge, London.

Agarwal, A and S Narain (1990), *Strategies for the Involvement of the Landless and Women in Afforestation*, Five Case Studies from India, ILO, Geneva.

Agarwal, B (1987), 'Under the cooking pot: the political economy of the domestic fuel crisis in rural South Asia', *IDS Bulletin*, Vol 18, No 1, pp 11–22.

Arora, D (1994), 'From state regulation to people's participation: case of forest management in India', *Economic and Political Weekly*, Vol XXIX, 19 March, pp 691–698.

Bose, S C (1970), *Geography of West Bengal*, National Book Trust, New Delhi.

Burgess, M (1992), 'Dangers of environmental extremism: analysis of debate over India's social forestry programme', *Economic and Political Weekly*, Vol XXVII, No 40, 3 October, pp 2196–2199.

Chambers, R, N C Saxena and Tushaar Shah (1989), *To the Hands of the Poor*, Intermediate Technology Publications, Oxford Publishing Co, New Delhi.

Chatterjee, M (1991), *Women in Joint Forest Management: a Case Study in West Bengal*, Technical Paper–4, Indian Institute of Bio-Social Research and Development, Calcutta.

Das, P K (1966), 'Jaldapara wildlife sanctuary', in *West Bengal Forests, Centenary Commemoration Volume*, Government of West Bengal, Calcutta, pp 251–258.

Das, V (1991), 'Forests and tribals of Jharkand', *Economic and Political Weekly*, 9 February, pp 275–276.

Desai, V (1991), *Forest Management in India – Issues and Problems*, Himalaya Publishing House, Bombay.

FAO (Food and Agriculture Organization of the United Nations) (1987), *Restoring the Balance: Women and Forest Resources*, Rome.

— (1989), *Forestry and Nutrition. A Reference Manual*, Rome.

— (1990), *The Major Significance of 'Minor' Forest Products: the Local Use and Value of Forests in the West African Humid Forest Zone*, Rome.

— (1991), *Women's Role in Dynamic Forest-Based Small Scale Enterprises*, Community Forestry study, Rome.

— (1992), *Forests, Trees and Food*, FAO, Rome.

Fernandes, W, G Menon and P Viegas (1988), *Forests, Environment and Tribal Economy*, Indian Social Institute, New Delhi.

Finger-Stich, Andréa (1991), *Shrinking Forests in India: Impact on Tribal Women*, M A thesis, Syracuse, May.

Government of West Bengal (undated), *State Report on West Bengal Forests 1991–2*, Office of the Principal Chief Conservator of Forests, Calcutta.

IIPA (Indian Institute of Public Administration) (1994), *Workshop on 'Exploring the Possibilities of Joint Management of Protected Areas'*, New Delhi.

Karuppaiyan, E (1990), 'Alienation of tribal lands in Tamil Nadu', *Economic and Political Weekly*, 2 June, pp 1185–1186.

Kelkar, G and N Dev (1991), *Gender and Tribe Women, Land and Forests in Jharkhand*, Kali for Women, New Delhi.

Kohli, Atul (1987), *The State and Poverty in India*, Orient Longman, Bombay.

Kulkarni, S (1991), 'Distortion of census data on scheduled tribes', *Economic and Political Weekly*, February, pp 205–208.

Kumar, R (1993), *The History of Doing*, Kali for Women, New Delhi.

Mallick, Ross (1993), *Development Policy of a Communist Government in West Bengal since 1977*, Cambridge University Press, Cambridge.

Mistry, M D (1992), 'The impact of the Forest Act on the household economy of the tribals', in A Agarwal (ed), *The Price of Forests*, Centre for Science and Environment, New Delhi.

Poffenberg, M (ed) (1990), *Forest Management Partnerships: Regenerating India's Forests*, Ford Foundation, New Delhi.

Report of the Commissioner for Scheduled Castes and Scheduled Tribes (1990), Twenty-Ninth Report, 1987–1989, New Delhi.

Rodda, A (1991), *Women and the Environment*, Women and World Development Series, Zed Books, London.

Sarin, M (1994), 'Leaving the women in the woods', *Down to Earth*, September.

Shiva, Vandana (1989), *Staying Alive*, Zed Books, London.

SPWD (Society for the Promotion of Wastelands Development) (1992), *Joint Forest Management: Concept and Opportunities. Proceedings of the National Workshop held at Surajkund*, August.

Thekaerkara, M M (1991), 'Undermining tribal culture?', *Economic and Political Weekly*, 5–12 January, p 26.

Viegas, P and G Menon (1991), *Forest Protection Committees of West Bengal: Role and Participation of Women*, ILO Workshop on Women and Wasteland Development, Geneva.

The World Bank (1994), *World Tables*, The World Bank, Washington, DC.

VI

LOCAL DEVELOPMENT AND PARKS IN FRANCE[1]

Andréa Finger-Stich and Krishna B. Ghimire

Introduction

French rural society is undergoing profound social, economic, demographic and environmental transformations. While some of these changes have deep historical origins, others, such as high unemployment, are abrupt and relatively recent phenomena. This chapter attempts to analyse these transformations in rural society by examining recent evolution in the areas of work, culture and nature. It will consider their interrelations in the current context of rural crisis characterized by economic vulnerability of significant portions of the population, socio-cultural disintegration and degradation of the physical environment. For the many formal institutions which are concerned with these issues, durable solutions are increasingly difficult to find.

Protected areas cover nearly 10 per cent of the territory of France, and are still expanding (Figure 6.1). They affect the local resource use patterns and economic opportunities of over 2 million inhabitants (Ministry of Environment, 1993; Fédération des Parcs Naturels de France, 1993a). How are the natural resources included within protected areas utilized and managed? To what extent do parks protect nature, create employment and income, and vitalize local culture? What, if any, ideas and measures aim at fostering local development in and around protected areas? Who benefits and what are the principal conflicts of interest involved?

---

1 This chapter is a condensed version of the following book in French: Finger-Stich, A. and Ghimire, Krishna B., *Travail, Culture et Nature: Développement Local dans le Contexte des Parcs Nationaux et Naturels Régionaux en France*, l'Harmattan, Paris, forthcoming.

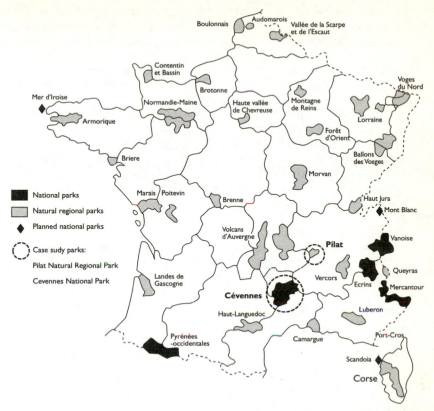

Source: Ministère de l'Environnement, direction de la Nature et des Paysages, 1992

Figure 6.1 *National and natural regional parks in France, 1992*

Study of the social impacts of protected areas has tended to focus mainly on developing countries, where the majority of the population is agrarian and highly dependent on the use of local natural resources. At the same time, the establishment of a protected area generally implies restrictions on the utilization of land, flora, fauna and most other resources found within its boundary. This frequently brings local populations into direct conflict with the park's administration, at times making it impossible to implement even limited conservation objectives (protection of flora and fauna, for example). The dominant protection agencies such as IUCN commonly note this dilemma in their strategic documents, but concrete policy measures are still mainly geared towards increasing areas under protection.

Many original attempts to combine nature conservation with local economic requirements have been attempted in France. The concept of peripheral development zones emerged in park management in France in

159

the 1960s, as did the innovative natural regional parks, which seek to integrate local economic, cultural and environmental needs in a more holistic manner. Since rural territories and populations are still numerically and economically — and to some extent politically — significant in France, the impact of parks, either national or regional, is a topical issue. With about half of the active rural population employed by industry, the French rural economy is suffering even more than urban areas as a result of current economic changes — in particular those related to the slow-down, displacement or automation trend of many industrial activities. Combined with a growing tendency on the part of the state to decrease its role in social provisioning, this 'rural crisis' is leading to a decline in the quality — and even the availability — of many public services such as schools, hospitals, roads and other infrastructure.

As an industrialized nation, France has considerable institutional and financial means to apply to the management of protected areas. It has confronted many difficult conceptual and practical policy issues. Conceptually, 'nature conservation' is largely a product of industrial society organized around service, commercial and consumer interests. Rural spaces are increasingly transformed to suit the leisure demands of urban populations. But the extent to which the establishment and management of protected zones can satisfy the employment and income needs of the rural inhabitants remains to be seen.

Relations between Work, Culture and Nature

Even though the concepts of 'work', 'culture' and 'nature' are broad and abstract, they nonetheless reflect important interactions in each society. Such interactions determine the way different social groups are formed and relate to one another. They also characterize the social organization of production, reproduction, levels of living, exchange of knowledge and the quality of the local physical environment. The exact outcomes of these interactions vary from one society to another depending upon time, location, population characteristics and social relations.

For example, in the context of the current crisis, in particular rising levels of unemployment, the conception of 'work' has changed. When economic growth is sustained, the term 'work' is associated mainly with 'employment' or 'salaried income'. The mechanization and globalization of production, as well as the more recent economic difficulties in the public sector, have led to increasing unemployment, which affected 12.2 per cent of the economically active population in France in 1995. According to some projections, the rate of unemployment may increase to 14 per cent by the year 2000 (ILO, 1995:160). Unemployment has touched both the industrial and agricultural sectors. In 1954, the agricultural sector occupied 27 per cent of the active population; in 1990 it had been cut to a mere 5 per cent. As a consequence of this process, more and more rural people have found themselves in economically and socially precarious situations. The policy measures formulated and partially applied by the successive left- and right-wing governments have attempted to address the socially damaging consequences of unemployment through early retirement, work-sharing, part-time work, reduced weekly working hours, etc. (Gorz, 1980; 1988; Roustang, 1982; Sauvy, 1980; Perret, 1994).

During the years of economic growth and with the increased importance of wage labour as a means to secure people's livelihoods, the 'leisure society' expanded as well, with the availability of free time creating a demand for rural landscapes, as places to live or for recreation. However, rising rates of unemployment have meant increasing competition for job opportunities, requiring certain categories of the population to work even harder than before. For these groups, there is little free time. Agricultural employment in some ways is characteristic of this situation, although it is relatively independent and may partially satisfy consumption needs. Land-use and crop patterns must evolve to suit emerging demands. More importantly, farmers from areas outside intensively cultivated zones must increasingly undertake multi-production activities (agriculture combined with tourism, for example).

'Culture' is the overall interaction of an individual with her or his environment. It covers the mode of economic life, social organization and form of expression. UNESCO considers it to be a fundamental part of the vitality of each society (UNESCO, 1977; Dupuis, 1991). Culture shapes and distinguishes the urban and rural lifestyles, as well as the relations between them. The rural world, which is often seen as traditional and customary, has its own norms in terms of working habits, gender relationships and exclusion of outsiders. It also retains different natural resource use and protection patterns. Different cultures value certain landscapes and species, although perceptions of what is valuable continually change.

In particular, rural lives tend to be profoundly influenced by ideas, goods and services coming from urban areas. For example, the 'culture of mass consumption' has led to a commoditization of both rural culture and nature. Tourism based on the exploitation of rural landscapes, products and customs has grown rapidly in recent years. In parks, especially natural regional parks, tourism is seen as a solution to rural economic and environmental decline, and as a way to increase the value of the local cultural identity. In practice, such impacts have remained mixed at the best.

'Nature' is likewise open to varying interpretations. For many, it is analogous to 'physical environment'. Various branches of the natural sciences define nature on the basis of the quantity and quality of the flora, fauna and the physical environment outside of strong human influence. This 'detached' vision of nature does not generally correspond to the perception of French or European populations. The North American concept of wilderness is scarcely relevant to the European context. In France, the popular interpretation of 'nature' is associated with the notion of 'landscape', 'countryside' and 'patrimony', where human influence is believed to enhance nature's attributes (Schama, 1995).

'Nature' is, in fact, a social concept, with different cultures having different ways of viewing and comprehending it and thus appreciating its value. Cultural perceptions of the protection and use of nature have also changed over time. Nature which was seen by many as primarily a source of raw materials during the period of agricultural modernization and industrialization is now considered by others to have an intrinsic value (Serres, 1990). These ways of perceiving and portraying nature and natural resources have emerged mostly from urban social contexts.

What is the best way to protect nature and what specific choices does a given society have in terms of its use? These difficult questions cannot be separated from political decisions. For example, should a given area be made into a nature reserve or be utilized for livestock grazing and agriculture? Or should it rather be under wood or grassland? If wood growth is favoured, who can or cannot exploit the wood? And if grassland is vacated for the preservation of floral diversity, will it generate sufficient hay for the nearby livestock-breeder? Will the shepherd give up her or his traditional way of grazing, often involving the practice of annual burning of grass and transhumance, and agree to become dependent on public subsidies? And who should manage protected areas, and with what institutional and financial means? Such decisions cannot be left to specialists alone. The issue of nature protection implies that a certain mode of resource utilization and specific social groups are likely to be favoured over others. The important points are that possibilities should exist for negotiations among different groups to prevent damaging residents' and local workers' interests, and that just compensation should be offered when livelihoods and cultures are threatened. The case studies on the Cévennes and Pilat parks, discussed below, offer some answers to these complex questions.

Cévennes National Park and Pilat Natural Regional Park: General Social Contexts and Outcomes of Conservation

There are many different protected area regimes in France, with varying protection objectives and institutions in charge of implementing them. National parks and natural regional parks cover the greatest proportion of the national territory under some form of protection. Six national parks cover a total area of 1,257,488 hectares, of which 352,600 lie in central zones and 904,888 in peripheral zones (Ministry of Environment, 1993) (see Figure 6.1). They represent about 2 per cent of the national territory and are inhabited by 158,131 people. Under a July 1960 law, national parks were originally placed under the Ministry of Agriculture. Since 1971, the central zones of parks have been under the jurisdiction of the Ministry of the Environment. Numerous regional, departmental, municipal, ministerial and scientific officials make up the Administrative Council and Permanent Commission of the country's national parks. Binding regulations tend to be absent from the peripheral zones of national parks, where operations are based on contracts established with regional and local authorities.

There are currently 26 natural regional parks in France, covering 4,128,000 hectares or 7.5 per cent of the country's territory. These parks were home to 1,845,250 people in 1991. The first natural regional park was established in 1967. Like national parks, regional parks were originally administered by the Ministry of Agriculture, albeit through an affiliated body (DATAR — Délégation à l'Aménagement du Territoire et à l'Action Régionale). While their official establishment is confirmed after a period of ten years by the Ministry of the Environment, the initial establishment, consecutive management and most of their finances are the responsibility of regional, departmental and communal administrations. Natural Regional Parks (NRP) are co-ordinated by the National Federation of Natural Regional Parks (a non-governmental, non-profit organization); each is directed by a team (called a 'Syndicat Mixte') composed of representatives from different regional, departmental, city, municipal, professional and cultural agencies, and managed by 25 to 30 professionals. A contract or charter lays out the fundamental objectives of each park. Every three to five years, the members of the Syndicat Mixte agree on a management plan for the park (Fédération des Parcs Naturels de France, 1993a).

National and regional parks have varying institutional (administrative, legal and financial) means and concern different kinds of territories. National parks cover mostly uninhabited and secluded, often high-altitude, areas. Regional parks are strongly 'human-influenced' areas, where landscapes may not be as spectacular as those of national parks. National parks are concerned mainly with the protection of wildlife habitat or specific national landmarks, although research and some degree of tourism are allowed in all of them. The NRP have three objectives: protection of the environment, rational planning of land use and fostering of the region's economic and social development.

Cévennes National Park is one of the largest, most inhabited and most used national parks in the country (Figure 6.2). It is composed of a central zone of 91,416 hectares and a peripheral zone of 237,000 hectares. In 1992, some 600 people lived in the central mountainous area and 41,000 in the peripheral zones. Pilat Natural Regional Park, albeit one of the smallest NRPs at 65,000 hectares, is representative of the general management style and outcomes of regional parks in the country (Figure 6.3). In 1989 some 39,254 people inhabited the park. Furthermore, the proximity of the major cities of Lyon and St Etienne allows the study of economic, political and cultural relationships between urban and rural constituencies.

Cévennes National Park

The idea of establishing a park in the Cévennes preceded the 1960 law on national parks. Proposals date back to the 1930s, when reforestation in the region around Mount Aigoual was begun 'in order to develop wood resources and tourism which could thrive on the expansion of forests' (*Revue Trimestrielle Club Cévenol*, 1992:138). The economic difficulties of the region were increasing with the decline in silk and chestnut production, and mining. A few local elites, mainly physicians, lawyers, teachers and university professors, pursued the idea of establishing a national park. Some proposed a large forested park, while others favoured the idea of a cultural park which would value the local customs, landscapes and architectural patrimony (ibid.). The local population was more immediately concerned with protecting their livelihoods. Mistrustful of both the elites and the national parks legislation, the Cévenol population resisted the establishment of the park for several years. When a regional referendum in 1969 finally brought together a small majority of voices in favour of the establishment of the Cévennes national park, several compromises for the use of the resources of the park were necessary. For example, people were allowed to remain inside the park. Peasants were promised support for improvement of their crop and livestock production. Their access to the park for collecting forest products, and fishing and hunting was also partly granted. However, the establishment of the park produced no immediately measurable benefits, and with management of the park going to outside administrators and some of the local elite, some residents felt alienated from their resources and cultural roots.

Over the last thirty years, the style of park management has undergone many compromises and changes. The Biosphere Reserve in the park, which includes the Galeizon Valley, has initiated a project aiming at a better integration of conservation and development. The valley suffers high unemployment and agricultural decline, but is nevertheless used for various agricultural, pastoral, fishery and forest related needs. The valley's natural wealth is relatively well-preserved, and it offers some cultural attractions and thus benefits from some tourist frequentation.

Agricultural decline has touched all areas of the park. Mechanization has led to reduced agricultural employment and growing competition from larger farmers for the lower altitude and flatter land areas. Smaller farmers have been forced to adopt more diverse forms of production. Farmers in the Galeizon Valley have combined cow and beef rearing with poultry, or with goat and pork, for example. Off-farm, part-time employment has also become crucial for household subsistence, as has out-migration for work and better living conditions in urban areas, which has led to a decrease in the valley's population.

Work and agriculture in the Cévennes region are becoming increasingly diverse. 'One needs to be able to do everything and to change when the wind turns direction', said one interviewee from the area.

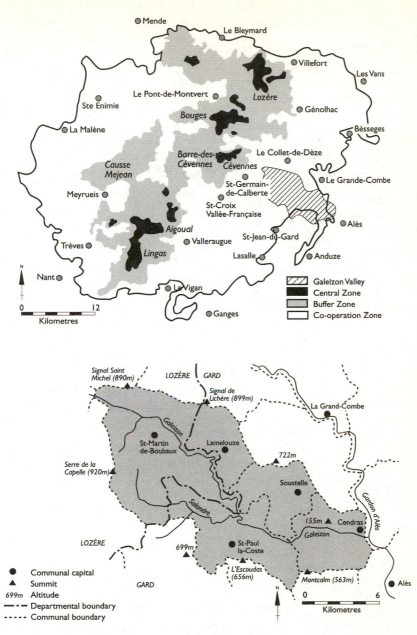

Source: Réserve de la Biosphère des Cévennes, and SIVU - Aménagement de la vallée du Galeizon, *La Vallée du Galeizon, un Projet de Conservation et de Développement*, leaflet, undated.

Figure 6.2 *Cévennes National Park and the Galeizon Valley*

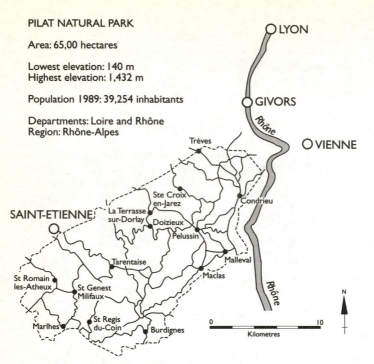

PILAT NATURAL PARK

Area: 65,00 hectares

Lowest elevation: 140 m
Highest elevation: 1,432 m

Population 1989: 39,254 inhabitants

Departments: Loire and Rhône
Region: Rhône-Alpes

Source: Parc Naturel Règional du pilat, *Circuit des artistes*, Pelussin, 1994

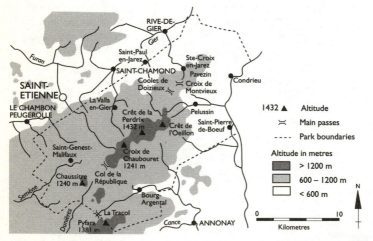

Source: Parc Naturel Règional du pilat, *Connaissance grandeur nature*, Pelussin, 1994

Figure 6.3 *Pilat Natural Regional Park: elevations*

166

Most farmers in both the central and peripheral zones of the park own little land, much of which is often infertile and inaccessible. Many keep sheep or goats and use rented land, or informally borrowed fields, to cover their pasture and hay needs. Some are also attempting to earn income from tourism.

Pilat Natural Regional Park

This regional park, created in 1974, is situated in the department of Loire and Rhône. Over 2 million people live within 50 kilometres of the park's boundaries, and the park itself is relatively populated, with a density of about 73 persons per square kilometre. It has nevertheless conserved a rural character. The communes closer to urban areas have tended to grow, while the most remote are losing population (Parc Naturel Régional du Pilat, 1993).

Forests cover about 30 per cent of the surface of the park, but their economic exploitation is low. Agriculture is diversified and spread throughout the territory of the park. Land around an altitude of 1000 metres is used mostly for livestock rearing and pasture. The north-east plain is used for market gardening and for arboriculture. The south and west slopes reaching down to the Rhône river are used for viticulture and arboriculture (including peach and apple trees).

The Pilat area has a long history of industrial and crafts development. It was particularly known for its textile industries, steelworks and sawmills which ran on local hydrological power. Nowadays, plastic, automobile and agro-food industries have become the dominant sectors. On the other side of the Rhône stands the nuclear plant of St Maurice l'Exil, which uses the river water for its cooling system. Next to it lie the facilities belonging to the petrochemical enterprise Rhône-Poulenc, which in recent years has offered no new employment opportunities.

According to the park's administration, less than 10 per cent of the park's population seeks outside employment. Most of the economically active population (33.2 per cent) are registered as being labourers in construction, textile production, mechanics, plastics or wood-working. The second largest group (15.9 per cent) are registered as cultivators (Parc Naturel Régional du Pilat, 1994:19).

The park's administration has attempted to improve land use, provide architectural restoration and construct new infrastructure. Another priority of the park has been to develop the capacity of the region to attract more tourism by offering information and cultural activities and by advising the private sector on accommodation, sports and other services. The park's administration favours small units and leisure activities which require little resource input, allow a wide distribution of costs and benefits among the population, and have limited effects on the natural environment.

The park has also supported local agriculture in a variety of ways. With limited financial means, the park has been modifying its role from one of allocating funds to one of counselling on organization, harmonization of land and other natural resources use, improvement of the quality of production and development of product marketing. One of the main actions of the park has been to support about 50 cultivators exploiting 350 hectares of orchards (producing 5000 tons of apples) in the organization of the building and management of a co-operative to stock and process the fruit. The apples are marketed under a legally protected label which certifies their origin and quality (Fédération des Parcs Naturels de France, 1989:160).

The park's administration is seeking to open an industrial museum and endow a prize for new industries in the park which adapt their structures and activities to the local architectural and natural surroundings. The park also helps new enterprises in the region to get acquainted with local institutions and to make contacts for building business partnerships.

The park supports a diversity of cultural activities, including the creation of small-scale 'eco-museums', and the organization of musical events and exhibits. For example, the *Maison de l'Eau* ('House of Water'), which presents the principal characteristics of local ecology, and the natural water resource system in particular, is part of a national network of environmental centres. The *Maison de l'Eau* also provides training and work experience in waterway maintenance, landscape design, erosion prevention, etc.

Local Level Social Impacts

In the context of local development in rural areas, the primary, secondary and service sectors must be seen as interdependent. These sectors depend on — and influence — their region's environment. Agricultural activities are a force in shaping rural landscapes and other local economic activities, especially tourism. The development of tourism depends upon public and private investments, which are in part derived from industrial development — even in rural areas. The industrial sector relies on local services, such as education, communications and financial transactions, which rely in turn on local tourism, and industrial and agricultural activities. Furthermore, in addition to land and housing taxes, the income of local municipalities depends to a large extent on the earnings of local industrial, service and agricultural enterprises.

Indeed, whether due to its intrinsic — 'existence' — value (ecological, aesthetic or recreational) or because of the use value of its resources and functions, the natural environment is inseparable from the rest of the rural economy's fabric. Not only are farmers, fisherfolk, forest workers and landscapers dependent on the quality of the environment, so are architects, construction-related entrepreneurs, and the tourism industry (in commerce, hotels and sports), since people prefer to visit, live and work in a healthy and pleasant environment.

Even if agriculture does not seem to be a determinant sector (in terms of employment or economic effects), its cultural and environmental roles are crucial in rural localities. Agriculture is increasingly appreciated for maintaining and enhancing the aesthetic, ecological and recreational value of rural areas (Pisani, 1994). In national and regional parks this environmental maintenance function is often valued more than any productive role.

The Camargue Natural Regional Park, well known for the flocks of pink flamingos which gather there in the summer, also illustrates these interactions. The saline water favoured by these migratory birds results in part from nearby salt-works; the protection of the species thus rests on the controlled activity of this extractive industry. The nature reserve protects an economic asset as well: the numerous tourists attracted to the flamingos' breeding grounds.

Parks also create employment directly. Approximately 400 park guards and 350 other professionals work in natural regional parks in France (*L'Avenir*, 1990). Cévennes National Park employs 63 persons permanently and hires 20 additional workers in season. More indirect impacts on employment are important but more difficult to quantify.

The economic impact of a park is often measured by the extent to which it fosters tourism. During the 12 last years, for example, tourist visits to the Cévennes National Park have increased fourfold. Since 1990, there have been an estimated 600,000 visitors per year, about 25 per cent of whom remained in the region for 13–20 days. Park administration has estimated that visitors generate about 1200 workplaces (directly and indirectly) — that is, 30 per cent of the jobs in the service sector (Parc National des Cévennes, 1993). Tourism has not developed evenly throughout all areas of the park. In the peripheral zone, for example, tourism cannot compensate for the decline of the mining sector, which is considered a main reason for the area's unemployment rate. In Pilat Natural Regional Park, the unemployment rate of 7.7 per cent is lower than the departmental (Loire, 11.6 per cent) and regional (Rhône-Alpes, 8.9 per cent) rates (Parc Naturel Régional du Pilat, 1994:7). These figures should be interpreted with caution as rural unemployment tends to be exported to urban areas, where people go to seek jobs or educational opportunities.

The impacts of parks on the agricultural sector vary from case to case. According to the administration of the Cévennes National Park, for example, the process of local agricultural decline has slowed down. The 83 farms in its central zone receive subsidies for renovations and to host tourists in some cases. The number of farms in the central zone has declined less dramatically (23 per cent) than in the peripheral zone (45 per cent) over the past 20 years. In Pilat Natural Regional Park the cultivated area of small farms (less than five hectares) doubled between 1979 and 1988, indicating the growing importance of farming as a part-time economic activity. This social phenomenon — called 'pluriactivity' — has been observed more frequently close to urban areas (Lyon and St Etienne). It is often the young, more dynamic, quite mechanized and educated farmers who adopt this means to earn their living. Pilat has encouraged this trend to keep farms functioning. In the more isolated areas of the south of the park, which are still predominantly agrarian, there is less pluriactivity, as well as a higher rate of out-migration.

Both national and European agricultural policies tend generally to be less supportive of the attempts of small- and medium-sized farmers to survive through the diversification of their economic activity. The European Common Agricultural Policy does, however, make a specific provision for agricultural support in remote and environmentally sensitive rural regions (Salvi, 1992; Goodmaker, 1988). Pilat Regional Park has undertaken an evaluation of 23 farms in the region to determine whether they are eligible for such subsidies.

While there is no co-ordinated agricultural policy for all natural regional parks, various means for maintaining local agriculture have been attempted. Some parks have encouraged farmers to form groups to acquire land. Others have worked to secure long-term use rights for farmers who rent land (Lamaison and Migault, 1989). Virtually all concentrate on using communal land zoning laws to safeguard agricultural land, while only occasionally renting or buying land themselves for conservation. Most parks have contributed some funds or provided advice to farmers for restoring their land and farming capital, and when possible have encouraged the younger generation to take over the farms of their parents (Fédération des Parcs Naturels de France, 1989).

Conflicts over Utilization, Representation and Property Claims

The 'value' of protected areas is often determined by urban culture and the perceived need for 'natural' areas. Urban perceptions of rurality depict a serene world to be used for leisure purposes (Bodiguel, 1986). Residents of urban areas — often backed by scientific and urban institutions — often claim the right to define and defend the 'common good' they see in rural and pristine areas. This claim is generally perceived by residents of rural areas as alienation.

Use Conflicts

As mentioned above, national and natural regional parks have very different policies regarding the use of their territories. National parks restrict use to preserve ecosystems, fauna and flora. These use restrictions concern the construction of infrastructure, intensive agricultural activity, hunting and gathering, and sometimes mass tourism. This approach to conservation can lead to conflicts between protection and the interests of local users. Such conflicts emerge less often in natural regional parks, where resource use is less restricted.

Pilat Natural Regional Park and, to some extent, the Cévennes National Park seek to maintain and enhance landscapes with existing settlements and populations and to contribute to the social (economic and cultural) development of their regions. According to the charter of the Pilat NRP, its objective is to become a zone of 'rural development where the population can progressively enjoy conditions of life equivalent to those in urban areas'. It emphasizes the need to invest in local infrastructure, the development of agricultural and cottage industries, and improvement of leisure opportunities (Parc Naturel Régional du Pilat, 1991).

But such an integrated approach is difficult to implement. A study conducted in the peripheral zone of the Cévennes National Park (the Galeizon Valley) has shown a decrease in agricultural land due to pressure from regular visitors constructing secondary residences. Between 1975 and 1990, such residences have almost doubled, representing 60 per cent of the area's housing. While farmers use about 25 per cent of the valley's land under more or less formalized user rights, they own only about 4 per cent of the valley's land. As demand for secondary residences puts upward pressure on local land and housing prices, local farmers feel pressure to sell on the one hand, and, on the other, are priced out of the market if they want to purchase land for agricultural use. The decline of cultivated land is an obvious consequence (Montero, 1991:68).

In the Cévennes National Park, a joint development and conservation programme for the Galeizon Valley has been developed by specialists and administrators from the UNESCO Man and Biosphere Programme, the park and the intercommunal authorities and local professional-cultural organizations. It addresses use conflicts and studies ways to encourage tourism while respecting local people's agriculture, forestry, fishing, hunting and gathering activities. It provides information to visitors on how to prevent fire hazards and damage to flora and fauna caused by picking and trampling. The programme also seeks to adapt land zoning policies in order to mitigate pressures on agricultural land, and on housing availability and prices.

The development of 'green tourism' aimed at complementing the shrinking revenues of farming communities can be difficult to implement. This kind of tourism takes place mostly in the summer, which coincides with an intense working time for farmers. The task of welcoming visitors and guests often falls to the female members of farming households, in addition to their other tasks. Of course, farming households benefit from their contacts with visitors, breaking the isolation of remote rural areas.

Differing Perceptions of Nature

Conflicting urban and rural perceptions and ways of portraying 'nature' are embedded in the various ideologies of 'conservation' and in the institutions which are meant to carry out such conservation initiatives. An idealized rural lifestyle and environment provide cultural roots to urban populations which are increasingly unsettled by rapid change and weakening community ties. This view of rural areas — as open, underdeveloped spaces — justifies their use by urban people and institutions for experimentation or as a resource for the realization of their projects and dreams. Indeed, a document of the co-ordinating organization of the natural regional parks refers to these areas as 'laboratories' for rural development policies (Fédération des Parcs Naturels de France, 1993b).

The conservation movement is generally composed of members of the middle class who are not directly involved in industrial and commercial work but are, nevertheless, both a product of modernization and promoters of its development through provision of technical and organizational skills — functionaries, technocrats, teachers and professors (Angeli, 1992). These socio-professional categories have the administrative power to institute regulatory measures and generally reinforce their own stakes by doing so. Opposing this official, rational or managerial stance of conservationists, local people have often developed other means to express their own perceptions, and disregard 'superior' objectives and knowledge.

One interesting colloquial illustration of such differences in perceptions has been reported in the Cévennes National Park. Residents do not always feel comfortable with the introduction of wild species like the lynx, vultures, eagles or the bear. Snakes are also considered dangerous or pests by most people. Shortly after a law was passed to protect vipers, a strange story began to circulate in the Cévennes, with people claiming that helicopters had been seen dropping boxes of vipers in the region. Park administrators have refuted this claim, and tried to find some explanation for the general confusion that the story has brought about among the population. In their version of the story, boxes called *Vibert* — sold in shops for use as worm containers for fishing — have been discarded along waterways in the area, leading to the misunderstanding (Campion-Vincent, 1988)!

Property Claims

In national parks, which are legally authorized to impose restrictions and to take over ownership in the central zones, the power or threat of constraint is real. With the exception of the Cévennes National Park, however, relatively few people live in the central zones of French national parks. Also, many protected areas have often been under some form of common property regime. For instance, the Vanoise National Park is mostly glacier, rock and some high altitude pastures; only 10 per cent of the central zone is under private property. The administration of that park has avoided disappropriating local pasture owners, preferring to rent their fields out if over-grazing became a problem (Lebreton, 1988:286). In the Cévennes National Park, however, where 60 per cent of the central zone belongs to private owners, the relationship between the administration and the farmers is indeed much tighter. The park subsidizes farmers to remain in activity, acknowledging that the landscapes they seek to conserve are the result of the residents' work and culture (Beede, 1992).

The national parks are confronted daily with dilemmas regarding property rights and conflicts over use claims (Parc National des Pyrénées, 1986; Faujas, 1994). The national parks derive much of their legitimacy from their claim to act according to scientific criteria, and their ability to implement this claim with support and backing from the government. National parks thus tend to adopt a rather legalistic and restrictive management approach, leading to 'problem solving' through compensation rather than negotiation and conflict resolution.

Natural regional parks tend to work with a larger population of residents and have fewer legal and financial resources to back their policies or ownership claims over the territory. Their style of management tends to emphasize negotiation and agreement among the local social actors. While private property — privately owned forests, for instance — may hamper the implementation of protection policies, Natural Regional Parks have no choice but to abandon their claim or to negotiate some form of joint management. Nevertheless, the ideological and institutional history of the conservation movement does also influence the management style of the Natural Regional Parks. As discussed below, Pilat Natural Regional Park showed little aptitude for encouraging the active participation of local associations.

Local Development: Evolving Views and Experiences

This section looks at how the concept of 'local development' has evolved, how it has been embraced by various social movements and ideologies, and how different parks have attempted to integrate it into their conservation programmes. The — sometimes dramatic — changes in the natural environment have often led to criticism of the processes of modernization. Conservation and environmental movements have built upon such criticism in a variety of ways. Some of the distinctions and commonalties between the century-old conservation approach and more recent social movements — in particular the associative movements of the 1930s, the 1968 movement, the anti-nuclear and peace movements, and the environmental movement from the 1970s on — will be considered briefly below.

The Administrative, Aesthetic and Naturalistic Approach to Conservation

The conservation movement has been shaped and strengthened by a convergence of administrative, aesthetic and naturalistic interests in nature. The 'administrative' interest in nature is based on the management of natural resources for the long-term development of the nation. The aesthetic interest seeks preservation of nature as a basis for cultural identity and as a source of creative inspiration. The naturalistic approach views nature as a collection of species, as a subject for scientific observation. The establishment of protected areas, lists of protected species, or regulations concerning the use of land, water and forest resources depends on the interplay of all three interests. At the same time, natural resources are required as inputs for industrial production. As those resources are limited, the state's role is to enact policies not only to further the economic growth of the nation but also to control the use of resources. For example, the French Ordinance of 1669 regulated the use of forests and water. It encouraged the planting of coniferous species, forbade pastoral fires and attempted to prevent erosion through the control of logging in mountain forests. The Forestry Code of 1827 was similarly meant to ensure the sustainable yield of forests for their timber production as well as for their 'common good value', in order 'to protect the right of future generations to enjoy and ... to respect the distinction between personal and collective interest'. (Code Forestier 1827, cited in Lebreton, 1988:276)

Remarkably, the first protected areas established by the French government were in its colonies. In 1881, for example, France instituted a forestry code in Madagascar to sanction the use of forest land for shifting agriculture, and by 1926 a network of nature reserves had been established across the country (Ghimire, 1991). In 1921 in Algeria, the general governor of Northern Africa constituted 13 parks on a total surface area of 27,600 hectares. In 1923 the French government constituted protected zones in the Kergelen Islands, St Paul d'Amsterdam and the Crozet Archipelago. While other European and North American countries had been establishing parks and reserves since the turn of the century, it was not until 1957 that the law on nature reserves was written, and not until 1960 that the first national park was established on French national territory (Leynaud, 1985:21–22).

The aesthetic side of the conservation movement was strengthened with the opening of the Barbizon landscape school in 1853, which led to the establishment of the first nature reserve near Paris, called the Série Artistique de Fontainebleau. At that time, naturalists were also playing an important part in defining conservation theories. The Jardins d'Acclimatation, a botanical and zoological park in the Bois de Boulogne of Paris, was a place where natural scientists met to design conservation measures for the colonies — from which they collected many exotic species — and the metropolis. Ornithologists were among the first to exert pressure for the creation of protected areas to protect the nesting grounds of migratory birds. In 1912, the French League for the Protection of Birds constituted a reserve on the seven islands at Perros Guirec off the North Atlantic coast. This artistic and naturalistic approach was reflected in the first French conservation legislation. Until 1930, sites to be protected were designated 'natural monuments' — to justify their eventual expropriation — before becoming 'natural sites' (Fromageau, 1985). These first conservation endeavours thus came mostly from an urban (often Parisian) elite that was also greatly under the influence of romanticism. Jean-Jacques Rousseau, for example, was a regular solitary hiker of the forests of Fontainebleau, cultivating the myth of the 'brave savage', of nature cleansing humans from the influence of their corrupt society (Schama, 1995:538–546).

The Associative Movement and the Urban Middle Class

The idealization of landscapes of France and their role in contributing to the wealth and unique 'patrimony' of the nation have grown with the increasing importance of state institutions. First, the nation-state institutions were able to evoke this 'common patrimony' as a unifying concept to nurture patriotic feelings. Second, as we saw, a class of city-based civil servants used the idealization of landscapes to instil a sense of responsible citizenship during a period of accelerated industrialization and growth of the mass-leisure society. Beginning with a new employees' act in 1936 that instituted the right to paid holidays, national tourism was promoted and infrastructures were built to meet the economic means and tourism expectations of more or less every social class. Tourism long remained an overwhelmingly urban pastime and a way to return to the countryside where many urban people had family connections.

The law of 1901, which legitimized the formation of non-profit and non-governmental organizations, reinforced the associative movement. Associations have been increasingly active in the post-war years in supporting cultural and sporting events and in furthering social issues such as health, education, housing, social security, and occupational and environmental protection. Associations have been mostly grassroots and practice-oriented, based on voluntary, secular social action and thus a function of the material, time, mobility and organizational opportunities of their active members — mainly teachers and administrators from the urban middle class. Economic and public-sector growth have reinforced the movement. The associative movement is still strong in France, although it has suffered from the same limitations which are hampering the environmental movement, as we will see below.

May '68: a Critique of Dominant Values and Structures

What has become known as the May '68 movement was both political and cultural: political in contesting the élitism and cynicism of political power-holders; cultural in calling for a change in lifestyles and social values. May '68 challenged the existing hierarchical system as well as fundamental institutions such as marriage and family values. Many members of the movement were in favour of going back to a more simple, autonomous rural lifestyle. Between the late 1960s and the 1980s, the argument drew many young people to rural areas, where they settled in abandoned farms and tried to build communities and make a living from agriculture (Léger and Hervier, 1979).

The Cévennes region saw thousands of these new migrants seeking to put their ideals in practice. Once they were settled they realized, however, that the rural area they imagined was suffering from agricultural decline and that the young rural people idealized urban comfort and were leaving for the city. The new inhabitants were often rejected by long-time rural residents who despised them as the spoiled and arrogant offspring of city-dwellers. Those who have remained in rural areas are still called the *néo-ruraux* ('new rural inhabitants'), which shows that their integration is not complete. Some of them have become more realistic about local problems and have become involved in local official institutions and grassroots organizations in order to improve the living conditions of the region. But in doing so they have established ties with — or themselves become members of — the local elite. Participating in protected-area initiatives was a way for the new rural populations to preserve rural areas according to their ideal perception, and to prevent their becoming like the urban area they had left behind. The May '68 movement explains in part why the conservation initiatives which developed in France during the 1970s had to integrate social issues — for the movement was only slightly influenced by the conservation ideology. Indeed, the environmental concerns emphasized by the movement — the nuclear menace and other threats to global survival — had little to do with the conservationists' concerns about natural resource scarcity and protection.

Recent Environmental Movements

Three main tendencies can be distinguished in environmental movements over the last twenty years or so. First, scientific ecology, which is closest to the conservation approach described above. Second, associative grassroots environmentalism, which builds on the legacy of issue-focused local voluntary associations. Third, the political ecology movement, which presents a wider social critique of modernization. These three tendencies have grown quite separately, each with its respective constituency. By the end of the 1980s, while the environmental discourse had become both more widely diffused and more mainstream, the scientific, technocratic conservation approach had achieved the most importance. Associative grassroots environmentalism and political ecology, on the other hand, had lost influence.

Yet the great conservation institutions such as the World Conservation

Union (IUCN) and the World Wide Fund For Nature (WWF) are claiming to be becoming more socially orientated, while still retaining rather restrictive nature conservation approaches. Environmental concerns in France have tended to remain limited to 'greening cities' — building in more filters and security measures in factories — or zoning land use — for supposedly 'efficient management' of natural resources — or fencing off some areas for their 'protection'. The conservation approach is pushed to its extreme when all values of nature are expressed in monetary terms — as illustrated by the current popularity of cost/benefit analyses. The state and the major economic forces (often multinational enterprises) are attempting to use the current environmental and social crises to strengthen their control of land, water, mineral, biological or genetic resources, as well as labour. The institutions which bear a great responsibility in these crises are now claiming to be the healers.

Because French culture — persisting in defending its identity for better or worse — has tended to evolve quite separately from international trends and debates, it has been less marked by the preservationist (now often called deep ecologists) versus conservationist debate prevalent in Anglo-Saxon countries, or the *realos* versus *fundis* splitting the Greens in Germany. The French have generally remained outside such intellectual debates from abroad. On a positive note, they have also remained less trapped in these often sterile dichotomies, and could thus more easily foster a more integrated and pragmatic approach to local development. In France, the distinction between more strictly protected areas such as national parks and less strictly protected areas — but socially more viable formula — such as regional parks, shows that the preservationist claim does not hold either. In practice, the preservationist approach is both too regressive and too restrictive — and national parks, as an expression of the preservationist approach, can only remain islands. Natural regional parks, on the other hand, have become a social experience which is more applicable to vast areas of territory and to changing overall social relationships between work, culture and nature.

'Local Development' in Practice

The concept of local development has evolved as an alternative for integrating more social and environmental criteria in economic development objectives — essentially by adapting them to local circumstances. In the 1970s, 'local development' was associated with interpretations such as Ernest Schumacher's book *Small is Beautiful*. The concept has been tried out in many local communities in France as well as in Third World countries as an alternative to mega-infrastructures and centralized modes of decision-making. In the 1980s, in the French context in particular, 'local development' was used more often as an official discourse on rural and regional development than as a true effort to decentralize the political and economic forces of the country. Laws were passed in 1982 giving considerable power to municipalities in matters of urbanization and over-all land zoning procedures. In the 1990s, the concept of local development is being used in a quite different social context (Biarez, 1989). It has become relevant to people who are experiencing the social and environmental crisis and are realizing that large institutions lack the means to deal with such problems. French rural populations, farmers in particular, have been politically active in defending their views on agricultural and rural development (Mendras, 1976). This dynamism was recently expressed during the GATT negotiations and the European Common Agricultural Policy resolutions (Pisani, 1994; Seibel, 1994). Local development was thus associated with self-help and cultural identity as counter-forces to cultural and political-economic globalization which affect livelihoods while being beyond the control of individuals and local communities.

Local development does not correspond to a social movement. It is a pragmatic, adaptive approach to social action. It aims at reinforcing collective exchange and negotiation by assembling and organizing the social actors of a given area, defining their common interests and complementary competencies. It is a holistic approach favouring integrated solutions which build upon a territory's or population's particular capacities. Local development goes beyond economic development — as it is too often defined on a national scale (GDP growth) — in order to adapt social and environmental development processes to the local territory and population. According to the National Federation of Natural Regional Parks: 'The territory is considered as a space of life, a basis for multiple activities, a system of resources and of actors ... the notion is better apprehended in a systemic logic than in a purely economic one.' (Fédération des Parcs Naturels de France, 1989: 187).

But, where the local begins and where it ends is a relative question, particularly in the context of globalization. And what does the territory mean to the people who reside in it, while their livelihood and many of their cultural references stem from outside that territory? Can local development foster intolerance towards social diversity? Can or should the rural areas develop apart from the urban perceptions and demands on that territory? Has the regional patrimony been enriched by exchanges throughout history with many parts of the world? Recognition of the uniqueness of this convergence of different influences in rural areas is fundamental to convince local people to invest in their region.

The local development project in the Galeizon Valley designed with the collaboration of the central administration of the Cévennes National Park, the Man and Biosphere Programme of UNESCO and local municipalities emphasizes the following areas for action: job creation, affordable housing, local services and commerce, local associations, local communication, agricultural and forestry development, controlled development of tourism, conservation and valorization of the patrimony, and management of water resources. In implementing the first area for action, the programme begins with an evaluation of local employment in order to seek new ways to develop local resources and job opportunities (Montero, 1991; Réserve de la Biosphère des Cévennes, et SIVU – Aménagement de la Vallée du Galeizon, undated). This experience seems to be unique in the context of national parks in France.

A second illustration of how local development is put into practice can be seen in the conditions being set by the National Federation of Natural Regional Parks for new regions seeking NRP status. An NRP needs 'to be a territory of fragile equilibrium and of a rich natural and cultural patrimony'. Furthermore, the conditions set by the law emphasize that natural regional parks must:

1   protect the patrimony by an adapted management of the natural milieu;
2   contribute to the economic and social development of this territory within the conditions fixed by the laws concerning the right and freedom of action of communes' department and region;
3   promote education and information of the public;
4   realize experimental and exemplary actions in the above cited matters and contribute to research programmes (Art. 1, Décret no. 88–443, 25 April 1988).

Generally speaking, the priorities of natural regional parks are rural renovation, development of tourism and the protection of the environment (Lebreton, 1988:230). There are nevertheless considerable disparities between these wide-ranging objectives of local development and their actual implementation. Natural Regional Parks and, to a more limited extent, national parks, seem to emphasize the development of tourism in integrating the protection and improvement of the natural environment with local development. Small-scale tourism in particular is seen as a means to support farmers by providing them with some extra revenue opportunities.

It may also be difficult for parks to reconcile local development and conservation because of the multiple institutions defending their special interests in a given region. The ministries of agriculture, forestry, culture, energy and transportation all have regional and/or departmental representatives with their own agenda. When the administration of a park — a natural regional park or the peripheral zone of a national park — seeks to integrate its environmental policy in all these areas, it needs to meet the agreement of numerous actors.

The difficulty with integrating the protection of nature with social development is particularly obvious in the national parks and their territorial division into central and peripheral zones (Faujas, 1994). Some administrators of the Cévennes and the Vanoise National Parks were trying to work with a more integrated concept like the 'big park' or 'park space', to avoid the term of 'peripheral' zone, which defines the inhabited territory in relation to the 'superior' unpopulated and pristine central zone. In order to increase their say in the communities of the periphery, national parks would have to adopt a more co-operative management approach similar to that in natural regional parks, but the institutional history of national parks cannot be undone. Contrary to natural regional parks, which are only adopted once the concerned communes and regions formally agree on a contract, national parks can only propose ad hoc negotiation. National parks have been adopting a compensatory approach when addressing the livelihood questions that some of their environmental policies imply for local people. Natural regional parks, on the other hand, are obliged to discuss the content of their environmental policies with the concerned actors — mainly municipalities and regional administrations — in order to avoid harming the interests of local residents and users.

The Role of Parks in the Context of Decentralization and Participation: Potential and Limitations

The aim of the decentralization policies being implemented since 1982 has been to reduce interregional disparities, and 'to entrust competency to authorities which are closer to the citizens, who will therefore be able to call them to account' (Giblin, 1994:194). In practice, however, the country's 36,000 municipalities, which are the main beneficiaries of these decentralization policies, are often hardly accountable to the people who elect them every six years. Decentralization measures are in some cases slowing down the widening of interregional disparities, but are barely able to prevent them altogether. For those who work in the area of environmental protection, the increased power of the municipalities — particularly in matters of urbanization — is making their work even more difficult. The regulatory approach to environmental protection necessitates well co-ordinated (if not centralized) institutions.

The disadvantages of decentralization policies are thus increasingly recognized and the constitution of larger administrative and management units is again being encouraged by the state. But intercommunal organizations also have problems ensuring transparency and participation, and may also be open to corruption (Paringaux, 1994). In the Marais de Poitevin Natural Regional Park in western France, a conflict between the intercommunal syndicate (SIVOM) and the park's administration led to the dismantling of the latter and the end of a local users' institution which had existed for over a century. The SIVOM — with the support of larger governmental institutions including the Ministry of Agriculture — was defending land- and water-use management policies based on private property that favoured intensive agriculture in a certain area of the park. The park's administration, on the contrary, was attempting to accommodate local users' varied interests, seeking to defend commons used as temporary pastures, and as fish and crustacean nursery territories, and to maintain the overall diversity of the ecosystem valued as a tourist attraction. In order to de-legitimize the park's administration, the SIVOM exploited local perceptions of the park's management as an outsider group of ecologists disappropriating residents. It is likely that the SIVOM won the case also in large part because it is easier to value private interests than common property resources.

The French NRPs are an original conservation institution because the request for their establishment comes from regional and communal institutions. These institutions together with concerned professionals have often had a hard time following contradictory and inconsistent national policies, on land use in particular. For instance, the drying of wetlands had long been subsidized until some of these areas became protected. The planting of forests was encouraged by cutting taxes on forested land, but there was no policy to avoid the planting of (mostly all-coniferous) monocultures, to consider the surrounding land uses and landscapes, or to develop means to commercialize the wood (Groupe de Recherche pour l'Education et la Prospective, 1988). Moreover, the role of NRP administrations was reduced to complying with those policies, while trying to mitigate their contradictions or to complement them with more locally adapted measures. For example, Pilat Natural Regional Park encouraged forest co-operatives in order to favour deciduous trees and to support joint investments in the infrastructure needed for the maintenance and exploitation of forests. The park has, of course, no influence on the market forces which may make the exploitation of wood economically unattractive. It can, however, facilitate the commercialization of wood products by supporting enterprises making furniture or toys out of the locally grown wood — as was done in Vercors Natural Regional Park (Fédération des Parcs Naturels de France, 1982).

Both national and natural regional parks resemble state institutions in their methods of operation. Both also work closely with the public sector at regional and departmental levels.

> *A NRP is a hybrid institution ... it is difficult to tell whether it is hiding state objectives concerning environmental and rural development, or whether it is — as its mode of functioning seems to indicate an emanation of the local counsellors — one of the places where there is an autonomous exercise of local power. (Billaud, 1986:14)*

While the financial contribution of communes to a NRP's budget is on average only 20 per cent (the main share coming from the region and the department), the municipalities remain the principal counterparts of NRPs.

Because NRPs depend upon a variety of local and regional institutions, because they work mainly with non-binding regulatory instruments, and because their budgets are renegotiated every five years, their 'conserva-

181

tion' approaches and policies are a good example of intercommunal compromise. They tend to go beyond practical managerial and economic considerations, and to take a long-term perspective on the overall development of the region. This type of cross-institutional activity can also improve their accountability. However, it is possible that NRPs may tend to focus too much attention and effort on more official, secure institutions, and thus neglect local residents and their non-governmental organizations. For example, some local associations, such as the Association des Agriculteurs du Parc du Pilat, have dissolved. This could be because they realized that the park was not going to harm their particular interests, but may also be because they were not given an active or independent role in the management of the park. The melting of all the local associations in one pot, under the name Association des Amis du Parc (Friends of the Park), reveals the lack of autonomy granted to them.

In establishing parks, territorial considerations may take precedence over the needs and concerns of the residents — for geographic zones may not correspond to social and economic units. Indeed, purely conservation objectives — which quite often would justify large parks — might be ill-adapted to social development criteria.

Conclusions

Sustaining economic lives, valuing regional culture, and protecting species and ecosystems is a complex task. Must nature be protected under any circumstances, even at the expense of social considerations? The above discussion shows that dominant institutions cannot remain indifferent to the problems of unemployment, agricultural decline and of population loss in rural regions. As social institutions, parks are not an exception. In the present crisis, the institutions related to the state and to the market are anxious to affirm their influence or legitimacy, although they are often ill-prepared to confront the problems facing rural populations in diverse contexts in France.

We have tried to demonstrate how the French park administrations have attempted to link the protection of nature with local development. On the one hand, the national parks have promoted inhabited 'peripheral zones'. On the other hand, the natural regional parks have attempted to go beyond the restrictive conservation approach by promoting forms of development that are more adapted to local social and environmental realities. National parks have found the task relatively difficult in their peripheral zones, where their regulatory and compensatory tools are pushed to their limits.

In the case of natural regional parks, however, the notions of 'culture' and 'nature' are more closely integrated. Although economic and political realities make their full implementation extremely difficult, regional parks seem to have beneficial impacts on rural economies since their numbers are still increasing. Their common underlying idea is to discourage the build-up of heavy infrastructure and to develop a more diversified economy, compatible with the maintenance of the local quality of life and regional landscapes. Tourism is frequently seen as a prime tool of this kind of development, especially in view of compensating the decline in agriculture and reviving craftsmanship. It is argued that the ecological and cultural impacts of small-scale tourism in natural regional parks are more benign than large-scale tourism, and that it is potentially more socially just since its economic benefits are more widely distributed among the resident population.

Tourism is, however, not a panacea; it is hardly a remedy for the most profound causes of the decline in agricultural activities on small and medium holdings. Development of the necessary physical infrastructure to receive tourists requires substantial financial investment (for construction of accommodation), training and time (for administration, reception, housekeeping, cooking, etc.). At the same time, the tourism season coincides with the period in which there is a great demand for work on the land and with the animals.

It is difficult to determine the precise impacts of parks on employment, culture and the protection of ecosystems. To begin with, the territories included in the parks are under the influence of a multitude of other institutions in addition to the administration of the park. It is not easy to distinguish the impacts on the local economy, culture and the environment of these institutions from the impacts of the park. Parks also do not systematically follow social tendencies within their boundaries, such as the trends on demographic dynamics and employment.

Although the approach of natural regional parks, in particular, is better adapted to the local division of responsibilities and negotiation of compromises with other institutions, these parks do not quite succeed in attracting the active participation of the resident population in the regular park management or in determining wider social objectives within its territory. Similarly, although the natural regional parks are frequently found associated with various professional and cultural organizations and administrative units at regional, departmental and communal levels, many of the activities of these latter institutions, especially in the areas of urbanization, infrastructure building and commerce, are not always transparent, nor are they necessarily compatible with the environmental, cultural and social goals desired by the local populations or defined by the parks. Also, the priorities of residents and local workers may differ from those of the park and from those of these various institutions.

The 20 years of experience of natural regional parks nevertheless reveals an approach rich in interesting lessons. Other industrialized countries, such as Germany and Great Britain (see Chapters III and IV in this volume), and Scandinavia (Nissi, 1995), have tended to emphasize compensation of affected individuals and groups rather than compromise in establishing and managing protected areas. The experience of the natural regional parks goes beyond the provision of compensations. It makes local development an inseparable objective of the protection of the natural and cultural 'patrimony'.

It may be recalled that France played an important role in the creation of the IUCN in 1948. Its influence has receded in favour of a more Anglo-Saxon, conservation-oriented management style that has not favoured promoting approaches like the natural regional park. The financial, ideological and political powers of IUCN in the area of protected-area management are well known, but this and many other dominant environmental organizations, such as WWF, are on the whole engaged in promoting a more restrictive approach to conservation. The critique of the conservation ideology in the context of the institutional history and cultural background presented above helps us to understand why such influential institutions have preferred to pursue a more restrictive approach.

To sum up, it can be said that even if their financial, technical and policy inputs in local development projects are relatively modest, the social impacts of parks in France are in most cases positive. The French parks (and those in other industrialized countries) do not come under pressure from the surrounding peasant populations, as they often do in developing countries. While their prime function remains 'decoration' of rural landscapes for recreational purposes, regional parks in particular nevertheless address the socio-economic difficulties characteristic of rural areas. Given the current social crisis in France, including unemployment, agricultural decline, growing social marginalization, reduced public social provisioning and a deteriorating physical environment, the social purposes of natural resource use and protection need to be reflected upon and debated more openly. Further adoption of the approach taken in the French natural regional parks would not lead to a slackened capacity to protect nature; on the contrary, it could contribute to longer-term and possibly larger-scale social and environmental repair through 'local development'.

References

Angeli, Franco (1992), *La Natura in Vetrina: le Basi Sociali del Consenso per i Parchi Naturali*, Casa Editrice Osti G — Franco Angeli, Milan.

L'Avenir (1990), 'L'Environnement: Emploi et formation' (special edition), No 415, juin, pp 1–69.

Beede, Susan (1992), 'Le Parc National des Cévennes' in Patrick West and Steven Brechin, *Resident Peoples and National Parks: Social Dilemmas and Strategies in International Conservation*, The University of Arizona Press, Tucson.

Biarez, Sylvie (1989), *Le Pouvoir Local*, Economica, Paris.

Billaud, Jean-Paul (1986), 'L'Etat en perspective: l'Etat nécessaire: aménagement et corporatisme dans le Marais de Poitevin', *Etudes Rurales*, Nos 101–102, January-February, pp 73–111.

Bodiguel, Maryvonne (1986), *Le Rural en Question: Politiques et Sociologues en Quête d'Objet*, L'Harmattan, Paris.

Campion-Vincent, Véronique (1988), *Histoire du Lacher de Vipères, Une Légende Française Contemporaine*, paper presented at the Sixth International Seminary of Perspectives on Contemporary Legends (Sheffield, 25–28 July 1988).

Dupuis, Xavier (1991), *Culture et Développement: De la Reconnaissance à l'Evaluation*, UNESCO, Paris.

Faujas, Alain (1994), 'Le dilemme de Bonneval-sur-Arc: l'un des villages les plus écologistes de France peut-il porter atteinte au sanctuaire du Parc National de la Vanoise au nom de sa survie?', *Le Monde*, 6–7 February, section 'Régions', p V.

Fédération des Parcs Naturels de France (FPNF) (1982), *Interventions Economiques dans les Parcs Naturels Régionaux*, Compédit Beauregard, La Ferté-Macé.

— (1989), *Guide de la Valorisation Economique des Ressources Locales*, Syros Alternatives, Paris.

— (1993a), *Données de Base des Parcs Naturels Régionaux*, mimeo, FPNF, Paris, mai.

— (1993b), *Contribution de la Fédération des Parcs Naturels Régionaux de France au Débat sur l'Aménagement du Territoire Conseil d'Administration du 25 novembre 1993*, FPNF, Paris.

Finger-Stich Andréa and Krishna B Ghimire (forthcoming), *Travail, Culture et Nature: Développement Local dans le Contexte des Parcs Nationaux et Naturels Régionaux en France*, l'Harmattan, Paris.

Fromageau, Jérôme (1985), 'Réflexions relatives à l'histoire du droit et de la protection de la nature', in A Cadoret (ed), *Protection de la Nature: Histoire de l'Idéologie de la Nature à l'Environnement*, L'Harmattan, Paris.

Ghimire, Krishna B (1991), *Parks and People: Livelihood Issues in National Parks Management in Thailand and Madagascar*, Discussion Paper No 29, UNRISD, Geneva, December.

Giblin, Béatrice (1994), 'L'Etat et les collectivités locales, le bilan des années Mitterrand', in *L'Etat de la France 93–94*, La Découverte, Paris, pp 194–199.

Goodmaker, Anne Marie (1988), 'Ecological perspectives of change in agricultural land use in the European community', in M G Paoletti, B R Stinner and G G Elsevier (eds), *Agricultural Ecology and Environment*, Amsterdam Proceedings of an International Symposium on Agricultural Ecology and Environment (Padova, Italy, 5–7 April 1988).

Gorz, André (1980), *Adieu au Prolétariat: au-delà du Socialisme*, Galilée, Paris.

— (1988), *Métamorphoses du Travail: Quête de Sens*, Galilée, Paris.

Groupe de Recherche pour l'Education et la Prospective (1988), 'La forêt sur la place publique', *Pour*, No 117, Privat, Paris.

ILO (International Labour Organisation) (1995), *World Employment 1995*, Geneva.

Lamaison, Pierre and Catherine Migault (1989), *La Déprise Agricole: Réflexions à propos des Parcs Naturels Régionaux*, Ministère de l'Agriculture — Direction des Exploitations de la Politique Sociale et de l' Emploi, Paris.

Lebreton, Philippe (1988), *La Nature en Crise*, Sang de la Terre, Paris.

Léger, Danièle and Bertrand Hervier (1979), *Le Retour à la Nature: Au Fond de la Forêt l'Etat*, Seuil, Paris.

Leynaud, Emile (1985), *L'Etat et la Nature: L'Exemple des Parcs Nationaux Français Contribution à une Histoire de la Protection de la Nature*, Parc National des Cévennes, Florac.

Mendras, Henri (1976), *Les Sociétés Paysannes*, Collection U, Armand Colin, Paris.

Ministry of Environment (1993), *Annuaire des Parcs Nationaux*, Paris, June.

Montero, S Graf (1991), *Occupation et Gestion de l'Espace dans la Vallée du Galeizon: Réserve de la Biosphère*, Centre National d'Etudes Agro-Economiques des

Régions Chaudes, Réserve de la Biosphère des Cévennes, Cendras.

Nissi, Sari (1995), *Modernization and Nature Conservation in Finland*, draft thematic paper, UNRISD, Geneva.

Parc National des Cévennes (1993), *Dossier de Presse*, Parc National des Cévennes, 26 August.

Parc National des Pyrénées (1986), *Pourquoi Parc? Regards sur le Parc National des Pyrénées*, Parc National des Pyrénées, Tarbes.

Parc Naturel Régional du Pilat (1991), 'Charte Constitutive', Art 4, in PNR du Pilat, *Annexes de la Charte Révisée du Parc Naturel Régional du Pilat*, Annexe VII– 1.

— (1993), *La Population du Parc du Pilat*, Fiche documentaire, May.

— (1994), *Contrat de Pays de Développement Economique du Haut Pilat*, Pelussin, January.

Paringaux, Roland (1994), 'Sombre fin de mandat pour Olivier Guichard', *Le Monde*, 29–30 May, p 11.

Perret, Bernard (1994), 'La France et son chômage', *Esprit*, August-September.

Pisani, Edgar – Groupe de Seillac (1994), *Pour une Agriculture Marchande et Ménagère*, Editions de l' Aube, Paris.

Réserve de la Biosphère des Cévennes, and SIVU (Syndicat d'Initiative à Vocation Unique) — Aménagement de la vallée du Galeizon (undated), *La Vallée du Galeizon, un Projet de Conservation et de Développement*, leaflet.

Revue Trimestrielle du Club Cévenol (1992), 'Causse et Cévennes', Vol XVII, No 1, January–February–March.

Roustang, Guy (1982), *Le Travail Autrement*, Dunod, Paris.

Salvi, Isabelle (1992), *A Propos de l'Article 19 dans les Marais de Rochefort: Quand le Concept d'Environnement Prend sa Place dans la Gestion du Territoire*, Ecole National du Génie Rural, des Eaux et des Forêts and Institut National Agronomique Paris, Grignon, Paris, novembre.

Sauvy, Alfred (1980), *La Machine et le Chômage*, Dunod, Paris.

Schama, Simon (1995), *Landscape and Memory*, Alfred A Knopfe, New York.

Seibel, René (1994), 'Des paysans en campagne', *Collectif, Mouvement Syndical et Dynamique Sociale*, No 24, December, pp 12–14.

Serres, Michel (1990), *Le Contrat Naturel*, François Bourin, Paris.

UNESCO (United Nations Educational, Scientific and Cultural Organization) (1977), *Thinking Ahead*, Paris.

VII

CONSERVATION AND SOCIAL DEVELOPMENT: AN ASSESSMENT OF WOLONG AND OTHER PANDA RESERVES IN CHINA

Krishna B. Ghimire

A whole array of issues must be addressed in considering people and conservation. How were protected areas established and managed and what were their impacts on basic needs of local social groups? Have the conservation measures undertaken enhanced existing livelihood opportunities and alleviated poverty and other aspects of human deprivation? Have they encouraged any self-reliance? Or, have they led to resource alienation, marginalization and increased local resentments?

These questions are addressed in this chapter by examining panda protection initiatives in China. The discussion of panda reserves is important not only because pandas are so well-known, but also because they are considered 'unique' and as a 'flagship species' by dominant conservation scholars and organizations. There has been enormous scientific interest in the species, beginning towards the end of the nineteenth century, but socio-economic aspects of panda protection initiatives have not been carefully examined.

Panda Protection Initiatives in China and at the International Level

China's already wide network of strictly protected areas is increasing very rapidly. In 1965, parks and reserves covered only 0.07 per cent of the national territory. But by 1991, nearly 6 per cent of the territory, or 560,000 sq km (an area slightly larger than France) was included in parks and reserves (NEPA, 1992). Recent official information suggests that the government intends to establish as many as 1000 nature reserves by the year 2000 (*China Daily*, 1993).

It should be noted, however, that many parks and reserves established up until the early 1980s were 'paper parks'. Much of the official emphasis was limited to showing the outside world that increasing areas of national territory were being brought under strictly protected regimes although actual implementation was often neglected. The concept of strict protection was essentially contradictory to the existing government policy of land reclamation, agricultural extensification, natural resources extraction and rural industrialization. But there has been a marked shift from the past lukewarm conservation efforts to a more rigorous protection in recent years, in large part to attract external financial resources.

There are currently 13 panda reserves. Of these, 11 reserves are found in Sichuan and one each in Gansu and Shaanxi. By the end of 1980s, these reserves covered a total area of 6227 square kilometres (see Table 7.1 and Figure 7.1).

Many of the initial efforts aimed at formulating comprehensive legislation for the protection of pandas. In recent years, laws have been tightened further. People convicted of poaching pandas can now receive sentences ranging from short-term to life imprisonment and capital punishment.

It is difficult to estimate how many pandas still live in the wild. The survey carried out between 1974 and 1977 by Chinese authorities estimated the panda population to be in the range of 1000 to 1100. Another survey carried out in 1985 and 1988 by China and WWF gave an even more wide-ranging figure of 880 to 1360 pandas (MacKinnon et al., 1989:12–14). Conservationists and government officials frequently have a tendency to quote the lowest number thus amplifying the declining trend in panda numbers, as well as to justify tougher legislation, an increased network of reserves and additional funding. The fact that pandas are difficult to breed in captivity has also provided conservationists with another reason why they should be protected in their natural habitat.

Pandas have been a species of special interest in the West among explorers, mammalogists, zoologists, biologists and animal collectors since the late nineteenth century. The first descriptions of pandas provoked a great deal of scientific interest when they were brought to Europe by a French missionary explorer, Père David, in the 1860s. Many expedition teams from the United States, Britain and Germany subsequently visited panda habitats. Possession of a live panda became a goal of many zoos and scientists. However, given the long travel involved and difficult feeding habits, a live panda was not brought to the West until 1936 (Sheldon, 1975:XVII–XIX). The 1949 Chinese Revolution and the breakdown of contacts with the West created further Western inquisitive-

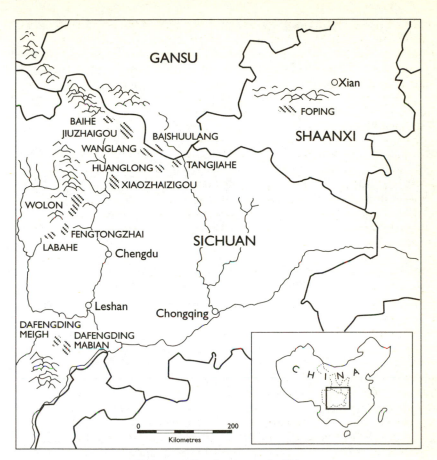

Figure 7.1 *Panda reserves in China*

ness over pandas. For many, pandas are just alluring, tender, furry and designed for hugging (Schaller, 1993:42).

Recent impetus to 'save' pandas by establishing strictly protected areas emanated from the evolving conservation ideology in the West, and internal political changes in China. The protection of attractive birds and spectacular mammals in Africa, Asia and Latin America during the colonial heyday was an issue of some concern among natural scientists as well as hunters and animal traders, and these causes were taken up by environmental movements in the West after the Second World War. IUCN was established in 1948; WWF was founded in 1961. This momentum continued until the creation of UNEP in 1972, plus the establishment of many new environmental NGOs. These movements have generally been highly preservationist.

189

Table 7.1 *Panda reserves in China*

Name	Date of establishment	Province	County	Area (square kilometres)
Baihe	1963	Sichuan	Nanping	200
Baishuijiang	1963	Gansu	Wen	953
Labahe	1963	Sichuan	Tianquan	120
Wanglang	1963	Sichuan	Pingwu	277
Wolong	1963	Sichuan	Wenchuan	2,000
Xiaozhaizigou	1975	Sichuan	Beichuan	167
Dafengding Mabian	1978	Sichuan	Mabian	300
Dafengding Meigu	1978	Sichuan	Meigu	160
Fengtongzhai	1978	Sichuan	Baoxing	400
Foping	1978	Shaanxi	Foping	350
Juizhaigou	1978	Sichuan	Nanping	600
Tanjehai	1978	Sichuan	Qingshuan	300
Huanglong	1983	Sichuan	Songpan	400
Total				6227

Source: MacKinnon et al., 1989.

WWF has attached great importance to the protection of pandas and their habitat. It has used the panda as its logo since its inception; in recent years, it has devoted considerable resources to the management and expansion of panda reserves. Although the agency has recently sought to broaden its vision by changing its name (i.e. World Wide Fund For Nature instead of World Wildlife Fund), many of its activities in the field seem still mainly concerned with the preservation of specific species (cf. WWF, 1993). This narrow, species-centred focus of some of WWF's activities is well illustrated in the case of the panda reserves.

Attempts to capitalize within China on the West's growing interest in pandas began in the early 1960s. Pandas became a prized gift in various countries. The capture and exhibition of pandas in zoos were increasingly sought, and the Chinese government allocated some resources for research on care and breeding of pandas in captivity. Following the foundation of WWF and subsequent selection of the panda as its symbol, the Chinese government established three panda reserves in the early 1960s. This was an attempt to elevate the richness of the country's natural heritage as well as a response to emerging external scientific, political and economic interests. Following China's open-door policies in the late 1970s, WWF was the first foreign conservation organization to be invited to support research and project activities for the preservation of the panda habitat. By this time, a group of powerful, often widely travelled and well-read Chinese natural scientists had became influential in the bureaucracy. They were able to appreciate the financial and other advantages of foreign aid and press for the diversion of more resources to the environmental sector, as well as for closer contacts with agencies such as WWF.

Human Interaction with Pandas and their Habitat

We now turn to examining more closely the social and environmental impact of panda reserves at the local levels, highlighting the interactions between human beings and pandas. For this, it is crucial to understand both the physical and social components of local ecosystems. Demographic structure and trends, settlement patterns and production activities, as well as the nature of reserve management, are all important factors.[1]

Physical Setting of Wolong Reserve

The 2000-square-kilometre Wolong reserve is situated in north-west Sichuan. It lies in the Qionglai mountain range and forms part of the Min

---

1 This chapter is based on the review of available publications, consultations with a number of panda experts and, more importantly, fieldwork in Jiuzhaigou and Wolong panda reserves. Jiuzhaigou is one of China's best-known natural reserves for its scenic beauty involving the alpine landscape, pine forests, clear lakes and waterfalls. About 300,000 tourists, mainly Chinese, visit the area annually. As the reserve has a small population of pandas, it has been included in the national conservation management plan for pandas. The plan proposes removal of three villages inside the boundary of the reserve and alignment with neighbouring reserves by establishing corridors (MacKinnon et al., 1989:48). Tourist accommodation centres inside the reserve have rapidly expanded in recent years, using vacant land as well as a large quantity of wood for construction. To attract more tourists, roads have been widened and the construction of an airport is planned. These infrastructures are also sought by local populations as this allows them to break out of their long isolation from the wider world. Many of these dilemmas and contradictions are not unique to Jiuzhaigou, but are common in most panda reserves.

Most of the field work was carried out in Wolong reserve. A reconnaissance visit and consultations with reserve authorities in Jiuzhaigou indicated that many of the processes observed there could be found in Wolong as well. But Wolong had many additional features. For example, it is China's oldest and largest panda reserve. It has the highest density of pandas and other wildlife. An international panda research centre has been set up here. It has also remained a centre for many eminent scientific studies on pandas and has been included in UNESCO's Man and Biosphere (MAB) network. Unlike most reserves which are generally administered by provincial authorities, it is under the direct command of central government (i.e., the Ministry of Forestry). Finally, like Jiuzhaigou, many groups of people are resident in the reserve, and future tourism potential is high because of its close proximity to Chengdu (the provincial capital of Sichuan). For an investigation of panda reserves, Wolong appeared the most illuminating case; and this chapter deals mainly with the socio-economic and environmental settings found in this reserve. Dialogues with the reserve officials and interviews with 32 local people representing different location, ethnic, economic, gender and age groups formed the main research techniques. Personal impressions have also been important. The author was assisted in the field by two prominent Chinese scholars from the Rural Development Institute and Institute of Forest Conservation in Beijing. Also, his limited previous exposure to Tibetan culture and language in Nepal was helpful.

191

river system, one of numerous water sources for irrigation and agricultural development downstream. Since the construction of a dam on the fast-flowing Min river and a vast network of irrigation canals in the third century, the Sichuan basin has been one of the most important grain-producing areas in China. It is also the country's most populous region.

The reserve spreads over several climatic zones due to varying altitudes: a sub-tropical zone below 2000 metres, a temperate zone from 2000 to 3500 metres, a cold zone from 3500 to 5000 metres, and a zone of perpetual ice and snow above 5,000 metres. Temperatures vary greatly between these specific zones. There are long, cold and rainy/wet periods. Precipitation is high (1500 to 1800 millimetres annually).

Soil types vary, depending largely upon the topography. Alluvial soils are found on the banks of the Pitiao river and lower ridges of the mountains. Alpine meadow and tundra soils are concentrated above 3500 metres (Zhou, 1992:355)

The diversity in topography, hydrology, climate, rainfall and soil formations has given rise to many distinctive plant and animal species. About 97 per cent of the reserve is believed to contain forests, grasslands and rocks and rivers. Of these, forests and grasslands cover 45 and 38 per cent respectively and rocks and rivers occupy the remaining 14 per cent of the reserve (Li et al., 1992:319). Over 3000 species of plants and some 46 species of mammals, 225 of birds and 17 of reptiles have been identified in the reserve (Li and Zhao, 1989:83). The giant panda has been the prime protection target since the inception of the reserve. Nearly 15 per cent of the total pandas in the wild are found in this reserve. The abundance of bamboo has been cited as the main reason for this high density. But the reserve is vast, and is capable of accommodating a panda population many times this size. About 100 pandas existed in the wild in late 1993; and there were 19 pandas in the research centre; but it is unclear how many of the pandas that were given away as gifts, lent or kept in different zoos in China had been removed from Wolong. Pandas are concentrated mainly in the Zheng and Zhong-xi drainage areas in the northern and eastern parts of the reserve (see Figure 7.2).

Settlement Patterns, Population and Livelihood Activities

There are two townships (known previously as communes) within the reserve: Gengda and Wolong. Each township has three main villages. Many of these villages are comprised of several hamlets (see Figure 7.2). Most human settlement is concentrated in a narrow valley-strip of the Pitiao river. One source indicates that human settlements occupy about 3 per cent of the reserve (Li et al., 1992). However, according to information provided by the township authorities, they occupy 5879 mu (392 out of 20,000 hectares), which is less than 2 per cent of the reserve.

Documented evidence and personal conversations with knowledge-

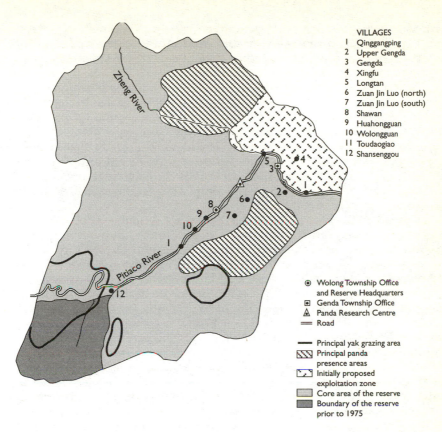

VILLAGES
1 Qinggangping
2 Upper Gengda
3 Gengda
4 Xingfu
5 Longtan
6 Zuan Jin Luo (north)
7 Zuan Jin Luo (south)
8 Shawan
9 Huahongguan
10 Wolongguan
11 Toudaogiao
12 Shansenggou

⊙ Wolong Township Office
    and Reserve Headquarters
▣ Genda Township Office
△ Panda Research Centre
═ Road

━ Principal yak grazing area
▨ Principal panda
    presence areas
▧ Initially proposed
    exploitation zone
▨ Core area of the reserve
▨ Boundary of the reserve
    prior to 1975

Figure 7.2 *Wolong nature reserve*

able elderly people suggest that all the villages in the townships were established a long time ago and, in any event, much earlier than the reserve. Some people had moved to the area from the Tibetan plateau during the second half of the seventeenth century when the Chinese Qing dynasty sought to colonize the area with Tibetan people (Ma, 1989:202). The motive behind this was to increase royal revenue and to receive political support from the Tibetan chiefs, who were then made administrators of the area and were allowed to keep a certain portion of the revenue generated. The newly-arrived 'settlers' too were given incentives in the initial period of settlement in the form of reduced taxation. Since the lowland Han people were unwilling to move to an altitude as high as Wolong, it was logical to attempt to attract the highlanders. Also, as most Tibetans specialized in mountain livestock raising, combined with a limited degree of upland agriculture, Wolong and its surroundings represented a highly suitable settlement area for them. Unlike most parts of Tibet, the area had more favourable rainfall and soil conditions for pasture regeneration and crop production. There was also plenty of game to supplement food supplies.

These highland pastoral people seem to have remained on higher altitudes until the introduction of maize, probably during the early eighteenth century. Because maize could only be grown at lower elevations, which also had more productive land, people found it advantageous to move lower down the slopes. This was further encouraged by the introduction of potatoes and cabbages of European varieties at the lower altitudes (Schaller, 1993:133). Lower elevations meant warmer temperatures and faster ripening of crops. It was also easier to construct canals for irrigation.

This led to the emergence of more compact settlement units, as well as permanent and larger agricultural fields. It also allowed raising of lowland animals such as pigs. Similarly, crops and livestock could be better protected from wildlife as settlements became compact. These developments led to an improved standard of living for these people.

From the beginning of the twentieth century, a limited upward movement of Hans took place, especially in the Gengda area (the main entry point from the Sichuan basin). These migrants, originally collectors of medicinal plants, generally followed the river course. However, immigration from this side of the reserve was never very significant. This is reflected in the fact that people of Tibetan origin still constitute the majority of the population, even in the Gengda area. Table 7.2 shows that in 1992, 60 per cent of the population in Gengda consisted of people of Tibetan origin. In Wolong Township they represented nearly 80 per cent of the population whilst in the reserve as a whole the Tibetan people represented 70 per cent of the population. Han and Qiang formed the remaining 26 and 3 per cent respectively.

In 1993, a total of 4229 people lived inside the reserve. An improvement in general health care in the 1950s and 1960s led to a significant population growth in the area during those decades, but growth has stagnated in recent years. For example, population grew by 583 persons between 1982 and 1992, and the total population declined from 4277 in 1990 to 4229 in 1992 (see Table 7.2).

The origin, ethnic composition and size of the local population, as well as the prevailing natural conditions have important implications for the way people live and their subsistence needs. Han people introduced pigs into the area, as well as cows from the plains. Pork soon became a major component of the local diet and nutrition, and in recent years pigs have become one of the principal sources of cash income. Cross-breeding between lowland cows and yaks has resulted in a breed that yields more meat, gives more milk and has more draught power. The Han people also brought many types of new crops.

Tibetans were more familiar with the different types of local plants and their uses. They were also skilful hunters. They were ingenious in raising yaks at high altitudes. Furthermore, many aspects of their housing and livelihood practices were better adapted to cold and high elevations.

Many traditional practices have continued but with constant adjustments by both communities. Crop production is now the main subsistence activity. Even the Tibetan households, which traditionally relied more on livestock raising, have begun to depend heavily on agriculture. Maize, potatoes, wheat, green vegetables and fruits are grown using mainly hand implements, natural manure and oxen. Livestock raising is the second most important source of livelihood. Yaks are raised in significant numbers, but there are also cows, goats and sheep. Nearly all households keep pigs and poultry.

Table 7.2 *Population characteristics and ethnic composition in Wolong reserve*

Population characteristics	1982	1987	1990	1992
Gengda	2,046	2,147	2,234	2,248
Wolong	1,600	1,990	2,043	1,981
Total population	*3,646*	*4,137*	*4,277*	*4,229*
Number of households				
Gengda	—	—	—	479
Wolong	—	—	—	360
Total	—	—	—	*839*
Average household size				
Gengda	—	—	—	4.6 persons
Wolong	—	—	—	5.5 persons
Average for the reserve	—	—	—	*5.0 persons*
Ethnic composition				
% of population, 1992	*Tibetan*	*Han*	*Qiang*	*Other*
Gengda	60	36	3	1
Wolong	80	15	3	2
Average for the reserve	70	26	3	*1*

Note: — 'not available'.
Source: Author's fieldwork in Gengda and Wolong Townships, 1993

Forests are important not only for grazing yaks, cows, goats and sheep, but also for collecting medicinal plants. As will be discussed in the next section, income from medicinal plants is crucial for most households. Collection of wood, bamboo, fodder and many edible items is carried out in different seasons. The recent official restraints on the use of forest resources have thus had a profound effect on local livelihood security.

Reserve Management Style and Goals

Wolong reserve was established in 1963, covering an area of 200 square kilometres. In 1974, after a national panda survey which showed that the reserve had the highest local density of pandas amongst all the panda reserves and that international interest in pandas had been rising, the government decided to enlarge the reserve to 2000 square kilometres. Much of this new area involved isolated high mountains where no or little human impact existed. However, expansion also meant incorporating the communes of Gengda and Wolong, as well as the areas used for formal logging along the Pitiao valley. The main office complex of the logging operations was transformed into the reserve's headquarters.

There have been five principal reserve management goals and activities. The first one is a classic park or reserve management task involving efforts to improve the existing physical infrastructure such as roads and trails, check posts, office buildings, staff quarters, a research centre, shops and visitor accommodations. In Wolong reserve, some of these existed previously such as the office buildings and roads built for logging, but many required improvements, and other new facilities had to be constructed. A sustained budget from the government, together with occasional financial contributions from abroad, have permitted reserve authorities to install most basic facilities. However, maintenance is generally poor. The central problem is that the reserve has no source of income of its own, and the government and outside funding agencies have tended to provide assistance for construction only. This, for example, is the case with the WWF-assisted panda research centre. WWF provided funding only for the construction and initial equipping of the centre, and made no provisions for its maintenance. The centre has been severely handicapped in its functioning, in large part as a result of the natural wear and tear, and the breakdown of many imported ultra-modern instruments which are expensive to replace.

The organization and facilitation of research has been another important management activity. Wolong has long been a centre for academic and scientific research by Chinese students and scholars. For example, the panda research centre was established in the early 1980s to breed pandas in captivity. This was backed by studies by Western naturalists on panda behaviour and regeneration of bamboo. Researchers and scientists also carried out an enumeration of the flora and fauna of the region, which was completed at the end of the 1980s (MacKinnon et al., 1988:8).

A third management activity is the protection of wildlife. Access to the reserve by outside people was curtailed by establishing a checkpoint at a narrow gorge at the boundary of the reserve, and imposing an entry pass on visitors. Dates for the annual collection of medicinal plants have been regulated, and people both from inside and outside the reserve require a permit. A permit — which is time consuming to obtain and rarely granted — is also necessary to cut wood for construction. Extraction of bamboo and firewood by villagers is tolerated at best, as is grazing. Crop production and hunting inside the reserve are severely punishable. Surveillance has been made more effective by increasing the number of reserve guards per square kilometre and improvements in their training.

Fourth, rehabilitation of degraded areas through tree planting has been a key management goal since the early 1980s. Reforestation is a major effort throughout China, often accompanied by various incentive schemes. Much of the 'degraded' areas inside the reserve include lands previously used by peasants for crop production or grazing. By 1992, a total area of 132,677 mu (8845 hectares) was afforested through rehabilitation programmes which included both reforestation as well as enrichment planting activities (personal communication, Wolong Reserve Headquarters, 1993). Peasants were given minimal compensation for the loss of their land, as well as for looking after the trees planted during the initial years. In the 1980s, the World Food Programme (WFP) subsidized many of these activities. Until 1982, most afforestation was carried out in isolated or peripheral fields where peasants had trouble protecting their crops from wildlife and thus there was no strong opposition from the peasants. But their attitude changed as trees were increasingly planted on prime agricultural land.

Finally, the removal of human settlements from the reserve has remained a central objective. Ever since the establishment of the reserve, the existence of the settlements has been considered incompatible with the protection of panda habitat. In the early 1980s, the division of the reserve into three principal zones was sought. A core area was proposed at the centre part of the reserve, surrounded by scientific research and management (human settlement) zones (Li et al., 1992:353; MacKinnon et al., 1988:16–18). This zoning put the Wolong township in the core area. An attempt was subsequently made to remove the people from the township and resettle them in the Gengda area, which was considered to be in the buffer zone. As a first step, people settled closest to the panda habitat were to be removed, and WFP provided financial assistance to construct Western-style apartment buildings to house some 100 families. However, this resettlement scheme made no provision for agricultural land, and off-farm employment was non-existent. Understandably, people refused to move to the new location. Some opposition was also shown by the receiving population, as they would have been obliged to compete with the newcomers for existing jobs, grazing sites and firewood collection. In addition, the Wolong people were accustomed to living in wooden houses with extended kitchen gardens and pig-yards, which the new apartment buildings could not offer. People were also unwilling to move because they knew the proposed site was more windy and warmer due to the lower altitude. In the end, no one moved out of their village, and the apartment buildings have remained empty, deteriorating rapidly. In 1989, the national conservation management plan for the giant panda, prepared by the Ministry of Forestry and WWF, proposed the complete removal of people from Wolong to somewhere outside the reserve. The plan also proposed the removal of people from Gengda township to make the reserve entirely free from human settlements. If this was not feasible, the plan recommended excluding some 200 square kilometres of settlement and forest area covered by the township from the reserve boundaries. But the removal of people from the reserve seems to have been the option chosen in the plan, as funds were already appropriated for this purpose. The resettlement item in fact constitutes over 65 per cent of the reserve's budget for five years (MacKinnon et al., 1989:48,134).

Where is the Conflict?

Figure 7.3 shows the settlement and forest structure in Wolong township. This is similar in Gengda, but the base-altitude is lower. The most striking feature that can be observed in this figure is the existence of mutually non-conflicting activities at different elevations. Most human settlement is situated on the valley floor. Small isolated hamlets and agricultural plots are found up to 2000 metres. People collect firewood and graze cows and goats up to 2500 metres where mixed deciduous evergreen forest exists. Beyond this point rising up to 3500 metres lies the typical panda habitat. Villagers interact very little with this tract, except for the annual collection of a few bundles of bamboo-sticks by some households. Above the panda habitat lies the alpine grassland where yaks are grazed and medicinal plants are collected. It is here that most hunting was previously carried out. Neither the activities related to crop production and livestock raising below, nor the yak grazing and medicinal plant collection above, come into direct conflict with the pandas and their habitat. Most villagers have not seen a panda in their entire lifetime. This is in part because pandas are elusive animals and live in a belt that is not frequented by villagers. Pandas seldom descend to the settlement areas. They come in some contact with yaks during the peak winter season when herds are brought down to the lower altitudes. But as yaks prefer to remain in the grassland, they are not a threat in terms of destroying the panda habitat which consists of woody and bamboo vegetation. They are near the panda belt for at most a couple of weeks each year before moving up the mountain. This suggests that the existing conflict between human activities and the panda habitat is almost negligible.

However, the reserve management plan implies that present human activities are causing the reduction and degradation of forest areas available for pandas. It should be recalled that the reserve represents an extended area of 2000 square kilometres and that human activities are concentrated in areas outside of the panda habitat. Part of the problem seems to have arisen as a result of the way the zoning of the reserve has been carried out. The concept of establishing specific zones for strict conservation and human activities developed by the MAB programme of

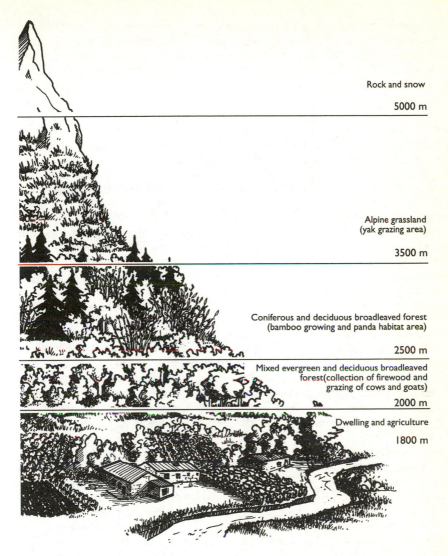

Rock and snow

5000 m

Alpine grassland
(yak grazing area)

3500 m

Coniferous and deciduous broadleaved forest
(bamboo growing and panda habitat area)

2500 m

Mixed evergreen and deciduous broadleaved
forest(collection of firewood and
grazing of cows and goats)

2000 m

Dwelling and agriculture

1800 m

Figure 7.3 *Typical settlement and forest structure in Wolong township*

UNESCO indicates that the core area should consist of 'minimally disturbed ecosystems' (Batisse, 1986). Under this criterion, the area where the pandas currently live (i.e., the northern and southern flanks of the reserve) should have been the principal 'core' zone (see Figure 7.2). Instead, the plan considers the central area where human settlements have long existed as the core of the reserve.

Another argument explicit in the management plan is that the

199

villagers are engaged in excessive use of reserve resources. This deserves some clarification. Despite people's critical reliance on certain forest products, the actual level of local resource use in the reserve has remained low. As discussed above, the use of the reserve for agricultural expansion has totally ceased. In fact, there has been a continuous decline in the area under agriculture and pasture adjacent to villages. There has been a drastic reduction in local hunting, in part as a result of vigorous surveillance and tough anti-hunting laws. In any event, pandas were never a target for hunting by local people. The collection of medicinal plants is allowed for just over a month annually. Timber from the forest, generally in small quantities, is sought mainly for house construction and repair, and is extracted, where possible, once every few years. The management plan singles out the collection of firewood by local people, which is estimated to be 1817 cubic metres per year (MacKinnon et al., 1988). But it does not take into account the fact that many households regularly supplement firewood with agricultural residues such as maize cobs, straw and farmland trees. Also, a few households use electricity for heating. Furthermore, a significant number of households living near the Pitiao river collect wood that is brought by the annual floods during June and July. This occurs principally in Wolong township, where the river bed is flat and most villages are situated close to the river.

The main issue of concern amongst the reserve authorities and conservationists has been the size and growth trends of the local population. The national panda management plan sees population growth as the 'greatest threat' to pandas (MacKinnon et al., 1989:37). Schaller, a reputed natural scientist, emphasizes the 'inexorable population growth' that is threatening the future of pandas and other wildlife (Schaller, 1993:208). The Wolong reserve management plan is even more explicit. It states:

> *Undoubtedly the biggest constraint on the reserve management is the problem of handling the very large population of human residents in the reserve. These residents cause most of the damage that threatens the well-being of the ecosystem, slow down efforts to restore the ecosystem and place a huge workload on the administrative offices of the reserve staff (MacKinnon et al., 1988).*

Three specific points are worth noting here. First, the population density in north-west Sichuan, where pandas are found, is much lower than in the Sichuan plain or many other parts of China. The ratio between population density and resources available is quite favourable. Indeed, much of Wolong reserve, and most other panda reserves, is still inaccessible and largely uninhabited. Second, as noted above, the human population in Wolong is quite small in relation to the surface of the reserve. Inhabitants are constrained by wildlife laws and reserve guards in their ability to extract forest products. There is no in-migration to the reserve.

Finally, recent population dynamics hardly suggest an 'inexorable population growth' trend. As mentioned above, the total population in the reserve has actually declined in recent years as a result of the official relaxation on people's movements. Some seemed to have moved to urban centres, attracted by higher wages and better education and living conditions, whilst others have moved to neighbouring areas to join family members. The offer of compensation, which ranged from 3000 to 5000 yuan per household, must have also encouraged people to leave the reserve, especially when their future in Wolong seemed so uncertain. Even though most people in the area, especially those of Tibetan origin, are not required to follow the official one-child policy, the majority seem to have already chosen to do so. The common practice of intermarriage between Han and Tibetan people has especially facilitated the adoption of the one-child policy. The Chinese national culture and educational system have also had a considerable influence in promoting population control. Hence, the perceived conflicts between humans and pandas are in many ways dubious.

Social Development through Conservation

The concept of social development can be divided into three sets of issues: basic social provisioning, economic security and improvements, and social integration and popular participation. These are, however, very broad categories. They also frequently overlap. For instance, basic social provisioning could easily include many aspects of livelihood security and social integration, or vice versa. But for the present purpose, the goal is to throw light on key parameters of social development, organized primarily around these three categories. The central question for discussion is: has the establishment of the reserve contributed to meeting basic needs, improving standards of living, and promoting cultural development in the area, together with its conservation objective?

Basic Social Provisioning

The people of Wolong aspire to improved conditions of housing, health care, education and food security, as do the people in other parts of rural China and, indeed, the world. They also desire better roads and access to electricity. Individual households and communities, for their part, have made numerous efforts to fulfil 'primary needs'. How are these endeavours supported by the reserve management?

Let us begin with the issue of housing. Although the general housing conditions in Wolong have improved over the past decades, they are far from adequate. Despite a prolonged winter each year, walls and roofs are badly insulated. People traditionally lived in wooden houses with roofs of stone slates, which were considered warm and were easy to construct. In recent years, in part as a result of the restriction on extracting wood and stone from the reserve, people have been more inclined to use concrete blocks, bricks, tiles and zinc sheets for roofing, as well as glass for windows. Modern houses are also seen as a status symbol. Even though they offer more living space, with bigger verandas and courtyards, they generally tend to be damper and colder than the traditional houses. Also, the construction of these houses can prove to be a financial burden for most households. There is no official assistance or compensation for house construction. The abandonment of the commune system and influence of modernization have also meant a steady decline in the previous reciprocity system of neighbours helping each other with house building.

The reserve has done little to improve health care and sanitation. Although there has been some improvement in health in general, critical health problems persist, including insufficient health facilities, poor sanitary conditions and practices, and the prevalence of contagious diseases. There are three small dispensaries in the reserve, established following the 1949 Revolution. Salaries and equipment costs are covered by the provincial authority. Health care costs were previously subsidized by the respective commune office, but now individuals seeking medical care are required to pay themselves. For treatment of serious disorders, people must make the costly trip to Chengdu.

During 1950s basic education facilities were provided with the opening of one primary and one middle school. Over the following decades, three pre-primary schools, two additional primary schools and one high school were established. The majority of the people in the reserve are literate; and primary school attendance is high. Schooling is obligatory for children, but parents need to pay for books and make other contributions to the local school. The provincial government pays the teachers' salaries, but as the pay is lower than in the Sichuan basin, it is difficult to attract enough good teachers. Furthermore, schools lack many teaching instruments. Hence, the educational standard in the area is low.

The establishment of the reserve has played a positive role in two specific areas: the construction of a road and a few hydroelectric plants. The road which joins the Pitiao valley to the Sichuan plain was initially constructed in 1961 for logging. Since the establishment of the reserve, it has been much improved. As it is a principal road leading to the Aba autonomous region, the government has provided considerable sums of money for its periodic improvement. However, much of this has been spent on the maintenance of the stretch between the plain and reserve headquarters in order to facilitate easier mobility of reserve staff and visitors. Very recently, the work to surface this section of the road and replace wooden bridges with concrete ones was completed. The construction of this road has allowed the peasants to transport their produce to larger commercial centres, and thus sell for higher prices than locally. They are also able to purchase necessary household items, which are generally cheaper in these centres. But most roads leading to different villages, and trails within villages, remain in poor condition.

There are at present five hydroelectric plants in the reserve, with a total capacity of 1695 kilowatts. The first two were constructed to provide electricity primarily to the reserve staff, and to a limited extent to Shawan and Gengda villages. In the 1980s, three more hydroplants were set up, with the specific aim of reducing villagers' demand for firewood. Earlier plants were constructed by the Chinese government, but the newer ones are funded by foreign agencies. Regular maintenance and staffing of these hydroplants is supervised by the reserve management. Nearly 99 per cent of the households now have access to electricity (Li et al., 1992:324), although much of it is used for lighting only. Most households pay about 20 to 30 yuan (US$ 3–5) annually for lighting, but this rises substantially if the electricity is used for cooking as well. A few more prosperous households use electricity for some heat during the winter months and to heat water for showers, but none of them use it for cooking.

Food and nutrition is an important area of social provisioning. Because of limited access to land resources, mountainous terrain, a long cold season and simple agrarian technology, food remains the primary preoccupation of the majority of households. The government's drive to intensify agriculture during the 1950s, 1960s and 1970s (see e.g. Perkins, 1969; Rawski, 1979; Croll, 1982) had some impact in Wolong as well. In particular, the widespread use of hybrid varieties of potatoes and maize led to a significant increase in production of these crops. The government also introduced plastic sheets to cover and allow germination of maize seeds during the cold periods, thereby permitting the ripening of maize before the arrival of the following winter. These plastic sheets are still subsidized by the government. Several new types of beans and green vegetables have made their way into the area. Despite all these efforts, however, food availability is lower than the regional and national levels, and there is seasonal variation in food availability. Furthermore, people's preference for rice as a main diet staple means that they must exchange maize and potatoes for rice, despite the higher price of the latter. Each household receives a subsidy for 500 kilograms of rice annually from the government, but the rate of the subsidy has remained the same for many years, even though the price of rice has increased many-fold. In recent years, the loss of agricultural land to the reserve (i.e., a 23 per cent reduction in area previously tilled) on the one hand, and the increasing destruction of crops by wildlife as a result of the rapid growth in their numbers, on the other, has had negative effects on the production of such crops as potatoes and maize. Indeed, the total quantity of food availability per person declined between 1985 and 1991 from 104 kg to 93.6 kg (see Table 7.3). Yet during this same period, average agricultural production elsewhere in China increased, due in part to market incentives and the rising application of agricultural inputs (China Agricultural Yearbook 1992, 1993:283). In 1991, the local per capita grain production was about one third of the national or provincial figures.

The level of food availability and the type of food eaten have many implications for nutritional standards. No precise information is available on local per capita supply of calories, proteins and other nutrients. The per capita grain production in Wolong is less than half of the national per capita grain consumption (see Table 7.3), which suggests a clear shortfall in food consumption for an average household. Furthermore, the local diet is heavily dependent on cereals, with little consumption of meat, eggs and fish. Pigs and poultry, which form the main local sources of meat, are now raised increasingly for the market. Beans, various kinds of green vegetables and fruits are commonly eaten, but in much smaller quantities than rice. Moreover, they are available only seasonally. There is a local taboo against catching fish. This indicates that local diets may be deficient in both calories and proteins. It is difficult to determine whether the prohibitions on hunting wild game and collecting medicinal plants have also had an impact on people's nutrition.

Table 7.3 *Agriculture and food production in Wolong reserve, 1980–92*

	1980	*1985*	*1992*
Area under agriculture (in mu)			
Gengda	3,920.0	—	3,571
Wolong	3,685.5	—	2,308
Total	7,605	—	5,879
Average land holding per household (in mu)			
Gengda	—	—	7.3
Wolong	—	—	6.4
Average for the reserve	—	—	7.0
Grain production per person/annum (in kg)			
Reserve	90.0	104.0	93.6*
Sichuan province	—	—	400.4*
China	326.7	360.7	378.0*
Grain consumption per person/annum (in kg)			
Reserve	—	—	—
Sichuan province	—	—	253.4*
China	257.0	257.0	257.0*

Note: — 'not available'; * 1991 figure
Sources: Author's fieldwork in Gengda and Wolong Townships, 1993; *China Agricultural Yearbook, 1992, 1993*; State Statistical Bureau, 1992

Economic Security and Improvements

We have examined the significance of the reserve in terms of housing, health care, education, food and physical infrastructure for people in Wolong. Economic protection and amelioration is another critical, and related, issue. Has the reserve played any role in reducing poverty through employment creation and income generation, or provided conditions for higher social mobility?

Employment

Making a decent living has been a major challenge for most households in Wolong, more so since the establishment of the reserve. Crop production and livestock raising are the dominant sources of employment. Yet, agricultural activities have been severely restricted. As noted above, the area under agriculture has steadily declined, and the average land holding per household is less than half a hectare (see Table 7.3). This extremely small farm size means that even with maximum labour intensification, little additional employment can be generated. Obviously, this also hinders the creation of wage employment in agriculture.

The livestock sector, too, has failed to generate further employment. Constant official harassment for grazing their livestock within the reserve boundary has led peasants to reassess their livestock raising practices. As Table 7.4 shows, between 1982 and 1992, the number of grazing yaks remained about the same, but there was a sharp drop in the numbers of sheep and goats. The increase in the number of cows raised reflects the need for each household to maintain its own animals as a result of the 'householdization' of the production system since the late 1970s, as well as the cows' high market value. Cows are now increasingly stall-fed. It is probable that restrictions on grazing have also encouraged pig-raising.

The use of forest resources is a vital component of household employment strategy. The collection of medicinal plants, wild fruits, nuts, mushrooms, wood and bamboo, as well as hunting of game, where possible, requires a significant amount of labour, and these are activities which congenially supplement household subsistence needs. One important aspect of forest use by local communities is that extraction activities are carried out when labour demand in agriculture is low, mitigating seasonal unemployment. However, these opportunities have been continuously eroded by laws and regulations intended to protect the reserve.

The issue of employment has been entirely neglected in management of the reserve. By the end of 1993, the reserve had a total of 375 staff members, very few of whom came from the area. There was no policy to employ local people. Villagers are occasionally hired for construction works (e.g. construction of hydroplants, office buildings and road repair), especially when bringing in outside labour is not advantageous.

Underemployment is becoming a serious problem, and the reserve has done little to alter the situation. Households have to devise their own strategies. A few households with some savings have established small

Table 7.4 *Livestock-populations in Wolong reserve*

	1982	1990	1992
Gengda			
Yak	105	120	119
Cow	318	682	910
Sheep/Goat	549	120	154
Pig	1,238	1,344	1,365
Wolong			
Yak	1,128	—	1,100
Cow	208	—	200
Sheep/Goat	630	—	350
Pig	900	—	1,500
Total for the reserve			
Yak	1,233	—	1,219
Cow	526	—	1,110
Sheep/Goat	1,179	—	504
Pig	2,138	—	2,865

Note: — 'not available'
Source: Author's fieldwork in Gengda and Wolong Townships, 1993

shops and stalls in village centres, or become engaged in itinerant trading. Most households, however, must seek seasonal work in construction and road-building sites outside the reserve. Although the current dynamism of the national economy, especially in urban areas, provides promising prospects for wage employment, due to the physical isolation of the area and the need to travel a relatively long distance, people from Wolong are generally disfavoured.

Income Generation

The nature and extent of employment available is closely related to income-generation opportunities. Hence, where employment is restrained, income levels remain correspondingly low. At the same time, with the increased insertion into the market system and rising demands for consumer goods, cash needs are becoming more compelling. Peasants are frequently required to sell their meagre produce in the market.

Meanwhile, many traditional or prevailing sources of income have terminated or are seriously threatened, in large part as a result of the restrictions imposed on resource use within the reserve. To offset this, peasants are more inclined to use hybrid varieties of potatoes and maize, even if it implies buying seeds and plastic sheets each year. They use their small plots much more intensively. For example, four-season beans are cultivated on the plot boundaries, and vegetables (e.g. radish, turnips) are planted immediately after the harvest of potatoes, whilst maize still occupies the field. Yellow beans are grown in between the maize plants on the same row. To increase yields, nearby water sources are neatly canalized, pig manure, goat/sheep pellets and cow dung are spread in the field. Potatoes, maize and green vegetables are some of the main sources of cash income when sold and are usually exchanged for rice. But only about one third of the peasant households are actually able to market grain and vegetables in moderate quantities (Table 7.5).

Table 7.5 *Selected sources of cash income in Wolong reserve, 1992*

	% of households with income from:	Average income (in yuan) among households with income:
Grains	33	1,008
Vegetables	26	410
Livestock	50	651
Medicinal plants	43	699
Subsidies	100	158
Trading/labouring	90	1,912

Note: sample size = 42 households
(Source: RDI/FRI, 1993)
Average income per person/annum for the reserve: 700 yuan (gross) or 538 yuan (net) (Source: author's fieldwork in Gengda and Wolong townships)
Average rural household net income in 1991: 590 yuan in Sichuan; 708 yuan in China (Source: State Statistical Bureau, 1992)

Many households used to receive significant income from yaks and goats. Both these sources have now shrunk — especially the income from goats — because of the increasing restrictions on grazing in the reserve. There has been an increase in pig-raising, as there is a ready market for pork in the plains. Overall, the income from livestock has declined. In 1992, only 50 per cent of the households were able to generate cash income from livestock sales (see Table 7.5).

Peasants used to earn some cash through the collection and sale of such forest products as mushrooms, fruits and nuts. The collection of medicinal plants remains the most important source of income from the forest. Despite a reduction in the price of medicinal plants — largely due to widespread availability of modern medicine — 43 per cent of the sampled households earned on average 699 yuan in 1992 from collecting medicinal herbs, which was more than the income from livestock and about half that of crop sales (Table 7.5).

Petty trading and wage labouring are clearly emerging as the most dominant sources of income in Wolong. In 1992, as many as 90 per cent of households engaged in these activities and earned on average 1912 yuan

(Table 7.5). Although the above figures must be interpreted cautiously, for it was the surfacing of the road in the reserve (which is not regular employment) which provided much of the wage employment in 1992, there is a clear tendency to become increasingly engaged in off-farm daily labouring activities as cash needs grow.

Social Mobility

The possibilities for upward social mobility are also limited. For example, during the field study, only five individuals out of the entire reserve population were found holding stable jobs. Individual enterprise and family support have played a more important role in allowing these people to achieve limited occupational advancement than has formal social provisioning by the government or the reserve.

Social mobility was, to some extent, frustrated in the past by official restrictions on migration, which limited access to urban employment, higher wages and better educational facilities. In recent years, control of migration has been more relaxed. Nonetheless, for people who are generally unskilled and hardly speak mandarin Chinese, securing housing and employment in urban centres is far from easy.

Sociologists, generally in the context of industrial societies, have shown a close link, in particular, between the level of education attained and employment enhancement, which enables upward social mobility (e.g. Barber, 1957; Coxon and Jones, 1975; and Lipset, 1981). In Wolong, both the facilities available for and the standard of education are poor. Although basic education opportunities exist, minimum school education can often lead nowhere. Evidence suggests that as many as 98 per cent of the pupils attend primary school, but only 65 per cent of them go on to middle school (Li et al., 1992:325). The percentage of students actually completing high school is even smaller.

Students have to be exceptionally bright to secure a scholarship to attend university. Sending children to university privately is hardly conceivable, as households cannot afford the costs of food, clothes, books, and in certain cases, accommodation. This has become even more difficult under the new reforms to make universities economically self-reliant, which require students and their parents to pay even more.

Likewise, the family and local social environment are scarcely conducive to higher education and occupational mobility. There is little motivation for education. Children have to learn the skills of using sickles, hoes and axes even before they go to school; and frequently they are obliged to spend more time in the field than at school. Moreover, as children usually get married early, they tend to separate from the main family at a relatively young age. Household responsibilities make it impossible to leave the farm even for a few days.

Social Integration and Participation

Social integration, in a normative sense, is used to express 'the specific goal of promoting harmonious interaction and solidarity' amongst different groups of people (UNRISD, 1994). Despite the growing influence of market forces and an increasing operation of production activities at household level, people in Wolong still strongly identify themselves as 'us', and any other persons, including those from the plains, as 'others'. Tibetan and Han cultures have interacted in the area for a long time, resulting in the emergence of a unique and tolerant 'sub-culture'. In particular, the practice of intermarriage between the two communities has helped to create a distinct identity. Both cultures had their own specific contributions to make to crop production, livestock and foraging practices. Initially, the Tibetan culture was dominant and the Han people had to make many adjustments in living and production practices. In recent decades, the influence of the Han culture has grown through the schooling system and political thinking, as well as through state intervention in general. But even this more recent outside influence has so far not led to the emergence of any clear cultural contradictions between the two communities.

It is certain that economic differentiation will increase in the future. Because of declining income from crop production, livestock raising and collection of forest products, especially medicinal plants, on the one hand, and the growing influence of consumerism, on the other, many households are likely to find themselves in poorer situations. Televisions, radios, wrist watches, water heaters and modern clothes are now highly sought-after items, and the social position of a household is often associated with the possession of these goods. People may cut down on subsistence expenditures or divert savings from agriculture in order to purchase such consumer items. When an off-farm income is available, it is normally used for buying consumer goods. Borrowing is also prevalent, but it generally involves small amounts and loans are given for one agricultural season only. As the state is still the owner of land, households cannot sell or buy it, which has prevented the emergence of classes of landless and rich farmers (see e.g. McKinley, 1993). Households which are able to run shops and businesses, in addition to agriculture, are usually better off. Most of these households invest their savings outside agriculture, although a few of them were found buying more yaks in the area. Certain individuals have become more 'successful' in business and other new income-generating activities, and they are drawn from both communities. Importantly, there is no sign of one ethnic group becoming rich at the cost of others.

For a vast majority of the people, regardless of their ethnic origin, making a living is an arduous task, and they have little say in the opportunities for livelihood improvement through formal planning or the reserve management. The extended impact of the notion of 'democratic centralism' and the rite of technocratic efficiency is that people are discouraged from taking part in conservation activities. This is further exacerbated by the negative attitude of conservation officials towards local people, who are essentially seen as an uncompromising threat to wildlife.

Conclusions

The above description and analysis suggest that the establishment of Wolong reserve has brought about much uncertainty for local livelihoods. The whole reserve management exercise is geared towards 'saving' pandas by the creation of extended habitat zones free from human interference. For this purpose, people living inside the reserve are either removed or severely restricted in their customary resource extraction activities. This phenomenon is common in other panda reserves as well.

Project documents in panda reserves fail to consider social development as an issue at all, even though elsewhere it is becoming fashionable to talk of integrated resource management through people's participation (e.g., Wells et al., 1992; IUCN, 1993). Social development of a population is most legitimate. People should have continued access to local resources to maintain their subsistence, ensure their livelihood security and, ultimately, realize higher social mobility. Moreover, a socially stable and conscious population will be capable of taking better care of its environment. In fact, in the case of the Wolong reserve, social development could occur even in the absence of official conservation, as people would be freer to bring more land under crop production, to improve livestock raising and to undertake sustainable forest harvesting. But conservation goals will fail in the long run if socio-economic objectives are neglected — especially as local people become increasingly impoverished and disgruntled.

The resettlement of people living in the Wolong reserve is not necessary socially, environmentally or economically. In fact, there are just over 5000 people in all panda reserves (with a total area of 6287 square kilometres.). If it had been decided from the start that people could remain in their villages, in the case of Wolong, the costs of constructing the empty modern apartment building and the planned resettlement, amounting to several million yuans, would have been avoided. They could have been used for improving agricultural or production support services in the area for many decades. Alternatively, they could have been used for conservation purposes, for instance, maintaining the panda research centre which is now dilapidated due to lack of funds. A further disadvantage of the attempt to remove people from their settlements is that it has probably discouraged local people from making any significant investment in land, livestock and other productive activities because of the insecurity of their tenure.

The Chinese authorities, with an interest in peasants' welfare and economic improvements, were generally opposed to moving people against their will. This is clearly reflected in the absence of the official use of coercive means to remove people, or house them in the new apartment buildings. International agencies such as the WWF have missed an opportunity provided by political conditions that actually favoured letting people remain in their villages. This was basically due to their pursuit of a conservation ideology that saw the existence of people in the reserves as inherently contradictory to the protection of pandas. However, in recent years, official conservation thinking in China has been much influenced by Western dogmas, in part due to expectations of increased foreign aid and investments in the environmental sector. The opportunity that was missed may thus not present itself again.

A more flexible attitude in establishing and managing protected areas could help to explore many socially desirable initiatives. There are extraordinary opportunities afforded by the occurrence of distinct panda habitat and human activities zones at different elevations. In Wolong, the existing population could enjoy a much higher standard of living if the potential for yak farming were fully exploited by allowing peasants to graze more yaks and organizing market outlets. There are also good prospects for assisting peasants to increase pig breeding as a source of income. More yaks and pigs could also contribute to animal protein and fat in the local diet while posing no dangers to the pandas.

The collection of medicinal plants is one of the major sources of household cash income. Given this situation, the period that the peasants are allowed to enter the reserve for this purpose could be lengthened. They could be offered wages or food to regenerate medicinal plants if certain species were to be over-exploited. Some of the medicinal plants might be grown by peasants themselves in their own fields with technical and financial assistance from the reserve. There are many types of forest foods (game, honey, nuts, vegetables, fruits) which could be both consumed and sold without damage to panda habitat.

Local food availability could be increased by intensifying land use as well as by bringing back to agriculture some of the land appropriated for protection. Marginal areas or the land adjacent to the reserve boundary might be used for agro-forestry. Currently, both expropriated and adjacent areas are used by the reserve for planting monoculture pine trees.

As the reserve is large and undertakes many administrative and protective activities, there are many potential opportunities for local people to be employed in offices, infrastructure construction and maintenance and protection work. It would seem natural for local communities, which are obliged to bear the burden of the establishment of the protected area, to be given preference for employment in the reserve.

There is much local interest in running shops and itinerant business. The reserve could help people by extending credit for such activities. They could also be given incentives to establish small lodges and restaurants for tourists. Small-scale cottage industries related to the production of tourist handicrafts, processing of forest foods, bottling of fresh water, etc. are some other areas where the reserve could probably help.

Indeed, an in-depth investigation might show many other possibilities. Nonetheless, it can be seen from the above that, for a population of just over 4000, the opportunities mentioned above are extensive. Improved living conditions would permit peasants to invest more in health and children's education. This in turn would probably lead to smaller families. It may also discourage out-migration to the already overcrowded cities, although much will also depend upon the 'pull' factors originating in the cities (e.g., job opportunities, higher wages, better schooling and healthcare). In conclusion, there exist many opportunities to improve the social conditions of local communities without degrading the panda habitat, but they have not been exploited.

References

Barber, B (1957), *Social Stratification*, Bruce & Co, New York.

Batisse, M (1986), 'Developing and focusing the biosphere reserve concept', *Nature and Resources* (UNESCO), Vol XXII, No 3.

China Agricultural Yearbook 1992, (1993), Agricultural Publishing House, Beijing.

China Daily, 'China will link up its Nature Reserves', July 13 1993.

Coxon, A and C Jones (1975), *Social Mobility*, Penguin, Suffolk.

Croll, E (1982), *The Family Rice Bowl: Food and the Domestic Economy in China*, Food Systems Monograph, UNRISD, Geneva.

IUCN (World Conservation Union) (1993), *Parks for Life*, IUCN, Gland.

Li, C, S Zhou, D Xian, Z Chen and Z Tian (1992), 'Study of the management of Wolong nature reserve', in Wolong Nature Reserve and Sichuan Normal College (eds), *The Animal and Plant Resources and Protection of Wolong Nature Reserve*, Sichuan Publishing House of Science and Technology, Chengdu.

Li, W and X Zhao (1989), *China's Nature Reserves*, Foreign Languages Press, Beijing.

Lipset, S M (1981), *Political Man: The Social Bases of Politics*, Johns Hopkins University Press, Baltimore.

Ma, Y (ed) (1989), *China's Minority Nationals*, Foreign Languages Press, Beijing.

McKinley, T (1993), 'Agrarian transformation and the distribution of fixed productive assets in China', *Development and Change*, Vol 24, No 3, July.

MacKinnon, J, F Bi, M Qiu, C Fan, H Wang, S Yuan, A Tian and J Li (1989), *National Conservation Management Plan for the Giant Panda and its Habitat*, Ministry of Forestry, Beijing and WWF, Gland.

MacKinnon J, M Qiu, F Bi and K Zhang (1988), *Draft Management Plan for Wolong Nature Reserve*, WWF mimeo, Gland.

NEPA (National Environmental Protection Agency) (1992), *CES Yearbook 1992*, Chinese Environmental Science Press.

Perkins, D H (1969), *Agricultural Development in China 1368–1968*, Aldine Publishing Co, Chicago.

Rawski, T G (1979), *Economic Growth and Employment in China*, The World Bank/Oxford University Press, New York.

RDI/FRI (Rural Development Institute/Forestry Research Institute) (1993), *Sources of Cash Income in Wolong Reserve*, leaflet, RDI/FRI, Beijing.

Schaller, G (1993), *The Last Panda*, University of Chicago Press, Chicago.

Sheldon, W G (1975), *The Wilderness Home of the Giant Panda*, University of Massachusetts Press, Amherst.

State Statistical Bureau (1992), *China Statistical Yearbook 1992*, China Statistical Information and Consultancy Service Centre, Beijing.

UNRISD (United Nations Research Institute for Social Development) (1994), *Social Integration: Approaches and Issues*, Briefing Paper Series No 1, World Summit for Social Development, UNRISD, Geneva.

Wells, M, K Brandon and L Hannah (1992), *People and Parks: Linking Protected Area Management with Local Communities*, World Bank/WWF/USAID.

WWF (World Wide Fund For Nature) (1993), *WWF List of Approved Projects*, Vols 1–6, WWF, Gland, October.

Zhou, S (1992), *China Provincial Geography*, Foreign Languages Press, Beijing.

VIII

ECOTOURISM AND RURAL RECONSTRUCTION IN SOUTH AFRICA: REALITY OR RHETORIC?

Eddie Koch

South Africans put an end to apartheid when they voted in the country's first non-racial elections in April 1994. Since then, an ambitious reconstruction and development programme has been put into place by the government of national unity to correct the economic inequalities inherited from the past. Most sectors of the economy, however, are either stagnating or are not growing rapidly enough to generate the resources needed to ensure an effective redistribution of wealth. The trade in tourism, however, is an exception. Statistics show the number of visitors to the country is steadily climbing, with an average annual increase of 10 per cent in the last three years. The year of the elections, abnormal because of the unprecedented number of political missions that came into the country from abroad, saw an increase of between 20 and 25 per cent.

Proponents of nature tourism argue that, were it not for the endemic violence that wracks some parts of the country, the travel industry could equal the contribution of the mining sector to South Africa's gross domestic product. Some entrepreneurs and conservationists believe that nature-based tourism is the solution to poverty and underdevelopment, especially in the rural backwaters of the country. Ecotourism, they say, creates economic growth without smokestacks. It can turn grave robbers into tour guides, guerrillas into game rangers. Is this all wishful thinking, a romance dreamed up by people keen to convince politicians that the conservation of biological diversity, and the money that can be made from it, is a panacea for the country's economic problems?

This chapter examines the political economy of nature tourism in South Africa. It includes a critical evaluation of various scenarios put forward by proponents of ecotourism and concludes that it can be used as a tool to reconstruct some local areas of the rural economy — but only if serious efforts are made to address obstacles that inhibit genuine community participation in these ventures. The industry should not be seen as a magical solution to rural poverty in South Africa. If it is to live up to its potential in specific localities, its practitioners must take into account factors that constrain ecotourism's ability to generate and redistribute benefits to the poorest members of society.

The Politics and Economics of Ecotourism in South Africa

Conservation in South Africa has a reputation for being implemented with scientific and technical rigour. Among the urban middle classes, the protection of game parks has generally been considered a righteous cause unsullied by involvement in the country's turbulent political conflicts. This belief, however, is based on a romanticized history of wildlife protection. In reality, argues historian Jane Carruthers, protectionist attitudes and actions have always been deeply embedded in the country's political economy. Far from being politically neutral, the practices of conservationists have always been highly politicized and contested (Carruthers, undated (a):1–2).

During the early part of the twentieth century, colonial governments in various parts of the country began proclaiming game reserves, mainly on marginal agricultural land, and afforded 'Royal Game' status to certain threatened species. The Pongola Game Reserve, established in July 1889 by the government of the Transvaal Republic to prevent the *snelle uitroeing* (rapid extermination) of game, was probably the first to be proclaimed in South Africa. The Pongola reserve's new warden promptly expelled all Africans living in the area and forbade them to return. These provocative actions were cited by the British government as a reason for its decision to annex Maputaland in the late nineteenth century (Carruthers, undated (a):5–6).

At the same time Africans were subjected to a range of harsh and discriminatory legal restrictions. They were not eligible for hunting licences, which were issued only to white settlers, they had no legal access to firearms, they were not allowed to kill wildlife that damaged their crops and their right to own packs of hunting dogs was severely curtailed. Curbs on fishing were imposed in parts of the country, depriving people of an important source of protein.

Many of these restrictions were part of the ruling classes' efforts to create a cheap labour force for the mines and other industries that mushroomed after the discovery of gold. As one colonial official remarked in 1903: 'The destruction of game by natives... enables a large number of natives to live by this means who would otherwise have to maintain themselves by labour' (cited in Carruthers, undated (b):2).

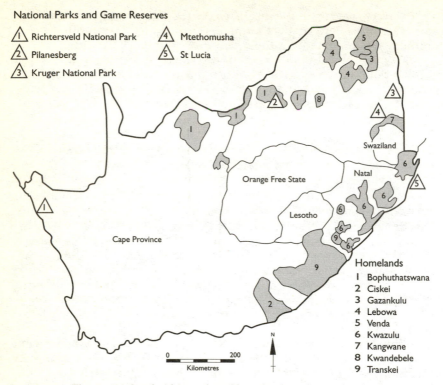

National Parks and Game Reserves

△1 Richtersveld National Park   △4 Mtethomusha
△2 Pilanesberg   △5 St Lucia
△3 Kruger National Park

Swaziland

Orange Free State   Natal

Lesotho

Cape Province

Homelands
1 Bophuthatswana
2 Ciskei
3 Gazankulu
4 Lebowa
5 Venda
6 Kwazulu
7 Kangwane
8 Kwandebele
9 Transkei

N

0   200
Kilometres

Figure 8.1 *South Africa: selected homelands and game reserves*

Wildlife protection was thus one of the many mechanisms used to create a black proletariat during the Transvaal's industrial revolution in the late nineteenth and early twentieth centuries. The creation of the Kruger National Park, currently the flagship of South Africa's conservation programme, involved severe hardship for the Tsonga communities who lived in and around the park. After the Anglo-Boer War at the turn of the century, the new British administration acquired the Sabi Game Reserve that had also been established by the Boer Republic on a strip of land between the Sabi and Crocodile rivers in the eastern Transvaal. In 1904 a new reserve was established to the north, called the Singwitsi Game Reserve, between the Great Letaba and Olifants Rivers. These two were to become the basis of the Kruger National Park (Figure 8.1).

It is estimated that about 3000 people lived in the Sabi reserve in 1902. The first warden, James Stevenson-Hamilton, adopted a harsh policy from the start and evicted large numbers from the area. When he was given the task of managing the reserve in 1902, Stevenson-Hamilton confessed that 'it had been impressed on me that the first difficulty would probably be with the natives, since these and the game could not be

216

expected to exist together, and I had already decided in my own mind that... the Reserve would have to be cleared of all human inhabitants' (cited in Archer and Fig, 1992:6).

These policies earned him the Tsonga name *Skukuza* (he who sweeps away, or he who turns everything upside down), which the colonial authorities proudly adopted as the name for the first rest camp in the park. Members of the local community voiced what was to become a common refrain in South Africa's conservation record: 'The government wants to drive (us) away from the Lowveld (the eastern Transvaal area where the park was established) so as to include these parts in the game reserve' (cited in Carruthers, undated (b):3).

Removals, forced labour and poll taxes — all features of South Africa's conquest at the hands of white settlers — were not restricted to the Kruger Park. From the western border of the country, where indigenous San people were removed to make way for the Kalahari Gemsbok Park in the 1930s, to the eastern shores of South Africa, forced removals were part and parcel of wildlife protection programmes. H.J. van Graan, Secretary of the Department of Native Affairs in the 1930s, had resisted earlier efforts to remove the Makuleke people from the Kruger Park. He apparently had a degree of acumen rare amongst government officials at the time. 'I foresee in this gain of today,' he said, 'the future germ of destruction of the whole park' (cited in Carruthers, undated (b):5).

A BBC documentary on the politics of conservation in South Africa, broadcast in 1992, begins with a scene of youths from the township of Matsulu, located on the southern fence of the Kruger National Park, singing and dancing in the gravel road that separates their homes from the reserve. 'Weep Kruger, you shall weep,' says their song. The angry youths went out into the streets to protest about 'Kruger' — a place where animals are able to roam in freedom while people who venture over the fence to collect firewood or poach game are arrested — because they associate game parks with forced removals, restrictions on freedom of movement and paramilitary game rangers (*The Weekly Mail*, 15–21 November 1991). The history of conservation in this country has ensured that similar sentiments are found across the South African landscape.

According to a report prepared by the former apartheid government, tourism is the world's largest and fastest-growing industry. It is claimed that international travel grew by 260 per cent between 1970 and 1990. In at least 17 countries it accounts for more than half of all foreign exchange earned and it is estimated that today one out of every 14 workers is employed in travel and related enterprises. This excludes those employed in industries created by 'multiplier effects' of tourism projects (Ministry for Administration and Tourism, 1992:2).

The South African white paper follows optimistic international accounts of the potential for travel and tourism to generate growth and development. In one study, tourism is said to have generated 5.9 per cent of the world's GNP in 1990, the equivalent of US$ 1.1 trillion. Of this, it is estimated US$ 62.5 billion went to developing countries.

Some writers claim it is the only industry in the world that allows a net 'North–South' flow of wealth from industrial countries to developing countries — although these figures do not compute the negative impacts, such as cultural and environmental degradation, that can be caused by tourism (Brandon, 1993:3 and 31). It is now commonplace to suggest that travel to wilderness areas is one of the fastest-growing sectors of the world's travel industry. There are, however, a number of serious problems associated with ecotourism.

The most common factor that prevents ecotourism from redistributing wealth in rural backwaters is the leakage of profits out of the host country to developed countries as well as from the countryside to the cities. The World Bank estimates that 55 per cent of tourist spending in developing countries eventually leaks back to developed countries. Some studies suggest that leakages of up to 90 per cent of revenue generated by tourism may apply in countries that lack substantial local ownership of services such as airlines, hotels and transportation companies (Brandon, 1993:32). A study conducted in Fiji, one of the most developed tourist resorts in the Pacific, found less than 25 per cent of the revenues from tourism actually stays on the island. The rest goes to multinational corporations which own and control the industry (*Southern Africa Political and Economic Monthly*, Tourism Supplement, Vol. 6, No. 11). Some 70 per cent of the money spent by foreign tourists on a beach holiday in Kenya returns to developed countries. 'The money goes to travel companies and for consumer goods to satisfy western tastes. Few developing countries can meet these sophisticated consumer demands internally' (*New Internationalist*, July 1993).

A related impediment to successful rural development through tourism is the failure to integrate ecotourism schemes into larger development plans. Examples abound of ecotourism projects that receive state subsidies only to be under-utilized because they are inadequately marketed or because there are no roads or other forms of transport into the region. Ecotourism, by its very nature, has limited linkages with other sectors of the rural economy and does not generate many additional local economic activities. Despite the optimistic claims of some commentators, it is possible for ecotourism projects to operate in relative isolation from the surrounding local economy. Capital, consumer goods and services can easily be imported from the outside. There is no economic imperative to link up with local industries, and this is a major reason for tourism's failure to stimulate further growth in some countries (Healy, 1992).

In this chapter, 'ecotourism' is used as it has been defined by the Ecotourism Society as purposeful travel to natural areas in order to gain an understanding of the culture and natural history of the environment. It implies that care is taken not to alter the integrity of the ecosystem and that economic opportunities are provided which make the conservation of natural resources beneficial to local people (Box 8.1).

> **Box 8.1** *Potential Benefits of Ecotourism*
>
> Benefits that ecotourism can provide to local people include:
>
> - the generation of revenue for continued efforts to maintain biological diversity in a particular area;
> - the simultaneous generation of revenue that can be used for the benefit of people living in or around the conservation area;
> - the encouragement of people's participation in the management of enterprises that use natural resources for the purpose of sustainable development;
> - the provision of appropriate institutions and skills to facilitate this kind of 'empowerment';
> - the enhancement of appreciation and understanding on the part of outsiders, tourists as well as conservation specialists, of local knowledge and culture involved in protection of the environment;
> - the growth of awareness by members of local communities of the need for environmental protection and sustainable development and an acceptance by local people of techniques, imported by scientists and specialists, that can enhance this objective.

South Africa currently attracts about 0.2 per cent of the world's travellers. In 1992, 2.7 million foreign visitors came to South Africa. Of these 2.1 million came from the African continent, mainly to conduct business, shopping or work-related activities, while 559,913 came from overseas. In 1993 the figures increased to 3 million with 2.4 million coming from Africa and 618,508 coming from abroad (Satour, 1993).

It has been estimated that in 1992 foreign tourism earned some SAR 2.5 billion (about US$ 800 million) in foreign exchange and provided 300,000 people with jobs, about one out of every 14 actively employed people in South Africa (Ministry for Administration and Tourism, 1992). In 1990, tourism was the fifth highest foreign exchange earner in South Africa. Manufactured exports earned SAR 30 billion, gold earned SAR 18 billion, mining and quarries SAR 6.3 billion and agriculture SAR 2.7 billion (Conservation Corporation, undated:4). The value of foreign tourism in 1992 increased by about 26 per cent to SAR 3.4 billion (Hughes, 1994:5). Despite the political violence that has swept the country in the past few years, there has been an average 10 per cent increase in the number of visitors from abroad (excluding Africa) (Satour, 1993).

A variety of land-use studies conducted locally show that nature conservation and tourism in arid and semi-arid regions of the country are able to generate greater revenues than more conventional agricultural land uses. A study of the new Madikwe game reserve in the north-west province, for example, shows that only 80 jobs would be generated by cattle farming compared to 1200 jobs in six luxury lodges being planned for the reserve. Income for labourers involved in cattle ranching would average SAR 3000 (about US$ 860) annually compared to SAR 7200 (about US$ 2057) from the ecotourism projects. Commercial projects that involve some degree of wildlife conservation currently constitute one of the few growth areas in the South African economy:

> *Up till now South African business has concentrated on the global competitive advantage it has in non-renewable resources such as the country's mineral wealth. Attention is at last being paid to the renewable resources such as wildlife in which we also have a global competitive advantage.* (Financial Mail, *20 September 1991*)

However, optimistic scenarios for tourism frequently do not take into account the heavy subsidies from state coffers that are required to maintain protected areas. The Pilanesberg National Park, generally regarded as one of the most successful ecotourism ventures in South Africa, has only just reached the stage where it generates a profit. After more than 10 years in existence, the park continues to rely on funding for both development and operational costs. A recent study estimates Pilanesberg made a loss of some SAR 500 million (about US$ 143 million) in the 1989/90 and 1990/91 fiscal years. Total investment in the park by the homeland government since its inception has been estimated at more than SAR 78 million (about US$ 23 million) (Davies, 1993).

Statistics published by the Natal Parks Board show that conservation in that province is also heavily subsidized. Its ecotourism programmes run at a break-even level or generate only a few hundred thousand rand in profits. Overall the parks in Natal cost millions of rand more to run than they generate in revenue (Parris, 1993:5). According to one conservationist:

> *Only a minority of conservation areas in South Africa can be regarded as financially viable. They rely largely on an annual allocation of funds from respective governments. Therefore, when a significant percentage of revenue is allocated to tribal neighbours it amounts to these people receiving an indirect handout from the government. In effect the areas are being rented by the state.* (Anderson, 1992:7)

This reflects the situation in most southern African countries, where there is at present 'a general disparity between profitable, well-managed private-sector tour companies enjoying the fruits of the under-funded management efforts of government agencies' (Kaufmann, undated:11). According to one conservationist, protected areas in South Africa attracted tourist expenditure in the vicinity of some SAR 3 billion (about US$ 0.85

billion) in 1992 while the national parks captured less than 10 per cent of this revenue. The rest, it is assumed, went to private game parks, hotel chains, car hire companies, local airlines, etc. (Hughes, 1994:5).

The Conservation Corporation believes that ecotourism is an industry which creates small business opportunities in the areas of laundry services, vegetable production, transportation, mechanics, medical and educational services, handicrafts, carpentry, construction and the supply of building materials. 'The service industry is labour intensive with a wide range of skills required thus presenting opportunities for training and multi-skilling of the people from the local economies' (Conservation Corporation, undated:4). But there are indications that community benefits are overstated by tour operators, probably to attract political and financial support for ecotourism, while efforts on the ground to promote effective improvements in the local economy are neglected.

Unlike cattle farming or agriculture, ecotourism can involve a long turn-around time between initial investment and the production of tangible benefits. In situations where rural communities depend on farming for their day-to-day survival, for example, people simply cannot afford to wait a couple of years before they start reaping benefits from ecotourism. This is the case in many parts of South Africa where land scarcity along with the recent drought, which continues in some areas, forces people to seek new lands for farming and grazing.

All too often operators make a decision to initiate ecotourism projects on the basis of their own feasibility studies without initially consulting with all sectors of the affected community and discussing the range of land-use options available to them. Recent history is replete with examples of popular resistance to tourism because conservationists and tourism entrepreneurs are insensitive to this issue. Efforts to pull local communities into some form of participation in the project are frequently strategies in damage control, incidental rather than integral attempts at promoting genuine participatory rural development.

Conservation Reform and Tourism-Based Development Initiatives in South Africa

Conflict between parks and people, between game reserves and their neighbours, between animals and communities are common themes in most parts of the world where national parks, wildlife reserves and other types of protected areas are at the forefront of efforts to protect biodiversity.

It has now become fashionable if not mandatory for conservation movements to claim they are implementing community-based programmes, or to use a term coined by World Bank and World Wide Fund For Nature (WWF) consultants, integrated conservation and development projects (ICDPs) to solve these problems. The World Conservation Union (IUCN) began to show concern about the clash of interests between game reserves and local people from the early 1980s. The organization's 1980 World Conservation Strategy stressed the importance of linking protected-area management with the economic activities of local communities.

Professional conservationists adopted the idea that their work should be community-friendly and promote development at the 1982 World Congress on National Parks in Bali, calling for increased support for communities through education programmes, revenue-sharing schemes, participation in the management of reserves, and the creation of appropriate development schemes near protected areas.

The World Bank's 1986 policy on wildlands recognizes that the protection of natural areas must be integrated into regional economic planning. In 1985 WWF launched its Wildlife and Human Needs Programme, which consists of some 20 projects in developing countries that attempt to combine conservation and development. According to Wells et al.:

> These projects attempt to ensure the conservation of biological diversity by reconciling the management of protected areas with the social and economic needs of local people. The smaller ICDPs include biosphere reserves, multiple-use areas, and a variety of initiatives on the boundaries of protected areas, including buffer zones.

However, the authors found that, almost without exception, these projects manifest a significant gap between the theory and practice. (Wells et al., 1992:ix and 63–64).

Southern Africa: The CAMPFIRE Initiative

In southern Africa, these international approaches were mirrored by the emergence of Zimbabwe's pioneering CAMPFIRE (Communal Area Management Programme for Indigenous Resources) programmes, indigenous experiments in combining conservation with community development. The CAMPFIRE programmes purport to have three main benefits: they improve the livelihoods of rural people, they impart a sense of self-management and self-reliance and they provide an incentive for rural communities to protect wildlife. Currently CAMPFIRE programmes are centred primarily around communal management of wildlife resources, but there are plans to expand the model to include management of other types of rural resources, such as forests and lakes.

The essence of CAMPFIRE is an attempt to harness the economic value of wildlife, which derives primarily from recreation and tourism, for the benefit of rural people. Some of these programmes have demonstrated to rural communities that conservation of wild animals and their management in ecotourism programmes can be more beneficial than cattle farming, especially on marginal lands.

Critics of CAMPFIRE point out that some projects fail to facilitate genuine community participation because they are still seen as externally imposed models with conservation of wildlife, rather than social development, as their primary objective. A recent assessment of CAMPFIRE notes a number of projects have failed to promote effective community participation in wildlife management because local village and ward committees have often been used merely to implement centrally conceived programmes and plans, rather than as participatory institutions for local development planning and implementation (Murombedzi, 1993).

Interest groups outside the community involved in CAMPFIRE projects — such as tour operators, the organizers of safari hunts, and various government agencies — tend to exercise more power than ordinary people and their organizations in the wildlife management schemes. There is also concern that CAMPFIRE projects which cannot provide trophy hunting and rely instead on photo-safaris may fail to generate any significant revenues from foreign visitors (Murombedzi, 1993:20–25).

The CAMPFIRE approach has achieved some credibility and popularity among professional conservationists and rural development planners in South Africa. A number of projects have been initiated in different parts of the country which attempt to apply CAMPFIRE principles to local South African conditions so as to offset the hostilities that have been engendered by conservation practices in the colonial and apartheid periods. There is a growing awareness that South African conditions are very different to those in the rural areas of Zimbabwe. For example, settlements in, or around, conservation areas are frequently heavily populated and do not lend themselves to the relatively simple participatory mechanisms devised by CAMPFIRE programmes. Some settlements that border on game reserves are, in fact, located in peri-urban rather than rural areas where it is far more difficult to establish 'proprietorship' or 'ownership' by a relatively cohesive community over a given set of natural resources.

In this context of congestion and scarcity, it becomes far more difficult to use resources from a game reserve to generate enough revenue to come anywhere near alleviating poverty and generating effective development. While the principles of CAMPFIRE are being emulated in South Africa, some conservationists have warned that simple importation of these programmes could create unrealistic expectations among people affected by conservation programmes, thereby compounding the historical hostility that is directed at game reserves in the country.

Surveys conducted in the former KwaZulu, Bophuthatswana and KaNgwane homelands indicate that in some of these areas the number of people, and their needs, are so great that natural resources are simply not capable of providing sustained and meaningful development to a significant proportion of the population.

> *Unlike Zimbabwe, where substantial wildlife populations have enabled the development of their CAMPFIRE programme, based on resource allocation, the resource in most tribal areas in South Africa is severely depleted. We do, however, have wildlife populations in conservation areas which can provide the basis for populations to develop projects similar to CAMPFIRE in our tribal areas. (Anderson, 1992:10)*

Mthethomusha: the New Way of Doing Things

Perhaps the best known 'CAMPFIRE' project in South Africa is the Mthethomusha Reserve, a small 'tribally owned' park located on the southern border of the Kruger Park, in the KaNgwane homeland. There was initial resistance in 1984 when the KaNgwane Parks Corporation (KPC) first raised the idea of starting a tribal resource area on land owned by the isiSwati-speaking Mphakeni people. The local chief and his councillors initially feared the community would lose their grazing land but were won over to the alternative idea of ecotourism/conservation when KPC officials pointed out that the area was mountainous and without enough water for all-year grazing. The promise of new jobs in the project also helped convince the tribal leaders and they gave their consent, naming the new project Mthethomusha ('the new law' or 'the new way of doing things').

Some 200 jobs were created, most of them filled by people from the nearby villages. Meat, and the wood to cook it, is provided once a year for a large celebration in the reserve. Sixty per cent of income from an upmarket lodge in the game park goes to the tribal authority, which remains the owner of the land. The parks authorities also work closely with the local association of traditional healers, allowing this influential group to undertake controlled trips into the area for the purpose of collecting herbs and roots. Local contractors were used, wherever possible, to build the reserve's lodge, which is now managed by a large hotel chain (*New Ground*, 1991/92, No. 6:16).

A trust, which includes representatives from the tribal authority and the conservation agency, has been set up as the main institution for administering the project. Decisions about how to use revenue, which has been spent mainly on classrooms and creches, are made primarily by the tribal authority. Until recently, there appears to have been no effective participation by people elected to civic and other 'democratic' organizations from the three main villages around the reserve. However, KaNgwane's parks authorities, prompted by criticism that they have ignored the voice of constituencies that are not represented in the old tribal structures, are looking at ways of broadening popular participation in the Mthethomusha project as well as other community-based projects in the homeland (van Wyk, interview, 1992).

From Casinos to CDOs

An older attempt to initiate a CAMPFIRE scheme in South Africa is the Pilanesberg National Park, located in the Bophuthatswana homeland about 700 km to the west of KaNgwane. The small park, some 58,000 hectares in size, is ringed by some of South Africa's most luxurious hotels and casinos including the Lost City, Sun City and the Marula Lodge. It derives a substantial part of its revenue from up-market tourists who come to this part of South Africa to combine the high-life of casino gambling with an ecotourist venture into the wild.

A study conducted in 1984 found that the creation of the Pilanesberg reserve caused serious problems for the original inhabitants and people living in settlements surrounding the park. According to the study, the reserve's original inhabitants lost access to grazing land for cattle. Researchers uncovered allegations of corruption in the tribal authority and tardiness in providing compensation for the loss of land.

> *People perceived the tribal authority as using the establishment of the park as a means of extending its domination and exploitation of villagers. The villagers' perception that this was condoned by the Bophuthatswana government was reinforced by a number of issues that arose in relation to the presence of the Sun City hotel complex on the border of the park. These related to the rustling/impounding of cattle entering Sun City property, unfair remuneration of Sun City employees and the Bophuthatswana government's action during a labour dispute [at Sun City]... [These] issues were all perceived to be linked within the context of the wider political economy resulting in a negative perception of the park. (Duthie, undated:3)*

Nevertheless, in the past few years, the parks board has encouraged community development organizations (CDOs) in the settlements around Pilanesberg. These independent institutions, with equal numbers of representatives nominated by the tribal authority and chosen from among ordinary residents, take key decisions about management and the use of revenue derived from the park. This initiative, a little more than two years old, is seen as an effective way of reconciling the need for popular participation with traditional structures of local government.

Recent research indicates the parks board's new policies have also succeeded in overcoming local hostility towards the Pilanesberg park. A survey based on a sample of 400 people from the surrounding communities found that the majority would not like to see the park deproclaimed and the land redistributed to the people (Davies, 1993:iv).

Contract Parks

A recent initiative in South Africa is the 'contract park' in the remote Richtersveld region of the north-western Cape. This model has its genesis in a land struggle during the late 1980s between the indigenous inhabitants of the area and the (South African) National Parks Board, which wanted to declare the area a nature reserve and have the pastoralists who live in it move out.

The Richtersveld region is unique in South Africa in that it combines mountain and desert conditions. The area's biodiversity has long been acknowledged by conservationists. The area hosts small mammals and reptiles but is most famous for its *!khureb* or *halfmensboom* (*Pachypodium namaquanum*) which can grow to two metres and has a half-human appearance. It hosts more than 1000 endemic species of succulent plants. One of the Namaqualanders, famous for their wit and a colourful dialect of Afrikaans, had the following to say when he heard the pastoralists were to be deported in the interests of conservation: '*Hulle gee om vir die halfmens, maar wat van die volmens?* (They care about the half person but what about the whole person?)' (Archer and Fig, 1992:5).

Backed by human rights groups in Cape Town as well as a number of sympathetic academics, the local communities refused to move and began to formulate an alternative plan that involved popular involvement in the running of the proposed park. They negotiated the right to remain in the area, to continue grazing their stock, and to receive royalties and jobs from the park. They persuaded the National Parks Board to give them a say in the management of the park as well as the right to review the agreement in its entirety after a period of 30 years (Fig, 1992:119). This breakthrough initiated a series of reforms by the National Parks Board.

Rhetoric and Reality in Maputaland

Conservation authorities in KwaZulu-Natal — responsible for administering a number of reserves in the Maputaland region of KwaZulu-Natal province — claim to have a community-friendly approach to conservation. In 1989 KwaZulu's Chief Minister, Mangosuthu Buthelezi, said his old homeland 'has clearly understood that people must be the cornerstone of any conservation effort and that unless conservation is made relevant to ordinary people, it has no hope of gaining their support' (AFRA, 1990:9).

The KwaZulu Department of Nature Conservation (KDNC), in line with this policy, allows people into the reserves to collect reeds for use in building houses, fish are harvested in the Kosi Bay estuary by a small group of fishermen using a centuries-old *kraal* fishing system. The department's policy is to give the local tribal authorities 25 per cent of all revenue derived from gate takings so that these can be used for 'social upliftment' projects. Its official newsletter claims: 'All conservation efforts are doomed to fail if there are not tangible benefits for the people involved. This is especially true in a Third World situation such as ours. We believe that our policy of sharing will continue into the future because it was developed with the people in mind' (*Isigijimi*, No. 1, 1992:4).

Reserves in Maputaland — Kosi Bay, the Tembe Elephant Park and the Ndumu Game Reserve — have each received negative publicity because of a significant gap, at least in the past, between their rhetoric and practice. However, the KDNC has recently attempted to implement some of its stated principles more effectively. For example, the department has promoted private-sector investment in its reserves, so as to mobilize funds for the development of lodges and tourist camps. These are to be run in partnership with local communities with a renewed emphasis on providing benefits for local people from revenues generated in this way.

White Businessmen and Black Entrepreneurs

A number of South Africa's exclusive private reserves, which cater for foreign tourists willing to pay up to SAR 1000 (about US$ 300) per night for their bush experience, have begun to devise ways of making their businesses contribute to the social improvement of black neighbours. The Conservation Corporation, which runs the Londolozi Lodge in the eastern Transvaal and the Phinda Lodge in Maputaland, is a prime exponent of this approach. Workers are paid above standard wages and management has expressed a willingness to negotiate salaries and conditions of employment with their black workers, unlike most employers in the rural areas of South Africa. Another key component of what has become known as the 'Londos strategy' is to create business opportunities, financial backing and skills-training for local black entrepreneurs around the lodges.

The Londolozi reserve, for example, has contracted a local taxi operator to provide transport from its airstrip to the lodge. Management of the Phinda reserve has employed a community relations officer and plans to stimulate a charcoal industry for entrepreneurs from the surrounding communities. The Corporation has set up a Rural Investment Fund to raise capital for, and promote, major infrastructural projects in the depressed areas around their reserves. These include new roads, a water reticulation project, entertainment centres and a SAR 6 million (about US$ 1.7 million) airport for the Gazankulu homeland. This fund had, by early 1993, also negotiated a donation of SAR 100,000 (about US$ 28,000) for small businessmen in the areas surrounding Phinda. Funds raised through the trust are used to subsidize the building of schools and clinics.

Within the context of the current socio-political environment in South Africa, we are firmly committed to acting as a catalyst for responsible development — not only through investment in the luxury end of the eco-tourist market. Our major drive this year,

through the Rural Investment Fund, is to encourage the develop-
ment of business peripheral to luxury lodges and to assist the
development of infrastructure in the adjacent communities. We
believe that only through achieving socio-economic development
and growth will our eco-tourism industry be ensured of legitimacy
in the new order of South Africa. Our approach is, we believe, the
only means of ensuring that our wilderness areas remain econom-
*ically viable. (*Conservation Corporation News, *No. 3, April*
1993:2)

Other luxury reserves are following the example set by the Conservation
Corporation. The Sabi Sabi Private Game Reserve, located not far from
Londolozi, is another example of how sound ecological management can
make big business. The primary objective is 'maintenance and improvement of the current species and habitat diversity, thus optimising the
commercial returns through visual gain and minimizing the detrimental
impact of the environment' (Sabi Sands press release, 1992). The reserve
sells local crafts to visitors and supplies bursary schemes for training
black rangers. Its management has set up a feasibility study for the Sabi
Sabi Pfunani Project that aims to establish 'linkages' between the reserve
and neighbouring communities and to obtain funding for local development schemes (Hearn, 1992).

Pulling Down some Fences

Management of the Kruger National Park has also recently embarked on
an effort to improve the image of the reserve in surrounding communities. During the drought of the 1980s, the worst this century in southern
Africa and one that still affects this part of the country, water was
provided by the park management to villages in parts of the KaNgwane
homeland. Black artisans from neighbouring villages have been encouraged to manufacture and sell crafts and curios to Kruger's visitors, and
tourist shops inside the park are encouraged to stock their shelves with
local products. According to senior parks officials, there are fairly
advanced plans to build small business estates in some of the large townships near the park and recycling projects have been started in
Namakgale, a black township near Phalaborwa on the western border of
Kruger, which provide revenue and jobs for the residents.

Park officials train residents of surrounding villages to plant communal gardens and trees are supplied from a nursery inside the park for
village wood lots. Herbal gardens have been initiated by park officials in
some villages so that traditional healers can harvest roots and plants used
in indigenous medicines. Subsidized day trips for local school children
are provided and 'ecoclubs', designed to show the benefits of conservation, have been created in neighbouring schools with the help of
headmasters and teachers (*The Weekly Mail*, 30 October–5 November

1992). Management of the park has recently decided to create popular forums in each of the homeland areas surrounding Kruger. These involve an effort to promote participation by tribal authorities, political organizations and civic organizations in negotiations about issues that range from land claims to investment of park revenue in development projects (Marais, interview, 1994).

Evaluation

In their comparative study, Wells et al. note that 'eliciting authentic participation in projects is difficult and time-consuming in developed countries and even more so in developing countries' (1992:43). Few of the programmes they reviewed in different parts of the world had effectively promoted 'participation in decision-making, problem identification, project design and implementation, and in project monitoring and evaluation'. Many of the organizations and institutions set up to achieve these goals are still young and require more time to operate effectively. Most are still dependent on outside agencies for some form of support, either financial or for the provision of skills. Yet there are encouraging signs, say the authors, of some popular enthusiasm for local participation in resource management (Wells et al., 1992:63–64). This trend could be maximized in South Africa by paying attention to the following key issues.

Land Reform

The government of national unity has begun a complex process of land reform that aims to redistribute 30 per cent of all arable land in the country to disadvantaged black groups within five years. As part of this programme, people who were forcibly removed from their land during the colonial or apartheid periods are able to lodge claims for the restoration of their title to a special land court that has been established.

A number of rural groups, including at least two tribal chiefs whose people were removed from the Kruger National Park, have already lodged such claims. A number of similar cases are expected in other areas of the country where the creation of wildlife estates involved racial removals. These are viewed by some conservationists as a threat. However, there are also signs that these claims can lead to negotiations about ways of including rural people as real partners in joint management of protected areas and attendant nature tourism programmes. The land reform programme does not stipulate that people who regain title will automatically reoccupy land that was alienated from them — thus allowing for creative arrangements in which conservation areas can be maintained and managed by existing authorities while being used for tourism-based development schemes that benefit the original owners.

Tribal Authorities and Civic Organizations

Residents of settlements adjoining parks frequently complain that tribal authorities do not represent all sectors within the community. In Maputaland residents have alleged there is corruption within local authorities and that profits from game reserves are spent on expensive motor cars rather than schools and creches (GEM, 1993). A youth from the village of Mzinti in KaNgwane, where a small tribal resource reserve has been started by the KPC, complained that the local chief used money from the reserve to build a new tribal office. 'The money was used to build a place where people have to go and pay their fines.' In addition the chief is said to have located the office next to his market, thus attracting people to his stalls and making money out of the process (interview, November 1992).

Residents from youth groups and civic organizations active in the villages surrounding Mthethomusha complained that the local chief was unwilling to accept the views of these organizations (GEM, 1993: section 8). Some members of civic associations in the Gazankulu homeland are also critical of their local chiefs. 'The government recruited chiefs and used them against the people. Many are not acceptable to the community. The community has different layers, different age groups and views and these are not taken into account' (GEM, 1993).

However, there appears to be widespread acceptance, even among left-wing civic organizations, that traditional authorities are an integral part of local government in most of South Africa's rural areas and cannot be dispensed with. Pilanesberg and Mthethomusha have attracted a fair amount of local co-operation, primarily because the chiefs there have some degree of support and credibility. Where chiefs are seen as being imposed from the outside, as in Maputaland and some areas of Gazankulu, working with tribal local authorities is a much less effective means of harnessing popular support for ecotourism.

A number of conservation agencies have accepted the need to work with 'democratic' organizations as well as tribal authorities. They have begun to look at ways of implementing models similar to the Bophuthatswana CDO or the Richtersveld management committee. However, it has been pointed out that the CDO for Pilanesberg is not an elected body even though a serious effort was made to ensure that it represents a wide cross-section of the local community. It is a fairly stable institution primarily because it has the support of the local chief and operates in a homogeneous community. Efforts to create similar structures in regions where there are hostile local authorities as well as more severe ethnic and social tensions will pose a number of challenges (GEM, 1993).

The next problem is an inverse of the first. Conservationists in South Africa are showing increased willingness to work with grassroots organizations but frequently find these to be fragile and unstable. When there is conflict between civic organizations and tribal authorities, conservation agencies face the dilemma of which body to work with. 'We don't want to offend one by talking to the other' is the way one official expressed the conundrum. Some conservation agencies argue that civic organizations eligible for participation in the running of a conservation area must be elected and be able to demonstrate they have a mandate to talk for the constituency they claim to represent.

Access to thatching, meat, herbs and other resources inside the conservation areas is an important contribution to local people's subsistence. However these resources, especially in heavily congested settlements, make little difference to the livelihoods of most people. They are sometimes seen as 'handouts' from above rather than a form of development capable of working a real transformation in the rural economy. A similar perception sometimes applies where a proportion of entrance fees is paid to local communities by a conservation agency. In the words of a member of the Pilanesberg CDO: 'The parks board gave token money as a "present" to the community. This was apparently 10 per cent of the profits, but people have not been informed of where the money comes from, or how the amount was decided on.' The creation of a community development organization with rights to decide on how to distribute and invest the money is a potential solution to this problem (GEM, 1993).

Education and Indigenous Knowledge

A fairly common perception in settlements surrounding game reserves is that the parks do not employ enough local people. Conservationists stress that there is a limit to the number of people who can be absorbed into these projects, and that community-based conservation schemes should not be seen as a magical remedy for high unemployment rates in rural areas. Many community groups make the point that, instead of handing out meat and other resources, wildlife products should be sold and the proceeds put into a scholarship fund for local youth to study conservation and other skills needed for parks management (GEM, 1993).

Residents frequently complain that conservationists use 'book knowledge' for the management of resources and ignore the store of local knowledge. There have been strong recommendations that local approaches to conservation be studied and applied wherever possible in the management of the reserve and its resources.

A common criticism is that there is not enough communication between the body managing a game reserve and members of the community. Even where education programmes exist, as in the case of most community-based programmes, it is still common to find people in the community who know little about the aims and objectives of the project. 'What is this thing called a park?' is a common question raised in the Richtersveld. The need to increase and expand education and recreation activities associated with ecotourism schemes is reinforced by these perceptions (GEM, 1993).

231

Development and Division

There is a growing awareness in South Africa that efforts to promote community participation in development projects can engender new forms of conflict and fragmentation. Events in Maputaland, where the setting up of community-based game reserves has promoted secessionist organizations, are an example.

An even more extreme case occurred in Phola Park, a large shanty-town settlement some 40 km east of Johannesburg, where a non-governmental organization, Planact, set up what it believed was a democratic development committee to plan and implement a scheme for upgrading the informal settlement. Members of the committee were elected and reported back to the community at mass meetings called especially for this purpose. Funds for a site-and-service scheme that would have allowed families to build brick homes with basic amenities were provided by the large funding organization and were to be administered by the development committee. Phola Park was seen as the model of participatory development.

Yet on the day the scheme was to be implemented, members of the development committee were attacked by gun-wielding men in the shack that served as their office; one of them was killed. Others were forced out of the township and their names, along with those of officials from Planact, were put on a death list. Despite their best intentions, the planners and the local community leaders had failed to reach and incorporate the most marginalized groups in the settlement in their planning.

These groups — made up of illegal Mozambican immigrants, criminal gangs and migrant workers who wanted a temporary place to stay in the urban areas so that they could remit most of their earnings to their homes in the rural areas — relied on the illegal and informal nature of the settlement to sustain the lifestyle they had developed. Police stations, street lights, site and service rents were inimical to their interests. The very way of life of these people involved the creation of clandestine networks hidden from the view of policemen, officials as well as civic leaders. This alliance of interest groups expressed their opposition only at the last moment, and then in the most direct and violent way (Baskin, 1993a).

A committee set up by the Goldstone Commission, a body of judges and lawyers whose task it is to probe the causes of political violence in South Africa, has noted a basic paradox that underlies many development schemes in this country.

> *Socio-economic development must be undertaken concurrently with the elimination of the triggers of violence and the re-imposition of law and order. We acknowledge that it will frequently be very difficult to undertake development in the area because of the violence and that such development itself might in fact initially*

*aggravate the level of conflict within the community. (Goldstone
Commission, 1992:61)*

An official who worked with Planact believes the starting point for all
development officials is to understand that the word 'community' is a
misnomer. The term masks the harsh, and sometimes unpleasant, reality
that most settlements are made of fragmented and deeply divided
factions. Instead of assuming an in-built inertia towards consensus, planners should assume their programmes will impact in different ways on
groups within poor 'communities' and that varied and conflicting
responses will be elicited from them. Before any development programme
is even conceptualized, a detailed survey of the different stakeholder
groups in each community should be conducted and the way their interests are likely to be affected by the development process should be
outlined.

> *This further implies that the present method of feedback and
> mandate gathering is inadequate and must be adjusted to incorpo-
> rate an outreach programme aimed at bringing in the different
> interests. Thus the role of the civic [organization] changes from
> representing the community to facilitating and mediating commu-
> nity interests and conflicts. It is thus more an enabling role than a
> controlling one.*
>
> > *It is precisely because many interest groupings find it impos-
> sible or inappropriate to organize themselves formally or to engage
> in open debate that they are forced to use random violence to stop a
> development perceived to be threatening... By defining such inter-
> ests beforehand the opportunity exists to engage with groupings
> which normally are invisible but have the capacity to destroy. Such
> early engagements will help to define the conflicts early in the
> process thus enabling creative ways to be found to accommodate
> them. This can only be done if the civic actively seeks out and gains
> the confidence of such groupings. (Baskin, 1993a:6)*

Some ecotourism planners have suggested that environmental impact
studies should be mandatory before any scheme is given official
approval and financial backing, and that these studies should include
an assessment of the project's social impacts. Project proposals based
on, and the results of, such studies should be made available to the
public for review and conscious strategies should be devised to ensure
proper dissemination and open-ended discussion with a wide range of
community groupings.

> *Developers should be required to provide data and evaluations on
> proposed tourism developments. This should include environmen-
> tal, social, and economic impacts. There should be a governmental*

and public review process and a method of denying development requests and mandating mitigation of impacts. (Ashton and Ashton, undated:52)

Another important lesson from the Phola Park experience is that development programmes should have a set of short-term objectives that can be easily met while the longer-term process of building deep and effective community participation is in process. These short-term goals should be designed to show that a project is capable of meeting some urgent needs while a sound social base and participatory institutions for bigger and more ambitious aspects of the programme are being built.

There can be no development without a community organization. This doesn't come easily and there has to be a concentrated programme to build up and facilitate. Talking to one or two elders is not community building. Then there is no such thing as long-term development without short-term progress. People have to be able to see that they are starting to benefit from the project (Baskin, 1993b:11).

Integration of Conservation Administration

More seriously, for our purposes, fragmentation in the ecotourism sector has negative social and economic consequences. Brandon notes that a common difficulty in promoting ecotourism to Third World countries is the lack of integration between national and local initiatives:

While countries may be quick to promote ecotourism as a source of regional economic growth, promotion is often emphasized at the expense of planning. In many cases, a lack of integration of local level plans with national level policy has led to greatly reduced potential for ecotourism. (Brandon, 1993:51)

A common complaint from rural people affected by 'community-based' conservation is that there is a confusing array of approaches to the implementation of such projects. This has led to suggestions that a future government draft broad national policy which requires each conservation agency to follow standard procedures that, at the same time, are designed to allow for regional variation and diversity. Clearly it is also vital that there be rationalization in the number of agencies charged with responsibilities for ecotourism and conservation. This would help to reunify fragmented ecological zones and prevent potential benefits from being reduced and dispersed.

The Kruger Park and the private sector are leading the way in this respect. Fences between the private reserves and the park have been taken down. Liaison bodies have been set up to deal with common resource management issues while each reserve is able to maintain its different style and approach to ecotourism: the private lodges continue with their upmarket safari drives and hunting expeditions, the Kruger Park provides a more modest set of facilities catering for tourists with a wider range of incomes. Kruger's management has also begun discussions with the Gazankulu conservation authorities and the KaNgwane Parks Corporation about eventually linking the Manyeleti and Mthethomusha reserves more closely to the Kruger Park (*The Weekly Mail*, 30 October–5 November 1992).

Conservation agencies have begun discussing the need for a more co-ordinated approach to their work and the possibility of institutional reform to overcome the artificial divisions created by apartheid. However, some of the most interesting efforts at community involvement in tourism took place in the independent or semi-independent homelands that were set up under apartheid. This indicates that local and regional agencies, charged with the responsibility for economic development in relatively backward rural areas, are more likely to respond to the challenge with innovative initiatives. New institutional arrangements should not stifle the creativity that stems from this situation.

According to the director of the KwaZulu Department of Nature Conservation: 'This suggests that the concept of federalized conservation and management as opposed to unitary control in one or two monolithic bodies may be a better option in the "new" South Africa'. Given the considerable cultural and environmental diversity existing in South Africa and the increased need for sensitivity and experience in dealing with the variations, the idea of existing conservation bodies enjoying a degree of regional autonomy under a centrally placed policy making 'umbrella type' organization may be the answer.

However, rationalization may prove every bit as difficult in the conservation arena as it currently is in the political field. 'Winner-take-all concepts are likely to be vigorously resisted, beginning perhaps with the first hint of group structures to protect the interests of professional conservation staff in the future'. (*Isigijimi*, No. 1, 1992:3)

The National Parks Board has noted the need for a more detailed categorization of different types of game reserves in South Africa. It wants to maintain the concept of national parks as areas large enough to host exceptional biological and physical diversity in an integrated ecosystem that is granted the 'highest form of government protection'. It suggests that certain areas have a national, and aesthetic, set of values which will have to be balanced against the needs of local communities when it comes to devising policy and protectionist measures (National Parks Board, 1992:6). Jeremy Anderson, director of the KaNgwane Parks Corporation, envisages a 'patchwork quilt' scenario in which national parks, resource reserves, community-run projects, privately owned lodges, joint-partnership schemes, safari hunting companies and even mixed resource areas can co-exist, each having their own local management structures which abide by, and are governed by, a central agency and set of principles (Anderson, interview, 1992).

Conclusions

This chapter has identified serious obstacles that need to be addressed if ecotourism is to improve the livelihoods of people in rural areas — and has suggested a number of policies that may help to ensure that it can. They include the need for land reform, the restoration of title wherever feasible to indigenous owners, so that rural people can participate effectively in decisions about whether their land is to be used for ecotourism schemes. Legal and constitutional reforms designed to reinforce a feeling amongst local people that they are the proprietors — the guardians if not the owners — of the natural resources that exist on their land are also important. Support for forms of land tenure, including communal arrangements, that lend themselves more to sustainable use and can be less environmentally damaging than individual ownership is likely to facilitate this process.

The creation of new democratic institutions, which can operate alongside the traditional tribal authorities, that will maximize people's participation in local development projects is a popular demand in South Africa. But it is also vital that so-called 'mass democratic organizations' recognize the need to demonstrate that they have real support and an effective mandate from the groups they represent if they are to help make ecotourism projects achieve their full potential.

It has become abundantly clear that skills training and support for community organizations to enhance the ability of their members to participate in ecotourism and natural resource management schemes is a priority for the tourism industry and the state. This should be based on an understanding that 'communities' are, in reality, agglomerations of diverse and fractious groupings and that each of these experience development in different — and often contradictory — ways. Mandatory environmental and economic impact assessments for all ecotourism schemes should examine social impacts as well. They should facilitate governmental and public review, and require mitigation of negative impacts.

A standardized approach to the implementation of ecotourism projects and rationalization of the many different state — and parastatal — bodies currently involved in the administration of these will be a major task facing South Africa's new government. This reorganization should be undertaken with the objective of limiting the leakage of revenue derived from ecotourism and associated activities out of the area and maximizing the funds available to stimulate local development.

The rural poor of South Africa need real reconstruction not rhetoric. It is necessary to guard against romantic notions that ecotourism is a magical panacea for poverty. For it to be used as an effective tool in community development requires a massive effort to redistribute the benefits and revenues generated by the tourism industry.

References

AFRA (Association for Rural Advancement) (1990), *Conservation and Removals*, Special Report No 6, Maputaland.

Anderson, J L (1992), *Case Studies of Conservation Agency: Tribal Neighbour Agreements in South Africa*, unpublished Kangwane Parks Board mimeo.

Archer, F and D Fig (1992), *Empowerment and Environment: Towards Effective Community Conservation in the Richtersveld*, unpublished GEM mimeo.

Ashton, R and P Ashton (undated), *An Introduction to Sustainable Tourism (Ecotourism) in Central America*, Water and Air Research Inc, Florida.

Baskin, J (1993a), *The Phola Park Development Project and Possible Implications for Urban Planning and Development in the PWV*, unpublished Planact manuscript.

— (1993b), *Community Participation in Conservation Projects*, paper presented to GEM's People and Parks Conference (Magaliesberg, 21–23 May) (included in proceedings of conference published by GEM).

Brandon, K (1993), *Bellagio Conference on Ecotourism: Briefing Book*, Rockefeller Foundation Conference (8–12 February).

Carruthers, J (undated-a), *Nature Protection in South Africa: an Historical Perspective*, mimeo, University of South Africa, Pretoria.

— (undated-b), *'Police Boys' and Poachers: Africans, Wildlife Protection and National Parks, The Transvaal 1902 to 1950*, mimeo, University of South Africa, Pretoria.

Conservation Corporation (undated), *Tourism: South Africa's Economic Re-awakening*, mimeo.

Davies, R J (1993), *Cost Benefit Analysis of Pilanesberg National Park*, draft research report for masters degree in business leadership, University of South Africa, Pretoria, August.

Duthie, A (undated), *Pilanesberg National Park's Neighbouring Communities, An Historical Profile*, unpublished GEM information paper.

Fig, D (1992), 'Flowers in the desert: community struggles in Namaqualand', in J Cock and E Koch (eds), *Going Green: People, Politics and the Environment in South Africa*, Oxford University Press, Oxford.

GEM (Group for Environmental Monitoring) (1993), *Record of the People and Parks Conference* (Magaliesberg, 21–23 May), mimeo, GEM, Johannesburg.

Goldstone Commission (1992), *Report of the Inquiry Into Causes of Violence on the East Rand*, Goldstone Commission, November.

Healy, R G (1992), *The Role of Tourism in Sustainable Development*, unpublished mimeo circulated at Bellagio Conference on Ecotourism (8–12 February 1993).

Hearn, G (1992), *Reconnaissance Survey of Rural Communities Bordering the Sabi Sabi Wildtuin and the Identification of Some Possible Linkages*, Sabi Sands Pfufanani Project Interim Report, Institute of Natural Resources, November.

Hughes, G (1994), *Can Ecotourism Promote Rural Reconstruction in South Africa?*, proceedings of GEM workshop on Natal Parks Board's Plans for

Ecotourism, GEM, Johannesburg.

Kaufmann, D (undated), *The Tourism Sector*, unpublished paper produced for the African Development Bank.

Ministry for Administration and Tourism (1992), *White Paper on Tourism*, Republic of South Africa, Pretoria.

Murombedzi, J (1993), *State Versus Local Control of Natural Resources: the Case of The CAMPFIRE Programme in Zimbabwe*, Centre for Applied Social Sciences mimeo, University of Zimbabwe, Harare, December.

National Parks Board (1992), *Methodology and Approach in the Selection of Proposed National Parks for a New South Africa*, National Parks Board, Pretoria.

Parris, D (1993), *Management of Conservation Areas*, paper presented to GEM's People and Parks Conference (Magaliesberg, 21–23 May), (included in proceedings of conference published by GEM).

Satour (South African Tourism Board) (1993), *Foreign Arrivals Statistics*.

Wells, M, K Brandon and L Hannah (1992), *People and Parks, Linking Protected Area Management with Local Communities*, World Bank/ WWF/USAID, Washington.

The following newspapers, magazines and television programme were also drawn on during research for ths chapter:

Conservation Corporation News, Financial Mail, Isigijimi, New Ground, New Internationalist, Sabi Sands press release, *Southern Africa Political and Economic Monthly, The Weekly Mail, Fair Game*, Television Documentary, produced by BBC Natural History Unit, 1991.

Interviews were conducted with: Jeremy Anderson, Director, KaNgwane Parks Corporation, South Africa (November 1992); Avrie van Wyk, Senior Conservation Officer for the KaNgwane Parks Board, South Africa (November 1992); and Chris Marais, Official in charge of community relations in the Kruger National Park, South Africa (March 1994)

IX

MANAGEMENT OF WILDLIFE, TOURISM AND LOCAL COMMUNITIES IN ZIMBABWE

Chris McIvor

Introduction

National parks constitute some 12.7 per cent of the total land area of Zimbabwe. These parks are home to an exotic variety of wild animals in a relatively unspoiled natural habitat, and constitute the cornerstone of Zimbabwe's tourist industry. It is an industry which now earns the country a major percentage of its foreign exchange. Yet while the economy enjoys this revenue and while the tourists enjoy the unique variety of wild animals, what of the communities that live on the edge of these estates?

Hwange National Park in the southern part of the country reveals some of the issues in the relationship between people and parks in Zimbabwe (Figure 9.1). Covering some 1.5 million hectares of land, it is one of the most popular destinations on the African continent. Its brochure to attract visitors is typical: 'Come and enjoy an African wilderness untouched by human presence. Enjoy the provision of expert guides, modern air-conditioned vehicles and a luxury rest camp from which one can watch the wildlife from the comfort of one's own veranda'.

Yet the price of maintaining this illusion is high — not so much in terms of the cost to the tourist as in the consequences for the communities living around this area from which they are excluded. Inhabitants of a low-rainfall area with infertile soils and inadequate resources, these communities are among the poorest in the country. The thatched huts here, unlike those in the park rest camps nearby, are not waterproofed

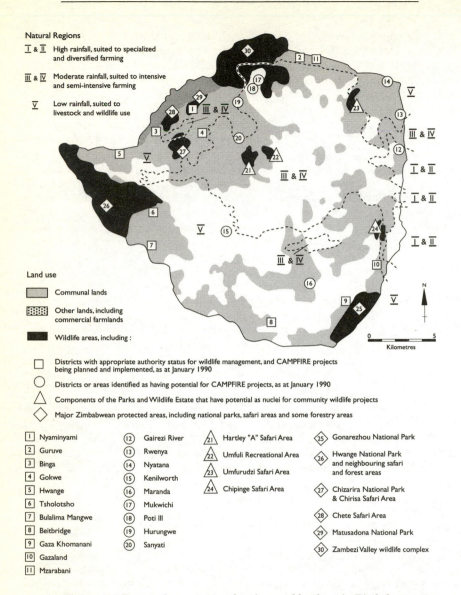

Natural Regions

I & II High rainfall, suited to specialized and diversified farming

III & IV Moderate rainfall, suited to intensive and semi-intensive farming

V Low rainfall, suited to livestock and wildlife use

Land use

Communal lands

Other lands, including commercial farmlands

Wildlife areas, including :

☐ Districts with appropriate authority status for wildlife management, and CAMPFIRE projects being planned and implemented, as at January 1990

○ Districts or areas identified as having potential for CAMPFIRE projects, as at January 1990

△ Components of the Parks and Wildlife Estate that have potential as nuclei for community wildlife projects

◇ Major Zimbabwean protected areas, including national parks, safari areas and some forestry areas

1 Nyaminyami	12 Gairezi River	21 Hartley "A" Safari Area	25 Gonarezhou National Park
2 Guruve	13 Rwenya	22 Umfuli Recreational Area	26 Hwange National Park and neighbouring safari and forest areas
3 Binga	14 Nyatana	23 Umfurudzi Safari Area	
4 Gokwe	15 Kenilworth	24 Chipinge Safari Area	
5 Hwange	16 Maranda		27 Chizarira National Park & Chirisa Safari Area
6 Tsholotsho	17 Mukwichi		
7 Bulalima Mangwe	18 Poti III		28 Chete Safari Area
8 Beitbridge	19 Hurungwe		29 Matusadona National Park
9 Gaza Khomanani	20 Sanyati		30 Zambezi Valley wildlife complex
10 Gazaland			
11 Mzarabani			

Figure 9.1 *Protected areas, natural regions and land use in Zimbabwe*

against rain or air-conditioned against the heat of summer. The water from stagnant wells is very different from the imported refreshments enjoyed by the tourist. The revenues from tourism end up in pockets other than those of the people nearest the tourist destinations.

It is evident from talking to people from these villages that they not only feel largely excluded from the park's benefits, but that they are actively prejudiced by its existence. Many communities surrounding Hwange view the park not as a romantic wilderness, but as a place from where wild animals emerge to trample and destroy the few crops they have managed to grow. Protected areas have allowed wildlife populations to expand to a level where, in order to survive, they must raid the fields of farmers on the edges of the park. Yet levels of compensation for crop damage, farmers point out, are either minimal or non-existent.

Local resentment does not end here. Older villagers recall a time when the land, now enclosed by park boundaries, was theirs to use for agriculture, grazing their livestock, collection of firewood, etc. But during the colonial era, the best agricultural lands in Zimbabwe were appropriated for a small elite of European farmers and communities were evicted from their traditional homes to make way for recreational reserves and safari hunting areas that benefited only the small European population in the country or visitors from abroad. While tourism may have brought some jobs and even stimulated a craft industry around a few of the parks, it is that sense of alienation and dispossession that has remained uppermost in the minds of the people interviewed by the author.

The first part of this chapter looks at the era of colonial dispossession and the early roots of antagonism. The second part discusses the resources lost to and opportunity costs suffered by local communities when commercial farms and national parks were created. Next, the growth of tourism in Zimbabwe and the centrality of wildlife to its international appeal are discussed. The chapter then goes on to describe how Zimbabwe has been attempting to reduce local hostility through a programme called CAMPFIRE, which aims to return benefits to the people most affected by wildlife and tourism. The conclusion discusses the need for devolution of further responsibilities for management, organization and ownership to local communities if an attempt such as CAMPFIRE is to achieve its objective of fully reconciling people and parks in contemporary Zimbabwe.

Control and Dispossession

When the 196 men of the Pioneer Column crossed from South Africa into what was later to become Southern Rhodesia on 11 July 1890, they expected to find a land of wealth and riches. For decades travellers had brought back stories of abundant gold to be found north of the Limpopo river, in what was called the kingdom of the Mashonas. The English explorer, Frederick Selous, related that as far back as the fifteenth century Arab traders along the coasts of south-eastern Africa had spoken of extensive gold mining in the interior (Selous, 1893:335). Given impetus by the discovery of the gold fields around Johannesburg in the 1880s, these stories turned the attention of prospectors further north in the hope that the fortunes realized in the Transvaal could be replicated in Zimbabwe.

The Pioneer Column was funded by Cecil John Rhodes, a wealthy British politician and businessman who had established his fortune in South Africa with the discovery of diamonds. On the pretext that colonial intervention was necessary in Mashonaland to protect the indigenous Shona people against the fierce and intrepid Ndebele, a branch of the Zulus who had entered their region several decades earlier, Rhodes negotiated with the British government for a royal charter for the British South Africa Company (BSAC), which he established in 1889. This charter gave him the right to occupy and exploit the land and its resources. With the promise of mining concessions and guarantees of land, the 196 volunteers he recruited and supplied penetrated to the heart of Mashonaland and, on 12 September 1890, raised the British flag at what was to be called Fort Salisbury. These men were soon joined by a wave of prospectors, administrators and adventurers from further south. By 1894 the European presence in Mashonaland had risen to over 5000.

For the indigenous population, claims by these newcomers that they were there to protect them against the depredations of the Ndebele must have seemed a bitter mockery. Within a few years, the BSAC had constituted itself into a de facto government and established an administrative and legal infrastructure to run the country. Much of the financing for this was raised by taxing the local people. Refusal to pay resulted in confiscation of their land which was handed over in turn to the growing wave of settlers arriving in the country.

Six years after the invasion the Shona and Ndebele rose in revolt, much to the surprise of the Europeans who had preferred to believe that both groups would never unite in opposition to them. Hostilities continued for over a year and it was only with the arrest and subsequent hanging of the leaders of the rebellion that the conflict finally ended. This war, however, which was popularly known as *Chimurenga*, was to inspire a later generation of Zimbabweans to fight for independence. From the arrival of Rhodes's pioneer column in 1890 to the establishment of democratic government in 1980, the reasons for conflict between the indigenous population and European settlers remained the same: the control of land and its wealth.

Creating Commercial Farms and National Parks

Despite the establishment of numerous mines, the fabled gold did not materialize to the extent that had been hoped for. When the directors of the BSAC toured the colony in 1907 they found that it was almost bankrupt. Yet the mineral wealth that the country lacked was compensated by vast tracts of rich, arable land in many areas. Shortly after the visit, the BSAC adopted a policy to diversify away from mining and began to encourage the development of the European commercial farming sector.

To attract settler farmers the state offered free agricultural training and services. In 1912 an agricultural bank was established to provide

European farmers with loans for the purchase of farms, livestock and agricultural equipment, as well as to finance improvements in irrigation and fencing. Fertilizers, seeds and stocks were made available at subsidized prices. Roads and other facilities were constructed close to European settlements. By 1914 there were 2040 European farms covering 183,400 acres, compared to the 20,000 acres that had been worked a decade earlier (Schmidt, 1992:66).

During the first few decades of settler rule, peasants provided most of the produce for the local market — especially maize, livestock and vegetables to the mines and urban areas. In order to ensure that the commercial farms were not undercut by cheaper peasant produce, the BSAC and subsequent governments in Rhodesia pursued a policy of discrimination against the indigenous population. Their first strategy was to appropriate the best agricultural land for the establishment of European farms. This policy was enshrined in law in 1920 with the adoption of the recommendations of the Native Reserves Commission. African farming areas were to be reduced, through forcible eviction of people, by 1 million acres of the most fertile, well-watered land close to markets and communication routes. This land was then to be handed over to European settlers. The indigenous population in these areas was removed to what were called African Reserves and later Tribal Trust Lands (TTLs). After independence these areas were renamed Communal Lands.

Tribal Trust Lands were situated on arid, impoverished soils. Tsetse fly was prevalent, causing sleeping sickness in humans and a disease called *Nagana* in cattle, which decimated the herds of African farmers. Hunting of wild game was prohibited on TTLs, depriving local communities of a traditional source of food. In 1923 wild animals were categorized as 'royal game' belonging to the state. The indigenous people thus effectively suffered a double expropriation, denied both the better land suitable for agriculture and the wildlife which could survive in the marginal areas to which they had been removed.

The establishment of commercial farms continued unabated. A series of acts throughout the colonial era systematically undermined the productivity of African farmers, enforcing their removal from white farming areas, their prohibition from entering certain markets and their exclusion from subsidies and infrastructure offered to the white commercial farming sector. By the time of independence in 1980 some 5000 commercial farms existed in Zimbabwe, in units covering areas of 2000 to over 100,000 acres. They occupied over 43 per cent of the total land area of the country and accounted for most of its agricultural revenue through exports of tobacco, tea, coffee, sugar and cotton.

Already by the 1930s the TTLs were unable to support the number of Africans who had been relocated to them. Most of these reserves were situated in Natural Regions III to V, those parts of the country with low rainfall and poor soils, and unsuitable for extensive crop production or large numbers of livestock. The more fertile Regions I and II had largely become the exclusive domain of European farmers.[1] Yet despite their poor agricultural potential the Communal Lands in the 1970s had a population density of approximately 28 people per square kilometre compared with only 9 people per square kilometre in commercial farming areas (Whitsun Foundation, 1983:26). It was estimated that by the time of independence the population of these reserves, approximately 7 million, had exceeded their carrying capacity by two million people (Jordan, 1979:134).

While forced evictions took place during the colonial era predominantly for the creation of European-owned commercial farms, large tracts of land were also seized for the establishment of parks and recreational areas. Recreation for many of the early European settlers consisted of trophy hunting of the wildlife that was abundant throughout the country. This fuelled demands for 'protected' areas as well as prohibitions on local communities against hunting of game, even for subsistence needs. J. H. Peterson, in his history of wildlife utilization in Zimbabwe, wrote, 'With the establishment of a colonial Government, all wildlife became the property of the state. Since the state was in the hands of white settlers, this effectively meant that legal utilization of wildlife was exclusively the property of whites' (Peterson, 1991:3).

Although most of the land set aside for national parks and other protected areas was found in Natural Regions IV and V, which were unsuitable for intensive agriculture, their establishment did involve the eviction of indigenous people. The Shangaan, for example, originally inhabited the immense lands of what is now the Gonarezhou National Park in Zimbabwe, the Kruger Park in South Africa, and adjacent areas of Mozambique. Shangaan communities were displaced from these areas as recently as the 1960s for the creation of parks to protect the wildlife that was rapidly vanishing from the white commercial farms and the more densely inhabited communal lands of these countries. The Shangaan, mainly the women, traditionally practised some agriculture, but the primary subsistence of the community was from hunting and large-scale fish drives on the region's major rivers. These options were closed when the park was established, and the Shangaan were forcibly resettled on the edges of the park where intensive agriculture was inappropriate (Peterson, 1991:6).

---

1 Rhodesia was classified into five main Natural Regions, depending on agricultural potential as follows:
Natural Region I: Specialized and diversified farming region with a rainfall of over 1000 mm a year.
Natural Region II: Slightly lower rainfalls of 750–1000 mm suitable for intensive crop and/or livestock production.
Natural Region III: This zone has 650–800 millimetres of rain per year suitable for semi-intensive farming.
Natural Region IV: Rainfall in this region drops to 450–600 mm per year and land is mainly suitable for livestock production.
Natural Region V: The low erratic rainfall in this area means that land is suitable only for extensive cattle and game ranching.

The Law and Institutions

Game laws which effectively prohibited hunting by indigenous communities were administered in Zimbabwe by the Director of Agriculture until 1923. Efforts were aimed at protecting large game species through regulation of hunting rights and the establishment of services and areas for this activity. The first government officers to be employed full-time on the protection and control of wild animals were appointed in the Forestry Department as far back as 1928. With the Game and Fish Preservation Act of 1929 this Department acquired full responsibility for game and fish preservation, which it retained until 1950 (Pittman, 1992:16–21).

In 1950 the Department of National Parks was created under the Minister of Internal Affairs. Its main objective was 'the protection and preservation of wild animal life and vegetation'. A number of national parks were also created during this time, including Hwange which remains one of the largest in the country. Between 1953 and 1963 'nature conservation' was administered under two separate acts by two separate agencies — the Department of National Parks and the Department of Wildlife Conservation. The former was concerned mainly with public enjoyment and recreation. Most of the 14 reserve areas proclaimed during the 1950s now form the basis of the country's recreational parks and botanical gardens. The larger areas, which provided the basis for today's major parks and safari areas, were administered by the Department of Wildlife Conservation in the form of game reserves, non-hunting reserves, and controlled hunting areas. In 1964 the situation was partly rationalized by the merging of these two agencies into a single Department of National Parks and Wildlife Management. It became responsible for 14 national parks, 8 game reserves and 5 controlled hunting areas.

In 1975 a new structure was created to administer national parks areas. The legislation that brought this about was to abandon the concept of 'royal game' in conformity with a perception that unless wildlife became a resource of benefit to indigenous people, the conflict between the two would continue and the costs of policing and control to curb poaching and the destruction of fences would rise. Nevertheless this legislation was not implemented among communities bordering such areas until the late 1980s. At independence, therefore, the parks and wildlife estate comprised a large area of the country to which local communities were hostile. The parks and wildlife estate is managed by the Department of National Parks and Wildlife Management which is under the Ministry of Environment and Tourism.[2] It covers some 5 million hectares and is divided into six categories of protected area: botanical reserves, botanical gardens, national parks, game sanctuaries, safari areas and recreational parks (Child et al., 1989:55–58).

---

2 'Parks and wildlife estate' or 'estate' is used to refer to the totality of all protected areas of all kinds in Zimbabwe that are administered by the Department of National Parks and Wildlife Management.

Deprivation and Hardship for Communities

When F. C. Selous explored the land of the Mashonas in the 1890s he found a land replete with wild animals, in contrast to South Africa whose population of large mammals had been decimated by sport hunting and agricultural clearance by immigrant settlers. The indigenous Shona and Ndebele managed these resources in a more sustainable fashion, killing only those animals that were necessary for their own needs when the agricultural season had been a poor one. Wildlife was accessible to most communities and hunting was an integral part of local tradition. Reflecting on the pre-colonial era, one old man interviewed in 1979 recalled:

> *It was a simple life. At that time we could go hunting anywhere we liked. No one claimed possession of wild game. Not everyone could hunt the elephant. Only special people could hunt and inflict injuries on them. When we returned home we would celebrate. Elephant meat is good meat. It is a mixture of all game and has big chunks of every type. Everyone was invited to come and take out the meat he wanted to carry home. When an elephant had been killed the word went round. (Cited in Jensen, 1992:36)*

The subsequent establishment of national parks during the colonial era brought several adverse consequences for indigenous populations. The first resource taken away from the local people was the land, which in many areas was fenced off and declared prohibited territory to the people who had formerly lived on it or were settled around it. It was not only from Gonarezhou, south-eastern Zimbabwe, that communities like the Shangaan were forcibly evicted. The declaration of a non-hunting reserve at Mana Pools along the Zambezi River in the 1960s resulted in the removal of one community to the more inhospitable and less agriculturally rich escarpment away from the river (Interview, Child, 1993). Tonga villagers further south were also moved when the Chizarira National Park was created around the same time. Recreational areas, such as those established around Lake Kyle, Lake McIlwhaine and other dam sites near urban centres, also resulted in eviction of African peasant farmers.

Access to wildlife was not the only resource lost to indigenous communities in those areas. Fuelwood collection was also prohibited, resulting in the further depletion of trees in the overcrowded and increasingly barren Native Reserves. Honey could no longer be collected by communities from state land, despite the minimal interference of this activity with the environment. Traditional healers were also restricted from entering forest areas to gather the herbs they used for medicinal purposes.

The creation of national parks was reinforced by the establishment of punitive laws against those infringing the above regulations. Cattle caught grazing in these areas were confiscated. Hunting or being caught with traps in the numerous police raids on villages bordering parks resulted in heavy fines or prison sentences, increasing the poverty of families which had prompted them to infringe such regulations in the first place. It is little wonder that under these circumstances local people came to see parks, the animals within them and the increasing number of tourists with hostility. In an interview with the author in July 1993, the chairperson of the CAMPFIRE Association, founded in the late 1980s to promote the rights of indigenous communities in wildlife utilization, pointed out that local people manifested their hostility in acts of destruction. Fences were routinely damaged around park areas. Fires were started within the park lands. Poaching increased to a level where the state had to invest more and more revenues in policing activities. This further increased the antagonism of local communities who came to see parks officers as no different from the army and police that the colonial government had to increasingly rely upon to defend its interests.

Protection of wildlife within the parks increased the animal population. It has been estimated that the elephant population increased from around 10,000 in the early 1900s to well over 50,000 by the late 1970s (Peterson, 1991:6). Yet such numbers exceeded the carrying capacity of the land covered by the estate. The result was the frequent migration of animals such as elephant, buffalo and hippopotamus out of the parks and into the surrounding areas in search of food.

Widespread destruction of crops by wildlife ensued and was estimated in Nyaminyami district in the early 1980s to be some 50 per cent of possible yields. Farmers were routinely killed defending their fields against problem animals, something which has continued until the present day. One farmer indicated that, from April through July, he slept in his fields in order to protect his harvest from marauding elephants and buffaloes (Interview, farmer in Mola district, Nyaminyami, 1990). At the same time the prohibition on hunting of wild game meant that local people were not allowed to kill the animals that raided their villages, under penalty of imprisonment or fine.

Given this history it was perfectly understandable that in a survey in 1980 of African farmers in Gokwe district, which borders several national parks in western Zimbabwe, communities indicated their opposition to wild animals and the foreign visitors who came to see them.

> *African farmers reasonably asked, why not shoot all the elephants and other wildlife. All benefits from wildlife go to foreign visitors, or to a central treasury or to a district council. The benefits do not come to the village much less to the households suffering losses. Yet elephants are seen in the fields every night. Granaries are robbed and people killed. Local farmers are not only protecting their families when they encourage in more immigrants, bring in more cattle, clear more land for fields, and request people to shoot any elephants which come into their area. (Peterson, 1991:52)*

The Challenge after Independence

Independence in 1980, which was largely brought about through popular support for land redistribution, was also accompanied by heightened expectations among local communities in parks areas that their own access to park resources would be enhanced and that land would be available for their use. Agricultural options in Natural Regions IV and V had been increased in the years leading up to independence through several tsetse-fly-eradication campaigns. These opened up areas, which had previously been restricted to wildlife use due to the threat of sleeping sickness, for cattle ranching. The popular demand was for eradication of wildlife, the withdrawal of restrictions on entry to parks and the conversion of these areas for agriculture and cattle.

The post-independence government, however, found itself in a dilemma. Despite popular pressure for large-scale land reform there were several factors that forced them to maintain the status quo in relation to park land management. The first was the realization that if Zimbabwe was to build up its tourist potential it had to maintain vast areas of natural habitat in which large mammals could exist without competition from humans. Despite a fall in tourist revenues during the war years (1974–1979), evidence was available that Zimbabwe had a unique niche to offer in the tourist market centred around its attractiveness as a sport-hunting venue and as a country which retained a large wildlife population in its natural environment. With foreign exchange shortages a major impediment to economic growth, the new government felt unable to sacrifice this interest in favour of popular pressure for land reform.

The second consideration, increasingly highlighted in the years after 1980 as evidence accumulated, was that agricultural expansion in Natural Regions IV and V of the country was severely limited by environmental factors. Areas freed from tsetse fly and opened up for agriculture were experiencing large-scale soil erosion, destruction of trees, siltation of rivers and declining crop yields as migrant farmers struggled to scrape a living from the poor soils. Several surveys in the mid- to late 1980s also began to show that in terms of economic returns, wildlife — through its attendant tourism and controlled hunting — was a more attractive option than settled agriculture. One study, which measured potential revenue per kilogram of biomass, estimated that whereas extensive cattle ranching would generate about US\$ 4 per hectare, wildlife management involving tourism and sport-hunting could potentially generate US\$ 12 per hectare.[3]

The final consideration that influenced government policy was a desire to avoid the political turmoil that might result from large-scale

---

3 In a detailed study of part of the south-eastern lowveld of Zimbabwe, Child determined that while game ranching per se is only marginally more productive than cattle ranching and is handicapped by a variety of technical and commercial constraints, wildlife utilization associated with different forms of tourism may be anything from twice to four times as profitable (see Child, 1988).

redistribution of land in favour of peasant farmers. The terms of the Lancaster House Agreement in 1980, which paved the way for independence, set limits on the capacity of the new government to honour its previous pledge to the people, namely that commercial farm land would be expropriated by the state and redistributed to the overcrowded inhabitants of the communal areas. The terms of the Agreement stipulated that land could only be acquired by the government on a willing-buyer-willing-seller basis and at market prices, which it could ill afford. The substantial international and internal lobby raised by commercial farmers to defend the status quo in terms of land ownership ensured that this policy was enforced and indeed extended beyond the decade of the Lancaster House period. Quite simply, therefore, the government did not make the sweeping changes to land ownership patterns either in commercial farming areas or national parks estates that communities had expected. The result was a further escalation in hostility which continued throughout the first decade of independence.

The Shangaan communities around Gonarezhou park in southern Zimbabwe illustrate this trend. According to one report there was a general perception that the ownership of wildlife had 'changed hands' as a result of independence. This led to an upturn in illegal hunting, arrests of villagers and increasing tension between the authorities and the people of the district. When villagers asked why the land could not be returned, they were informed that the government needed the foreign exchange brought in by the tourists who came to see the wildlife. This response became an added incentive to poach the animals in the park, since people reasoned that if there were no animals there would be no tourists. Without tourists there would be no need for a park and the government might return the land to the people. In one raid in 1982, 81 arrests were made and ivory, skins, fish and traps were recovered from many of the village houses (Zimbabwe Trust, 1990:18–20).

In many of the areas surrounding national parks, in-migration of farmers from other areas of the country was actively encouraged by the local population. A survey in 1988 established the priorities of one group of villagers.

> *The people in Simchemba ward see development of their area coming from increased agriculture and cattle and mining, not from utilization of wildlife. They welcome increased in-migration as forcing the government to provide more schools, and clinics, and making possible more development. They believe more people will force the government to erect fences around the national parks and safari areas to keep wild animals out of communal lands. (Peterson, 1991:50)*

The system which excluded communities from a substantial share of park benefits was also effectively maintained following independence.

Throughout the 1980s, therefore, hostility towards wildlife and tourism continued. By the late 1980s it was increasingly realized that unless a system was created which returned revenues from these areas more effectively to communities, Zimbabwe's national parks and its tourism industry would probably collapse under popular pressure for change.

The Development of Tourism in Zimbabwe

The nature of tourism in Zimbabwe has dramatically changed since the 1970s. After the Unilateral Declaration of Independence (UDI) by Ian Smith's Rhodesian Front in 1965, rejecting Britain's plans for a transition to majority rule, there was an initial decline in foreign visitors apart from South Africans. (The importance of South Africa to tourism in Zimbabwe changed in the 1980s when visitors from Europe and the United States began to outnumber South Africans in visitor statistics.) Despite sanctions by the international community against Rhodesia for its opposition to black majority rule, the number of foreign visitors soon picked up again. In addition, with Mozambican independence in the early 1970s local tourists lost their access to the traditional cheap holiday resort of Beira, on the Indian Ocean coast. Currency restrictions also affected the customary holidays in South Africa for local residents, so that an increasing number of Rhodesian whites began to spend their holidays in the country. By 1972, tourism, both internal and foreign, had reached its highest recorded level at 339,000 visitors (Central Statistics Office, 1988).

However as the war increased in intensity in the mid- to late 1970s, foreign tourism dropped rapidly and even the South African market eroded. With a vast expanse of territory to cover, the Rhodesian security forces were unable to control large parts of the country, including national park areas. The killing of several tourists and the shooting down of a civilian aeroplane in 1978 caused a fall in tourist numbers to a low of some 70,000 (largely comprised of visitors to the Victoria Falls). Many recreational areas near urban centres were also closed for security reasons and the local visitor trade dropped significantly. Several hotels closed down and others struggled along, barely covering their costs or even running at a loss.

Tourism numbers picked up again at independence in 1980 but it was only after 1986/87 that it exceeded its high of the early 1970s. Again, political instability seems to have accounted for the hesitant rise in numbers during those years. The conflict in the south of the country between the Ndebele and the majority Shona from the early 1980s until 1987 severely undermined the attractiveness of holidaying in the national parks, most of which were situated in that region. Six tourists were abducted and murdered in 1982 by forces hostile to the new government. Others were fired upon in Matopos National Park, south of Bulawayo, resulting in its closure for several months in 1984. The Unity Accord between rival political parties in 1988 dramatically improved the security situation in Matabeleland, paving the way for a significant rise in the number of tourists after that time, which reached 658,000 in 1992 (Zimbabwe Tourist Development Corporation, 1993).

Throughout the 1980s the type of tourist visiting Zimbabwe's parks and wildlife areas also changed. The vast majority of visitors prior to that time had been local people and South Africans, many of whom had relatives or friends in the country. Partly as a result of this, tourism was not a high-spending industry in Zimbabwe. Many residents did not demand expensive hotels and did not bring in significant amounts of foreign exchange. The declining importance of local/regional tourism was to occur after independence for several reasons. The first was the large-scale exodus of whites from the country. Fearing that black majority rule would seriously undermine the rights and privileges they had so far enjoyed, many left for South Africa, Australia and Britain. In the end their fears were not justified. Seizure of land, confiscation of private property, rigid socialism, reprisals for war atrocities, etc. never occurred. But the Rhodesia Front government's propaganda effort had forecast that these would occur under black majority rule, leading some 150,000 whites, half of the European population, to leave the country during the first two years of independence (Herbst, 1990:223).

The same fears about black majority government also affected the number of white South African visitors. Many were discouraged from visiting Zimbabwe by Rhodesian exiles whose own feelings about the country were predominantly hostile. At the same time, political relations between South Africa and Zimbabwe worsened after 1980 as a result of the latter's opposition to apartheid. The increasing marginalization of South Africa on the continent and its policy of regional destabilization through a mixture of economic and military measures made South Africans reluctant to visit neighbouring states.

These groups, which had formed the core of the tourist industry in the 1970s, were not replaced by their black counterparts after independence. Research into user characteristics in the major resort areas in the mid- to late 1980s indicated that the proportion of black Zimbabweans visiting these areas never comprised more than 3 per cent of the total number of visitors. This was not only due to financial constraints. The increasing number of African middle-class families with disposable income did not spend their money on visiting national parks or utilizing the country's tourist resorts. According to one researcher, their reluctance was largely a question of perception. 'It was felt that the recreational areas were developed by White Rhodesians for White Rhodesians and do not necessarily offer what the majority of Zimbabweans want when on holiday' (Heath, 1986:30).

Relative political stability in Zimbabwe throughout the latter part of the 1980s and the early 1990s, and the increasing attractiveness of the wilderness experience in the international tourism market, have prompted a rapid expansion in the number of foreign visitors to the country. The number of tourists rose from 375,000 in 1988 to 658,000 in 1992 and is expected to increase by an average of 8 per cent per year until the end of the decade. The expansion in the number of high-paying foreign visitors has made tourism the third largest foreign exchange earner in the country, after agriculture and mining. In 1990 the entire value of tourism to the economy was estimated to be in the region of US$ 70 million, excluding fares for the national carrier, Air Zimbabwe. Numerous hotels have been built or renovated. Between 1987 and 1990 the number of beds available in hotels throughout Zimbabwe almost doubled. There are currently over 50 registered operators organizing safaris in national park areas. Requests for permits for canoeing tours along parts of the Zambezi river rose from fewer than a hundred in 1985 to 750 some five years later. Employment generated from tourism is currently estimated at some 36,000, although this figure does not include informal-sector craft production. Major employment areas are hunting and trophy guides, restaurant and hotel personnel, transport services including air carriers, public administration, amusement and recreational services, and staff for museums and botanical gardens. Between 1990 and 1991, tourism in Zimbabwe registered a 20 per cent increase in direct employment, compared to a 0.5 per cent growth in the agricultural sector.

Avoiding the Problems of Mass Tourism

Like several other southern African destinations, Zimbabwe is relatively inaccessible to many potential visitors. Air fares to the country from Europe and North America are among the most expensive to the continent, with few opportunities for significantly cheaper package deals. At the same time Zimbabwe's attractiveness to the potential tourist depends on a very specific and somewhat exclusive taste. Ninety-five per cent of Zimbabwe's tourist industry, claimed a recent report (Price Waterhouse and Environmental Resources, Ltd., 1992:4), is 'nature based', catering in particular to those with an interest in viewing the continent's large mammals in a relatively undisturbed environment.

Partly in order to guard that niche in the market, Zimbabwe has opted for a policy of what is called 'low-volume, high-quality tourism'. While this limits the amount of revenue that can be realized, it has protected Zimbabwe from many of the adverse consequences of mass tourism found elsewhere. The relatively unobtrusive nature of tourism in Zimbabwe has also meant that conflicts between visitors and local communities in terms of dress, behaviour and social practices have not materialized to anything like the extent witnessed in several North African destinations such as Morocco, Tunisia and Algeria (see Smaoui, 1975 and McIvor, 1986, for example).

The low number of tourists in Zimbabwe has allowed the country to bypass the issue of competition for scarce resources. Hotels and other tourist facilities do not deprive local communities of water, electricity and other municipal facilities. The Victoria Falls resort, the principal tourist complex in the country, is not situated in an area of high population density which might result in such competition. Since the local community is now largely dependent on tourist revenue for its welfare, including the provision of a new hospital and several schools partly funded by revenues raised from the hotels, residents are not marginalized to the extent that has been witnessed elsewhere.

A solid and diverse agricultural base and a reasonably developed manufacturing industry (textiles, furniture, construction materials, pottery, crafts, etc.), as well as local managerial and administrative capacity have also allowed Zimbabwe to establish considerable linkages between tourism and other aspects of the economy. It has been estimated that, on average, 81 per cent of the direct investment costs associated with tourism were met by local capacity and only 19 per cent from foreign exchange (Price Waterhouse and Environmental Resources, Ltd., 1992). These statistics compare favourably with other tourist destinations. A study conducted in 1987, for example, estimated that of the money generated by tourism in the Pacific islands only 25–30 per cent stayed on the islands. The other 70–75 per cent of revenues leaked out of the country.

The existence of a hotel training school in Bulawayo, southern Zimbabwe, which offers courses in hotel management, catering and administration, has also meant that the industry has not had to import skills from outside the country, which in other places has caused a drain on revenues. Nor does Zimbabwe suffer from the kind of ownership patterns found elsewhere, with hotels and tourist establishments in foreign hands. ZIMSUN (with 14 hotels), CRESTA and Sheraton (of which the government controls the major share) are locally controlled companies, providing the bulk of residential and entertainment facilities for foreign visitors to the country.

In Zimbabwe, guides in the national parks, safari operators and trackers for the lucrative hunting industry are local people, many of whom have come through the national parks establishment and training facility. Employment is generated by tourism in many other sectors as well, as noted above, and this trend is expected to continue. Nevertheless tourism is a seasonal industry in Zimbabwe, peaking from July to September, the prime game-viewing season in Zimbabwean parks and the summer holiday period in the northern hemisphere. A decline in visitor numbers during the early part of the year does lead to shedding of jobs. Fluctuations in the tourist market can obviously have adverse consequences for local labour, as was witnessed in the 1992 season when publicity concerning Zimbabwe's drought led to a decline in visitor arrivals from outside the country and a consequent loss of jobs.

Problems Associated with Tourism

Despite the government's stated intention to maintain low-volume, high-quality tourism in Zimbabwe, no limits have been set either at national or resort/park level. Some observers are concerned that the recent growth in tourism of some 8 per cent per year in Zimbabwe, and the expectation that this will continue for the rest of the decade, will undermine long-term considerations in the interest of short-term benefits (see McIvor, 1994). According to some conservationists, the tourist carrying capacity for some of the fragile park ecosystems in Zimbabwe has already been exceeded. Soil compaction, caused by trampling and vehicles in several parks, has led to increased water run-off, erosion and changes in vegetation. Excessive trampling of vegetation by walking, photographic and hunting safaris may affect plant diversity and lead to the loss of several species (Heath, 1989:39). As in several of the Kenyan national parks, observable changes have also been noted in animal behaviour. Loss of ground cover, changes in water quality and increased noise have disrupted mating and feeding habits. Some animals have begun to rely upon food supplements acquired through campsite raids. This is already evident among the honey-badger, hyena and elephant populations at the Mana Pools National Park in northern Zimbabwe. Whether due to increased familiarity with human presence or irritation at their behaviour, attacks by crocodiles, hippopotami and buffalo along the Zambezi river have also been witnessed in recent years. In several cases this has led to the shooting of animals which have become too persistent. One bull elephant in Mana Pools recently had to be shot due to its habit of overturning cars in search of oranges (interview, park officers, 1993).

In a 1992 study carried out on the Matusadona shores of Lake Kariba, where houseboat tourism is popular, researchers noted several adverse consequences of the increasing number of visitors (Rogers, 1992). While the study pointed out that pollution, disruption of animals, etc., had not reached the levels found in other countries, the findings were worrying enough for the researchers to advocate the government's intervention to control the unchecked growth of tourism in this area. From 100 boats some five years ago, over 2,000 were registered on the lake at the time of the study, most of which were licensed for tourist purposes. A particularly popular area was the Sanyati basin, which forms the eastern boundary of Matusadona Game Park where the Sanyati River enters the Lake. Some 1579 vessels, predominantly houseboats, were registered for these waters at the time of the research, a figure which exceeded by several hundred the number the area could sustain without damaging the environment and destroying its particular wilderness appeal.

Pollution of water by sewage was also recorded, with an unacceptably high level of faecal coliforms. Since these levels were found in relatively close proximity to some local fishing communities, there was some worry about the possibility of contamination of drinking water. Also of concern was the use of chemicals to deodorize sewage before it left the vessels. For example, bleach kills not only bacteria, but also other microscopic forms of life which may be essential for the food chain. The impact on the behaviour of animals along the Matusadona shores also gave grounds for concern. Parks staff had observed the displacement of hippos from rivers and inlets, increased aggressivity of crocodiles, disappearance of bird species from their nests as a result of disturbance by boaters and the disappearance of herds of elephant from their former habitat near the lake.

Several parks staff and conservationists interviewed for the study felt that the high numbers of boats and visitors along the Matusadona shores were undermining the wilderness appeal of the area. The survey found, for example, that in one location 188 boats were parked overnight despite a recommendation by park authorities that the maximum number should be confined to 55 boats at any one time. Such stipulations, however, were found to be inadequately enforced, which might reflect the government's unwillingness to antagonize private tour operators and limit revenues realized from such activities.

Yet the short-term economic gains in increased revenue from large numbers of tourists need to be compared to the possible damage to an environment whose very appeal is its unspoiled quality where animals, birds and flora can be observed in a relatively undisturbed habitat. Parks staff in Mana Pools, for example, have heard increasing complaints from international visitors that the large numbers of people to be found there conflicted with their prior expectations of visiting a relatively unspoiled and remote area. Similar complaints were heard by the present author on a visit to Victoria Falls in 1992.

Ecological damage is often difficult to reverse. This is evident in Victoria Falls whose unique rain forest, watered by the spray from the Zambezi river, is said by some botanists to be in a state of almost irreparable damage due to the excessive trampling of vegetation by the thousands of visitors who frequent the area (see McIvor, 1994). Yet as tourism becomes bigger and bigger business, and as the government is pressured to issue more licences for more operators, safari companies and canoe enthusiasts, the lure of quick money for an economy desperate for foreign currency is difficult to resist. But perhaps some of the negative consequences of unregulated wildlife tourism in Eastern Africa can provide an instructive warning:

> *Though East African states have a policy for the conservation of wildlife through the establishment of national parks and reserves, tourism still has disastrous effects. The lure of reward from wealthy foreign visitors often induces tour guides to harass the animals in the parks. In the Kenyan Abozoli National Park a lion was demeaned and humiliated by hordes of tourists who wanted to photograph it. On another occasion, a cheetah, a shy creature, nearly starved to death because tourists never gave it peace to hunt.*

Speeding vehicles, driving off roads and night driving have contributed to wildlife mortality and alteration of wildlife habitats. Unregulated sewage and garbage disposal around lodges and campsites also creates problems as it attracts animals and disturbs traditional feeding patterns. (O'Grady, 1990:35)

Distributing the Benefits

Despite the potential offered by Zimbabwe's wildlife and parks to realize significant amounts of foreign exchange through tourism, financial control of the industry seems to be haphazard. The majority of financial benefits revert to private operators rather than the state, which bears the brunt of the costs. A 1992 study conducted in the Zambezi Valley Complex, which features six safari areas and one national park, concluded that total gross income from tourism in this area was in the region of US\$ 4.2 million per year (Coulson and Bowler, 1992:40). The Department of National Parks and Wildlife Management only received some US\$ 500,000 of that amount. Canoe operators, private hunting safaris, crocodile ranchers, hotel owners, and commercial game-viewing companies realized the vast bulk of the profits despite the fact that the cost of protecting the animals and environment which guaranteed their business was borne by the state.

Furthermore, of the US\$ 500,000 realized by the Department, 75 per cent had to be returned to their stations in the Zambezi for the payment of salaries and recurrent costs. But patrol and anti-poaching activities were seriously under-funded, which effectively meant that the Department was unable effectively to protect the wildlife under its care. This has in part resulted in the virtual extinction of rhinoceros in the area, poached by armed gangs from the Zambian side of the river who receive lucrative amounts of money for the horns of these animals. The low salaries of game wardens, retrenchment of parks staff due to shrinking budgets, and old and obsolete equipment have also meant that the government has lost this war to the poachers, claimed the director of the Zambezi Society, a local conservation group (Interview, Pittman, 1993).

The Department's small budget has had other adverse consequences. Facilities for visitors to the estate are often run down and officials acknowledge that in this area they are losing a competitive edge to other destinations on the continent. While animals may be more abundant and less harassed than elsewhere, visitor facilities in national parks are behind those found in Kenya, for example, observed a warden at Mana Pools, who had received complaints from international visitors about the lack of accommodation and poor toilet and waste disposal facilities.

At the same time, with most of the revenues flowing to private operators, the government has been unable to realize the kind of income that would allow it to allocate substantial funds for improvements to local communities in order to convince them of the benefits of having large areas reserved for wildlife. Provision of schools, clinics, roads and electricity still lag behind the rest of the country in communities surrounding parks, for whom tourism continues to be peripheral to their welfare and, in many cases, an inconvenience. Tourism, therefore, needs to be rehabilitated in the national consciousness if it is to enjoy popular support. There is still the perception among indigenous people that it is a luxury for the rich, white Zimbabwean and the international visitor — a perception reinforced by the financial inaccessibility of park facilities and resources to the majority of local people. As the proportion of international visitors increases (e.g. from 16 per cent in 1981 to 57 per cent of tourists to Mana Pools in 1991), there is a danger that this discrepancy could prompt further demands for alternative forms of land use in such large areas set aside for wild animals. The real challenge for tourism in Zimbabwe is to resolve that conflict. This was summarized by a contributor to a 1990 conference on tourism in Southern Africa.

> *The most vital question of wildlife tourism, both for game viewing and for safari hunting, is the increasing competition with other forms of land use, especially agriculture and livestock. The classical way of protecting a wildlife area, which has been to expel the rural population ... and ... to ban all other forms of land utilization including firewood collection, can neither be justified nor defended ... any more. The participation of the rural population in wildlife resource management, and the return of some kind of benefit from protected areas needs urgent attention. (Beutzler, 1990:10)*

Reconciling People and Wildlife in Zimbabwe

Wild animals have always posed some threat to people. Some destroy crops and trample property. Others attack farmers defending their fields. Before colonialism, however, these disadvantages were compensated by the meat, skins, tusks, etc. that wildlife could provide. As a source of potential benefits, therefore, wild animals were considered an integral part of communities' support systems, which led to the development of rules of conservation and management. Traditional prohibitions, for example, existed against the killing of pregnant female animals. Sanctuaries were created where all hunting was forbidden. These *Marambatemwa*, as the Shona called them, were venerated as holy sites and upheld by the sanction of the community against anyone infringing sanctuary regulations.

Colonial policies and legislation destroyed this relationship between wildlife and its human neighbours. By declaring such animals state property, the colonial government denied indigenous communities the benefits they traditionally obtained from the resource. Antagonism between local people and wildlife was exacerbated by the displacement of indigenous populations to areas that could barely sustain them. Alienation of Zimbabwe's rural population from the resources they had once enjoyed was to fuel the liberation war that brought independence.

The antagonism that had developed between people and parks was not only witnessed around the time of independence. During the 1960s it had been realized that the survival of wildlife outside heavily protected areas was dependent on the goodwill of rural communities and that these would be unwilling to conserve something that brought them more problems than benefits. As a result, a modest return of resources, mainly generated from sport hunting, was granted to local communities primarily in the form of meat for distribution during times of drought and food shortages. Nevertheless these benefits were intermittent and involved no participation of local people in the management or distribution of the wildlife resource. The predominant relationship between animals and local people remained conflictual.

During the mid–1970s a pilot project was developed in the Sebungwe region, south of Lake Kariba, under a programme launched by the Department of National Parks and Wildlife Management, which it called CAMPFIRE (Communal Areas Management Programme for Indigenous Resources). For the first time in the official documentation of the Rhodesian state, the phrase 'community access' appeared in policies related to wildlife management. The idea behind CAMPFIRE was that if communities developed appropriate institutions for decision-making and control, distribution of benefits could be decentralized and targeted towards the people most affected by wild animals. An experiment, called Operation Windfall, was carried out in the Sebungwe area. Some revenue and meat generated by the culling of elephants were returned to local people. The results were mixed. According to an evaluation:

> *There was an immediate decrease in illegal hunting in the area, and signs of a change in attitudes toward wildlife on the part of local people. But communities in the area were denied participation in decision making and management, and were unable to exert influence over the distribution of the proceeds. Operation Windfall was not sustained, and its effects soon waned (Zimbabwe Trust, 1990:6).*

Also in the 1970s, the ground was set for establishing a legal framework for community access to wildlife resources that offered post-independence Zimbabwe a possible means of reconciling the conflict between people and parks. In 1975 the Parks and Wildlife Act relinquished the notion that wildlife was the exclusive property of the state and permitted landowners to make use of such animals as an economic resource within the constraints of sound conservation practice. Under the Act, private landowners could apply for 'appropriate authority' status to manage wildlife. As farmers realized that the combined benefits of meat production and recreational value could exceed the revenues from cattle or agriculture, especially in the large southern ranches prone to sustained drought, increasing areas of commercial farmland were converted into wildlife reserves.

The effects of the Act were felt more slowly in communal lands where the state was and still is regarded as the landholder. This did not mean that rural communities were unable to benefit from wildlife in any way. Hunting concessions in communal lands with populations of wild animals were sometimes sold to commercial operators by the central government, and during the late 1970s it was expected that some of these revenues should be returned to those communities on whose land the hunts were to be conducted. But these revenues passed through the central treasury, which then returned a grant to the district councils the following year for such developments as roads, schools and clinics. In practice, only a fraction of the money realized from wildlife utilization in these areas was returned to local communities. In general, less than a quarter of the revenues realized by the state from wildlife-related activities in communal areas returned to local communities (Murphree, 1991:9).

A more serious flaw was that neither district councils nor community members had any say in the distribution or management of these resources. Grants from the government were thus seen as a hand-out from the central treasury which had no connection with the wild animals that continued to ravage the fields of the local people. Indeed communities believed that the revenue returned to them was compensation in response to their arguments about the inconveniences of wildlife, rather than a benefit resulting from its presence. Redistribution thus did not reduce prevailing antagonism. Nevertheless, the 1975 Act did raise, for the first time in legal terminology, the concept of economic benefit for the people most affected by wildlife, an idea which was to form the central component of the CAMPFIRE programmes of Zimbabwe in the post-independence period.

Origins and Early Years of CAMPFIRE

Surveys in several parts of Zimbabwe during the 1980s began to show that the most sustainable form of land use in many areas with marginal soils and low rainfall was the exploitation of their wild animal populations. A study done on Buffalo Ranch, south-eastern Zimbabwe, showed a drastic decline in productivity of conventional cattle ranching, especially during drought years. A wildlife section on the ranch showed little advantage when it was used solely for production of meat and other products. However, when recreational values of wildlife were properly marketed, through safari hunting and photographic tourism, the section generated returns three times as high as those for cattle. Such findings, however, were of little consequence to local communities who saw such revenues disappear into the coffers of the central treasury and for whom wildlife continued to be a menace.

A clause in the 1975 Act, however, provided the legal framework for resolution of this conflict. Although 'appropriate authority' status had only been granted to private landowners, the Act did make provision for a similar devolution of responsibility to communities through their local councils if it could be proven that they had the institutional and management capacity to utilize and conserve wildlife for the benefit of their people. Under the umbrella of the Department of National Parks and Wildlife Management, which was increasingly convinced that the survival of the parks depended on local involvement and support, an alliance was formed with the University of Zimbabwe's Centre For Applied Social Sciences (CASS), Zimbabwe Trust (a non-governmental organization) and a branch of the World Wide Fund For Nature (WWF) to begin a programme to assist rural development by aiding district councils to achieve the required level of management capacity of wildlife which would enable the government to confer appropriate authority status upon them. Four years after the alliance was formed the district council of Nyaminyami was granted this status, paving the way for a similar devolution of authority to other councils in areas of wildlife concentration.

Nyaminyami provided an ideal setting for the implementation of the first significant CAMPFIRE programme. Situated in the remote north-western region of the country, it covers some 363,000 hectares of land. It surrounds the Matusadona National Park on three sides and includes a large part of the Lake Kariba shores. The climate is hot and harsh with low and often erratic rainfall of 400–800 millimetres per year. Soils are generally poor and most of the area falls within Natural Region V, unsuitable for any agricultural activity apart from extended grazing. The population in the mid–1980s was estimated at 35,000.

The bulk of the population resident in this area had been forcibly resettled from the Zambezi Valley after the construction of Lake Kariba in the 1950s and the subsequent flooding of their homes. Their resentment is still coloured by the memory of the relatively fertile area they left behind. At the same time the once closely knit and homogeneous Tonga community of the valley was broken up and its people dispersed on both the Zambian and Zimbabwean sides of the lake.

Because of the general lack of development in Nyaminyami there was an exceptionally high rate of malnutrition and protein deficiency among both children and adults in the early 1980s, and the population relied on food aid programmes for several years. (Zimbabwe Trust, 1990). Local resentment was fuelled by the widespread destruction by wild animals of the meagre crops that farmers were able to produce. The nearby Matusadona Park hosted large herds of elephant and buffalo. Under the protection of the parks officers and through the strict prohibitions on killing these animals, wildlife populations had increased to a level which the Park itself could not sustain, resulting in migration of animals in search of food and continuous raiding on farmers' fields. In the mid–1980s, for example, an average of four farmers per year were killed in Nyaminyami as a result of wildlife attacks. Long periods of time were also spent by men, women and children protecting crops during the harvesting season or avoiding problem animals around their homesteads. School attendance rates were said to be among the worst in the country, as children were kept back in the fields to scare away the wild animals.

Ironically, this wildlife came to be seen as offering the people of the district their principal chance of escaping poverty. Prior to 1988, Nyaminyami had realized some revenues from wildlife through the sale of licences to hunters and safari operators among whom the district was extremely popular. But since the local council lacked appropriate authority to manage the resources, all revenues were returned to the central treasury. By the time this money had passed through the bureaucracy only a small percentage was returned to the area for infrastructural developments such as roads, schools and clinics. A survey in 1988 estimated that during the previous five years less than 50 per cent of revenues realized from wildlife-based activities came back to the area.

These factors, as well as the increasing proof from the private sector of the economic potential from proper wildlife management, prompted the Nyaminyami district council to solicit support to achieve more direct control of its wildlife resources. This was done through the establishment of a trust intended to contribute to the development of institutional capacity for wildlife management. Much of the early debate focused on the composition of the trust and its representative structure. Was it designed to boost the income of the district council or was it to become a genuine grass-roots project with popular participation? In many of the areas under its authority, the district council was almost as remote as central government in the minds of the people. Some observers felt that if the district council had full rights over allocation of resources, people's perceptions that they controlled resources would be lost. Without this sense of proprietorship, they argued, wildlife and its related activities — hunting and tourism — would continue to be perceived as an imposition, something which the communities would have no stake in defending. After three years, Nyaminyami made its bid for recognition by the government that it was competent to manage its own wildlife resources (Zimbabwe Trust, 1990:14).

During the first year of operations in 1989 most of the Trust's income was generated by sport-hunting in the Omay communal lands and through the sale of trophy rights to safari operators. The Department of National Parks and Wildlife Management set limits on the number of animals that could be hunted, so as not to jeopardize their populations. With limited resources at its disposal, the Trust requested safari operators to provide their own resources and facilities.

The distribution of benefits took different forms. Some 160 families, for example, were compensated in 1989 for the destruction of their fields by wild animals. More than 30,000 kilograms of meat were distributed at cheaper than commercial prices for consumption by local communities.

Fencing was erected in several areas to protect fields against marauding herds of elephant and buffalo. The first year's surplus stood at US$ 37,150 which, after the deduction of administrative costs for the district council, left a total of US$ 27,715 for distribution to local communities. (This figure does not take account of the initial capital investment in the project by Zimbabwe Trust and other NGOs.)

The Trust opted to divide the income equally between the 12 wards within the council area. This gave rise to some criticism that income had not been sufficiently channelled to communities which bore the highest social and other costs of wildlife in their areas. Further concern was raised about the lack of perception by communities that revenues returned to them were directly related to the utilization of animals with which they had been in conflict for many years. Informal conversations with individuals in Nyaminyami in 1989 suggested that many people did not understand the workings of the wildlife programme nor had they come to believe that the wildlife 'belonged' to them (Peterson, 1991:35). As with Operation Windfall of 1975 (described above), members of the community still believed that the government had handed over revenues in response to their complaints. The link between community cost and benefit, input and outcome, was neither direct nor clear.

The continuing dependence on outsiders (NGO workers, safari and hunting operators, government officials) for much of the running and organization of the scheme was also criticized. Safari operators, for example, imported all necessary resources and much of the personnel without transference of skills to local community members. Project planners, such as the Department of National Parks and Wildlife Management, and NGOs, were dependent on their own staff for all the management, administrative and ecological inputs to the project. A study of the scheme in 1990 found that 'There is little or no transfer of skills to the rural communities under present arrangements and the short-term nature of the contracts provide little incentive for the safari operator to invest in permanent facilities' (Zimbabwe Trust, 1990:15).

Yet both of these issues are symptomatic of a more fundamental problem that the Nyaminyami project did not adequately tackle: the issue of community ownership. Did the people of Nyaminyami, and in particular those families who were most affected by the presence of animals in their area, come to see this wildlife as their own resource to be managed, utilized and protected in order to sustain the benefits it might bring? The fact that district council officers, national parks staff and NGO personnel were still trying to educate people about the value of wildlife in this area was, according to Peterson, a demonstration that it was still not perceived as having a direct value for them (Peterson, 1991:129). One of the reasons seems to be that authority had not yet genuinely descended to the community level.

Most of the African farmers studied by Peterson claimed that the district council was 'almost as remote and incomprehensible as central government' (Peterson, 1991:35). Farmers in Mola, for example, interviewed by the present author in 1991 had little knowledge of the workings of local government in the Nyaminyami area. They indicated that community identity and authority was at the village level, where chiefs and headmen, social gatherings of elders and peer pressure, were more real than the occasional visits they might receive from district council officers. This distance between the communities which bear the direct costs of wildlife and the structure which manages, organizes and disburses benefits has thus meant that the community has not perceived wildlife as its own property, with all the attendant responsibilities of good proprietorship that this would bring. The temptation to poach animals, to cut down trees in parks areas, to allow cattle to graze on park land might have been reduced by the council's disbursement of revenues, as was indicated by parks staff in 1991, but it could never be wholly eradicated unless the community gained genuine ownership. The major flaw in a project like that of Nyaminyami was that proprietorship and responsibility did not go to the local people (Murphree, 1991:9).

Expansion and Diversification of CAMPFIRE Projects

By 1992, 12 district councils had acquired the status of appropriate authorities and some 40,000 square kilometres — almost equal to the land set aside in the formally protected parks and wildlife estate — was under wildlife management in communal lands. Several more councils have applied for 'appropriate authority' status, assisted in planning, research and development by the CAMPFIRE Association of District Councils. Formed in the early 1990s, this association of affiliated producer communities is now taking over many of the advisory functions previously carried out by the Department of National Parks and Wildlife Management, and collaborating NGOs.

The nature of CAMPFIRE projects has varied. In the district of Guruve, for example, the council has employed its own professional hunter to market and operate safaris in the main wildlife project area. This contrasts with Nyaminyami, which has relied on private companies to undertake safari operations. There have been some problems in Guruve with marketing, since the external contacts developed by established tour operators and their considerable experience have been difficult to compete with. But in the belief that local skills need to be tapped and utilized, the council is ensuring a maximum level of local support. It is also gaining direct experience that it believes will be reflected in the future viability of its own operations. But Guruve has also taken a further step by distributing benefits in proportion to community costs. Unlike Nyaminyami, Guruve district council established a method of distribution based on the quota of animals taken in each area. On this basis, Kanyurira ward received the largest share of the revenues, some US$ 6715 in 1990. This money was allocated to a fund for the construction of a village clinic and the purchase of school furniture, and also allowed payment of almost US$ 30 to each household. The impact of this dividend, according to observers, was profound (Murphree, 1991:10). It allowed the community to make a much more solid connection between wildlife and benefits than if the revenue had been invested by an external agency in a welfare project over which they might have had no say or control. According to Murphree, the establishment of this sense of ownership explains the change in attitudes witnessed in Kanyurira. A survey in 1988 showed a negative attitude to wildlife and a positive attitude to in-migration of other agricultural settlers. The local people were without a school or a clinic. They felt that if there were more people the district council would more quickly provide these and improve roads. By 1990, the importance of preserving habitat became clearer; for the first time in many years destructive late dry-season bush fires did not occur. At the same time the community had become increasingly aggressive in its claims for full proprietorship (Murphree, 1991:11).

Most CAMPFIRE projects have earned the bulk of their revenues from game hunting and safari operations. Nevertheless, several councils have begun to explore the financial viability of more tourism-based activities such as photographic safaris, walking trails, canoe safaris and pony-trekking. The most developed CAMPFIRE project centred directly on tourist activities is at Mavuradona Wilderness area in the far north of the country. Established by the Muzarabani District Council, the 450-square-kilometre area is located in a scenic part of the Zambezi escarpment. It is bounded on the south by commercial farmland and in the north by an area of the low-lying Zambezi Valley that was until relatively recently sparsely populated. The eviction of farm workers from nearby estates in the wake of mechanization and other financial pressures has, however, led to the establishment of communities in this area. Many of these farm workers are of migrant descent and consequently have no traditional land-use rights in other parts of the country. Their increasing search for land in the Mavuradona area prompted the local council to look at several land-use options in order to choose the one that would be most appropriate to preserve its unique scenic attractiveness while realizing a financial benefit for these people that might reduce their demands for agricultural land.

The mountainous nature of the terrain and its lack of surface water, however, made it unsuited to dense wildlife populations. Over-hunting in the past had also led to the virtual disappearance of large mammals, such as elephant and buffalo that used to pass through the region. Unlike Nyaminyami or Guruve, therefore, revenue from safari hunting was not possible. Feasibility studies carried out in 1988 by the Department of National Parks and Wildlife Management indicated that non-consumptive use of the area was financially viable. Their suggestions included horse-trails, backpacking and hiking, rock climbing, camping and bird watching. An area manager was employed in 1989 and, with financing from a local NGO, a single camp site with basic cooking and sanitation facilities was constructed.

According to projections of the Department of National Parks and Wildlife Management and WWF, Mavuradona is capable of achieving financial viability over a five-year development period (Zimbabwe Trust, 1990:22). However, several factors affect this prediction. The first is the marketability of the area in the competitive tourist industry. Mavuradona, unlike other regions which offer the prospect of large populations of elephant, giraffe, hippopotamus, buffalo, etc., occupies a more specialized niche in the market. Its ability to sell effectively what it has to offer to both local and international tourists is therefore crucial. Yet advertising can be expensive and takes considerable time to attract attention. Furthermore, the international tourist market often demands high quality accommodation and other facilities. Although the basic provisions at Mavuradona have appealed to a more 'adventurous' clientele, financial returns in terms of accommodation and entry fees have been small. In order to maximize revenues in this area Mavuradona has received assistance from WWF to construct more fully equipped and comfortable lodges that can generate much higher returns than the basic facilities now on offer.

But perhaps the most crucial issue that faces Mavuradona and other areas like it wishing to exploit their tourist potential is the impatience of the communities that surround them. Whereas fairly rapid and sizeable returns can be realized through the lucrative hunting market, tourist potential takes a longer time to develop. Given the pressure from agricultural settlers to open up the area, the slow pace of this development has been an issue. Several incursions by the local community into the wilderness area have already occurred: fuelwood collection is common, some agricultural activities have been started on the edge of the area, animals have been poached. Complaints to the district council from local communities that financial benefits have not adequately filtered through to them are also increasing. This has necessitated council attempts to improve public relations by informing local communities about the potential that can be realized if the project is allowed the space and time to develop. As the district council was given appropriate authority status in 1990, some reprieve from popular pressure may occur after the sale of a limited number of elephants, which had subsequently entered the area, to sport-hunters.

Conclusion

Independence brought demands for change in land distribution patterns, particularly in commercial farm areas. But political considerations prevented a large-scale redistribution of land. Economic constraints, especially the high cost of commercial farm land, also meant that the government was limited in the amount of land it could purchase as well as the support it could give to relocated peasant farmers.

Even where resettlement did take place an effective handover to the community was avoided. Resettled land remained state property, held in tenure by peasant farmers but without genuine ownership. The result has been environmental abuse, soil erosion, cutting down of trees and over-utilization of natural resources — as on the communal lands from where most of these resettled farmers have come. By refusing to confer proprietorship to peasant communities, state land continues to be regarded as an open access resource to be exploited for personal gain rather than cared for and protected because of a perceived long-term interest in its development.

Zimbabwe's programme of land redistribution after 1980, therefore, seems to replicate the fundamental mistrust towards peasant potential that characterized the period before independence, when local communities were regarded as inherently incapable of looking after and managing their environment. The degradation of communal lands has been cited as proof of this contention. Yet communities were never given a chance to manage adequately the lands to which they were relocated during the colonial era. The conditions for a genuine communal property rights regime were denied. They had no powers to refuse the in-migration of evicted peasants from other areas of the country nor did they have user rights such as access to wildlife and, in some cases, water. Land-use policy both before and after independence, therefore, has assumed two options: privatization in the hands of a select few commercial farmers or nationalization, with effective ownership and management in the hands of the state.

To achieve effective community ownership of land and its resources requires more than decentralizing administration or promoting community participation or increasing economic benefits arising from resources. No matter how well-intentioned these moves might be, they will still fail to establish in the minds of local people that there is a direct relationship between their own activities and benefits that they might derive from resources. Revenues obtained from a distant authority continue to be seen as handouts. The connection between benefits and community or individual activities will only be made if ownership is genuine: the right to use a resource and the right to benefit from that exploitation. Just as post-independence Zimbabwe has hesitated to confer this responsibility on resettled peasant communities on commercial farm land, its policy of reconciling people and parks has also run into similar difficulties. The state has failed to relinquish its authority to the people most affected by wildlife.

This is evidenced in the issue of 'producer communities'. Currently the CAMPFIRE model has largely focused on the district council as the base unit of decentralization. As we have seen, this can be as abstract and remote as the central government. Decisions made by such an institution, including the allocation of benefits, have not encouraged a sense of responsibility and involvement of local people. Some CAMPFIRE promoters are thus pressing for a further decentralization of appropriate authority to ward or village level.

CAMPFIRE programmes could also involve communities much more in their planning, organization and management stages in order to go beyond the simple distribution of financial benefits. Yet this involves promoting a model of development which sits uneasily with government bureaucracies where project blueprints are often established with only token consideration of local circumstances and where structures of decision-making are hierarchical and authoritarian. No matter how successful a project might be in financial terms, if there is little genuine participation in project design and management there is little learning as a result.

While CAMPFIRE has had internal difficulties, there have been other obstacles to its effectiveness as well. One of these is the hostility of some international organizations and conservation lobbyists towards its linking of wildlife conservation with wildlife utilization. Economic arguments are often anathema to conservationists who insist on protected wilderness areas with minimum human interference where only non-consumptive uses are permitted. Yet a major source of revenue for communities involved with the CAMPFIRE programme is the lucrative safari hunting business. The international ban on the sale of ivory because of the demise of the African elephant in other parts of the continent has deprived Zimbabwe of a potential source of revenue from a resource which is now stockpiling in its warehouses.

Another problem concerns the actual protection of wildlife resources. Even with local support for wildlife there is every reason to believe that poaching will continue in Zimbabwe, since many of the poachers that have been apprehended come from outside the country. Furthermore, the centralized mechanism for accessing funds from tourism and hunting in wildlife areas currently performs poorly. As we have seen, only a small percentage of the revenue from tourism actually finds its way into the coffers of the Department of National Parks and Wildlife Management, despite the fact that the latter bears most of the costs of policing the parks and providing visitors' facilities. Profits flow to private tour operators and safari concerns, some of which pay less than a fraction of 1 per cent of their gross annual turnover in lease fees.

In order to ensure sufficient funds for wildlife protection, a redistribution of profits away from private operators is essential. This is not to advocate unprofitability for such concerns. But they are dependent both on the parks officers to protect the wildlife that brings them tourists, and on communities for their willingness to bear the costs of the presence of wildlife and other forgone opportunities.

The low number of visitors from among the indigenous black population of Zimbabwe has also left the national parks without a solid base of popular support. Talks on conservation and wildlife issues, and animal rights campaigns continue to be patronized almost exclusively by a richer European clientele. As we have seen, this is partly due to local perceptions of how 'protected' areas originated in the first place. Also, entrance fees remain relatively high for the majority of the population. An effort to rehabilitate parks in national public opinion is required through positive promotion in schools, clubs and other grassroots organizations — for whom sponsored access should be encouraged. Unless the younger generation of Zimbabweans is exposed to the aesthetic value of such areas and the country's wildlife, as well as given evidence of their potential economic returns to local communities, the legacy of antagonism to parks will continue to fuel demands for their conversion to other types of economic activity.

In conclusion, the management of wildlife, tourism and local community benefits offers Zimbabwe an opportunity to partly resolve a century-old conflict caused by the displacement and dispossession of rural people by the colonial powers. While CAMPFIRE is a step in the right direction, it does not go far enough towards realizing its aim. What prevents it is a final act of faith in these communities: the extension of ownership to the people who have had to live with the adverse consequences of the presence of wildlife for many years.

References

Beutzler, W (1990), *Wildlife as the Backbone of Tourism in SADCC Countries*, paper presented at the Southern Africa Development Co-ordination Conference (SADCC)/Deutsche Gesellschaft für Technische Zusammenarbeit (GTZ) Workshop, Zambia, August.

Central Statistics Office (1988), *Monthly Migration and Tourism Statistics*, Central Statistics Office, Harare.

Child, G (1988), 'Assessment of wildlife utilization as a land use option in the semi-arid rangelands of Southern Africa', in A Kiss (ed), *Living with Wildlife: Wildlife Resource Management with Local Participation in Africa*, The World Bank, Washington, DC.

Child, G, R Heath and A Moore (1989), 'Tourism to parks in Zimbabwe, 1969–1988', *Geographical Journal of Zimbabwe*, No 20.

Coulson, I M and M Bowler (1992), *The Zambezi Valley Complex: Tourism and Economics*, The Zambezi Society, Harare.

Heath, R (1986), 'The national survey of outdoor recreation in Zimbabwe', chapter 13 in *Zambezia*, University of Zimbabwe Publications Office, Harare.

— (1989), 'The role of tourism in development', *Geographical Education Magazine*, Vol 12, No 1.

Herbst, J (1990), *State Politics in Zimbabwe*, University of Zimbabwe Publications Office, Harare.

Jensen, S (1992), *Our Forefathers' Blood*, Dokumentation No 4, Mellemfolkeligt Samvirke (MS), Danish Association for International Cooperation, Copenhagen.

Jordan, J D (1979), 'The land question in Zimbabwe', *Zimbabwe Journal of Economics*, Harare, No 1, pp 129–138.

McIvor, C (1986), 'Tourism in Algeria: Who benefits?', *Development and Cooperation*, No 2.

— (1994), 'Zimbabwe: Tourism may kill the golden goose', *New African*, No 316.

Murphree, M W (1991), *Communities as Institutions for Resource Management*, University of Zimbabwe Publications Office, Harare.

O'Grady, A (1990), *The Challenge of Tourism*, Ecumenical Coalition on Third World Tourism, Bangkok.

Peterson, J H (1991), *CAMPFIRE: a Zimbabwean Approach to Sustainable Development through Wildlife Utilization*, University of Zimbabwe Publications Office, Harare.

Pittman, D (1992), *Wildlife: Relic of the Past or Resource of the Future?*, Zimbabwe Trust, Harare.

Price Waterhouse and Environmental Resources, Ltd (1992), *Wildlife Management and Environmental Conservation Project*, Price Waterhouse and Environmental Resources, Ltd, Harare.

Rogers, Cathy (1992), *The Impact of Tourism on the National Park Shoreline, Lake Kariba*, The Zambezi Society, Harare.

Schmidt, E (1992), *Peasants, Traders and Wives*, Baobab Books, Harare.

Selous, F C (1893), *Travel and Tourism in South East Africa*, Century Publishing, London.

Smaoui, Ahmed (1975), *Tourism and Employment in Tunisia*, Tunisia National Tourism Office, Tunis.

Whitsun Foundation (1983), *Land Reform in Zimbabwe*, The Foundation, Harare.

Zimbabwe Tourist Development Corporation (1993), *Zimbabwe Tourist Statistics*, Zimbabwe Tourist Development Corporation, Harare.

Zimbabwe Trust (1990), *People, Wildlife and Natural Resources: The CAMPFIRE Approach to Rural Development in Zimbabwe*, Zimbabwe Trust, Harare.

Interviews were held with: a farmer, Mola District, Nyaminyami, 1990; park officers, Mana Pools National Park, Zimbabwe, April 1993; Dr G. Child, Director of National Parks, July 1993; Mr D. Pittman, Chairman of The Zambezi Society, July 1993

X

PROTECTED AREAS, CONSERVATIONISTS AND ABORIGINAL INTERESTS IN CANADA[1]

James Morrison

Introduction

The Canadian Wilderness Charter, an initiative of World Wildlife Fund Canada, suggests that conservationists and aboriginal people share common aims and objectives with regard to wilderness areas and wilderness use (Hummel, 1989:275). The broader Canadian public certainly subscribes to this view, one easily reinforced by the alliances formed between aboriginal people and environmental activists to create new parks in the far north, or to prevent the logging of old-growth forests in the provinces of Ontario and British Columbia.

But as the prominent native leader Georges Erasmus[2] has pointed out, aboriginal interests are not identical to those of the conservation community. The creation of parks and protected areas, he says, is only one part of a larger political question — one 'bound up with the thorny issues of treaty rights, aboriginal title and land claims'. The indigenous people of Canada are seeking both recognition of their inherent right to govern themselves, and a land and resource base adequate to support their communities (Erasmus, 1989:93–98).

---

1 This chapter is based on a discussion paper by World Wildlife Fund Canada and new material collected by the author.
2 Georges Erasmus, a Dene from the Northwest Territories, is former Grand Chief of the Assembly of First Nations. Since 1991, he has been Co-Chair of the Royal Commission on Aboriginal Peoples.

Since the late 1980s, the broader implications of these political goals have caused cracks in the facade of common interests. While Inuit people in the Arctic have been instrumental in having new wilderness parks set aside as part of recent land-claims settlements with the federal government, Cree and Dene people living in the northern part of the province of Manitoba have publicly objected to the creation of four new parks within their traditional territories (Figure 10.1). They argue that the establishment of parks without their active involvement or consent is a violation of their rights; and they have therefore asked conservationists to withdraw their earlier support for the provincial government's initiative.

Long-standing parks have also become the object of aboriginal protest for many of the same reasons. In the Rocky Mountain region straddling Alberta and British Columbia, the Siksika (Blackfoot) Nation has laid claim to a portion of Banff National Park (Canada's oldest and most famous) on the grounds that those lands had once been reserved for their use and illegally taken by the federal government. In the province of Ontario, similar aboriginal protests over parklands have already had tragic consequences. In September of 1995, a group of Chippewa people from the Kettle and Stony Point First Nation occupied Ipperwash Provincial Park on the eastern shore of Lake Huron. They argued that the park, once part of their traditional lands, contained sites which were sacred to their people. In an ensuing confrontation with provincial police, one of the protesters was shot dead and two others were wounded.

In addition to issues of land title, aboriginal land use itself is becoming a subject of controversy. Many conservationists believe that aboriginal people should be excluded entirely (as is now the case in most provincial jurisdictions) from hunting, fishing or gathering within parks; and they argue that, in areas where such activities are permitted, aboriginal people should be prevented from using motorized boats or vehicles. In Ontario, for example, the conservation community reacted first with surprise, then outrage when — as part of land-claim negotiations — the provincial government announced in 1991 that game legislation would not be enforced against members of the Golden Lake First Nation found hunting within the bounds of Algonquin Provincial Park. Among conservationists, there is an increasing view that aboriginal rights should be interpreted in the context of modern principles of resource management — which place controls on all users of natural resources, regardless of their ethnic origin.

Such differences in goals between conservationists and aboriginal people will clearly have major consequences for ongoing campaigns to protect endangered spaces in Canada from the impacts of large-scale resource development. In order for there to be future joint action, therefore, these differences must first be understood and addressed. A major source of disagreement, as we will see in the next section, are profoundly contrasting views of wildlife and wilderness.

271

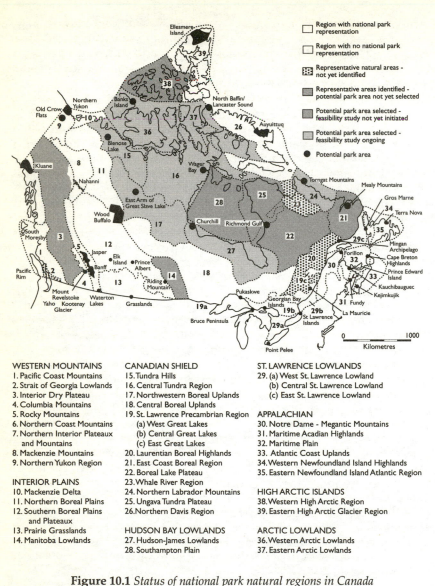

Figure 10.1 *Status of national park natural regions in Canada*

WESTERN MOUNTAINS
1. Pacific Coast Mountains
2. Strait of Georgia Lowlands
3. Interior Dry Plateau
4. Columbia Mountains
5. Rocky Mountains
6. Northern Coast Mountains
7. Northern Interior Plateaux and Mountains
8. Mackenzie Mountains
9. Northern Yukon Region

INTERIOR PLAINS
10. Mackenzie Delta
11. Northern Boreal Plains
12. Southern Boreal Plains and Plateaux
13. Prairie Grasslands
14. Manitoba Lowlands

CANADIAN SHIELD
15. Tundra Hills
16. Central Tundra Region
17. Northwestern Boreal Uplands
18. Central Boreal Uplands
19. St. Lawrence Precambrian Region
    (a) West Great Lakes
    (b) Central Great Lakes
    (c) East Great Lakes
20. Laurentian Boreal Highlands
21. East Coast Boreal Region
22. Boreal Lake Plateau
23. Whale River Region
24. Northern Labrador Mountains
25. Ungava Tundra Plateau
26. Northern Davis Region

HUDSON BAY LOWLANDS
27. Hudson-James Lowlands
28. Southampton Plain

ST. LAWRENCE LOWLANDS
29. (a) West St. Lawrence Lowland
    (b) Central St. Lawrence Lowland
    (c) East St. Lawrence Lowland

APPALACHIAN
30. Notre Dame - Megantic Mountains
31. Maritime Acadian Highlands
32. Maritime Plain
33. Atlantic Coast Uplands
34. Western Newfoundland Island Highlands
35. Eastern Newfoundland Island Atlantic Region

HIGH ARCTIC ISLANDS
38. Western High Arctic Region
39. Eastern High Arctic Glacier Region

ARCTIC LOWLANDS
36. Western Arctic Lowlands
37. Eastern Arctic Lowlands

A Wilderness Ethic and Differing Conceptions of Nature

Although there is no single definition of wilderness, many conservationists would acknowledge the philosophy expressed in the first great piece of American wilderness legislation. These ideals were popularized at the turn of this century by conservationists like John Muir,[3] who argued that there had to be spaces free from urbanization and industrial development, where the human species could recognize its own insignificance and retain a sense of awe at the wonders of creation.

Muir was reacting to — and rejecting — the modern conception of nature as an enormous reservoir of energy and resources that the human race can dominate and exploit with impunity. His view had much in common with the views of indigenous societies, who have consistently placed mankind in a subservient position to the rest of creation. To aboriginal people the idea that humans are a superior species who can dominate the natural world is blasphemous (King, 1992: 42–43).[4] Indeed, as more and more people worldwide now realize, it is the modern conception of nature which has led to the destruction of the environment.

Despite their apparent similarity, there are fundamental differences between indigenous and non-indigenous conceptions of nature. As poet and naturalist Gary Snyder has explained (1990), one thread of the conservation movement is profoundly romantic, in that it sees the human species as an intruder, not as a part of the natural world. Protected-area management on the Northern American continent has tended to reflect that philosophy. Canada's national parks policy, for example, speaks of protecting and managing natural resources in parks 'to ensure the perpetuation of naturally evolving land and water environments and their associated species' (Department of the Environment, 1979). The expression 'associated species' does not necessarily include humans.

By contrast, indigenous societies both past and present place mankind at the axis of the natural world — subordinate to the whole, but essential. Nowhere was this more apparent than among the pre-Columbian Olmecs and Aztecs of Mesoamerica. There, Mexican poet Octavio Paz tells us, humanity's role was as the giver of blood. It was human sacrifice which drove the world, enabling the sun to rise and the corn to grow (1990:18–21). If less terrifying, similar cosmologies have prevailed in all aboriginal cultures. Without proper offerings to show respect for the spirits — or what Cecil King, in his own language, calls the *manitous* — hunts will fail, the fish will vanish and the universe will come to a halt.

To indigenous people, wilderness itself — in the sense of areas 'untrammelled by man' — does not exist. Geographer Peter Usher has shown that Canada's wildest areas are far from being empty spaces (1987; see also Usher, Tough and Galois, 1992). Even if they appear to be underutilized, they are occupied by indigenous people on the basis of detailed knowledge going back hundreds or thousands of years. Graves and habitation sites dot the landscape. The mountains and hills, lakes and streams,

---

3 John Muir (1838–1914). Naturalist, advocate of US forest conservation, who was largely responsible for the establishment of the Sequoia and Yosemite national parks in California (USA).
4 Cecil King, an Odawa educator from Manitoulin Island in Ontario.

trails and portages all have names, and stories or legends associated with them. This is as true today for Mi'kmaq and Maliseet fishers on the Restigouche River in Quebec and New Brunswick — who have been in continuous contact with Europeans since the sixteenth century — as it is for Inuit or Dene hunters in the remote Arctic and sub-Arctic regions of the country.

At the core of the indigenous relationship with nature is a reciprocal connection with the plant and animal world. Because of this, many aboriginal people share with conservationists what can reasonably be called a wilderness ethic. A clear, deep, spring-fed lake is as positive a value to an Ojicree trapper in north-eastern Manitoba as it is to a recreational canoeist from Winnipeg. And an eagle is as worthy of respect and love — both for its innate beauty and for its connection with the thunderbird of native legend. In aboriginal communities across Canada, physical well-being is closely associated with nature. 'Country food', such as wild fish and game, is uniformly perceived as healthy, store-bought food as unhealthy.

Like many indigenous leaders today, Georges Erasmus insists that native peoples 'have a keen interest in preserving areas as close as possible to their original state' (Erasmus, 1989:93). In part, this is because they have experienced the alternative. Mississaugas living on the New Credit Reserve near Brantford remember Etobicoke (Adoopekog) as the 'place of the alders' near Lake Ontario. What was part of Mississauga territory in the mid-nineteenth century is now a suburb of Toronto. The alders are gone, the lake and creek are polluted and the fish no longer thrive (Smith, 1987).

Without renewable resources to harvest, as Georges Erasmus puts it, aboriginal people lose both their livelihood and their way of life. That way of life is not a folkloric remnant. In his latest book, former British Columbia Supreme Court Justice Thomas Berger argues that most Canadians misunderstand the native 'subsistence' economy (1991:126–139). Because our world is industrial, we tend to see aboriginal people as anachronistic. Either natives are living a precarious existence on the edge of starvation and must be weaned into the mainstream economy, or — a view held by many environmentalists — they should be permitted to continue their subsistence activities, provided they adhere to 'traditional' methods and patterns of harvest.

The second view is certainly more benign. The first — which sees the native economy as 'unspecialized, inefficient and unproductive' — has, Berger claims, resulted in enormous social upheaval. During the 1950s, especially in northern Canada, governments evacuated aboriginal people from their habitual areas and resettled them in new villages in the hopes that paid employment would eventually be provided. Those jobs, with few exceptions, have never materialized, and are unlikely to do so.

The alternative is an economy based on hunting, fishing and trapping, supplemented by occasional wage labour or transfer payments. In northern Canada, such an economy remains traditional in the sense that it continues to bind people together in an older web of rights and obligations. In the Cree communities of eastern James Bay, the best hunters still enjoy the greatest social prestige and game or fish are distributed according to age-old patterns (Scott, 1989).

Such practices also survive in native communities in southern Canada. The residents of Walpole Island Indian Reserve on the St Clair River, upstream from the automobile metropolis of Detroit, still consume far more fish, waterfowl and game — and far less store-bought protein — than their non-native neighbours. Indeed, the overall quantities of country food in the native diet can be quite startling. Based on his own studies in aboriginal communities across the country, Manitoba resource economist Fikret Berkes (1990) estimates that native people eat seven times as much fish as the average Canadian. The figures are even higher for wild game.

In one important respect, however, the subsistence economy is anything but traditional. Thomas Berger points out that native people everywhere now use outboard motors, snowmobiles or all-terrain vehicles (ATVs) in their hunting and fishing activities — much as in earlier generations, they adopted canvas canoes and muskets in the place of bark or skin boats, spears and bows. Dene from northern Saskatchewan even fly into the Northwest Territories to hunt caribou, rather than travel overland by canoe or snow-shoe. Indigenous people, then, do not share the antipathy felt by many in the conservation community towards technology — including mechanized forms of wilderness travel; these modern devices simply make it easier to earn a living.

For their part, conservationists raise legitimate fears about the long-term effects of new technology on wildlife survival. This is the real nub of much of the current conflict between the two sides. Do modern methods make it easier to harvest, and therefore threaten the very existence of wildlife species? Such concerns appear to be reinforced by demographic trends. By all estimates, native people have the highest birth-rate in Canada. On Indian Reserves across the country — in marked contrast to the ageing general society — children and adolescents now constitute the largest single population group. Assuming that traditional harvesting continues at the same rate, then a larger native population could put added pressure on fish and wildlife species.

This observation should be balanced against another social trend. Over the past few years, there has been an astonishing rate of aboriginal migration from rural to urban centres. This applies not only to large cities like Toronto, Winnipeg, Regina and Vancouver, but also to smaller centres in most regions. In Ontario alone, some 40 per cent of native people already live off-reserve and this number is growing rapidly (Bobiwash, 1992:58–60). This trend is also of concern to some conservationists. In virtually all urban areas — as well as in many rural or northern native communities — young aboriginal people have either lost or are losing traditional bush skills. Without the wilderness ethic of their elders, would aboriginal people continue to show respect for wildlife?

Yet despite such questions, aboriginal people are only a small part of the perceived problem. Most of the anger and frustration voiced by conservationists is related to the diminishing supply of wild places — due to urbanization — throughout Canada.[5] The lack of planning and development controls in rural municipalities has also led to the destruction of unique vegetation and wildlife habitat, as has the inexorable march of industrial development on Crown lands. In much of southern Ontario, to give a prominent example, there is no longer sufficient wild country to allow for the creation of fully representative protected areas (Hackman, 1992: 276).

Against this background, aboriginal issues can be seen either as a distraction or as a luxury. In his contribution to a recent volume celebrating the centenary of the Ontario parks system, John Livingston vigorously attacks the ideology of human proprietorship over nature. In the contemporary discussion of native claims, he points out, both aboriginal people and different levels of government consistently focus on the 'management' of wildlife 'resources' as a primary goal. Management, he notes bitterly, 'is the usual euphemism for deciding on what numbers of what species of living beings may be killed, where, when, by whom, and by what means' (Livingston, 1992:238).

Rather than concentrating on perhaps irreconcilable policy differences, conservation groups like World Wildlife Fund Canada have devoted much of their energy to counting and monitoring wildlife populations. As part of this goal, however, they too seek answers from aboriginal people and their political organizations. Echoing John Livingston, they ask whether an apparent fixation on treaty and aboriginal harvesting rights leaves any room for conservation.

This concern has been sparked by disturbing recent events. In 1992, to give an example, Fisheries and Oceans Canada (formerly the Department of Fisheries) agreed to recognize an exclusive native food fishery along the Fraser River in British Columbia. While some First Nations complied with their own or governmental regulations — and, indeed, counted and monitored fish populations — other native people along the Fraser have been accused of transporting large quantities of fish to markets in the United States.

Aboriginal people have not responded directly to these issues or questions. As the following sections of this chapter suggest, there are several reasons why they have instead tended to concentrate on issues of title and rights. For one, their experience with the creation of parks and protected areas, as well as with the enforcement of fish and wildlife regulations, has made many of them deeply sceptical of the goals and motives of both government and the conservation movement. Too often over the past century, say native leaders, governments have either ignored or violated their aboriginal and treaty rights — sometimes at the urging of conservationists concerned about aboriginal harvesting practices.

---

5 The struggle to preserve the Rouge River valley in suburban Toronto is one example.

Aboriginal Harvesting Rights and Land Claims

Aboriginal people are the only sector of Canadian society who have constitutionally recognized — and 'protected' — rights to harvest fish and wildlife. This reality does not sit well with the animal rights movement, nor does it appeal to groups such as the Ontario Federation of Anglers and Hunters. Although members of the latter usually cite the impact of native rights on conservation policies, in reality their disagreement is more fundamental. To them, native harvesting rights are undemocratic because they confer special privileges on one group of people. This opinion is widely shared by non-native people in rural and remote areas of the country.

The idea of one Canada for all Canadians — whatever their origins — was popularized by former Prime Minister Pierre Trudeau, who fully intended that the concept be extended to aboriginal people. In a policy paper published in 1969, the Trudeau government proposed abolishing the walls separating native people from the rest of society — largely symbolized by the Indian Act[6] — and transferring federal responsibility for the delivery of programmes and services to the provinces. To Trudeau, it was unthinkable that one sector of society should have treaties with another. Bringing native people into the mainstream would help solve glaring problems of poverty and powerlessness.

The virulence of the native reaction to these proposals took the government by surprise. Rejecting assimilation as a product of Western theories of racial superiority, aboriginal people argued that the Indian Act — though a colonialist document — was a testimony to the direct and special relationship they had always enjoyed with the Crown. This relationship entirely bypassed 'white settler' governments — which were represented, after Confederation, by the provinces. Aboriginal people made it clear that they sought their own governing institutions within Confederation, ones which would be parallel, not subordinate, to provincial governments (Marule, 1978: 103–116).

The modern era of native claims and litigation — and of the enforcement of treaty and aboriginal rights — can be said to date from the rejection of the White Paper. The federal government's position was further changed by the 1973 decision of the Canadian Supreme Court in the Calder case. In 1968, the Nisga'a people of northern British Columbia — represented by Thomas Berger — had sought a declaration that their aboriginal title to their ancient tribal territories had never been extinguished. Although the Nisga'a lost, three out of seven judges actually agreed with them, and the government was obliged to consider the possibility of some future, more favourable, definition of aboriginal rights.

---

6 The first federal Indian Act dates from 1868. It and succeeding amendments created rigid legal definitions for 'Indian status' and established virtually complete federal control over Indian reserve lands.

The result, in August 1973, was a two-part federal policy on future native claims. 'Specific claims' were defined as those involving breaches of treaty or the government's lawful obligations to aboriginal people (Government of Canada, 1982). This included unfulfilled land entitlements under the 11 major treaties — covering much of northern and western Canada (Figure 10.2) — which were made between 1871 and 1930, as well as grievances arising out of the surrender or sale of Reserve lands or breach of the Indian Act.

The new federal policy also defined 'comprehensive claims' as those applying to areas of Canada where the native interest had not been extinguished by treaty or superseded by laws (Government of Canada, 1986). Basically, this covered much of Quebec, British Columbia west of the Rocky Mountains, and portions of the north and the Maritime provinces.

To aboriginal people, treaties embody the special relationship between themselves and the Crown. In their view, these agreements symbolize the fact that Canada is not simply a settler society — but it is instead linked formally to the distinct aboriginal societies that were here when the Europeans first arrived. Harvesting rights are an important part of that special relationship, and are still integral to most aboriginal societies in Canada. This helps explain the tenacity with which native groups have, over the past two decades, fought to have those rights respected (Price and Smith, 1993–94:54–55, 70–73).

While fisheries regulations are clearly federal — being delegated to the provinces for administrative purposes — native groups have consistently argued that the provinces have no right to regulate their Treaty rights to hunt or trap. In northern Ontario, at least, such arguments have received Court backing.

But arguments about treaty rights have not been limited to agreements made after 1867. In the 1985 Simon case, the Supreme Court of Canada upheld Mi'kmaq hunting rights under a 1752 Treaty covering the Maritimes. And in the 1990 Sioui case, the Court overturned the conviction of a resident of the Huron Reserve near Quebec City who had cut down saplings in Laurentides Provincial Park for traditional ceremonial purposes. Such rights, the Court held, were guaranteed under a 1760 treaty with the British Governor of Quebec.

Even in areas not covered by treaty, aboriginal people have been successful in using the courts to enforce their prior rights. The most important recent example is the Supreme Court's 1990 decision in the Sparrow case. A fisherman from the Musqueam Band near Vancouver had appealed his conviction under federal fisheries regulations for having an improper net, arguing that he had an aboriginal right to fish. The judges ordered a new trial, on the grounds that the government had not proven that the aboriginal right in question had been clearly extinguished. The mere exercise of a regulation, they said, could neither extinguish nor delineate the nature of the aboriginal right.

The Court did acknowledge federal power to regulate the aboriginal

PRE-CONFEDERATION TREATIES

■ Peace & Friendship Treaties Area

Upper Canada Treaties Area

Province of Canada Treaties

▲ Vancouver Island Treaties

POST-CONFEDERATION TREATIES

Numbered Treaties (1871 to 1930)

Williams Treaties (1923)

Note: Some of these treaty boundaries are in dispute
Source: Department of Indian and Northern Affairs, 1992

Figure 10.2 *Indian treaty zones in Canada*

fishery — but subject to Section 35(1) of the 1982 Constitution Act, which acknowledges and confirms existing aboriginal and treaty rights. The government, said the judges, had a clear responsibility to ensure conservation of the resource. But after valid conservation measures had been implemented, Indian food fishing was to be given priority over the interests of all other user groups — including sports anglers and commercial fishermen.

The Sparrow case has had important ramifications. In the fall of 1991, the federal Minister of Fisheries and Oceans informed his provincial and territorial counterparts that their fisheries regulations did not meet the Sparrow test — in that they neither justified any interferences with treaty and aboriginal rights nor assigned priority to the native food fishery. The provision of an exclusive native food fishery along the Fraser River is one concrete outcome of the Court decision.

The implications of the decision for provincial and territorial wildlife regulations are certainly profound. And the case has sparked a continuing backlash among anglers and commercial fishermen. Aboriginal people have had difficulty convincing non-natives that these court decisions have not created new rights, but have simply recognized existing ones. Part of their difficulty has been the non-recognition of aboriginal and treaty rights for so many years. And at its core, the disagreement also raises questions about the overall content and purpose of government conservation policies.

Competing Theories of Wildlife Conservation

The founder of the Jack Miner Bird Sanctuary at Kingsville, Ontario, is justly famous for his efforts to protect waterfowl from hunting pressure or habitat disturbance. His skilled political lobbying, combined with a knack for publicity — a clear and simple message, and a folksy speaking style which later transferred wonderfully to radio — led directly to the passing of the Migratory Birds Convention Act of 1917. Miner's spiritual descendants are active today in groups like Ducks Unlimited and the Canadian Nature Federation.

But among the aboriginal people who live along the flyways of those same migratory fowl — the Chippewas of Lake Huron, for example, or the Cree of James and Hudson Bays — Jack Miner is far less fondly remembered. To them, he was just another white man who lacked understanding of aboriginal hunting culture — yet was prepared to impose alien rules in the name of conservation. In their view, laws such as the Migratory Birds Convention violated the British Crown's solemn assurances over the centuries that native people would always have priority of access to wildlife for their own support.

Many of the first generation of conservationists were sports hunters and anglers — as was Jack Miner himself (1969). The pages of *Rod and Gun in Canada* and other sporting publications from the turn of the century are filled with dispatches under his pseudonym of 'Gorilla Chief', detailing the glories of his northern expeditions in search of caribou, moose, or trophy fish. However, Miner later regretted his own role in what Farley Mowat has so aptly called the 'sea of slaughter' (Mowat, 1984).

That aboriginal people played a part in the massive assault on North American wildlife in the late nineteenth and early twentieth centuries cannot be denied. The exigencies of the commercial fur trade and the markets in fish, wild meat and hides guaranteed as much. But the question is one of degree. Throughout the first four decades of this century, Jack Miner and other exponents of 'scientific conservation' — including the major organizations of anglers and hunters — assigned an enormous share of the blame to native people.

Taking a major role in provincial and territorial commissions on fish and wildlife management of this period, these early conservationists insisted that laws be implemented to reflect their views. Cree and Ojibway hunters in northern Ontario and Quebec were accused of slaughtering such enormous numbers of geese, moose and deer that the survival of these very species was in doubt. Similar accusations were levelled at Ojibway sturgeon fishermen in Manitoba and north-western Ontario, at

280

Dene caribou hunters in the Northwest Territories, and at native salmon fishermen on both the east and west coasts. Except through officials of the Indian Affairs Department, however, aboriginal people were unable to respond. At the various investigative hearings on wildlife management, they were neither invited nor present (Tough, 1991).

The accusations themselves have been largely discredited. Their scientific accuracy is roughly equivalent to the charges levelled at wolves and other 'vermin' predators in the same historical period. As the Plains Cree and Blackfoot Nations are quick to point out, natives are certainly not to blame for the disappearance of the plains bison in the nineteenth century. Nor can aboriginal people be charged with responsibility for the extinction of the passenger pigeon.

In the case of Lake Sturgeon in north-western Ontario and the Lake Winnipeg drainage, a recent study has shown that Ojibway bands managed fish populations at their maximum sustainable yield until the late nineteenth century. According to Van West, it was not aboriginal over-fishing, but government licensing of non-native commercial fishermen — coupled with habitat destruction from lumber and pulp mill effluent — which eventually caused populations to crash (1990: 31–65). Similar reasons lie behind the collapse of native fisheries in northern Manitoba, as well as on Lake Huron and the west coast of British Columbia (Tough, 1984; Lytwyn, 1990; Berringer, 1987).

Nevertheless, indigenous people gradually found themselves, as Georges Erasmus puts it, regulated by the provinces and territories 'to the level of other users who do not possess aboriginal or treaty rights' (Erasmus, 1989:94). Despite the explicit guarantees contained in many treaties, such as those covering northern Ontario and the west, the Department of Indian Affairs — the supposed guarantor of those same rights — generally acquiesced before such conduct.

These developments did not pass without protest. The comments of Temagami Chief Aleck Paul — addressed to an American anthropologist in 1913 — are typical. Governments, he said, were clearly favouring white hunters and trappers, who were killing the game 'for sport and not for support' (cited in Speck, 1913:23–24). Native people were finding it increasingly difficult to make a living. Lacking political or legal redress, many of them either openly flouted what they believed to be illegal laws, or quietly ignored new regulations on quotas, seasons and methods of harvest. In those parts of northern Canada which were far from the frontier of settlement, this form of protest was generally successful. But in more settled areas, fines and occasional incarceration — along with a growing reputation as chronic offenders against the rule of law — were frequent outcomes.

At least part of the aboriginal protest has been a reaction to what they see as Western scientific arrogance. Provincial and territorial wildlife officials have generally given short shrift to traditional knowledge of fish and wildlife species, even though that knowledge is based on extremely detailed observation of habitat and population fluctuations. It was only the publication of European studies showing the effect of low-level flights on wildlife species that brought about a change in attitude.

Anthropologist Milton Freeman has consistently criticized wildlife biologists for scanting traditional knowledge. He cites the example of caribou hunting on Ellesmere Island. Government wildlife managers told local Inuit they should hunt only large and/or male caribou, and only a few animals from each herd. The Inuit argued that this would destroy the population — a prediction which came true when caribou numbers dropped sharply, despite a far lower hunt. The Inuit understanding was based on their observation that older or larger animals, being stronger, are better able to dig through the snow for food. They also calm the more nervous younger animals or pregnant females. This makes them important to the survival of the group (cited in Mander, 1991: 257–258).

The authors of *Whales Beneath the Ice* recommend that, when setting biologically sustainable and culturally desirable levels of harvest with native groups, 'it is important that the idea of a quota which is enforced by a "policeman" who distrusts the harvest, be avoided as much as possible. The result is often resentment and non-compliance' (WWF, 1986: 27). This, in fact, has been the history of wildlife management in Canada for much of this century. It helps to explain the hostility native groups frequently manifest towards provincial government officials — and the continuing difficulty of securing conservation agreements on shared management principles.

The need for cross-cultural training for government biologists, and fish and wildlife managers is evident. Even today, most such individuals are hired without any specific knowledge of aboriginal culture or traditions. But, as Georges Erasmus points out, it is aboriginal people themselves who should be playing the most important role in preserving wildlife (Erasmus, 1989:98). The reason will be clear from a look at national population distribution. Most Canadians live within 500 kilometres of the US border, principally in the St Lawrence-Great Lakes corridor, the southern prairies and the southernmost parts of British Columbia. In the rest of the country — which represents well over 70 per cent of Canada's land mass — aboriginal people are either an absolute majority or a significant minority of the population (Barsch 1994:8–9). Yet that fundamental reality is not yet reflected in the personnel of provincial or territorial resource management agencies.

Aboriginal involvement in fish and wildlife management could take various forms. Some native organizations have urged governments to create specific training programmes for aboriginal people, in order to prepare the ground for affirmative action within existing resource management agencies. Others have argued that aboriginal people should have an equal share in management decisions. The Beverly-Qamanirjuaq Caribou Management Board, for example, includes both federal and provincial wildlife officials and native harvesters from Manitoba,

Saskatchewan and the Northwest Territories.

Some native organizations, however, have preferred to concentrate their efforts on setting up their own systems, arguing that self-regulation is a necessary component of self-government. In Nova Scotia, Mi'kmaq people now follow regulations drafted by the Union Chiefs. Harvesters carry with them booklets outlining species, seasons and techniques. In Ontario, the United Chiefs and Councils of Manitoulin Island have been trying to negotiate a pilot project which would see them take over from the province the regulation and supervision of aboriginal harvesters.

Formative Native Views of Parks and Protected Areas

In 1893, when Algonquin Park became Ontario's first official protected area, the Administrative head of the Crown Lands Department received a report from a fire ranger on the Petawawa River. He had spotted several Indians setting up camp within the new park, where they intended to hunt and trap; already, he said, they had moose meat, and beaver and otter pelts in their possession.

Assistant Commissioner White acknowledged that aboriginal interests were not among those considered by his government when the park reserve was being created. But he decided — for a variety of reasons, including the fact that white trappers had already been ordered out — that it was far too late to make any special exceptions for Indians. He instructed his officials to explain to the people concerned — as carefully and tactfully as possible — that hunting and trapping were no longer permitted within the boundaries of Algonquin Park (Saunders, 1963:98–99).

The current land claim of the Golden Lake First Nation is based, at least in part, on a sense of historic grievance. Whether or not the Golden Lake people have a valid interest in all of what is now Algonquin Park is still an open question, as is whether or not Ontario should make amends by reopening the park to hunting. It is nevertheless apparent that, after 1893, Algonquin people were excluded from this new protected area without their consent (Tough, 1991).

The creation of most early protected areas in North America involved the exclusion of aboriginal people. Aboriginal interests were ignored, for example, when Riding Mountain National Park was established in southwestern Manitoba. In 1896, the Department of Indian Affairs set aside 728 acres on Clear Lake as a fishing Reserve for the Keeseekoowenin Band of Saulteaux. Some thirty years later, the federal government declared the enabling order in council inoperative and included the fishing reserve in the new National Park, which was formally created in 1933. The Keeseekoowenin Band were evicted, and their houses burned down (personal communication, Klein, 1992).

As the example of Algonquin Park suggests, provincial governments behaved no differently. Quetico, located in the boundary waters area of north-western Ontario, became a provincial park in 1913. Since protection of game was stated to be the park's chief objective, the province forbade local Ojibways to hunt or trap within park boundaries. Park fishing licences also prohibited the use of nets or spears, both of which were the usual native fishing tools at the time (Lambert and Pross, 1967:284–91).

Protected areas took more than one form in the early decades of the twentieth century. Both Quetico and Riding Mountain Parks were originally set apart as forest reserves. Many provinces also created game preserves within their jurisdictions. Aboriginal people, however, did not distinguish between the various categories, since most had similar impacts on their harvesting rights. In 1925, for instance, Ontario banned all hunting and trapping within the Chapleau Crown Game Preserve, a tract of several thousand hectares in northern Ontario. Not only did this action permanently affect the livelihood of a few hundred Ojibway and Cree people, it forced one of the Bands to surrender its Reserve in the centre of the Game Preserve. Ironically, those particular lands were eventually incorporated into Missinaibi Lake Provincial Park in the early 1970s.

It was the complete disregard for their dependence on traditional harvesting which most disturbed aboriginal people. There were few exceptions to this rule, one of which occurred in 1928, when Quebec banned non-native trappers from those parts of the province north of the Canadian National Railway line through Sanmaur and Amos. Quebec also co-operated with the Department of Indian Affairs in setting up the Nottaway Beaver Preserve Southeast of James Bay. In a unique experiment to replace the lost income from beaver trapping, aboriginal people were hired as 'tallymen' to count and monitor beaver populations within the Preserve (MLCP, 1987:27–28).

Quebec's policy, however, applied only in remote northern areas. In the Grand Lac Victoria Beaver Preserve near the headwaters of the Ottawa River, the same hunting and trapping restrictions applied to native and non-native people alike. After the Second World War, the Beaver Preserve was rolled into what is now La Vérendrye Park and Wildlife Reserve. Two very traditional Algonquin communities — Grand Lac and Rapid (Barrier) Lake — are still within park boundaries. While Quebec now tolerates some native harvesting, it has never legally recognized such rights. And because of the Park's legal status, it has been impossible for these Algonquin communities to expand their tiny land base.

The postwar period saw an exponential increase — at least in relative terms — in the number of protected areas across the country. But the various jurisdictions were no more solicitous of aboriginal interests than their predecessors. As Mike Murtha of British Columbia Parks told a 1993 protected areas conference, as late as the 1970s 'we just did not talk to native people at all' (CPAWS-Yukon, 1993:5). Tweedsmuir provincial park in British Columbia was created despite the long-standing native claim to portions of land within its boundaries. And both Bruce Peninsula National Park and Fathom Five National Marine Park in Ontario include lands and waters which have been claimed by the Saugeen and Cape Croker First Nations since the nineteenth century (ARC, 1992–93).

In 1974, the National Parks Act was amended to recognize aboriginal hunting, fishing and trapping in parks or reserves north of the 60th parallel. But, with the exception of Pukaskwa in Ontario, the same recognition has not been extended to southern properties. Until recently, provincial jurisdictions have generally refused to consider such native access to parks and protected areas.

Even good intentions have had unanticipated consequences. In the mid–1970s, Ontario's parks branch persuaded the Ojicree residents of Webequie, at the headwaters of the Winisk River in the remote Patricia District, that a proposed new provincial waterway park would help protect the area from resource development and safeguard their harvesting rights. But the Webequie community remains subject to parks regulations and development controls. They have also been unable to expand their community land base.

In North America, parks and protected areas have generally been created in the name of the public interest. Most conservationists fully support this concept — insisting that it is a governmental responsibility to protect significant regions of the country for the benefit of future generations. Aboriginal people, however, dispute the inclusiveness of the term 'public'. In their view, it automatically places the interests of the general society above those of minorities. They point out that governments also cited the public interest when imposing large-scale resource development projects on them — such as pipelines and hydroelectric dams. As the examples of the Oldman Dam and James Bay II hydro projects show, governments continue to use the same arguments today.

It is fair to say, therefore, that indigenous people have borne the costs of protecting natural areas, through the loss of access for hunting, trapping or other harvesting activities. As Georges Erasmus puts it, the doctrine of the public interests made 'an ancient way of life subject to the apparent modern-day whims of an alien culture, all in the name of conservation' (Erasmus, 1989:94).

Conservationists, nevertheless, vigorously defend the parks system. While they may concede a certain lack of historical sensitivity or understanding, they argue that the fundamental choice was never between protected areas and aboriginal interests, but rather between protection and industrial development. If anything, they say, the situation would have been infinitely worse without the skilled political lobbying of groups like the Algonquin Wildlands League and the Canadian Parks and Wilderness Society. The scale of clear-cut logging or mining on Crown lands would have been far more significant — and the damage to the habitat of the fish and wildlife sought by aboriginal people that much more severe.

Recent Parks, Claims and Conflicts

In recent years, more innovative approaches to protected area management have taken place in areas of federal jurisdiction such as the Northwest Territories and Yukon. Although some provincial jurisdictions have made policy statements or entered into talks with aboriginal groups, the overall climate there is far more conflictual. This section considers the parks provisions in proposed land claims settlements with the Inuvialuit, Yukon and Inuit native peoples, then at Parks Canada properties south of the 60th parallel. In Canada's north, the federal government has been negotiating for the past twenty years with various native organizations for the surrender of aboriginal title in exchange for specified treaty benefits under its 'comprehensive claims' policy (Government of Canada, 1986).[7] Many of these land claims settlements have provided the major vehicle for expanding the network of protected areas.

Inuvialuit Claim

In 1984, Canada reached a land claims settlement with the Inuit inhabitants of the western Arctic known as the Inuvialuit. The terms of the agreement included the establishment of an Inuvialuit Game Council (IGC) —responsible for native wildlife interests, including traditional harvesting — and an Inuvialuit Regional Corporation (IRC).

In July 1992, the federal government, the IGC, IRC and the Northwest Territories government reached an agreement to establish a new national park on Banks Island. The agreement gives the Inuvialuit exclusive rights to harvest wildlife in the park, and their fishing is given priority over sports angling. They will also have the power to screen archaeological research. The Canadian Wildlife Service will ensure the continued management of the Banks Island Bird Sanctuary.

The Inuvialuit are to be involved in the drafting both of the Interim Management guidelines for the Park and the final Management Plan, which is evidence of recognition of the potential contribution of Inuvialuit traditional knowledge to both planning and research. Other provisions give the Inuvialuit guarantees of employment and training as well as priority in contracts and park business licenses, including tourism development.

Yukon Claim

The long-standing land claims of Yukon native people have basically been settled. An Umbrella Final Agreement has been ratified by Canada and

---

7 The Royal Commission on Aboriginal Peoples, appointed in 1991, has recently recommended that the federal government no longer require the surrender or extinguishment of Aboriginal title as a condition of claims settlements, on the grounds that such concepts are offensive to Aboriginal peoples (RCAP, 1994).

native representatives, and First Nation Final Agreements are being implemented for Champagne and Aishihik, Nacho Nyak Dun (Mayo), Kluane, White River and Vuntut Gwich'in (Old Crow) First Nations. One major feature of the draft final agreements is the creation of special management areas to maintain important features of the Yukon's natural or cultural environment 'for the benefit of Yukon residents and all Canadians while respecting the rights of Yukon Indian People and Yukon First Nations' (Government of Yukon, 1993). Such areas are to include national wildlife areas, national parks or park reserves, territorial parks and national historic sites, special wildlife or fish management areas, migratory bird or game sanctuaries, designated heritage sites and watershed protection areas. Existing designated conservation areas will continue to be protected, though they will be identified as special management areas in accordance with the agreements. Existing harvesting rights of native people will be guaranteed. Generally speaking, ultimate management authority for special areas will fall to existing agencies such as Parks Canada, though native people will have a much strengthened role in planning and administration.

Inuit Claim

Canada's land claims agreement with the Inuit of the eastern Arctic and sub-Arctic — through the Tungavik Federation of Nunavut (TFN) — has been ratified by both parties. The most publicized part of the agreement is Canada's stated intention to create a new public government out of the eastern half of the Northwest Territories, to be known as Nunavut.[8] In common with the other northern land claim settlements, various provisions of the TFN Agreement provide for new protected areas. Existing spaces will also be protected.

The TFN agreement calls for three national parks, at Auyuittuq, North Baffin and Ellsmere Island. It was the Inuit themselves who pushed for the creation of these spaces. The chapter dealing with the new parks is very specific. Once again, there are provisions for native employment, preferential hiring and training — with appropriate targets. And the chapter also provides schemes for the management of areas adjacent to the parks, so as not to detract from park or Inuit values. The Inuit will have exclusive harvesting rights and renewable resource use with the parks. Any restrictions on the technology used in harvesting will require the consent of the Inuit themselves. According to the agreement, all resources will be managed using both modern science and traditional knowledge.

---

8 Because it will be open to all residents of the territory, regardless of their ethnic origins, the public government of Nunavut will not technically constitute Inuit self-government. However, this government will be dominated for the foreseeable future by Inuit, who currently make up more than 95 per cent of the population.

Parks Canada: Specific Claims

Parks Canada continues to take the position — based, presumably, on opinions of the Department of Justice — that aboriginal harvesting rights do not apply to its properties. That is because they have been occupied for 'other purposes'. Aboriginal groups have never accepted this argument —with regard to either parks or wildlife preserves.

- Riding Mountain National Park, Manitoba. The claim, referred to above, of the Keeseekoowenin Band was validated by the government of Canada. By federal Order in Council, the 728 acres in question have been returned to the band and de-designated as park land. Until the final legal transfer, the Keeseekoowenin Band have agreed to lease the land back to Parks Canada. They have also passed Band bylaws stipulating conservation measures for the affected tract. These are based on the existing park regulations (personal communication, Klein, 1992).
- Pukaskwa National Park, Ontario. The large wilderness area west of the Michipicoten River on the north shore of Lake Superior was set apart in 1978 by federal–provincial agreement. As part of that agreement, the various local Ojibway bands — then represented by the Robinson–Superior Treaty organization — were guaranteed employment and other economic benefits. To date, the major beneficiaries have been the Ojibways of Pic River (Heron Bay), whose Reserve is on the west side of the river opposite the park entrance. Half of the staff — about 20 persons in all — are native, which meets the original target set. Native people have access for the purposes of hunting, fishing and trapping — including the use of snowmobiles for winter harvesting. At the present time, however, all-terrain vehicles are banned. Since these machines are becoming increasingly popular in native communities, this is causing some resentment at the Pic Heron Bay Reserve.

    Parks Canada retains full management authority for Pukaskwa. Land claims may affect this reality. The Pic-Heron Bay First Nation has recently submitted a claim to extensive areas of the Superior north shore — including the National Park. The next decade might well see aboriginal people being formally brought into the Park's governing structure.
- Bruce Peninsula National Park, Ontario. In 1987, Canada and Ontario agreed to create a new national park in the Bruce Peninsula, that spectacular portion of the Niagara Escarpment which separates Lake Huron from Georgian Bay. The agreement involved the transfer of two existing provincial parks — Fathom Five Marine and Cypress Lake — to Parks Canada, as well as the acquisition of private lands.

The aboriginal people of the peninsula — represented by the Saugeen Ojibway of Nawash (Cape Croker) and Saugeen (Southampton) — argue that, in creating this park, the Crown has breached its obligations to them. They base their claim on an 1854 treaty, under which their ancestors surrendered some one and half million acres of land in the Bruce Peninsula to the Crown, so that it could be sold for their benefit. About 40,000 acres still remain unsold — and it is some of this land which has been transferred to Parks Canada for the Bruce National Park. The Saugeen Ojibway are demanding the return of these unsold Crown lands, as well as participation in the management of all parks.

No final agreements have been reached by the three parties. Parks Canada is willing to discuss an advisory role for the Saugeen Ojibway in park management, but is not prepared to concede that the lands in question do not properly belong in the national park. For its part, Ontario has promised the Saugeen Ojibway that the provincial parklands will not be formally transferred to Parks Canada until their claim has been settled (personal communication, Johnston, 1993).

Parks Canada: Comprehensive Claims

Within those parts of Canada where there have been no treaties or land claims agreements, Parks Canada and other federal government agencies have been attempting to work out interim arrangements on protected areas similar to those in regions north of the 60th parallel. This is true of British Columbia and Quebec, for example.

* Mingan Archipelago, Quebec. The Conseil Attikamègue-Montagnais (CAM) has a comprehensive claim to extensive areas of Quebec, including portions of the St Lawrence north shore. In 1989, Canada and CAM agreed to set up an interim joint advisory body for Mingan Park, with four native representatives and four appointed by the federal government. The body is charged with review of management plans for the park. Subsistence harvesting is permitted within the park area. The overall claims negotiations have been subject to the charged political climate in Quebec over aboriginal rights.
* Gwaii Haanas/South Moresby, British Columbia. The battle to preserve the island archipelago was led by a coalition of wilderness activists and the Haida people, rather than Parks Canada itself. The coalition spearheaded the move to protect the area in question from logging and other forms of industrial development.

The May 1990 agreement which established the new National Park Reserve — subject to the Haida claim — provided for a joint Archipelago Management Board, which would guarantee traditional Haida harvesting rights, and identify sites of special spiritual and cultural significance to native people.

But in the various northern agreements to date, Parks Canada has insisted on retaining ownership of all properties. Native people have obtained certain economic and cultural benefits, as well as a very strong advisory role, but the Minister of the Environment makes the ultimate decisions on park management. The Council of the Haida Nation, however, has made it clear that they will be seeking title to Gwaii Haanas Park in any ultimate land claims settlement. This is because, like most groups in British Columbia, they are refusing to surrender their aboriginal title — whatever the outcome of negotiations.

Provincial Ferment: British Columbia

There are many land claims dating back to the province's entry into the Confederation in 1871. Not only were there no treaties on the mainland west of the Rocky Mountains, but a joint federal–provincial Royal Commission appointed in 1912 recommended that 19,000 hectares — including areas long coveted by settlers — be eliminated from existing Indian Reserves and communities as surplus to their requirements (Usher et al, 1992:118–119). Relations between native people and the provincial government, therefore, have been notoriously conflictual.

This situation has started to change. In October 1991, Canada, British Columbia and aboriginal groups agreed to establish a treaty commission to resolve most of the outstanding land issues. It is obvious that achieving claims settlements will not be easy. Not the least of the problems will be the existing interests of third parties such as private landowners, municipalities and holders of tree-farm licences.

Nevertheless, there are encouraging signs that the creation of new protected areas is a priority for both aboriginal people and the provincial government. In 1994, the provincial government announced protection for the Kitlope Ecosystem in the Gardner Canal area of the north coast — something which had been urged by the Haisla (Tsimshian) of the community of Kitimaat, with the overwhelming support of the conservation community. And the government of British Columbia has embarked on an ambitious programme to double parkland in the province. One of the new parks is the Nisga'a Memorial Lava Bed Provincial Park (*Anhluut'ukwsim Laxmihl Angwinga'asanskwhl Nisga'a*), consisting of 17,683 hectares of land in the Nass Valley. It was the Nisga'a Tribal Council which approached the provincial government to create the park. This particular park is a relatively small area. A greater test will come with proposals to permanently safeguard large natural regions of the province.

The Kitlope represents an important precedent, since it constitutes the southern half of the traditional territory claimed by the Haisla and borders Tweedsmuir Provincial Park to the south-west. In general, aboriginal people and conservationists have expressed a shared interest in protecting wild areas from uncontrolled resource development. This has been true of Pacific Rim and the adjoining Carmanah and Walbran valleys on the west coast of Vancouver Island, of the Stein Valley and of the Kitlope.

Provincial Ferment: Ontario

The Province of Ontario — where the names of Temagami, Algonquin and Quetico have all made headlines — ranks next to British Columbia in controversy over wilderness values, parks and protected areas. In September 1991, then Premier Bob Rae formally signed a Statement of Political Relationship with representatives of Ontario aboriginal organizations. In keeping with these principles, Ontario has announced that the 'creation of all new provincial parks and protected natural heritage areas will respect all treaty and aboriginal rights'. A consultation process has been undertaken to that end.

How the consultation will work out in practice is still unclear. Relations in the past between parks personnel and the native community have ranged from cool to hostile. Although some aboriginal people have been employed within the system, Ontario is typical of the provinces in never having acknowledged treaty or aboriginal rights to harvest wildlife within parks. In the remote north of Ontario, it is government policy, not legal recognition, which has permitted native hunting and trapping. Like Parks Canada, Ontario has always considered parks to be 'occupied' Crown lands for the purposes of the treaties.

Aboriginal people are already demanding access to existing parks for subsistence pursuits. Others want park land for community purposes. Current negotiations between the Ontario Native Affairs Secretariat and the Nishnawbe-Aski Nation, which represents many of the northern First Nations, may result in a change of status for parts of Polar Bear and Winisk River Provincial Parks.

Unlike British Columbia, where there has been some convergence of interest between aboriginal people, conservationists and local residents in opposing large-scale resource development — the Alcan Kemano project, for example[9] — the situation in Ontario is becoming more polarized. Hostility to aboriginal harvesting — and to the settlement of land claims — is becoming a province-wide phenomenon. At least some of the antipathy to native hunting within Algonquin boundaries is based on resentment of aboriginal rights. Ontario's recent land-claims settlement with the Mississagi First Nation near Blind River — which has seen their existing reserve enlarged — has sparked protests from a coalition of tourist outfitters and local hunters and anglers.

Temagami

At least one potential model for co-operative land management did result from a long-standing native claim to 6000 hectares of north-eastern Ontario — and the related struggle over logging of old-growth forests. In

---

9 In 1995, widespread opposition from Aboriginal people, commercial and recreational fishermen and environmentalists led the government of British Columbia to withdraw permission for the Alcan Company to build a hydroelectric plant on the Kemano River to supply power to its aluminium smelter.

June 1990, the Teme-augama Anishnabai and the Ontario government agreed to set up a co-management body — called the Wendaban Stewardship Authority — for four townships in the Temagami region which included the Wakimika triangle, where much old-growth red and white pine was located. In the meantime, no new forest operations were to be carried on in the four townships. The exact form of this protection — as well as other aspects of the Stewardship Authority Plan and conservation measures generally — will have to await the report of the Comprehensive Planning Council.

Conclusions

Recognition of their inherent right to self-government is a crucial goal for aboriginal people, despite the fact that some members of Canadian society envision the creation of ethnic enclaves and fear the potential destabilization of the body politic. Self-government will have a particular impact on relations with the provinces and territories. While most aboriginal people see themselves as Canadians — and as Nisga'a, Inuit or Cree — few have ever regarded themselves as citizens of British Columbia, or Ontario, or Nova Scotia. To them, provincial governments have always been the representative institutions of non-native settlers.

This explains the frequent insistence by aboriginal leaders that talks now be conducted with them on a 'government to government' basis. They see their (eventual) self-governing institutions as being at least parallel in status to those of the provinces. Ontario was the first jurisdiction to formally acknowledge this fact, in the August 1991 Statement of Political Relationship.

The federal government and many provinces argue that native self-government will only apply to existing Indian reserves or community lands created through negotiation. This is definitely not the view of aboriginal political leaders. They point out that the 1982 Constitution Act already recognizes and affirms their existing aboriginal and treaty rights. As several recent Supreme Court decisions have made clear, these rights include priority of access to unoccupied Crown lands and waters for hunting, fishing, trapping and other subsistence pursuits. Governments may well have difficulty maintaining the view that parks and protected areas are 'occupied' Crown lands, thus preventing the exercise of treaty and aboriginal rights.

Claims settlements in the Northwest Territories and Yukon already acknowledge aboriginal interests in archaeological sites and areas of cultural or spiritual significance on non-settlement lands. This is a trend in provincial heritage legislation as well, one which gives native people a say in the management of lands off their Reserves or settlements. Parks and protected areas are bound to be included in this category.

The combination, therefore, of self-government initiatives, the settle-

ment of native claims, and constitutional recognition of treaty and aboriginal rights will have an obvious impact on protected area management in
general. Both Canada and aboriginal groups have agreed to provide for
new protected areas as part of land claims settlements. The Inuvialuit,
Inuit and other groups in the Yukon and Northwest Territories have also
ensured that their interests — including employment opportunities and
cultural survival through continued harvesting rights — are fully
protected as well.

Within the provinces, however, the situation is much more problematic. It has been complex enough to reach land claim settlements between
aboriginal people and the federal government — the addition of the
provinces and private or third-party interests makes agreements that
much more difficult. And in provinces like Ontario, the hostility of angler
and hunter groups to treaty and aboriginal rights has further complicated
the task.

Virtually all of British Columbia is subject to native claims of one sort
or another. The same is true of large portions of Quebec and the
Maritimes, which also have few, if any, treaties with their native inhabitants. The prairie provinces are blanketed with claims based on Treaty
entitlement. A September 1992 announcement in Saskatchewan commits
the three levels of government — Saskatchewan First Nations being the
third — to negotiate and settle the considerable areas of land still owing
to aboriginal people under treaties signed between 1874 and 1910. Some
lands with conservation potential may well be selected. In Alberta and
Manitoba, as already noted, claims have been advanced to parcels of
existing national parks. Ontario, too, has outstanding claims issues in
addition to the one involving Algonquin Park.

In much of the country, therefore, it is the native political agenda which
will influence protected-area programmes, not the other way around. In
northern Quebec, for example, the Cree are interested in park proposals
because they see them as one means of halting James Bay II. Their kins-
men in western James Bay have similar goals for the Moose River basin. If
parks or protected areas will prevent further hydroelectric development
on the rivers leading to the bay, then they are in favour. The same is true
of Montagnais from the lower north shore of the St Lawrence, who seek to
stop hydroelectric development in their traditional homeland.

However, in other regions of the country, like Ontario, tensions
between aboriginal groups and environmentalists are rising, as each side
pursues its own goals. Does allowing aboriginal people motorized access
violate the fundamental protected status of parks? Should the 'few rights
the aboriginal people have left' take precedence over the pleasure of
canoeists and campers? Or should treaties be interpreted only in the light
of modern principles of resource management?

As long as the argument pits native subsistence against the recreational needs of an urbanized general society, aboriginal people will have
the moral upper hand. Indeed, their message to conservationists — and

to government — is that, without respect for existing treaty and aboriginal rights, new conservation agreements will not be possible. They will no longer allow their rights to be sacrificed on the altar of some larger public interest. In the planning of new protected areas, aboriginal people also expect to be involved from the very beginning. They want protected-area managers to realize that their participation in planning and management is not a threat, but a guarantee of their own livelihood and a positive contribution to the preservation of wild spaces.

But another issue is the uncontrolled exploitation of natural resources 'regardless of the racial origin of the exploiters'. Wild spaces everywhere are generally shrinking as a result of human pressure. Even in a country as thinly populated as Canada, some plant and animal species have already become extinct, and more are vulnerable.

Conservationists do not accept that treaty and aboriginal rights should ever be an end in themselves, particularly if they substitute one type of human predator for another. In southern Canada, faced with the twin pressures of urbanization and industrial development, conservationists continue to see aboriginal interests as secondary to the ultimate survival of wildlife and natural areas.

While conservationists and aboriginal people may differ on their ultimate objectives, they do have common interests. One is a shared antipathy to the type of large-scale resource development which has ravaged much of Canada. Another is a commitment to the ethos expressed recently by naturalist Ron Reid — that, while humans have become the dominant species on earth, 'we still have a cardinal responsibility to share our whole planet with all other living creatures, plant and animal, that evolved here' (1992:46). As the example of Gwaii Haanas/South Moresby clearly shows, the advantages of common action far outweigh the disadvantages. To paraphrase a saying commonly used by aboriginal leaders, both groups do not have to travel in the same canoe. But they can certainly share a waterway — and even arrive at a common destination.

References

ARC (Aboriginal Rights Coalition) (1992–1993), 'Casting for justice: Saugeen Ojibways seek recognition of fishing rights', *Bulletin Solidarité Newsletter*, Vol 2, No 4, ARC, p 3.

Barsch, Russell Lawrence (1994), 'Canada's aboriginal peoples: Social integration or disintegration', *The Canadian Journal of Native Studies*, Vol XIV, No 1, pp 1–46.

Berger, Thomas (1991), *A Long and Terrible Shadow: White Values, Native Rights in the Americas, 1492–1992*, Douglas and McIntyre, Vancouver and Toronto.

Berkes, Fikret (1990), 'Native subsistence fisheries: a synthesis of harvest studies in Canada', *Artic 43*, No 1, pp 35–42.

Berringer, Patricia (1987), *Aboriginal Fishery Systems in British Columbia: the Impact of Government Regulations, 1884–1912*, paper presented to the 16th annual Congress of the Canadian Ethnology Society, Ottawa.

Bobiwash, Rodney (1992), 'The provision of aboriginal social services in a native urban self-government paradigm', in B Hodgins, S Heard and J Milloy (eds), *Co-Existence: Studies in Ontario-First Nations Relations*, Frost Centre for Canadian Heritage and Development Studies, Trent University, Peterborough, Ontario, pp 58–66.

CPAWS-BC (Canadian Parks and Wilderness Society-British Columbia) (1989), *Wilderness, Parks and Native Land Claims*, Henderson Book Series No 12, CPAWS-British Columbia Chapter, Vancouver.

CPAWS-Yukon (1993), *Northern Protected Areas and Wilderness: Summary of Proceedings and Recommendations*, Forum on Northern Protected Areas and Wilderness (Whitehorse, November 1993), CPAWS-Yukon, Whitehorse, 12 pp.

Department of the Environment (1979), *Parks Canada Policy*, Supply and Services Canada, Ottawa.

Erasmus, Georges (1989), 'A native viewpoint', in Hummel, op cit, pp 93–98.

Government of Canada (1982), *Outstanding Business*, Department of Indian Affairs and Northern Development, Supply and Services Canada, Ottawa.

— (1986), *Comprehensive Land Claims Policy*, Department of Indian Affairs and Northern Development, Supply and Services Canada, Ottawa.

Government of Yukon (1993), *Umbrella Final Agreement between the Government of Canada, the Council for Yukon Indians and the Government of the Yukon*, Supply and Services Canada, Ottawa.

Hackman, Arlin (1992), 'The job to be done', in Lori Labatt and Bruce Littlejohn (eds), *Islands of Hope: Ontario's Parks and Wilderness*, Firefly Books, Toronto, pp 276–281.

Hummel, Monte (ed) (1989), *Endangered Spaces: the Future for Canada's Wilderness*, Key Porter Books, Toronto.

King, Cecil (1992), 'And the last shall be first', *Compass: a Jesuit Journal*, Vol 10, No 4, September-October, pp 42–43.

Lambert, Richard S and Paul Pross (1967), *Renewing Nature's Wealth: a Centennial History of the Public Management of Lands, Forests and Wildlife in Ontario, 1763–1967*, Ontario Department of Lands and Forests, Toronto.

Livingston, John (1992), 'Attitudes to nature', in Lori Labatt and Bruce Littlejohn (eds), *Islands of Hope: Ontario's Parks and Wilderness*, Firefly Books, Toronto, pp 237–240.

Lytwyn, Victor P (1990), 'Ojibwa and Ottawa fisheries around Manitoulin Island: historical and geographical perspectives on aboriginal and treaty fishing rights', *Native Studies Review*, Vol 6, No 1, pp 1–30.

MLCP (Ministère du Loisir, de la Chasse et de la Pêche du Québec) (1987), *Présence Amérindienne en Abitibi-Témiscamingue*, Rouyn.

Mander, Jerry (1991), *In the Absence of the Sacred: The Failure of Technology and the Survival of the Indian Nations*, Sierra Club Books, San Francisco.

Marule, Marie Smallface (1978), 'The Canadian government's termination policy: from 1969 to the present day', in A L Getty and D Smith (eds), *One Century Later: Western Canadian Reserve Indians Since Treaty 7*, University of British Columbia Press, Vancouver.

Miner, Jack (1969), *Jack Miner: His Life and Religion*, The Jack Miner Migratory Bird Foundation, Kingsville, Ontario.

Mowat, Farley (1984), *Sea of Slaughter*, McLelland and Stewart, Toronto.

Paz, Octavio (1990), 'The power of ancient Mexican art', *New York Review of Books*, Vol XXXVII, No 19, pp 18–21.

Price, Richard and Shirleen Smith (1993–1994), 'Treaty 8 and traditional livelihoods: historical and contemporary perspectives', *Native Studies Review*, Vol 9, No 1, pp 51–91.

RCAP (Royal Commission on Aboriginal Peoples) (1994), *Treaty-Making in the Spirit of Co-Existence: an Alternative to Extinguishment*, Supply and Services Canada, Ottawa.

Reid, Ron (1992), 'Ontario parks: islands of hope', in Lori Labatt and Bruce Littlejohn (eds), *Islands of Hope: Ontario's Parks and Wilderness*, Firefly Books, Toronto, pp 45–46.

Saunders, Aubrey (1963), *Algonquin Story*, Ontario Department of Lands and Forests, Toronto.

Scott, Colin (1989), 'Knowledge construction among Cree hunters: metaphors and literal understanding', *Journal de la Société des Américanistes*, No LXXV, pp 193–208.

Smith, Donald B (1987), *Sacred Feathers: The Reverend Peter Jones (Kahkewaquonaby) and the Mississauga Indians*, University of Toronto Press, Toronto.

Snyder, Gary (1990), *The Practice of the Wild*, North Point Press, San Francisco.

Speck, Frank, G (1913), 'The Indians and game preservation', *The Red Man*, Vol 6, No 1, pp 20–28.

Tough, Frank (1984), 'The establishment of a commercial fishing industry and the demise of native fisheries in northern Manitoba', *The Canadian Journal of Native Studies*, Vol 4, No 2, pp 303–319.

— (1991), *Ontario's Appropriation of Indian Hunting; Provincial Conservation Policies vs Aboriginal and Treaty Rights, ca 1892–1930*, mimeo, Ontario Native Affairs Secretariat, Toronto.

Usher, P J (1987), 'Indigenous management systems and the conservation of wildlife in the Canadian north', *Alternatives*, Vol 14, No 1, pp 3–9.

Usher, P J, F Tough and R Galois (1992), 'Reclaiming the land: aboriginal title, treaty rights and land claims in Canada', *Applied Geography*, No 12, pp 109–132.

Van West, John J (1990), 'Ojibwa fisheries, commercial fisheries development and fisheries administration, 1873–1915: an examination of conflicting interest and the collapse of the sturgeon fisheries of the Lake of the Woods', *Native Studies Review*, Vol 6, No 1, pp 31–65.

WWF (World Wildlife Fund) (1986), *Whales Beneath the Ice: Final Report, Conclusions and Recommendations Regarding the Future of Canada's Arctic Whales*, WWF, Toronto.

Personal communications from: Darlene Johnston, (1993), Land Claims Research Co-ordinator, Saugeen Ojibway Land Claims, Chippewas of Saugeen, Southampton, Ontario; and Manfred Klein, (1992), Specific Claims West, Department of Indian and Northern Affairs, Vancouver, B.C.

XI

PARKS, PEOPLE AND PROFESSIONALS: PUTTING 'PARTICIPATION' INTO PROTECTED-AREA MANAGEMENT

Michel P. Pimbert and Jules N. Pretty

Coercion and Control in Nature Conservation

The pursuit of environmental conservation has been a significant theme in rural development in the twentieth century. Conservationist beliefs have generally held that there is an inverse relationship between human actions and the well-being of the environment. Professionals have widely agreed that problems such as soil erosion, degradation of rangelands, desertification, loss of forests and the destruction of wildlife require intervention to prevent further deterioration. At the same time, official policies have consistently defined local misuse of resources as the principal cause of destruction (Pimbert and Pretty, 1995).

Many protected-area schemes have overlooked the importance of locally specific ways of providing for food, health, shelter, energy and other fundamental human needs. Outside professionals and institutions have all too often failed to acknowledge differences in the ways and means of satisfying fundamental human needs. While fundamental human needs are universal, their 'satisfiers' vary according to culture, region and historical conditions (Max-Neef et al., 1989).[1]

---

1 A definition of the 'good life' implies different ways of satisfying fundamental human needs. Max-Neef and his colleagues (1989) have identified nine fundamental human needs, namely: subsistence (for example, health, food, shelter, clothing); protection (care, solidarity, work, etc.); affection (self-esteem, love, care, solidarity and so on); understanding (among others: study, learning, analysis); participation (responsibilities, sharing of rights and duties); leisure/idleness (curiosity, imagination, games, relaxation, fun); creation (including intuition, imagination, work, curiosity); identity (sense of belonging, differentiation, self-esteem and so on), freedom (autonomy, self-esteem, self-determination, equality).

Many rural communities value and utilize wild resources, and there is good evidence from many different environments for effective and sustainable local management (Scoones et al., 1992; Gómez-Pompa and Kaus, 1992; Nabhan et al., 1991; Oldfield and Alcorn, 1991). Individually and cumulatively, wild species can contribute to the food and financial security of rural households as dietary supplements, hedges against crop failure, income-generators, medicinal plants, construction materials, fodder and fuelwood. Despite this widespread use of wild products, protected-area management plans and resettlement schemes pay very little, if any, attention to the importance of wild resources for local livelihood security.

Some remarkable exceptions apart, resettlement housing for displaced people, health care and agricultural developments in park buffer zones, changes in tenure laws and other externally driven activities have, implicitly or explicitly, adopted the dominant cultural model of industrial society. In industrial societies fundamental human needs are almost exclusively catered by satisfiers that must be bought in the market and/or produced industrially.

People in and around many protected areas are thus seen as poor if they wear home-made garments of natural rather than synthetic fibre. They are perceived as poor if they live in houses constructed from natural materials like bamboo, thatch and mud rather than concrete. The ideology of development declares them to be so because they neither fully participate in the market economy nor consume commodities produced for and distributed by the market, even though they may be satisfying their fundamental needs through self-provisioning mechanisms. This neglect of human ingenuity and diversity ultimately reinforces the dominant model of development based on uniformity, centralization and control.

Tribal peoples, poor farmers, fishermen and pastoralists displaced by such coercive conservation have seen their needs and rights poorly met in their new, more risk-prone, environments. Lack of livelihood security ultimately undermines conservation objectives as poverty, rates of environmental degradation and conflicts intensify in areas surrounding parks and natural reserves. Indeed, it is when local resident people are excluded that degradation is more likely to occur. This reasoning represents a complete reversal for conservation policy and professional practice.

The Narrowness of Conservation Science and Normal Professionalism

The norms and practice of conservation science itself have been one of the major reasons for these failures of parks and other protected areas. Since the early seventeenth century, scientific investigation has come to be dominated by the Cartesian paradigm, usually termed positivism or rationalism. This posits that there exists a reality driven by immutable laws. Science seeks to discover the true nature of this reality, the ultimate aim being to discover, predict and control natural phenomena. Investigators proceed in the belief that they are detached from the world. Reductionism involves breaking down components of a complex world into discrete parts, analysing them, and then making predictions about the world based on interpretations of these parts. Knowledge about the world is then summarized in the form of universal, or time- and context-free, generalizations or laws. The consequence is that investigation with a high degree of control over the system being studied has become equated with good science. And such science is equated with 'true' knowledge.

But no scientific method will ever be able to ask all the right questions about how we should manage resources for sustainable protected-area management, let alone find the answers. The results are always open to interpretation. All actors, and particularly those stake-holders with a direct social or economic involvement and interest, have a uniquely different perspective on what is a problem and what constitutes improvement in a livelihood system. As Wynne has put it: 'the conventional view is that scientific knowledge and method enthusiastically embrace uncertainties and exhaustively pursue them. This is seriously misleading' (Wynne, 1992:115). The trouble with normal science is that it gives credibility to opinion only when it is defined in 'scientific' language, which may be inadequate for describing the complex and changing experiences of rural people and other actors in conservation and development. As a result, it has alienated many of them.

Reductionist Science and Disciplinary Specialization

Conservation scientists and field officers tend to perceive ecosystems through the narrow window of their own professional discipline. Their training has taught them to look at just that aspect of the ecosystem in which they specialize, which may be medicinal plants, rare orchids, trees, birds, elephants, tigers or ecosystem attributes like species diversity. This then becomes the main focus of their attention when they visit an area rich in biological diversity.

All too often, however, the disciplinary specialization of conservation professionals militates against understanding the factors behind the success of indigenous systems of natural resource management. As a result, opportunities to design culturally appropriate biodiversity conservation schemes are missed. What Nabhan et al. (1991:130) say about plant conservation illustrates the more general problem of Western, positivist, disciplinary science and its inherent ethnocentric bias:

> *Regardless of the potential for building on indigenous peoples' plant traditions to further the conservation of rare species, certain ethnocentric attitudes remain among Western-trained conservation biologists which keep this potential from being fully realised.*

> *Because many biologists are intent on analysing so-called natural systems, they often ignore that they are really observing relationships between organisms and environments that have been influenced by humankind over thousands of years... Even when they do not ignore human influences, such 'natural systems' biologists typically treat human presence as a purely negative phenomenon, a nuisance or intrusion.*

Another problem is that specialists commonly adopt just one or two criteria for deciding on priorities and measuring the performance of conservation projects. This might be the number of species saved, or the number of migrating birds wintering at a wetland site. But indigenous and rural people, as managers of complex systems, have many different criteria which they weigh up and combine in the choice of management activities that influence the fate of biological diversity, at a genetic, species and ecosystem level. This raises some important questions. Whose knowledge should count in the design of national parks and protected areas? Whose priorities and preferences should count for successful conservation of biodiversity? Those of the scientists or those of rural people?

Preservationist Ideology

Over the last century or so, some Western ideologies have exalted the values associated with both the preservation of unspoilt wilderness and the restoration of 'degraded' areas to a more pristine condition. During this time, a range of beliefs have been propagated. These include the assumptions that:

- wildlife conservation can only work by adopting a total position against killing and use of wildlife;
- biodiversity conservation can be achieved by not buying wildlife products, regardless of whether they were produced through approved management schemes;
- wildlife conservation in the developing world can succeed without generating economic returns to landowners and to the traditional custodians of biological diversity;
- all wildlife populations are fragile entities driven closer to extinction by any human use.

More recently, this preservationist ideology has been radically extended by a North American version of the 'deep ecology' movement (Devall and Sessions, 1985; Foreman, 1987). For deep ecologists, preserving nature has an intrinsic worth quite apart from any benefits preservation may provide to future human generations. Truly radical policy proposals have been put forward by deep ecologists on the basis of this argument. Interventions in nature, they claim, should be guided primarily by the need to preserve biological diversity and integrity rather than by the needs of humans. Some of the more militant deep ecologists have argued that a large proportion of the globe must be immediately cordoned off from human beings (Foreman, 1987). The radical conclusions of deep ecology have been criticized both in North America (Bookchin, 1990; Chase, 1991; Merchant, 1992) and by Third World scholars worried about the consequences of this obsession with wilderness (Guha, 1993).

However, while the tenets of deep ecology are no doubt valuable in challenging humankind's arrogance and ecological hubris, their growing influence on conservation planning is disturbing. For example, the international conservation elite is increasingly using the philosophical, moral and scientific arguments used by deep ecologists in advancing their wilderness crusade. Writing in the prestigious *Annual Review of Ecology and Systematics*, Daniel Janzen says that only biologists have the competence to decide how the tropical landscape should be used. As 'the representatives of the natural world', biologists are 'in charge of the future of tropical ecology', and only they have the expertise and mandate to 'determine whether the tropical agroscape is to be populated only by humans, their mutualists, commensals, and parasites, or whether it will also contain some islands of the greater nature — the nature that spawned humans, yet has been vanquished by them' (Janzen, 1986:305).

While clearly extreme, Janzen's views are by no means atypical. Five years after the Earth Summit in Rio, it is not uncommon to hear Western-trained conservation biologists argue in favour of taking over large portions of the world to expand the network of protected areas. They argue that the best way to establish priorities is to gather various key experts, who are invariably international and national scientists. In the words of two senior staff members of an influential international conservation organization: 'The best example of the short term approach to priority setting at the local level is to deploy the RAP team (for Rapid Assessment Program), which uses a small group of world class field biologists with cumulative tropical experience in excess of 100 years' (Mittermeier and Bowles, 1993:647).

However, in this context 'interdisciplinarity' is confined to well known tribes of botanists, zoologists and other natural scientists: the emphasis is on getting the 'science' right. Although it is recognized that priority-setting exercises should also integrate socio-economic data, land-use patterns and the like, advocates argue that:

> *it is best to avoid 'mixing apples and oranges' and instead focus on getting the biological priorities right in the first step of the process. Other kinds of data can then be superimposed on the biological foundation using a Geographic Information System (GIS) and thus develop meaningful and scientifically-based conservation agendas. (Mittermeier and Bowles, 1993:647)*

As Guha points out:

> This frankly imperialist manifesto highlights the multiple dangers
> of the preoccupation with wilderness preservation that is charac-
> teristic of deep ecology ... it seriously compounds the neglect by the
> American movement of far more pressing environmental problems
> within the Third World. (1989:76)

— environmental problems that impinge far more directly on the lives of
the poor, such as food, fuel, fodder and water shortages. Guha adds:

> But perhaps more importantly, and in a more insidious fashion, it
> also provides an impetus to the imperialist yearning of Western
> biologists and their financial sponsors....The wholesale transfer of
> a movement culturally rooted in American conservation history
> can only result in the social uprooting of human populations in
> other parts of the globe. (1989:76)

The Blueprint Approach of Normal Conservation Professionalism

The methods and means deployed to preserve areas of pristine wilderness largely originated in the affluent West where money and trained
personnel ensure that technologies work and that laws are enforced to
secure conservation objectives. During and after the colonial period, these
conservation technologies, and the values associated with them, were
extended from the North to the South — often in a classical top-down
manner. Positivist conservation science and the wilderness preservation
ethic hang together with this top down, transfer-of-technology model of
conservation. They are mutually constitutive elements of the blueprint
paradigm which still informs much of today's design and management
of protected areas in developing countries (Table 11.1).

The main actors in this approach are 'normal professionals' who are
concerned not just with research, but also with action. Normal professionals are found in research institutes and universities as well as in
international and national organizations, where most of them work in
specialized departments of government (forestry, fisheries, agriculture,
health, wildlife conservation, administration, etc.). The thinking, values,
methods and behaviour dominant in their profession or discipline tend
to be stable and conservative. Lastly, normal professionalism generally
'values and rewards "first" biases which are urban, industrial, high technology, male, quantifying, and concerned with things and with the needs
and interests of the rich' (Chambers, 1993:1).

The blueprint approach to conservation is also selectively promoted
by wider economic forces that can appropriate the commercial values of
biological resources in and around protected areas. For example, both the

Table 11.1 *Biodiversity conservation and natural resource management paradigms: contrasting blueprint and learning-process approaches*

	Blueprint	Process
Point of departure	Nature's diversity and its potential commercial values	The diversity of both people and nature's values
Keyword	Strategic planning	Participation
Locus of decision-making	Centralized, ideas originate in capital city	Decentralized, ideas originate in village
First steps	Data collection and planning	Awareness and action
Design	Static, by experts	Evolving, people involved
Main resources	Central funds and technicians	Local people and their assets
Methods, rules	Standardized, universal, fixed package	Diverse, local, varied basket of choices
Analytical assumptions	Reductionist (natural science bias)	Systemic, holistic
Management focus	Spending budgets, completing projects on time	Sustained improvement and performance
Communication	Vertical: orders down, reports up	Lateral: mutual learning and sharing experience
Evaluation	External, intermittent	Internal, continuous
Error	Buried	Embraced
Relationship with people	Controlling, policing, inducing, motivating, dependency-creating; people seen as 'beneficiaries'	Enabling, supporting, empowering; people seen as actors
Associated with	'Normal' professionalism	New professionalism
Outputs	1. Diversity in conservation, and uniformity in production (agriculture, forestry, etc.) 2. The empowerment of professionals	1. Diversity as a principle of production and conservation 2. The empowerment of rural people

Source: adapted from Korten, 1984

World Bank's private-sector lending arm, the International Finance Corporation (IFC), and the World-Bank-controlled Global Environment Facility (GEF), have begun talks with potential investors about the possibilities of selling biological diversity for a profit (Chatterjee, 1994). This biodiversity venture capital fund would work on a planetary scale. Three possible areas have been identified for funding so far, including ecotourism (the marketing of tourism in protected areas and natural habitats to wealthy tourists); screening of genetic materials (the study of species in protected areas and tropical ecosystems for medical and other properties useful for new natural product development — oils, perfumes, waxes, biopesticides); and the commercialization of existing knowledge of traditional medicines. More generally, the proposed biodiversity venture capital fund could help sell the rights to 'charismatic' ecosystems and protected areas to large corporations for public relations value (Chatterjee, 1994).

Increasingly powerful economic and political forces shape conservation science and technology: the practitioners, the conceptual frameworks, the research questions, the funding institutions that promote certain directions, and the official histories of their progress. The blueprint approach of normal conservation is thus much more than a collection of true or false facts. It is best understood as a set of definite choices of worldviews and power relations. Choices are not between pristine wilderness and human use but between different kinds of use and between different forms of political control. Moreover, the 'objectivity' claimed by this conservation paradigm is, in and by itself, a way of selecting from and shaping nature, or protected areas in this context.

At a time when many other aspects of knowledge and culture are being seen as expressions of contending social forces, science — conservation science in particular — still claims to be above the battle (Rose and Rose, 1976; Levidow, 1986; Dickson, 1984; Merchant, 1980; Levins and Lewontin, 1985). The official view that conservation science is in itself neutral, though open to use and abuse, has been reinforced in the post-UNCED period. Conservation experts and their products are, after all, being asked to play a dramatically increased role in the formulation of global environmental management strategies in the 1990s (Sachs, 1993).

However, conservation science still operates on a narrow intellectual base emphasizing categories, criteria, knowledge and procedures that serve the interests of professional control over the management of protected areas. Conservation priorities often turn out to be inappropriate, conservation packages are rejected, some conservation technologies do not fit, or are non-sustainable or inequitable because of an emphasis on purchased inputs in resource-poor contexts. The broader implications of recommended conservation technologies are largely ignored. Similarly, the ideologies which inform and legitimate dominant conservation practices are assumed to be valid for all people, all places and all times. These are features of the positivist paradigm. If conservation efforts are to become more effective, efficient and just, then they will have to move away from this paradigm to seek alternative values, methods and approaches.

Alternatives to the Dominant Paradigm

The positivist paradigm is so pervasive that, by definition, those inside it cannot see that alternatives exist. The absolutist position of positivism excludes other possibilities. Yet positivism is just one of many ways of describing the world. What are needed are pluralistic ways of thinking about the world and acting to change it (Kuhn, 1962; Feyerabend, 1975; Habermas, 1987; Giddens, 1987; Rorty, 1989; Pretty, 1994; Uphoff, 1992).

New paradigms are now emerging from advances in a wide range of disciplines and fields of investigation, such as mathematics, non-linear science and chaos theory, quantum physics, post-positivism, critical theory, constructivist inquiry, soft-systems and contextual science, the philosophy of symbiosis, post-modernism and stakeholder analysis. There are many others not listed here.

The advances in alternative paradigms have important implications for how we go about finding out about the world, generating information and taking action. All hold that 'the truth is ultimately a mirage that cannot be attained because the worlds we know are made by us' (Eisner, 1990:89). All suggest that we need to reform the way we think about methodologies for finding out about the world. This should not be surprising, as 'the language of reductionism and positivism does not entertain the very complex and dynamic phenomena associated with the quest for sustainable practices' (Bawden, 1991:263).

In parallel with these developments in other fields, there have also been recent advances in ecological theory and knowledge. It has become increasingly clear that existing ecological systems of plants and animals are a function of their unique pasts. Understanding the particular history of a modern community or ecosystem is critical to its current management. Ecosystems are dynamic and continuously changing, and this has very significant implications for management principles and practices.

A paradigm shift is occurring in ecological thinking with the realization that past management of animal populations and vegetation has been based on far too static a concept of ecosystems. For example, there is 'growing empirical evidence [to suggest] that moderate frequencies or intensities of disturbance foster maximum species richness ... To preserve biotic diversity and functioning natural ecosystems, then, conservation efforts must include explicit consideration of disturbance processes' (Hobbs and Huenneke, 1992:324). It has also been suggested that

Ecologists are becoming progressively sensitized to the importance of the effect of history on the structure and function of modern

communities and ecosystems... The conclusion is that it is inevitable that ecologists will simplify greatly the history of inferred human impacts on the forest. However, a consideration of the extensive and variable nature of human use of the landscape suggests that we bear in mind some understanding of this complexity (Foster et al., 1992:785).

Recent studies indicate that some of the biodiversity loss observed in protected areas stems from the restrictions placed on the activities of local communities. For example, with the expulsion of the Maasai from their lands in Tanzania, the Serengeti is increasingly being taken over by scrub and woodland, meaning less grazing for antelopes (Adams and McShane, 1992). The rich Serengeti grassland ecosystem was in part maintained by the presence of the Maasai and their cattle. Similarly, resource management policies to protect and control elephant populations in Tsavo National park in East Africa have led to severe deterioration of the land within the park boundaries (Botkin, 1990). The inhabited area around the park remained forested. The sharp demarcation of the park boundaries in the LANDSAT images and aerial photos appeared 'as a photographic negative of one's expectation of a park. Rather than an island of green in a wasted landscape, Tsavo appeared as a wasted island amid a green land' (Botkin, 1990:36).

These insights contrast with the conventional view, which has too long held that systems are largely a function of current operating mechanisms, and that any human interference will cause a depletion of biological diversity (Wood, 1993; 1995).

Five principles set out the crucial differences between these emerging paradigms and positivist science (Pretty, 1994). First, any belief that sustainability can be precisely defined is flawed. It is a contested concept, and so represents neither a fixed set of practices or technologies, nor a model to describe or impose on the world. Defining what we are trying to achieve is part of the problem, as each individual has different values. For us to prescribe a concrete set of technologies, practices or policies would be to exclude future options, undermining the notion of sustainability itself. Sustainable protected-area management is, therefore, not so much a specific strategy as it is an approach to understanding complex ecological and social relationships in rural areas.

Second, problems are always open to interpretation. All actors have unique perspectives on what a problem is, and on what constitutes improvement. As knowledge and understanding are socially constructed, they are functions of each individual's unique context and past. There is, therefore, no single 'correct' understanding. What we take to be true depends on the framework of knowledge and assumptions we bring with us. It is thus essential to seek multiple perspectives on a problem situation by ensuring the involvement of a variety of actors and groups.

Third, the resolution of one problem inevitably leads to the production of another 'problem-situation', as problems are endemic. The reflex of positivist science is to seek to collect large amounts of data before declaring certainty about an issue or problem. As this position is believed to reflect the 'real world', courses of action can become standardized and actors no longer seek information that might lead to another interpretation. Yet in a changing world, there will always be uncertainties.

Fourth, the key feature now becomes the capacity of all actors continually to learn about these changing conditions, so that they can act quickly to transform existing activities. They should make uncertainties explicit and encourage rather than obstruct wider public debates about pursuing new paths for conservation and development. The world is open to multiple interpretations, each valid in its limited context but not necessarily true in absolute terms.

Fifth, systems of learning and interaction are needed to gain an understanding of the multiple perspectives of the various interested parties and encourage their greater involvement. The view that there is only one epistemology (that is, the scientific one) has to be rejected. Participation and collaboration are essential components of any system of learning, as change cannot be effected without the full involvement of all stakeholders and the adequate representation of their views and perspectives. As Sriskandarajah et al. write, 'ways of researching need to be developed that combine "finding out" about complex and dynamic situations with "taking action" to improve them, in such a way that the actors and beneficiaries of the "action research" are intimately involved as participants in the whole process' (1991:4).

People in Conservation

These fundamental differences suggest that conserving biological diversity requires a far more subtle appreciation of both human and natural influences. They call into question the separation of people from nature and support the view that people are part of nature. In most terrestrial and coastal environments, both the form and the degree of biological diversity result from a combination of cyclical ecological and climatic processes and past human action. What Denevan (1992) says of forests also applies to wetlands, grasslands and other humanized ecosystems: human impacts may enhance or reduce biodiversity, but change has been continual at variable rates and in different directions. This implies that efforts to conserve biodiversity may need to give greater attention to ecosystem processes rather than ecosystem products (McNeely, 1994). And, perhaps more importantly, conservation efforts may need to identify and promote those social processes which enable local communities to conserve and enhance biodiversity as part of their livelihood system.

There is, of course, a long history of discussion on community participation in development activities. Indeed, the terms 'people's participation' and 'popular participation' are now part of the normal language of many development agencies, including non-governmental organizations (NGOs), government departments and banks (Adnan et al., 1992; Pretty, 1994). It is to be found in the public statements and stances of even those agencies which have nothing to do with people or participation. The problem is that the term means different things to different people.

In conventional rural development, participation has often centred on encouraging local people to sell their labour in return for food, cash or materials. Yet these material incentives distort perceptions, create dependencies, and give the misleading impression that local people are supportive of externally driven initiatives. This paternalism then undermines sustainability goals and produces results which do not persist once the project ceases. As little effort is made to build local skills, interests and capacity, local people have no stake in maintaining or supporting new practices once the incentives cease.

Like many other areas of rural development, conservation has been characterized by very different interpretations of participation. During the colonial period, management was characterized by coercion and control, with people seen as an impediment to conservation. Until the 1970s, participation was increasingly seen as a tool to achieve the voluntary submission of people to protected-area schemes. Here, participation was no more than a public relations exercise, in which local people were passive actors. During the 1980s, participation became increasingly defined as taking an interest in natural resource protection. And now, in the 1990s, participation is being seen by some as a means to involve people in protected-area management. There has been growing recognition that without local involvement, there is little chance of protecting wildlife. Moreover, the costs of park management are very high if local communities are not involved in caring for the environment.

It is thus essential for professionals to focus on the appropriate process of participation if sustainability and biodiversity conservation goals are to be met. Drawing on the range of ways that development organizations interpret and use the term participation, it is helpful to disaggregate participation into at least seven different types (Table 11.2).

The implication of this typology is that the term participation should not be accepted without appropriate qualification. The problem with participation as used in types 1–4 is that the 'superficial and fragmented achievements have no lasting impact on people's lives' (Rahnema, 1992:128). Such forms of participation can be employed, knowing they will not lead to action. If the objective is to achieve sustainable conservation, then nothing less than functional participation will suffice. All the evidence points towards long-term economic and environmental success coming about when people's ideas and knowledge are valued, and power is given to them to make decisions independently of external agencies.

Table 11.2 *A typology of participation*

Typology	Components of Each Type
1. Passive participation	People participate by being told what is going to happen or what has already happened. It is unilateral announcement by an administration or by project management; people's responses are not taken into account. The information being shared belongs only to external professionals.
2. Participation in information-giving	People participate by answering questions posed by extractive researchers and project managers using questionnaire surveys or similar approaches. People do not have the opportunity to influence proceedings, as the findings of the research or project design are neither shared nor checked for accuracy.
3. Participation by consultation	People participate by being consulted, and external agents listen to views. These external agents define both problems and solutions, and may modify these in the light of people's responses. Such a consultative process does not concede any share in decision-making and professionals are under no obligation to take on board people's views.
4. Participation for material incentives	People participate by providing resources, for example labour, in return for food, cash or other material incentives. Much in-situ research and bioprospecting falls in this category, as rural people provide the resources but are not involved in the experimentation or the process of learning. It is very common to see this called participation, yet people have no stake in prolonging activities when the incentives end.
5. Functional participation	People participate by forming groups to meet predetermined objectives related to the project, which can involve the development or promotion of externally initiated social organization. Such involvement does not tend to be at early stages of project cycles or planning, but rather after major decisions have been made. These institutions tend to be dependent on external initiators and facilitators, but may become self-dependent.
6. Interactive participation	People participate in joint analysis, which leads to action plans and the formation of new local groups or the strengthening of existing ones. It tends to involve interdisciplinary methodologies that seek multiple perspectives and make use of systematic and structured learning processes. These groups take control over local decisions, and so people have a stake in maintaining structures or practices.

309

| 7. Self-mobilization | People participate by taking initiatives independent of external institutions to change systems. Such self-initiated mobilization and collective action may or may not challenge existing inequitable distributions of wealth and power. |

Source: modified from Pretty, 1994

Those using the term participation must both clarify their specific application and define better ways of shifting from the more common passive, consultative and incentive-driven participation towards the interactive end of the spectrum.

In recent years, there has been a rapid expansion of new participatory methods and approaches. These have drawn on many long-established traditions that have put participation, action research and adult education at the forefront of attempts to emancipate disempowered people. These systems of learning emphasize the interactive participation of all actors (Chambers, 1992a; 1992b). There are many different alternative systems of learning and interaction, some more widely used than others.[2] Despite the different ways in which these approaches are used, they have important principles in common (Pretty, 1994). These are:

- A defined methodology and systemic learning process — the focus is on cumulative learning by all the participants and, given the nature of these approaches as systems of learning and action, their use has to be participative. The methods are structured into those for group and team dynamics, sampling, interviewing and dialogue, and visualization and diagramming.
- Multiple perspectives — a central objective is to seek diversity, rather than characterize complexity in terms of average values. Different individuals and groups are assumed to make different evaluations of situations, which lead to different actions. All views of activity or purpose are laden with interpretation, bias and preju-

---

2 These systems of inquiry include, for example, Agroecosystems Analysis (AEA), Beneficiary Assessment, Diagnosis and Design (D & D), Diagnostico Rural Rapido (DRR), Farmer Participatory Research, Groupe de Recherche et d'Appui pour l'Auto-Promotion Paysanne (GRAAP), Méthode Accélérée de Recherche Participative (MARP), Naturalistic Inquiry, Participatory Analysis and Learning Methods (PALM), Participatory Action Research (PAR), Participatory Research Methodology (PRM), Participatory Rural Appraisal (PRA), Participatory Rural Appraisal and Planning (PRAP), Participatory Technology Development (PTD), Participatory Urban Appraisal (PUA), Planning for Real, Process Documentation, Rapid Appraisal (RA), Rapid Assessment of Agricultural Knowledge Systems (RAAKS), Rapid Assessment Procedures (RAP), Rapid Assessment Techniques (RAT), Rapid Catchment Analysis (RCA), Rapid Ethnographic Assessment (REA), Rapid Food Security Assessment (RFSA), Rapid Multi-perspective Appraisal (RMA), Rapid Organisational Assessment (ROA), Rapid Rural Appraisal (RRA), Samuhik Brahman (Joint trek), Soft Systems Methodology (SSM), Theatre for Development, Training for Transformation, and Visualisation in Participatory Programmes (VIPP).

dice, and this implies that there are multiple possible descriptions of any real-world activity.

- Group learning process — all involve the recognition that the complexity of the world will only be revealed through group learning. This implies three possible mixes of investigators, namely those from different disciplines, from different sectors, and from outsiders (professionals) and insiders (local people).
- Context specific — the approaches are flexible enough to be adapted to suit each new set of conditions and actors, and so there are multiple variants.
- Facilitating experts and stakeholders — the methodology is concerned with the transformation of existing activities to try to bring about changes which people in the situation regard as improvements. The role of the 'expert' is best thought of as helping people carry out their own analysis and thus achieving something for and by themselves. These facilitating experts may be stakeholders themselves.
- Leading to sustained action — the learning process leads to debate about change, including confronting the constructions of others. This debate, in turn, changes the perceptions of the actors and their readiness to contemplate action. This leads to more sophisticated and informed constructions about the world. The debate and/or analysis both defines changes which would bring about improvement and seeks to motivate people to take action to implement the defined changes. Action is agreed, and implementable changes will therefore represent an accommodation between conflicting views. This action includes local institution building or strengthening, thereby increasing the capacity of people to initiate action on their own.

A more sustainable conservation, with all its uncertainties and complexities, cannot be envisaged without all actors being involved in the continuing processes of learning.

Towards a New Professionalism for Conservation

Empirical evidence from other areas of natural-resource management (forestry, agriculture, soil and water conservation) have highlighted the misfits between what normal professionals and bureaucrats perceive and do, and what poor rural people need for sustainable livelihoods. A new paradigm is clearly needed. The professional challenge for protected-area management is to replace the top-down, standardized, simplified, rigid and short-term practices with local-level diversified, complicating, flexible, unregulated and long-term natural resource management practices.

The reversals for diversity, democracy and decentralization which characterize this process oriented approach to biodiversity conservation are shown in Table 11.1. Chambers (1991:8) has best captured the essence of this paradigm shift:

> *Solutions can be sought through reversals, through turning the normal on its head. Professionally, this means putting people before things... It means permitting and promoting the complexity that poor people often want, presenting them with a basket of choices rather than a package of practices... Bureaucratically, it means decentralising power, destandardizing and removing restrictions. In learning, it means gaining insight less from 'our' often out of date knowledge in books and lectures, and more from 'their' knowledge of their livelihoods and conditions which is always up-to-date ... In behaviour, it means the most important reversal of all, not standing, lecturing and motivating, but sitting, listening and learning. And with all these reversals, the argument is not for an absolute or 'slot rattling' change, from one extreme to another; rather it is that only with a big shift of weight can an optimal balance be achieved.*

The devolution of planning, implementation, management, monitoring and evaluation of protected areas to villagers and low-income groups is a frontier that needs to be explored by modern conservation organizations and governments. People in and around protected areas should no longer be seen simply as informants, but as teachers, activists, extensionists and evaluators. These local specialists include village game wardens, beekeepers, village veterinarians, herbalists, wild-food collectors, fisherfolk, farmers, pastoralists and so on. An emphasis on village specialists and different resource user groups allows their skills and knowledge to shape protected area management priorities.

Clearly conservation professionals and rural people both have strengths and limitations. Conservation and other professionals have advantages at two levels. At the macro-level, computer-assisted geographic information systems can allow landscape ecologists to integrate temporal and spatial variation in ecological factors. Professionals can also rely on worldwide electronic communications networks and data banks to access and exchange scientific information. At a micro-level, conservation scientists have accurate identification techniques and taxonomic skills. But the collective knowledge that rural people have of their watersheds, forests, rangelands, coastal strips and wetlands gives them distinct advantages at the meso-level — where the protected-area management schemes are ultimately aimed. This is, after all, the ecological and social context in which rural people experiment, adapt and innovate.

Thus the advantages and skills of professionals (at the micro- and macro-levels) need to be effectively combined with the strengths of indigenous knowledge and experimentation by empowering people through a modification of conventional roles and activities. This participatory approach would permit the generation of diverse, locally negoti-ated conservation programmes which may be more sustainable in the long term than current projects. Design and management of protected areas thus rely on processes that seek to give more power to local commu-nities. Empowerment includes forms of interactive and spontaneous participation as well as 'organized efforts to increase control over resources and regulative institutions in given social situations, on the part of groups and movements of those hitherto excluded from such control' (Pearse and Stiefel, 1979:7–8).

In this context, the central concept for conservation and protected area management is that it must enshrine new ways of learning about the world. Learning should not be confused with teaching. Teaching implies the transfer of knowledge from someone who knows to someone who does not know. Teaching is the normal mode of educational curricula, and is also central to many organizational structures (Ison, 1990; Russell and Ison, 1991; Bawden, 1992; Pretty and Chambers, 1993). Universities and other professional institutions reinforce the teaching paradigm by giving the impression that they are custodians of knowledge which can be dispensed or given (usually by lecture) to a recipient (a student).

A move from a teaching to a learning style has profound implications for conservation institutions. The focus is less on what we learn, and more on how we learn and with whom. The pedagogic goals become self-strengthening for people and groups through self-learning and self-teaching, and 'the role and action of the researcher is very much a part of the interactions being studied' (Russell and Ison, 1991:1). Systems of participatory learning and interaction, therefore, imply new roles for conservation professionals, and these all require a new professionalism with new concepts, values, methods and behaviour. The challenge is to make the shift from the old professionalism to the new (Pretty and Chambers, 1993).

It should be emphasized that the success of community-based conser-vation projects depends on the behaviour and attitudes of outsiders. The notion that educated professionals may have something to learn from the uneducated and illiterate is still sheer heresy for some. As many have not been trained to put the views of local communities before considering their own potential contributions, training and re-orientation is essential.

To date, there have been few systematic attempts by conservation organizations (public-sector and non-governmental) to adopt participa-tory planning methods. Moreover, among those in favour of a transfer of park management activities to local communities, insufficient attention has been given to methodological research and development that promotes genuine people participation in the conservation and sustain-able use of biodiversity. And yet, recent experience shows that when outsiders behave differently and use new participatory methods, rural people show an unexpected creativity and capacity to present and analyse information, to diagnose, plan, manage and evaluate. They know the complexity and diversity of their livelihoods and environment. They are experts on their own immediate realities (Pimbert et al., 1996).

This new vision for conservation implies new roles for project staff and local people in protected-area management. This calls for a greater emphasis on training in communication rather than technical skills. Outside professionals must learn to work closely with colleagues from different disciplines or sectors, as well as with rural people themselves, including women and children. Judgement and interpersonal skills should be cultivated through the adoption and use of participatory methods. This may imply a significant shift in technique for conventional trainers, since training for participation must itself be participatory and action-based (Chambers, 1992a).

The challenge for top and middle management is to design appropriate institutional mechanisms and rewards to encourage the spread of participatory methods within their organization. Without this support from the top, it is unlikely that participatory approaches which enhance local capacities and innovation will become core professional activities. They will remain isolated and marginalized within NGOs and government departments responsible for conservation programmes.

But for the pioneers who embrace the new professionalism, this will be an extraordinary challenge. As Richard Bawden (1991) has put it, 'this is profoundly difficult ... I am quite aware that I risk fierce controversies, international name calling, and dissolutions of old friendships'.

Operational Components of an Alternative Conservation Practice[3]

Sustainable and effective protected-area management requires reversals in normal conservation professionalism, and an emphasis on community based natural-resource management and enabling policy frameworks. These are not easy options. Contemporary patterns of economic growth, modernization and nation-building all have strong anti-participatory traits. The integration of rural communities and local institutions into larger, more complex and urban-centred systems often stifles whatever capacity for decision-making the local community might have had and renders its traditional institutions obsolete. So the challenges of adapting the ingredients of these community based successes to the design and management of national parks and protected areas are enormous. To achieve this, considerable attention will have to be given to the following six operational features.

---

3 This section draws on analyses of case studies on sustainable development at the community or neighbourhood level (PEC workshop, 1990; Conroy and Litvinoff, 1988; Farrington et al., 1993; Bebbington et al., 1993; Wellard and Copestake, 1993; Pretty and Sandbrook, 1991; Pretty, 1994; Ghai and Vivian, 1992). While the concepts presented here have not penetrated the harder conservation literature and everyday field conservation practices, they may provide useful pointers for protected-area management in the near future.

314

Local Systems of Knowledge and Management

Local management systems are generally tuned to the needs of local people and often enhance their capacity to adapt to dynamic social and ecological circumstances. Although many of these systems have been abandoned after long periods of success, there remains a great diversity of local systems of knowledge and management which actively maintain biological diversity in areas earmarked for the expanding protected-area network (Kemf, 1993; West and Brechin, 1992).

Local systems of knowledge and management are sometimes rooted in religion and belief systems. Sacred groves, for example, are clusters of forest vegetation that are preserved for religious reasons. They may honour a deity, provide a sanctuary for spirits, or protect a sanctified place from exploitation; some derive their sacred character from the springs of water they protect, from the medicinal and ritual properties of their plants, or from the wild animals they support (Chandrakanth and Romm, 1991). Such sacred groves are common throughout southern and south-eastern Asia, Africa, the Pacific islands and Latin America (Shengji, 1991; Ntiamo-Baidu et al., 1992). The network of sacred groves in countries such as India has, since time immemorial, been the locus and symbol of a way of life in which the highest biological diversity occurs where humans interact with nature. A sacred grove is preserved by villagers, 'not because it represents the antithesis of their productive activities but because it safeguards their livelihoods and their continued existence ... When the commons of local communities are still protected by the Goddess, nature's diversity is preserved' (Apffel Marglin and Mishra, 1993). Clearly these pockets of biological diversity could be the focus for the conservation and regeneration of forest cover, so perhaps forming the basis of more 'culturally appropriate' protected areas.

Despite the pressures that increasingly undermine local systems of knowledge and management, protected-area management plans should start with what people know and do well already, so as to secure their livelihoods and sustain the diversity of natural resources on which they depend.

Local Institutions and Social Organization

Local organizations are crucial for the conservation and sustainable use of biodiversity. As Michael Cernea (1993:19) has put it, 'resource degradation in the developing countries, while incorrectly attributed to "common property systems" intrinsically, actually originates in the dissolution of local level institutional arrangements whose very purpose was to give rise to resource use patterns that were sustainable'. Local groups enforce rules, incentives and penalties for eliciting behaviour conducive to rational and effective resource conservation and use. In developing protected-area management schemes, increased attention will need to be given to community-based action through local institutions and user groups. They include, for example, natural-resource management groups, women's associations and credit management groups. Successful group initiatives include invest-ing in protecting watersheds and reafforestation; organizing community-run wildlife management schemes; establishing small process-ing plants for natural products derived from the wild. Available evidence from multilateral projects evaluated five to ten years after completion shows that where institutional development has been important the flow of benefits has risen or remained constant (Cernea, 1987). Past experience therefore suggests that if this type of institutional development is ignored in protected-area management policies, economic rates of return will decline markedly and conservation objectives may not be met.

Local Rights to Resources

Conservationists have begun to realize that effective resource protection is possible only if local communities are fully involved in protected-area planning and gain direct benefits from the project. One notable success is the Arfak Mountains Nature Reserve in west Papua. This recognizes both the ancestral land rights of the Hatam people, and the fact that Indonesian law does not secure them. Although the legal definition of the area as a Strict Nature Reserve makes indigenous resource use theoretically illegal, the project, which has local government approval, allows local people to continue to use the area until the law is changed in their favour. Aware of the benefits, the local people have begun to act as effective guardians in the forest reserve (Craven, 1990; Colchester, 1992). But it is not all plain sailing once local rights have been granted. In Papua New Guinea, for example, where collective land rights are strongly protected by law, communities have frequently negotiated away rights over their lands by leasing them to logging and mining companies. Only lately have they come to regret the damage that their environments have sustained from such activities (Colchester, 1992). One of the critical issues is that the law does not make clear who at local level has the rights to negotiate land deals, and this can lead to collective ownership being undermined.

Locally Available Resources and Technologies to Meet
Fundamental Human Needs

Protected-area projects seeking to provide benefits for local and national economies should give preference to informal innovation systems, reliance on local resources and local satisfiers of human needs. Preference should be given to local technologies by emphasizing the opportunities for intensification in the use of available resources. Sustainable and cheaper solutions can often be found when groups or communities are involved in identification of technology requirements, the design and testing of technologies, their adaptation to local conditions and, finally, their extension to others. The potential for intensification of internal resource use without reliance on external inputs is enormous. Greater self-reliance and reduced dependency on outside supplies of pesticides, fertilizers, water and seeds can be achieved within and around protected areas, by complicating and diversifying farming systems with locally available resources. Similarly, if local communities fully participate in the design, implementation and maintenance phases of projects designed to meet health, housing, sanitation, water needs and revenue-generating activities (such as tourism), then the results are likely to be more sustainable and effective than those imposed by outside professionals.

Local Participation in Planning, Management and Evaluation
Table 11.2 schematically presents seven different types of participation. The implication of this typology is that the meaning of participation should be clearly spelled out in all programmes. If the objective of conservation is to achieve sustainable and effective protected-area management, then nothing less than functional participation will suffice. Support is needed for learning approaches in which the main goals are qualitative shifts in the ways people and institutions interact and work together.

Process-Oriented Flexible Projects
In this new approach to protected-area management, the initial focus is on what people articulate as most important to them. This may mean embarking on tasks not central to the project's remit. Community-based conservation projects may remain small, or be combined into larger protected-area programmes once the participatory procedures and processes have been fully worked out. Error is treated as a source of information and flexibility permits continuous adaptation of procedures. Indicators are developed from those most important to local communities. These are seen as milestones rather than absolute, eternally fixed and illusory targets. Innovative extension methods promote group demonstrations, visits, village-level workshops, and community-to-community extension to achieve effective multiplication of conservation technologies, both in and around protected areas. Protected-area management schemes based on this participatory, open-ended approach must be of realistic lengths of time for real social development and natural resource conservation. Projects of short duration probably have a much greater chance of failure than long-term projects (five to ten years or more). Donors and conservation organizations must be prepared for low initial levels of disbursement and for changes in priorities.

Action in these six areas must also be supported by appropriate national and international policy frameworks.

Enabling Policies for Conservation

Although existing national and international policies may be trying to encourage conservation, they tend to do so in a way that excludes local people and leads to greater degradation (Conway and Pretty, 1991; Utting, 1993; Pretty, 1995). Governments apply a wide range of policy instruments to their agricultural, forestry and fishery sectors. To date,

317

these have not been used with a view to directing practices towards greater sustainability.

Throughout the world, conservation policy has been based on the predominant view that rural people are mismanagers of natural resources. There are great dangers in this conservation ideology. When local people reject new practices or technologies that are prescribed for them, policies have tended to shift to seeking success through the manipulation of social, economic and ecological environments. Eventually this leads to coercion. This is not the basis for sustainable management of natural resources.

Policies for Vernacular Conservation

National protected area policies must be based on an understanding that modern local environmental attitudes are in part a legacy of past people–nature interactions. This demands that policy makers and other professionals pay serious attention to ecological and social history.

This policy imperative is particularly well highlighted in the case of Guinea's Ziama forest reserve (Fairhead and Leach, 1994). The Ziama forest in Guinea is considered by conservationists to be a relic of the disappearing Upper Guinean forest. It was designated a forest reserve in 1932, and became a biosphere reserve in 1981. Rare animals and birds of Ziama, including the forest elephant, pygmy hippopotamus, zebra duiker, bongo, golden cat, yellow-throated olive greenbul and the bald-headed rock fowl have been publicized to attract international concern and funding. However, in valuing the apparently 'pristine' characteristics of the forest, modern conservationists overlook its long history of influence by people. While often portrayed as being at risk of clearance for the first time under modern demographic pressures, the Ziama forest biosphere was, in fact, one of the most populous and agriculturally prosperous parts of the Upper Guinean region in the mid-nineteenth century. Like many other African forests, Ziama is not an ancient relic of a forgotten past.

Fairhead and Leach (1994:30) argue that 'the mismatch between the locally lived history that has shaped local priorities and conservationists' representations of it is extraordinary. The local antagonism towards the reserve which has built since its establishment cannot be understood or addressed outside this historical context'. As the most senior elder of the region says:

> *This forest problem is complicated. If you see that we no longer have control over the forest, it is because of the forest agents who come with their papers and delimit the forest. If we are given responsibility for the forest, we are ready to act in the interests of conservation ... If we had full responsibility for the management of the forest, we could give you the assurance of protecting it. But as*

318

long as control is left in the hands of the State, we can do nothing.
(quoted in Fairhead and Leach, 1994:30)

'Participatory' protected-area management will not prove possible unless such historical claims to land and political authority are high up on the agenda. Following the recommendations of the village elders, policy makers will need to consider conservation agreements that cede tenurial control to local landholders, within the context of management agreements that fully recognize the value their lands now have for others.

Without secure rights of access to protected-area resources, rural communities will always consider parks and other protected areas as lost village resources that are not worth caring for in the long term. Protected-area policies will therefore need to be reformed to allow indigenous peoples and other rural communities to play a more central role in determining what is conserved, how and for whom. This requires that ancestral land claims be legally recognized and that indigenous communities be provided with effective control over the natural resources contained in national parks and all other protected area categories recognized by the World Congress on National Parks and Protected Areas (CNPPA).

Some indigenous peoples and rural communities have established protected areas that resemble the parks and reserves codified in the CNPPA's system and in national protected-area policies. In Ecuador, for example, the Awa have spontaneously decided to establish conservation areas. They have secured rights over a traditional area, which has been designated the Awa Ethnic Forest Reserve (Poole, 1993). Sacred places such as the Loita Maasai's forest of the lost child in Kenya (Loita Naimana Enkiyio Conservation Trust, 1994) are also widespread forms of vernacular conservation. Vernacular conservation is based on site-specific traditions and economies; it refers to ways of life and resource utilization that have evolved in place and, like vernacular architecture, is a direct expression of the relationship between communities and their habitats (Poole, 1993).

However, the similarities between vernacular and scientific models of conservation obscure the fact that motivations for setting up such areas are quite distinct from those leading to national parks, even though the ultimate contribution to biodiversity conservation may be identical. The crucial distinction is that such areas are established to protect land for rather than from use; more specifically for local use rather than appropriation and exploitation by outside interests. To support vernacular conservation, the CNPPA's categories will need to be reformed to acknowledge people's own definitions of what constitutes a protected area and how it should be managed.

Enabling Policies for Local Action

The success of people-oriented conservation will hinge on promoting socially differentiated goals in which the varying perspectives and priorities of community members, and local communities and conservationists, must be negotiated. Signed agreements between conservation professionals and local community organizations could promote responsible and accountable interaction. In the case of indigenous peoples, national protected-area policies need to be brought in line with internationally recognized human rights: they should allow indigenous peoples to represent their own interests through their own organizations and not through consultative processes controlled by conservation organizations. International law and other agreements already provide clear principles which professionals working for conservation should observe in dealing with indigenous peoples. These include ILO Convention 169, Chapter 26 of Agenda 21 of the UNCED agreements, and parts of the Biodiversity Convention (Colchester, 1994).

However, in many instances, meaningful changes may only come about as a result of strong popular mobilization at the local level in favour of greater access to resources within protected areas. These struggles may include many continually changing forms of interaction, including mutual accommodation between power holders and the disadvantaged; bargaining, persistent friction and informal political skirmishing; and armed confrontation and violent repression of the weaker groups by the local or national power-holders. The establishment of a nature reserve by the Kuna Indians in Panama, during the early 1980s, highlighted the crucial role of grassroots mobilization and organization in ensuring that conservation initiatives served the interests of local people (Utting, 1994). A proposal for local participation has also recently come about following action of Gujjar inhabitants over the proposed Rajaji National Park in Uttar Pradesh, India (Cherail, 1993). In seeking a new deal, excluded groups like the Kuna Indians and the Gujjars confront social arrangements that determine patterns of access to resources. The goal of these grassroots initiatives is:

> not to conquer or vanquish the state but to forge selective alliances with parts of the state and its bureaucracy while avoiding new clientelistic constraints. Such successful political action would gradually lead to what the excluded would view as a 'better' state, one where their claims and interests are taken more seriously and where the authorities may be willing to tip the balance of power in their favour .... In the last analysis, there may be no alternative to the joint efforts of a reformist state and a reinvigorated and organized civil society in which the excluded can make their voices heard. (Stiefel and Wolfe, 1994:204–205)

A national or local government which wants to include people in the management of protected areas will need to review the legal basis for such involvement. There are a variety of legal arrangements that can be introduced by government to assure local control over resources. The range of choices is not limited to private ownership of land: communal ownership of land and/or resources is often a more culturally appropriate option in much of the developing world (Bromley and Cernea, 1989). Where local communities have been granted secure usufruct rights over neighbouring forests, governments have witnessed clear reversals in forest degradation and its associated biodiversity (Fortmann and Bruce, 1988). As V.K. Bahuguna recently put it, 'The only solution to the present day crisis of depletion of forest resources, and the circumstantial alienation of people, is to opt for people's forests by involving local people in forest protection and development' (1992:10).

The key activity at the local level is the establishment of local rules for the protection and conservation of natural resources. These rules, with the necessary local institutions, are the foundation for sustainable development. In India, for example, forest protection committees have developed different types of local rules as indicated by the following remarks of villagers:

> *It was resolved by the committees that all those areas where the trees are marked with red paints along the boundary are closed for grazing and hence all of us unanimously resolve not to take our cattle for grazing in these areas, nor allow the villagers of other villages to do so. We shall keep our cattle at home and all cases of violation would be reported to the forest officer. (Bahuguna, 1992)*

For the protection of trees 'it was unanimously resolved that we shall not girdle any tree nor allow others to do so. We shall have some strict watch over illegal cutting of trees'. For goats 'it is resolved that all those villagers who are having goats with them must sell them within a period of 3 days, otherwise action will be taken'. As for firewood, 'no villager would carry the fuelwood head load for sale outside the village. The defaulters would be charged Rs 51 per head load' (cited in Bahuguna, 1992:12).

In some cases, social fines have been imposed not only on villagers but also on forest guards, and in others, communities have taken action on social issues, including punishment for anti-social drinking and abuse. In Madhya Pradesh, the benefits have included improvements in fuelwood, grass and crop yields; reduced poaching of elephants and other animals; changed relations between forest officials and local people; and the creation of democratic local organizations (Bahuguna, 1992).

Conditions for Joint and Co-management Partnerships

Enabling legal arrangements for communal access to biological resources is an essential starting point for co-management between governments and local communities. The concept of joint or co-management grew out of a recognition that centralized forms of control over resources have failed to halt resource degradation in many countries, and that local (village or user-group) level control may be more effective where there is local vested interest in exercising management control. Joint management means the management of resources by the sharing of products, responsibilities, control and decision-making authority between the local users and the government agencies. At the heart of co-management is some form of negotiated contract which specifies the distribution of authority and responsibility among the major parties to the contract. Joint management recognizes the capacity of local resource users to be active partners (usually with government) in a power-sharing arrangement. In this way, both the government's policy objectives and local people's use requirements have better chances of being met (Pye-Smith and Borrini Feyaerabend, 1994).

By combining formal ownership by the government with people's security of access through time, co-management schemes are well suited for the effective and sustainable management of protected areas — in forests, wetlands, coastal areas, mountains, grasslands and other biodiversity-rich ecosystems. One example comes from Uganda: two years after the National Park Service granted rights of access to beekeepers in one of the country's parks, local involvement in resource management and stewardship has already begun to benefit both people and wildlife. Joint forest management, participatory rural appraisal and visual communication techniques are used with communities to set up multiple-use areas and the sustainable harvesting, utilization and monitoring of species in Bwindi Impenetrable National Park, in south-west Uganda (Wilde, 1994).

Governments have much to gain by decentralizing control and responsibility for protected-area management. Such protection is likely to be more cost-effective and sustainable when national regulatory frameworks are left flexible enough to accommodate local peculiarities. However, local control and secure access to protected-area resources will not, in and by themselves, enable local communities to benefit fully from, and care for, biodiversity-rich sites. Governments will also need to pay attention to other requirements for effective and sustainable protected-area management at the local level.

In addition to security of tenure and access, local communities must have the right to retain their knowledge about biological and genetic resources in and around protected areas. They should be able to access all the information about the medicinal plants and other biological material they manage in protected areas. They will also need funds, if they are to develop their biological resources in and around protected areas. Local communities must also be free to develop their own technologies and to take advantage of other technologies they find useful. Lastly, recognizing that biological resources, information, funds and technologies function within cultural and marketing systems, a further requirement is for local communities to exercise their right to choose and retain those systems that best meet their needs.

The devolution of protected-area management to local communities does not mean that state agencies have no role. A central challenge will be to find ways of allocating limited government resources so as to obtain widespread replication of community initiatives in protected-area management. Honouring local intellectual property rights, promoting wider access to biological information and funds, designing technologies, markets and other systems on the basis of local needs and aspirations all require new partnerships between the state and rural people, and the organizations representing them.

Building appropriate partnerships between states and rural communities demands new legislation, policies, institutional linkages and processes. It requires the creation of communication networks and participatory research linkages between the public sector, NGOs and rural people involved in protected-area management. Legal frameworks should focus on the granting of rights, access and security of tenure to farmers, fisherfolk, pastoralists and forest dwellers. This is essential for the poor to take the long-term view. Similarly, the application of appropriate regulations to prevent pollution and resource-degrading activities is essential to control the activities of the rich and powerful — timber and mining companies, for example. Economic policies should include the removal of distorting subsidies that encourage the waste of resources, the targeting of subsidies to the poor instead of the wealthy, who are much better at capturing them, and the encouragement of resource-enhancing rather than degrading activities through appropriate pricing policies.

Such changes will not come about simply through the increased awareness of policy makers and professionals. They will require shifts in the balance of social forces and power relations. How far governments can be encouraged to create this enabling context for protected-area management depends on circumstances. This is clearly a problem where governance is not democratic and where reliance on strongly coercive conservation is the norm. Moreover:

> *governments are not neutral administrative bodies but political expressions of dominant social forces, and the poor and excluded are not part of these ruling forces and alliances unless, briefly, in revolutionary political conjunctures. Quite naturally, governments tend thus to resist any policy that entails dilution of power and above all participatory approaches that aim to empower the hitherto excluded. (Stiefel and Wolfe, 1994:212)*

Nonetheless, when empowerment of local communities has been a political priority, then the successes that have followed have been significant.

These include:

*   reduced environmental degradation;
*   more efficient use of resources;
*   reduced dependency on external resources;
*   reversal of migration patterns;
*   enhanced livelihood security, particularly in resource-poor areas; and
*   increased human capacity for conservation.

In practical terms, local empowerment and popular participation can generate more productive means of livelihood and, through local control and co-management agreements, maintain 'protected areas' that the state currently manages inefficiently or can no longer afford.

Emerging Constraints and Opportunities

Sustainable and effective protected-area management calls for reversals from the 'normal' towards greater diversity, democracy and decentralization. The vision for conservation presented here would establish and develop parks and protected areas with a view to strengthening local livelihood opportunities, and then integrate these measures with nature conservation objectives. This new paradigm asserts that the multiple livelihood activities of rural communities are not necessarily incompatible with the conservation of biological diversity. Indeed, under certain conditions, community participation in natural resource management can help maintain and actually enhance the diversity of nature in and around protected areas.

Popular participation in defining what constitutes a 'protected area', how it should be managed, and in whose interests, implies a shift from the more common passive, consultative and material-driven participation to more interactive and genuinely empowering forms of participation. Genuine people's participation in the conception, design, management and evaluation of protected areas implies new roles for conservation professionals and other outsiders. These new roles all require a new professionalism with new concepts, values, methods and behaviour. Enabling policies are also needed to provide favourable conditions and appropriate forms of support for local initiatives in protected-area management.

In this context, participation involves far more than the active and willing involvement of local people in the management of protected areas. It is primarily about empowerment — the organized efforts of marginalized groups within civil society to transform patterns of resource allocation and increase their control over material resources and decision-making processes. Empowerment often necessitates the creation of new forms of socio-economic or socio-political organizations that are more representative and accountable than the traditional ones. Strong community organization and mobilization are also features of a participatory process that seeks to ensure that conservation initiatives serve the interests of local people.

The challenges of adapting the ingredients of participatory, community based successes to the design and management of national parks and other protected areas are therefore enormous. But it would be socially irresponsible not to pursue this approach actively in contexts where rural people directly depend on biological diversity and natural resources for their food, health, fuel, shelter and cultural needs. Without participatory, learning-centred approaches that support local livelihood interests in protected-area management, it is likely that conservation will further aggravate resource degradation, economic deprivation, social tension and loss of biological diversity.

Naturally, governments will tend to shy away from approaches that seek to empower the hitherto excluded. International and national conservation organizations have a unique responsibility in this context. Through their political and financial influence they can encourage policy changes by openly supporting indigenous and rural peoples' rights to their lands, instead of supporting the actions of elites.

This is particularly important at a time when the role and importance of protected areas in national economies are changing as genetic resources increasingly acquire market value. Governments of biodiversity-rich countries are now making bilateral agreements with foreign research institutes and multinational corporations to organize the collection, identification and exploitation of useful genes in the fauna and flora of protected areas. Such bioprospecting agreements have already been signed between Glaxo and Ghana, U.K. research institutes and Cameroon, and Novo Industry and the government of Nigeria. The pharmaceutical company Mercks has recently signed a five-year contract with Costa Rica's National Biodiversity Institute (INBio). Mercks pays for its prospection rights (over US$ 1 million) and has agreed to share royalties on sales of products derived from useful genes and biochemical substances identified in Costa Rica's protected areas. Many more bilateral agreements of this type are reported by Reid et al. (1993).

The subsistence values of protected areas may be further marginalized by the potential commercial values of biological resources which government and local elites can more readily benefit from, with or without international help. Patenting regimes and other intellectual property rights enable industrial users to protect and profit from technological innovations based on the use of these genetic resources. Conversely, the knowledge and informal innovations of local people in conserving and extending the genetic diversity of species with medicinal or agricultural values may not be compensated for, as has been the case until now (Crucible Group, 1994).

As the capacities of developing-country governments become increasingly undermined by structural adjustment programmes, diminishing aid and worsening terms of trade, the tendency is to continue to use the existing conservation paradigm. This emphasizes the ecological and commercial values of biodiversity and only secondarily, if at all, the subsistence values on which local livelihood security depends. As a result, coercive conservation strategies, backed by outside private interests and careless ideologies, may be further extended to preserve wildlife for tourism and 'scientific research'. These trends may serve both the economic and political interests of developing-country governments but the long-term effectiveness of this conservation strategy is as questionable as the ethics of its militaristic approach (Peluso, 1993).

The inherent contradictions between state control and autonomous participation will best be resolved through jointly negotiated agreements between governments and local communities. National parks and other protected areas, including their vernacular definitions, could be managed under agreements between governments and rural communities. The jointly negotiated co-management schemes would establish mutually agreed processes to achieve both long-term conservation goals and livelihood security. Elements of these agreements could include government assistance for strong defence against powerful outside interests, such as cattle ranchers, mining and timber companies, and bioprospecting agents. The co-management agreements could also cover technical assistance from conservation biologists for monitoring and advice, and perhaps trust funds and local credit systems set up to improve access to health care, education and other locally defined community improvements.

It is this new vision for protected areas, in which conservation professionals and local people 'participate' together in joint or co-management, that will lead to greater conservation. It will require great changes in professionals, policies and institutions. Local people, biodiversity and natural resources depend on these changes.

References

Adams, J S and Thomas O McShane (1992), *The Myth of Wild Africa: Conservation without Illusion*, W W Norton and Co, New York.

Adnan, S, A Barrett, S M Nurul Alam and A Brustinow (1992), *People's Participation: NGOs and the Flood Action Plan*, Research and Advisory Services, Dhaka.

Apffel Marglin, F and P C Mishra (1993), 'Sacred groves: regenerating the body, the land, the community', in W Sachs (ed), *Global Ecology: a New Arena of Political Conflict*, Zed Books, London.

Bahuguna, V K (1992), *Collective Resource Management: an Experience of Harda Forest Division*, Regional Centre for Wastelands Development, Bhopal.

Bawden, R (1991), 'Systems thinking and practice in agriculture', *Journal of Dairy Science*, 74, pp 2362–2373.

— (1992), *Creating Learning Systems: a Metaphor for Institutional Reform for Development*, paper prepared for joint IIED/IDS Conference, Beyond Farmer First: Rural People's Knowledge, Agricultural Research and Extension Practice (London, 27–29 October).

Bebbington, A and G Thiele with P Davies, P M Prager and H Riveros (1993), *Rethinking Roles in Sustainable Agricultural Development. Non-Governmental Organizations and the State in Latin America*, Routledge, London.

Bookchin, M (1990), *Remaking Society: Pathways to a Green Future*, South End Press, Boston.

Botkin, D B (1990), *Discordant Harmonies: a New Ecology for the Twenty-First Century*, Oxford University Press, New York.

Bromley, D W and M M Cernea (1989), *The Management of Common Property Natural Resources*, Discussion Paper No 57, The World Bank, Washington, DC.

Cernea, M M (1987), 'Farmer organisations and institution building for sustainable development', *Regional Development Dialogue*, 8, pp 1–24.

— (1993), 'Culture and organisation: The social sustainability of induced development', *Sustainable Development*, Vol 1, No 2, pp 18–29.

Chambers, R (1991), 'In search of professionalism, bureaucracy and sustainable livelihood for the 21st century', *IDS Bulletin*, Vol 22, No 4, pp 5–12.

— (1992a), 'The self-deceiving state: psychosis and therapy', *IDS Bulletin*, Vol 23, No 4, pp 31–42.

— (1992b), *Rural Appraisal: Rapid, Relaxed and Participatory*, Discussion Paper 311, IDS, Brighton.

— (1993), *Challenging the Professions: Frontiers for Rural Development*, Intermediate Technology Publications, London.

Chandrakanth, M G and J Romm (1991), 'Sacred forests, secular forest policies and people's actions', *Natural Resources Journal*, Vol 31, No 4, pp 741–756.

Chase, S (ed) (1991), *Defending the Earth: a Dialogue between Murray Bookchin and Dave Foreman*, South End Press, Boston.

Chatterjee, P (1994), 'Biodiversity for sale', *Bankcheck*, January, pp 3–23.

Cherail, K (1993), 'Time to change: Wildlife conservation strategy', *Down to Earth*, Vol 2, No 13, pp 5–9.

Colchester, M (1992), *Sustaining the Forests: the Community-Based Approach in South and South-East Asia*, Discussion Paper No 35, United Nations Research Institute for Social Development, Geneva, May.

— (1994), *Salvaging Nature: Indigenous Peoples, Protected Areas and Biodiversity Conservation*, UNRISD/World Rainforest Movement/WWF-International, Discussion Paper No 55, UNRISD, Geneva, September.

Conroy, C and M Litvinoff (1988), *The Greening of Aid*, Earthscan Publications Ltd, London.

Conway, G R and J N Pretty (1991), *Unwelcome Harvest: Agriculture and Pollution*, Earthscan Publications Ltd, London.

Craven, I (1990), *Community Involvement in Management of the Arfak Mountains Nature Reserve*, WWF (Indonesia), Jakarta.

Crucible Group (1994), *People, Plants and Patents: The Impact of Intellectual Property on Trade, Plant Biodiversity and Rural Society*, IDRC, Ottawa.

Denevan, W M (1992), 'The pristine myth: the landscape of the Americas in 1942', *Annals of the Association of American Geography*, 82, pp 369–385.

Devall, B and G Sessions (1985), *Deep Ecology*, Peregrine Smith, Salt Lake City.

Dickson, D (1984), *The New Politics of Science*, Pantheon Books, New York.

Eisner, E W (1990), 'The meaning of alternative paradigms for practice', in E G Guba (ed), *The Paradigm Dialogue*, Sage Publications, Newbury Park.

Fairhead, J and M Leach (1994), 'Contested forests: modern conservation and historical land use in Guinea's Ziama reserve', *African Affairs*, 93, pp 481–512.

Farrington, J, A Bebbington, K Wellard and D J Lewis (1993), *Reluctant Partners? Non Governmental Organisations, the State and Sustainable Agricultural Development*, Routledge, London.

Feyerabend, P (1975), *Against Method: Outline of an Anarchistic Theory of Knowledge*, Verso, London.

Foreman, D (1987), 'A modest proposal for a wilderness system', *Whole Earth Review*, 53, pp 42–45.

Fortmann, L and J W Bruce (eds) (1988), *Whose Trees? Proprietary Dimensions of Forestry*, Westview Press, Boulder.

Foster, D R, Z Zebryk, P Schoonmaker and A Lezberg (1992), 'Post-settlement history of human land use and vegetation dynamics of a Tsuga Canadensis (hemlock) woodlot in central New England', *Journal of Ecology*, 80, pp 773–786.

Ghai, D and J Vivian (eds) (1992), *Grassroots Environmental Action: People's Participation in Sustainable Development*, Routledge, London.

Giddens, A (1987), *Social Theory and Modern Society*, Blackwell, Oxford.

Gómez-Pompa, A and A Kaus (1992), 'Taming the wilderness myth', *Bioscience*, Vol 42, No 4, pp 271–279.

Guha, R (1989), 'Radical American environmentalism and wilderness preservation: a Third World Critique', *Environmental Ethics*, 11, pp 71–83.

— (1993), 'Two phases of American environmentalism: a critical history', in F Appfel Marglin and S A Marglin (eds), *Decolonising Knowledge: from Development to Dialogue*, Clarendon Press, Oxford.

Habermas, J (1987), *The Theory of Communicative Action*, Volume II, Heinemann, London.

Hobbs, R J and L F Huenneke (1992), 'Disturbance, diversity and invasion: Implications for conservation', *Conservation Biology*, 6, p 3240.

Ison, R (1990), *Teaching Threatens Sustainable Agriculture*, Sustainable Agriculture Programme Gatekeeper Series, SA21, IIED, London.

Janzen, D (1986), 'The future of tropical ecology', *Annual Review of Ecology and Systematics*, 17, pp 305–306.

Kemf, E (ed) (1993), *Indigenous Peoples and Protected Areas — The Law of Mother Earth*, Earthscan Publications Ltd, London.

Korten, DC (1984), 'People centered development: towards a framework', in DC Korten and R Klauss (eds), *People-Centered Development*, Kumarian Press, West Hartford, Connecticut.

Kuhn, T (1962), *The Structure of Scientific Revolutions*, University of Chicago Press, Chicago.

Levidow, L (ed) (1986), *Radical Science Essays*, Free Association Books, London.

Levins, R and R Lewontin (1985), *The Dialectical Biologist*, Harvard University Press, Cambridge, Massachusetts.

Loita Naimana Enkiyio Conservation Trust (1994), *Forest of the Lost Child: a Maasai Conservation Success Threatened by Greed*, Narok, Kenya.

Max-Neef, M, A Elizalde, M Hopenhayn, F Herrera, H Zemelman, J Jataba and L

Weinstein (1989), 'Human scale development: an option for the future', *Development Dialogue*, 1, pp 5–80.

McNeely, J A (1994), 'Lessons from the past: Forests and biodiversity', *Biodiversity and Conservation*, 3, pp 3–20.

Merchant, C (1980), *The Death of Nature — Women, Ecology and the Scientific Revolution*, Harper and Row, San Francisco.

— (1992), *Radical Ecology — The Search for a Liveable World*, Routledge, London.

Mittermeier, R A and I A Bowles (1993), 'The global environment facility and biodiversity conservation: lessons to date and suggestions for future action', *Biodiversity and Conservation*, 2, pp 637–655.

Nabhan, G P, D House, S A Humberto, W Hodgson, H S Luis and M Guadalupe (1991), 'Conservation and use of rare plants by traditional cultures of the US/Mexico borderlands', in M L Oldfield and J B Alcorn (eds), *Biodiversity: Culture, Conservation and Ecodevelopment*, Westview Press, Boulder.

Ntiamo-Baidu, Y, L J Gyiamfi-Fenteng and W Abbiw (1992), *Management Strategies for Sacred Groves in Ghana*, a report prepared for The World Bank and Environmental Protection Committee (Ghana), Washington, DC.

Oldfield, M L and J B Alcorn (1991), *Biodiversity: Culture, Conservation and Ecodevelopment*, Westview Press, Boulder.

Pearse, A and M Stiefel (1979), *Inquiry into Participation: a Research Approach*, UNRISD, Geneva.

PEC Workshop (1990), *Lessons Learnt in Community-Based Environmental Management*, Proceedings of the 1990 Primary Environmental Care workshop (29 January–2 February 1990), Grazia Borrini (ed), Italian Ministry of Foreign Affairs and the Istituto Superiore di Sanita, Rome.

Peluso, N L (1993), 'Coercing conservation? The politics of state resource control', *Global Environmental Change*, June, pp 199–217.

Pimbert, M P and J N Pretty (1995), *Parks, People and Professionals: Putting 'Participation' into Protected Area Management*, UNRISD/IIED/WWF-International, Discussion Paper No 57, UNRISD, Geneva, February.

Pimbert, M P, B Guja, M K Shah (1996) 'Village voices challenging wetland management policies: PRA experiences from Pakistan and India', *PLA Notes* 27, IIED, London, pp 37–41.

Poole, P J (1993), 'Indigenous peoples and biodiversity protection', in S H Davis, *The Social Challenge of Biodiversity Conservation*, Working Paper No 1, Global Environment Facility, (The World Bank/UNEP/UNDP), Washington, DC, pp 14–25.

Pretty, J N (1994), 'Alternative systems of inquiry for sustainable agriculture', *IDS Bulletin*, Vol 25, No 2, pp 37–48.

— (1995), *Regenerating Agriculture: Policies and Practice for Sustainability and Self-Reliance*, Earthscan Books Ltd, London.

Pretty, J N and R Chambers (1993), *Towards a Learning Paradigm: New Professionalism and Institutions for Sustainable Agriculture*, IDS Discussion Paper 334, IDS, Brighton.

Pretty, J N and R Sandbrook (1991), *Operationalising Sustainable Development at the Community Level: Primary Environmental Care*, paper presented to the DAC Working Party on Development Assistance and the Environment, OECD, Paris, October.

Pye-Smith, C and G Borrini Feyaerabend (1994), *The Wealth of Nations*, Earthscan Publications Ltd, London.

Rahnema, M (1992), 'Participation', in W Sachs (ed), *The Development Dictionary*, Zed Books Ltd, London.

Reid, W, S A Laird, C Meyer, R Gomez, A Sittenfeld, D Janzen, M A Gollin and C Juma (1993), *Biodiversity Prospecting: Using Genetic Resources for Sustainable Development*, World Resources Institute, Washington, DC.

Rorty, R (1989), *Contingency, Irony and Solidarity*, Cambridge University Press, Cambridge.

Rose, H and S Rose (1976), *The Political Economy of Science: Ideology of/in the Natural Sciences*, Macmillan Press, London.

Russell, D B and R L Ison (1991), *The Research–Development Relationship in Rangelands: an Opportunity for Contextual Science*, plenary paper for 4th International Rangelands Congress (Montpellier, 22–26 April).

Sachs, W (1993), 'Global ecology and the shadow of development' in W Sachs (ed), *Global Ecology: a New Arena of Political Conflict*, Zed Books, London.

Scoones, I, M Melnyk and J N Pretty (1992), *The Hidden Harvest: Wild Foods and Agricultural Systems*, an annotated bibliography, IIED, London with WWF, Geneva and SIDA, Stockholm.

Shengji, P (1991), 'Conservation of biological diversity in temple-yards and holy hills by the Dai ethnic minorities of China', *Ethnobotany*, 3, pp 27–35.

Sriskandarajah N, R J Bawden and R G Packham (1991), 'Systems agriculture: a paradigm for sustainability', *Association for Farming Systems Research-Extension Newsletter*, Vol 2, No 2, pp 1–5.

Stiefel, M and M Wolfe (1994), *A Voice for the Excluded — Popular Participation in Development: Utopia or Necessity?*, Zed Books, London.

Uphoff, N (1992), *Learning from Gal Oya: Possibilities for Participatory Development and Post-Newtonian Science*, Cornell University Press, Ithaca.

Utting, P (1993), *Trees, People and Power: Social Dimensions of Deforestation and Forest Protection in Central America*, Earthscan Publications Ltd, London.

— (1994), 'Social and political dimensions of environmental protection in Central America', *Biodiversity and Conservation*, 25, pp 231–259.

Wellard, K and J G Copestake (eds) (1993), *Rethinking Roles in Sustainable Agricultural Development — Non-Governmental Organisations and the State in Africa*, Routledge, London.

West, P C and S R Brechin (1992), *Resident People and National Parks*, University of Arizona Press, Tucson.

Wilde, R (1994), *Community Participation in Planning Resource Utilisation from within a National Park — Bwindi Impenetrable National Park*, Uganda, mimeo, WWF-International.

Wood, D (1993), 'Forests to fields — Restoring tropical lands to agriculture', *Land Use Policy*, April, pp 91–107.

— (1995), 'Conserved to death: are tropical forests being over-protected from people?', *Land Use Policy*, Vol 12, No 2, pp 115–135.

Wynne, B (1992), 'Uncertainty and environmental learning — reconceiving science and policy in the preventive paradigm', *Global Environmental Change*, June, pp 111–127.

ABBREVIATIONS AND ACRONYMS

ABN	Arbeitsgemeinschaft Ehrenamtlicher und Beruflicher Naturschutz e.V.
ACYS	Association Communautaire de Yobe-Sangha (Central African Republic)
AEA	Agroecosystems Analysis
AFRA	Association for Rural Advancement
ANR	absolute nature reserve
ARC	Aboriginal Rights Coalition
ASA	Arbeits- und Studienaufenthalte in Asien, Afrika und Lateinamerika
ASOMPS	Asian Symposium for Medicinal Plants, Spices and other Natural Products
ATV	all-terrain vehicle
BOSTID	Board on Science and Technology for International Development
BR	biological reserve
BSAC	British South Africa Company
BSCRM	Bulgarian Society for the Conservation of the Rhodopi Mountains
BSR	biosphere reserve
BUND	Bund für Umwelt- und Naturschutz in Deutschland (Union for Environmental Protection and Nature Conservation in Germany)
CAM	Conseil Attikamègue-Montagnais
CAMPFIRE	Communal Areas Management Programme for Indigenous Resources (Zimbabwe)
CASS	Centre for Applied Social Sciences (University of Zimbabwe)
CATIE	Centro Agronómico Tropical de Investigación y Enseñanza (Tropical Agronomy Teaching and Research Centre)
CBD	The Convention on Biological Diversity
CCR	community controlled research
CDO	community development organization
CES	Chinese Environmental Science Press
CGIAR	Consultative Group on International Agricultural Research

CI	Conservation International
CITES	Convention on International Trade in Endangered Species of Wild Fauna and Flora
CNEARC	Centre National d'Etudes Agronomiques en Régions Chaudes
CNPPA	World Congress on National Parks and Protected Areas
CONAI	Costa Rican National Commission for Indigenous Affairs
CPAWS	Canadian Parks and Wilderness Society
D&D	diagnosis and design
DANIDA	Danish International Development Agency
DATAR	Délégation à l'Aménagement du Territoire et à l'Action Régionale
DENR	Department of Environment and Natural Resources
DFO	district forest officer
DGF	Costa Rican General Directorate for Forestry
DGVS	Costa Rican Wildlife Directorate
DRR	diagnostico rural rapido (rapid rural appraisal)
EC	European Community
EEC	European Economic Community
FAO	Food and Agriculture Organization of the United Nations
FDC	forest development corporation
FNNPE	Federation of Nature and National Parks of Europe
FÖNAD	Föderation der Natur- und Nationalparke Europas — Sektion Deutschland e.V.
FPC	forest protection committee
FPN	Costa Rican National Parks Foundation
FRI	Forestry Research Institute
GATT	General Agreement on Tariffs and Trade
GATT-TRIP	General Agreement on Tariffs and Trade — Trade Related Aspects of Intellectual Property Rights
GEF	Global Environmental Facility (World Bank)
GEM	Group for Environmental Monitoring
GIS	geographic information system
GRAAP	Groupe de Recherche et d'Appui pour l'Auto-Promotion Paysanne
GTZ	Deutsche Gesellschaft für Technische Zusammenarbeit
HDI	Human Development Index
ICBG	International Cooperative Biodiversity Groups
ICDP	integrated conservation and development project
ICIHI	Independent Commission on International Humanitarian Issues
ICIMOD	International Centre for Integrated Mountain Development
ICT	Costa Rican Tourism Institute
IDA	Agrarian Development Institute
IFC	International Finance Corporation
IGC	Inuvialuit Game Council

IIED	International Institute for Environment and Development (UK)
IIPA	Indian Institute of Public Administration
ILO	International Labour Organization
INA	International Conservation Academy (German Ministry of Environment)
INBio	Instituto Nacional de Biodiversidad (Costa Rica)
IPR	intellectual property right
IRC	Inuvialuit Regional Corporation
ITTA	International Tropical Timber Agreement
IUCN	The World Conservation Union
JAPDEVA	Junta de Administración Portuaria y Desarrollo de la Vertiente Atlántica
JFM	joint forest management
JPAM	joint protected area management
KDNC	The KwaZulu Department of Nature Conservation
KPC	KaNgwane Parks Corporation
MAB	Man and Biosphere programme (UNESCO)
MAG	Costa Rican Ministry of Agriculture
MARP	Méthode Accélérée de Recherche Participative
MFP	minor forest products
MIDEPLAN	Ministry of Planning and Economic Policy
MIRENEM	Costa Rican Ministry of Natural Resources, Energy and Mines
MLCP	Ministère du Loisir, de la Chasse et de la Pêche du Québec
NEPA	National Environmental Protection Agency
NGO	non-governmental organization
NM	national monument
NORAD	Norwegian Agency for Development Cooperation
NP	national park
NRP	natural regional park
NTFP	Non-timber forest product
OAS	Organisation of American States
PALM	participatory analysis and learning methods
PAR	participatory action research
PEC	primary environmental care
PRA	participatory rural appraisal
PRAP	participatory rural appraisal and planning
PTD	participatory technology development
PUA	participatory urban appraisal
RA	rapid appraisal
RAAKS	rapid assessment of agricultural knowledge systems
R&D	research and development
RAFI	Rural Advancement Foundation International
RAP	rapid assessment procedures
RAT	rapid assessment techniques
RCA	rapid catchment analysis

RDI	rural development institute
REA	rapid ethnographic assessment
RFSA	rapid food security assessment
RMA	rapid multi-perspective appraisal
ROA	rapid organisational assessment
RRA	rapid rural appraisal
SADCC	Southern Africa Development Co-ordination Conference
Satour	South African Tourism Board
SI-A-PAZ	International System of Protected Areas for Peace (Nicaragua — Costa Rica)
SINAC	Costa Rican National System of Conservation Areas
SIVOM	Syndicat d'Initiative à Vocation Multiple
SIVU	Syndicat d'Initiative à Vocation Unique
SPN	Costa Rican National Parks Service
SPWD	Society for the Promotion of Wastelands Development
SSM	Soft Systems Methodology
TFN	Tungavik Federation of Nunavut
TTL	Tribal Trust Land
UDI	Unilateral Declaration of Independence
UNCED	United Nations Conference on Environment and Development
UNDP	United Nations Development Programme
UNEP	United Nations Environment Programme
UNESCO	United Nations Educational, Scientific and Cultural Organization
USAID	United States Agency for International Development
VIPP	visualisation in participatory programmes
WCMC	World Conservation Monitoring Centre
WFP	World Food Programme
WRI	World Resources Institute
WRM	World Rainforest Movement
WTO	World Trade Organization
WWF	World Wide Fund For Nature
ZPA	Zambia Privatisation Agency

Land and Weight Measurements

15 mu = 1 hectare
One bigha is 0.68 of a hectare
One maund is about 36 kilograms

Currency Conversion

US$ 1 = 5.7 RMB (yuan) in October 1993
US$ 1 = 3.5 SAR (South African Rand) in 1993
US$ 1 = 14.5 Indian Rs (rupees) in 1988, and 32 Indian Rs in 1993

INDEX